ANCIENT INDIAN TRADITION AND MYTHOLOGY

Translated by
Board of Scholars

Edited by
Prof. J.L. Shastri

VOLUME 16

ANCIENT INDIAN TRADITION AND MYTHOLOGY SERIES

[PURĀṆAS IN TRANSLATION]

Volumes Released

ŚIVA 1-4
LIṄGA 5-6
BHĀGAVATA 7-11
GARUḌA 12-14
NĀRADA 15-19
KŪRMA 20-21
BRAHMĀṆḌA 22-26
AGNI 27-30
VARĀHA 31-32
BRAHMA 33-36
VĀYU 37-38
PADMA 39-48
SKANDA, PARTS I-XXIII, 49-71
VĀMANA 72-73

Volumes Under Preparation

BHAVIṢYA
BRAHMAVAIVARTA
DEVĪBHĀGAVATA
KĀLIKĀ
MĀRKAṆḌEYA
MATSYA
VIṢṆU
VIṢṆUDHARMOTTARA

THE NĀRADA-PURĀṆA

PART II

Translated and Annotated by

GANESH VASUDEO TAGARE

MOTILAL BANARSIDASS PUBLISHERS
PRIVATE LIMITED • DELHI

2nd Reprint: Delhi, 2013
First Edition: Delhi, 1981

ISBN: 978-81-208-0348-0

MOTILAL BANARSIDASS
41 U.A. Bungalow Road, Jawahar Nagar, Delhi 110 007
8 Mahalaxmi Chamber, 22 Bhulabhai Desai Road, Mumbai 400 026
120 Royapettah High Road, Mylapore, Chennai 600 004
236, 9th Main III Block, Jayanagar, Bangaluru 560 011
Sanas Plaza, 1302 Baji Rao Road, Pune 411 002
8 Camac Street, Kolkata 700 017
Ashok Rajpath, Patna 800 004
Chowk, Varanasi 221 001

UNESCO COLLECTION OF REPRESENTATIVE WORKS—*Indian Series*
This book has been accepted in the Indian Translation Series of the UNESCO Collection of Representative Works, jointly sponsored by the United Nations Educational, Scientific and Cultural Organization (UNESCO) and the Government of India

published by JP Jain for Motilal Banarsidass Publishers (P) Ltd,
41 U.A. Bungalow Road, Jawahar Nagar, Delhi-110007

PUBLISHER'S NOTE

The purest gems lie hidden in the bottom of the ocean or in the depth of rocks. One has to dive into the ocean or delve into the rocks to find them out. Similarly, truth lies concealed in the language which with the passage of time has become obsolete. Man has to learn that language before he discovers that truth.

But he has neither the means nor the leisure to embark on that course. We have, therefore, planned to help him acquire knowledge by an easier course. We have started the series of *Ancient Indian Tradition and Mythology* in English Translation. Our goal is to universalize knowledge through the most popular international medium of expression. The publication of the Purāṇas in English translation is a step towards that goal.

PREFACE

The present volume contains the *Nārada Purāṇa*, Part II (Chapters 42-62 completing the second Pāda in English translation). This is the Sixteenth Volume in the series of fifty volumes which we have planned on *Ancient Indian Tradition and Mythology*.

The project of the series was envisaged and financed in 1970 by late Lala Sundar Lal Jain of Messrs Motilal Banarsidass. Hitherto sixteen volumes of the series, including the present one (that is, four volumes of the *Śiva Purāṇa*, two volumes of the *Liṅga Purāṇa*, five volumes of the *Bhāgavata Purāṇa*, three volumes of the *Garuḍa Purāṇa* and the two volumes of the *Nārada Purāṇa*) have been published and released for sale.

The present volume, like all other volumes, is encyclopaedic in character. It deals with miscellaneous topics such as Cosmogony, Religion, Philosophy, Veda and its ancillaries—Etymology of Vedic words (*Nirukta*), Grammar (*Vyākaraṇa*), Mathematics and Astronomy (*Gaṇita* and *Nakṣatra-vidyā*), Horoscopy and Natural Astrology (Jyotiṣa) and prosody (Chandas). In Cosmogony it describes the process of creation of the Universe. In Religion and Ethics it places emphasis on the performance of duties of one's own profession (*Varṇa-dharma*) in relation to one's stage of life (*Āśrama*). In Etymology it gives the derivation of Vedic words. In Grammar, it presents a general idea of the Subject. In Prosody it prescribes rules for the metre by the method of Prastāra. In Jyotiṣa it explains the essentials in details. In occult science, it prescribes ritual for attaining particular ends. In spirituality it provides a discourse on meditation, gives an exposition of dharmas leading to liberation, narrates the story of Bharata and contains the dialogue between Śuka and Janaka as well as Śuka and Sanat Kumāra on detachment, renunciation and kindred ways of life which bring emancipation to the seeker in this very existence.

In the Sectarian grouping of the Purāṇas, the *Nārada Purāṇa* is classified as a Vaiṣṇava Purāṇa on the basis of the fact that among the deities glorified in the Purāṇa, Viṣṇu holds the Supreme position, though laudatory references to other deities—Śiva, Śakti, etc. are also made. In the obvious partiality for Vaiṣṇavism, the Nārada Purāṇa gives special treatment to Rādhā and Kṛṣṇa, even prescribes a hymn of 1000 names in their eulcgy and proclaims special importance to Ekādaśī Vrata in honour of Viṣṇu. It is the first to mention Rāma, Kṛṣṇa, Nṛsiṁha and other incarnations in connection with Tantric practices.

The variety of topics is very interesting but it is marred as some time it is couched in expression that needs elucidation—a task which cannot be accomplished by a mere translation. Hence, a provision has been made for the notes, which are attached to each chapter, separately, and not put at the foot of a page as has been the practice in the translation of other Purāṇas. We hope the reader will not feel embarrassed by this shift.

The translation is based on the Sanskrit text of the *Nārada Purāṇa* as published by Messrs Kṣemarāja Śrīkṛṣṇadāsa, Veṅkaṭeśvara Press, Bombay. This text constructed on the collation of mss and supported by the evidence of citations found in the Smṛti granthas, is fairly accurate.

We have included abbreviations in this part too and they will be repeated in successive parts as well, with such additions as are inserted in the notes in those parts. The Glossary and the General Index to the complete Purāṇa will be appended to the last part. For Introduction to this Purāṇa, the reader is referred to Part I of this book.

Acknowledgment of obligation:

It is our pleasant duty to put on record our sincere thanks to Dr. R. N. Dandekar and the authorities of the UNESCO for their kind encouragement and valuable help which render this work extremely useful. We are extremely grateful to Dr. G. V. Tagare who in the storm and stress of his pressing occupations has snatched time for the accomplishment of this national task. The lucid translation and the explanatory notes attached thereto are, in fact, his monumental contributions in the field of Indology. We are also grateful to Dr. K. V. Sharma and Professor M. R. Bhatt for translating chapters 54-56 on Mathematics and Astronomy, Horoscopy and Astrology and providing notes on them. We must also thank Shri T. V. Parameshwara Iyer for his valuable assistance in the preparation of translation. Finally we express our gratitude to all those who have offered suggestions for improving the same.

— Editor

ABBREVIATIONS

Common and Self-evident abbreviations such as ch(s)—chapter(s), p—page, pp—pages, v—verse, vv—verses, Ftn—footnote, Hist. Ind. Philo—History of Indian Philosophy are not included in this list.

ABORI	*Annals of the Bhandarkar Oriental Research Institute*, Poona.
AGP	S. M. Ali's *The Geography of Purāṇas*, PPH, New Delhi, 1973.
AIHT	*Ancient Indian Historical Tradition* F. E. Pargiter, Motilal Banarsidass (MLBD), Delhi.
AP	*Agni Purāṇa*, Guru Mandal Edition (GM), Calcutta, 1957.
AV	*Atharva Veda*, Svadhyaya Mandal Aundh.
Bd. P.	*Bhāgavata Purāṇa*, MLBD, Delhi 1973.
Bh. P.	*Bhāgavata Purāṇa*, Bhagavat Vidyapeeth, Ahmedabad.
Bm. P.	*Brahma Purāṇa*, GM, 1954.
Bnr.	*Bṛhan-nāradiya*—Pt. Hrishikesh Shastri, Chowkhamba, 1975.
Bs. P.	*Bhaviṣya Purāṇa*, Vishnu Shastri Bapat, Wai.
Bv. P.	*Brahma Vaivarta Purāṇa*, GM, 1955-57.
CC	*Caturvarga Cintāmaṇi* by Hemādri.
DB	*Devi Bhāgavata*, GM, 1960-61.
De or GDAMI	*The Geographical Dictionary of Ancient and Mediaeval India*—N. L. De, Orienta Reprint Delhi, 1971.
Dh. S.	*Dharma Sūtra* (preceded by the author's name such as Gautama).
ERE	*Encyclopaedia of Religion and Ethics*—Hastings.
GP.	*Garuḍa Purāṇa*, Ed. R. S. Bhattacharya, Chowkhamba, Varanasi, 1964.
GS	*Gṛhya Sūtra* (Preceded by the name of the author such as Āpastamba).

HD	*History of Dharma Śāstra* by P. V. Kane, G.O.S.
IA	*The Indian Antiquary.*
IHQ	*The Indian Historical Quarterly.*
KP	*Kūrma Purāṇa*, Venkateshwar Press Edt. Bombay. also Kashirāj Trust Edt., Varanasi 1971.
LP.	*Liṅga Purāṇa*, MLBD, Delhi, 1981.
Mbh.	*Mahābhārata*, Gita Press Gorakhpur, V. S. 2014.
MK.	*Mārkaṇḍeya Purāṇa.*
MN.	*Mahābhārata Nāmānukramaṇī*, Gita Press, Gorakhpur, V.S. 2016,
Mt. P.	*Matsya Purāṇa*, GM, 1954.
MW	*Monier Williams—Sk.-English Dictionary*, MLBD, Delhi, 1976.
NP	*Nāradiya* or *Nārada Purāṇa*, Venkateshwar Press, Bombay.
PCK	*Bhāratavarṣiya Prācina Caritra Kośa*—Siddheshwar Shastri, Poona, 1968.
Pd. P.	*Padma Purāṇa*, GM. 1957-1959.
PE	*Purāṇic Encyclopaedia* V. Mani, English, MLBD, Delhi, 1975.
PJ	*Purāṇa* (Journal of the Kashirāj Trust) Varanasi.
PR or PRHRC	*Purāṇic Records on Hindu Rites and Customs*—R. C. Hazra, Calcutta, 1948.
ṚV	*ṚG Veda*, Svādhyāya Maṇḍala, Aundh.
Śat. Br.	*Śatapatha Brāhmaṇa.*
SEP.	*Studies in Epics and Purāṇas* by A.D. Pusalkar Bharatīya Vidya Bhavan, (BVB), Bombay.
SG or SGAMI	*Studies in the Geography of Ancient and Mediaeval India*—D. C. Sircar MLBD, Delhi, 1971.
SKD	*Śabda-Kalpa-Druma*—Raja R. K. Dev., Chowkhamba, Varanasi.
Sk. P.	*Skanda Purāṇa*, GM. 1960-65.

SM	*Sādhana Mālā*—B. Bhattacharya, GOS, Baroda, 1928.
SMC	*Smṛti Candrikā*—Devanna Bhaṭṭa.
Smṛ	*Smṛti* (preceded by the author's name or simply the author's name e.g. Manu Smṛti or Manu. All GM editions in the Smṛti-Sandarbha. 1952-57.
Sv. P.	*Śiva Purāṇa*, Pandit Pustakālaya Kashi, V.S. 2020.
Va. P.	*Vāyu Purāṇa*, GM, 1959.
Vm. P.	*Vāmana Purāṇa*, Kashiraj Trust, Varanasi.
VP.	*Viṣṇu Purāṇa*, Gītā Press, Gorakhpur, V.S. 2026.
VR	Vālmīki Rāmāyaṇa, Gītā Press, V.S. 2020.
VRK	*Vālmiki Rāmāyaṇa Kośa*—Ramkumar Rai, (Chowkhamba Varanasi.)
Yaj	*Yājñavalkya* (Smṛti), etc.
YSP	*The Yoga System of Patañjali*—J. H. Wood.

CONTENTS

SECOND PĀDA

CHAPTER FORTYTWO

Cosmogony : The Origin of the Universe[1]

(A Dialogue between Bhṛgu and Bhāradvāja)

Nārada submitted :

1. O Brāhmaṇa, kindly narrate to me whence this universe comprised of the mobiles and immobiles was created and to whom it goes at the time of dissolution. O Sanandana !

2. By whom was this world created along with the oceans, the sky, the mountains, the clouds, the earth, the fire and the wind ?

3. How were the *Bhūtas* (Elements or living beings) created ? How were the different castes divided? What is the arrangement for their purity ? How do they get impurities ? What are their rules regarding *Dharma* and *Adharma* ?

4. Of what nature is the soul of the living individuals? Where do those who die go? May your honour recount everything from this world to the other.

Sanandana replied :[2]

5. O Nārada, listen. I shall tell you this ancient mythological anecdote, the scripture narrated by the sage Bhṛgu to Bhāradvāja who enquired of him about this.

6. On seeing the brilliant great sage Bhṛgu, of enormous prowess, seated on the top of mount Kailāsa, Sage Bhāradvāja enquired of him.

Bhāradvāja said :

7. O bestower of honour, how does the individual soul continuously transmigrate into the different forms of life (existence)? How is its liberation from the cycle of worldly existence effected?

8. (How is it) O revered sir, that he who is Lord Nārāyaṇa himself and god Brahmā, the self-born creator, always conduct themselves (as if) in the master-servant relationship?

9. How is it that the controller of universe in whom all the mobile and immobile beings enter at the time of dissolution (of the universe), is (as a matter of fact) devoid of all attributes and untinged (by anything)?

10-12a. How and by whom can he who cannot be specifically particularised and reasoned about, be realized? How do the Vedas respectfully eulogise this great *Ātman*, who cannot be pursued by *Kāla* (time) and *Śakti* and whose conduct is beyond comprehension? How does the individual soul transcend his *Jivatva*—(the state of being the individual soul) and merge unto the *Brahman*? O store-house of mercy, I wish to hear this. Kindly narrate it to me (in details)."

12b-13a. When the venerable one was thus asked about his problem by Bhāradvāja, the great sage resembling Brahman (or god Brahman) thereupon explained everything to him.

Bhṛgu replied :

13b-15. The primeval Lord Viṣṇu who was well known to the great sages by the designation *Mānasa*[3] is the god without the beginning and end, unageing and immortal. He is well known as the unmanifest, permanent, everlasting and unchanging. It is from him that the living beings are created. They are born of him and they die in him. That lord at first created the principle called *Mahat* (the great principle).

16-17. He is the lord that supports the elements. (He created what is well known as *Ākāśa* (ether). From *Ākāśa* originated the water[4] and from the water, fire and wind were evolved. As a result of the contact of fire and wind, the earth was evolved. Thereafter, a brilliant lotus was created by the selfborn deity.

18. From that lotus originated Brahmā, the creator who is the embodiment of the Vedas. He is well known as *Ahaṁkāra*[5] (the Cosmic Ego), the creator of other elements and the soul of them all.[6]

19-22. That highly brilliant one was Brahmā. The five elements were the five *Dhātus* (constituents or ingredients of the body). The mountains were his groups of bones (skeletal structure). the earth was the suet and the flesh. The oceans constituted his blood and the firmament his belly. The air (god) was his respiration. The *Agni* (fire) was his brilliance and the rivers were his blood vessels. Agni and Soma, the sun and the moon were well known as his eyes. The sky is the crown of his head; the earth constitutes his feet and the quarters his arms.[7] There is no doubt about this that he is incomprehensible, and his nature is inconceivable even by the Siddhas. He is the Lord Viṣṇu well known as Ananta (Infinite).

23. He is stationed in all living beings as their soul. He cannot be realized by those who are not self-possessed. He is the creator of *Ahaṁkāra* which is the cause of origin of all elements. Thence out of the elements was evolved the universe. And it is this that I have been asked by you.

Bhāradvāja said :

24. What are the magnitudes of the sky, the quarters, the surface of the earth, and the wind? Clear this doubt precisely.

Bhṛgu said :

25. Infinite is this beautiful sky inhabited by Siddhas and gods. It supports (in its expanse) all the things scattered about, but its limits could not be ascertained.

26-27. Neither the moon nor the sun sees its end although they go up and down. Even the gods who are self-refulgent like the brilliance of the sun or the fire and whose prowess is well known, cannot perceive the end of the firmament, as it is both inaccessible and infinite, say so, O bestower of respects.

28. This firmament which is over-crowded higher and higher up with highly blazing self-luminous bodies is incomprehensible even to gods.

29. At the extremity of the earth are the oceans. Darkness is remembered as existing at the (other) extremity of the oceans. They say that there is water at the end of that darkness and at the end of the water[8] there is only fire.

30. At the extremity (bottom) of *Rasātala* (the netherworld) there is water, and at the (lowest) extremity of water, there are lordly serpents. At its end, there is ether again and at the end of the ether, there is water again.

31. Ending with this limit of water is the magnitude of the lord which is more incomprehensible than that of fire, wind and water even to Devas.

32. The colours or nature of the fire, wind, and the surface of the earth are like those of the firmament. But they are distinguished, when the reality is viewed[9] or realized.

33. The sages read about it in the various scriptures as the magnitude of the three worlds and of the ocean, as has been laid down therein.

34. But who can tell the magnitude of what is invisible and what cannot be approached, and when the movement of Siddhas and Devas is restricted.

35-36. Therefore, the designation *Ananta* (connoting the un-accountability) of the immeasurable infinity (viz. Viṣṇu) has become famous. When the divine form of the noble-souled Mānasa (god Viṣṇu) who is so according to his designation (Ananta), decreases or increases again, who else is able to know it? If there be any other, he must be of His nature.

37. Thereafter from the *Puṣkara* (the lotus) was created the embodied omniscient lord Brahmā Who is Dharma incarnate, the first and the foremost Prajāpati (Lord of Creation).

Bhāradvāja said :

38. My doubt is that if god Brahmā is born of a lotus, the lotus becomes the elder (of the two). But your holiness stated that god Brahmā was the first-born (in the whole of creation).

Bhṛgu said :

39-40a. In order to offer a seat unto the physical form of Mānasa (Viṣṇu) that attained the state of Brahmā the earth is called *Padma* (Lotus). The pericarp of that lotus is the Meru which is as lofty as the sky

40b. This god Brahmā, occupying a seat in its middle, creates peoples and the universe.

Bhāradvāja said :

41. O excellent Brāhmaṇa, kindly explain how lord Brahmā seated in the middle of the Meru, creates different kinds of subjects outside the mount Meru.

Bhṛgu said :

42. Mānasa mentally[10] created the different subjects. In order to maintain and protect the living beings, water was created at the outset.

43. Water which is vital to all living beings was created at first. It is the very life of all beings and subjects grow and multiply thereby.

44. If they are abandoned by it, they perish. The whole universe is surrounded by it. The earth, the mountains, the clouds and all other embodied beings—everything should be known as Vāruṇa (presided over by Varuṇa, the deity of waters) The waters uphold and support everything.

Bhāradvāja said :

45. How was water produced? How were Agni (fire) and *Marut* (wind) created ? How was the earth created? My great doubt is in this respect.

Bhṛgu said :

46. O Brāhmaṇa, in a former Kalpa of Brahmā,[11] in the assembly of Brahmanical sages, some noble-souled (sages) had a doubt about the origin of the world.

47. Vying with one another, those Brāhmaṇas adopted silence and set meditating. They were motionless and they forsook all food. Thus they remained for a hundred divine years.

48. A speech originating from the Brahman (*or* words sacred as those of the Vedas) reached the ears of all. A divine speech came out of the atmosphere.

49. Formerly, the infinite firmament became still and unruffled like a huge mountain. As the sun, the moon and the wind were lost, it appeared as if it was sleeping.[12]

50. From that originated water, like a thicker darkness

from darkness. From the overflowing froth and foam of the water, the wind rose up.

51-52. Just as an abode[13] (or rather an empty vessel) without any outlet appears silent but when filled with water the wind makes it full of sound, so also, when the extremity of the firmament is continuously restrained by water, the roaring wind pierces through the surface of the sea and rises up.[14]

53. The wind originating from the over-flowing froth of the ocean moves amongst those. After reaching the place of the sky it does not calm down.

54. In the struggle between wind and water, fire of a mighty fire of great brilliance blazed up dispelling all darkness from the sky.

55. The fire in collaboration with the wind raises water to the sky, where it assumes the form of clouds due to the contact with fire and wind.

56. As it goes up the sky, another part of this (i.e. water) that stays behind due to sliminess solidifies into the earth.

57. This earth should be known as the source of origin of tastes, smells, sliminess as well as of living beings. It is from the earth that everything is delivered out.[15]

Bhāradvāja said :

58. (Defective) The five[16] subtle, *Dhātus* (properties of the five elements) which the lord created (are the Guṇas). These worlds are surrounded by what are termed as Mahābhūtas (great elements).

59. When the highly intelligent deity created thousands of *bhūtas* (living beings), how does *bhūtatva* (the state of being an element) is begotten in them specifically afterwards (in their post-creation stage).[17]

60. (Defective)[18] Innumerable/immeasurable are the great elements* (?). (From them) living beings are created. Hence the term "great element" (*mahābhūta*) is suitably applicable to them.

61. Our body is the aggregate of five elements since our *Ceṣṭā* (activity) is Vāyu (the wind), the cavity is

*Mahāṣṭāni is prob. a misprint vide Note 18, p. 511.

Ākāśa (ether), the heat is *Agni* (fire) the liquid portion is *Salila* (water) and the mass is Pṛthivī.

62. Hence, the mobile and immobile living beings do consist of these five elements. The ears, nose, taste, touch and vision are termed Indriyas (sense-organs).

Bhāradvāja said :

63. If (you say) that the mobile and immobile beings consist of five elements (I object to it) since in the body of the immobile beings, the five Dhātus (Primary elements) are not seen.

64. The five *Dhātus* are not perceived in the body of the trees, which are devoid of heat and activity and which are actually solid in form.

65. They do not hear, do not see, they are not cognisant of smell and taste nor do they perceive touch. How can they consist of the five *Dhātus* (elementary ingredients?).

66. There is no *Bhautika* feature (the state of being evolved out of the elements) in the trees due to their not being a liquid, not being a fire, not being the earth and not being the wind, not being *ākāśa* (the sky) as the sky is comprehensible and immeasurable.

Bhṛgu replied :

67. There is no doubt at all that though the trees are of solid nature there is ether in them. (Hence, the perpetual outcome of fruits and flowers from them comes to pass).

68. Due to heat the leaf withers; the bark, the fruits and flowers too wither and decompose. Hence, there is the (sensation of) touch in them.

69. The fruits and flowers become shattered due to the loud report of thunder and the (roaring) sounds of wind and fire. The sound is heard through the ears. Hence, trees do hear.

70. The creeper twines round the tree or spreads all round. The path cannot remain invisible. Hence trees can see.

71. Through merits and demerits and through scents and different kinds of incense, trees that are not affected by sickness, blossom.[19] Hence, trees do smell.

72. Since there is perception of happiness and misery, since the tree if lopped off grows again, I see a soul in the trees. They are not insentient.

73. (Defective) Hence, it takes up water; through fire and wind it consumes the food; as the food undergoes metabolism the growth of the tree takes place.

74. The five *Dhātus* (elements) are present in the body of all mobile beings. They act in diverse ways on the body whereby the body functions.

75. The skin, the flesh, the bones, the marrow and the fifth (*Dhātu*)—the sinews—these constitute the earth element in the body.

76. The Tejas element (energy) is the body, (the gastric) fire anger and the eyes as well as the body temperature. These five constitute the fire element in the body (the embodied being) which are created by the (element called) fire.

77. The five ether elements (i.e. the spaces) in the body of living beings are—the ears, the nostrils, the mouth, the heart and the belly.

78. Water elements always present in the bodies of the living beings are five, viz.—the phlegm, the bile, the sweat, the fat and the blood.

79-80. Five types of (organic elemental winds envelop the embodied being. It is through the *Prāṇa* that the living being delights (others) [20]* (?). The Vyāna is diffused throughout the body. The Apāna blows downwards. Samāna is stationed in the cardiac region. Through the Udāna the living being breathes and through all the five types it speaks.

81. The embodied being perceives the quality of smell from the earthly element and the taste from the water element in him. I shall recount in detail the quality of smell.

82-83. The smell is of nine varieties[21]—the agreeable, the disagreeable, the sweet one, the pungent one, that which spreads wide, that which is harmonious and compact. That which is bland and mild, that which is dreamy and sullied, that

*Probably a misprint for *praṇīyate*—moves about or respires. vide *Mbh. Śānti* 184.24.

which is manifestly calm. Such is the smell that pertains to the earth element. The embodied being sees the splendour through the eyes and perceives touch through the wind element.

84. The sound, the touch, the colour and the taste also are remembered as qualities (of water). I shall recount to you the knowledge of taste (i.e. the details of quality of taste). Listen even as I recount it.

85. 86a The taste has been mentioned to be manifold by the sages of renowned souls. Sweet, saline, bitter, astringent, sour and pungent. Thus, the six types of taste are remembered to be pertaining to the water element.

86b-89a. The fiery element is said to be possessing three qualities, viz., the sound, the touch and the colour. The fiery element perceives the colours and colours are said to be manifold (All types of features are included in the word colour—*Rūpa*). The *Rūpas* of the fiery element are sixteen (?), viz. short, long, stout, symmetrical, atomic, circular, white, black, red, blue, yellow, pink, hard, smooth, delicate, slimy, soft and rough.

89b-91. The ether has only one quality, viz. the sound. I shall tell you the diverse extension (varieties) of the sound —*viz*. *Ṣaḍja*, *Ṛṣabha*, *Gāndhāra*, *Madhyama*, *Dhaivata*, *Pañcama* and *Niṣāda*. The quality of the ether (viz. sound) is thus said to be of seven types.

92-93a. Thanks to its power, sound is present everywhere.[22] Yet it manifests itself in various kinds of drums such as drums, kettle-drums and Mṛdaṅga and the conch, clouds and the chariot. Thus the sound originating from the ether is of various kinds.[23]

93b-95. The special quality pertaining to *Vāyu* is the quality of touch. But the quality of touch is remembered (stated traditionally) to be of various kinds. The special quality pertaining to the wind is of eleven varieties, viz. hot, cool, pleasing and painful; soft, clearly manifest touch, the rough touch, the smooth touch, the slimy touch, the light touch and the heavy touch. *Vāyu* has two Guṇas, viz. the sound and the touch.

96. (Defective)[24] They say that the sound has been originated from the ether along with qualities of Vāyu unobs-

tructed. Whether perceived or not, its (*Vāyu's*) movement is uneven[25] (zigzag or irregular).

96. The *Dhātus* are always developed further by these *Dhātus*. The fire, the water and the wind—all these are always alert in the embodied beings.

98-99. They are the root cause of the body. They stay enveloping the *Prāṇas*.[26] When the powerful (*Prāṇa*) functions depending on the element called the earth, the Agni (fire element) rests on the top of the head and protects the body. Staying either in the cerebrum or in the fire, the Prāṇa functions.

100-101a. That creature is the *Ātman* of all living beings. It is the eternal Puruṣa. It is the mind, the intellect, the ego, the living beings and the object of the senses. Thus everywhere it is being protected[27] by the Prāṇas.

101b-102. From behind it is enabled to attain its respective movement, by the vital air called *Samāna*. The *Apāna* functions after resorting to the fire-element at the root of the bladder and the rectum where it makes the urine and the faecal matter flow out.

103. Experts in anatomical (spiritual) knowledge call that (particular organic wind) the *Udāna* which though single functions in three (spheres) viz. in exertions, in activities and in restraint.

104. The (vital) wind that abides in all the joints in the human bodies is called Vyāna.

105 The fire that is diffused in the arms[28] is urged by *Samāna*. It functions by creating the *Rasas* (lymphatic juices or secretions) and the many *Doṣas* (disorders in the three bodily humours) and functions.

106. In the middle of *Prāṇa* and *Apāna* the (gastric) fire attains its stable position and urged by *Prāṇa* and *Apāna*, it digests well.

107. (Defective) The digestive-system (?) extends from the mouth to the *Pāyu* (Anus) which is otherwise called *Gudā* (rectum). Hence, all the lymphatic vessels of the embodied beings produce Retas[29] (semen virile).

108. When the organic wind called a combined derangement of the humours[30] (causing fever) takes place, the heat

should be known as (gastric) fire. It digests the food of the embodied beings.

109. The *Prāṇa* that carries the force and heat of the fire goes down to the end of the anus and is obstructed at the extremity of the rectum. It comes up once again and casts the fire upwards.

110. The abdomen is beneath the umbilical region and the *Āmāśaya* (the receptacle of the raw or uncooked matter the upper part of the belly) is remembered to be above it. All the *Prāṇas* are stationed at the root of (*pakvāśaya*) the umbilicus of the body.

111. The *Nāḍis* (tubular vessels) proceed from the heart and go everywhere—to the sides, above and below. Urged by the ten *Prāṇas* they carry the nutritive juicy elements[31] (to all parts of the body).

112. The path of the Yogas is also this. Thereby the people attain that highest region. The self-possessed men of equanimity overcoming strain, keep the *Ātman* at the head (in the *Sahasrāra* Lotus)

113. When the Prāṇa and Apāna of the embodied beings function thus, *Agni* (fiery element) is generated and kindled as through in (or under) a cooking pot[32] (?).

CHAPTER FORTYTWO

1. The NP gives three theories of the evolution of the Universe: (1) 'The Popular Purāṇic Trinity Theory' wherein god Brahmā is regarded as the creator of the Universe (*Supra* 3.3-4) (2) 'The Śākta-Sāṅkhya theory' in which the *Parā Śakti* (Supreme Potency) of Mahāviṣṇu is credited with the creation. But the process of evolution is that of Sāṅkhyas. (3) The Third theory which may be called 'the Bhṛgu Theory of creation' is discussed in this chapter. The main feature is the special type of evolution proposed herein which is briefly as follows :

Mānasa (Viṣṇu)—*Mahat*—*Ākāśa* (the ether)—water—fire—wind—earth.

The NP has not only borrowed this theory from the *Mbh. Śānti* chs. 182-185 but has incorporated *Verbatim* the verses in these chapters. This shows the compilatory nature of the NP.

2. This corresponds to *Bhīṣma Uvāca* in the *Mbh.* (*ibid*) v. 5. The rest of the text is a copy of the *Mbh.*

3. Mānasa—NK (Nilakaṇṭha) the com. on the *Mbh.* explains by quoting a Śruti text which states :

"Out of *Asat* was evolved *Manas* which created Prajāpati. the progenitor of all beings; alternately, whatever is, exists in mind". Hence *Mānasa* is the name given to the cause of the origin of the Universe. But the adjectives used in vv 13b-15 show that Mānasa is identical with the *Brahman* or Mahāviṣṇu, NK shows how each of the adjectives is supported in the Upaniṣads.

4. The evolution mentioned here is different from that of the Sāṅkhyas. NK is hard put to it to explain this deviation. He states that the usual evolution—the sky—wind—fire—water--earth are implied here :

He states :

ākāśād abhavad vāri ityādipāṭha-kramo na vivakṣitaḥ kintu ākāśād vāyuḥ, vāyoragniḥ, agnerāpaḥ, adbhyaḥ pṛthivī iti śrauta eva jñeyaḥ.

NK further explains that the names of the elements (wind, etc.) indicate their subtle forms (*tanmātras*) before these elements were grossly divided. (*Tatra vāyvādi-sabdaiḥ sparśa-tanmātraṁ rūpa-tanmātram gandha-tanmātraṁ ca sūkṣmam apañcīkṛta-bhūtajātam ucyate.*

5. The Śrutis record that as soon as Brahmā was born he uttered the words "I am He" (*So'ham*). Hence, he is called *Aham* or *Ahaṁkāra*.

6. *Sarva-bhūtātmabhūtakṛt* : God Brahmā is the soul embodying all *bhūtas* (*sarva-bhūtātman*) as well as the creator of those *bhūtas* (*bhūta-kṛt*). As NK puts it : *Sarvabhūtāni sthūla-viyadādīni, tadātmā taccharīraḥ sa cāsau bhūtakṛc caturvidha-bhūtagrāma-sraṣṭā ceti samāsaḥ.*

7. The concept of the deity as the embodiment of the universe which is detailed here is an echo of the *Muṇḍaka Up.* II.1.4 where the deity is

called *Sarva-bhūtāntarātmā* and still the limbs of his body are said to have been constituted by the sun, the moon, the quarters, etc.

8. This repetition of water indicates the Lord who is the embodiment of water and he is unending—NK.

9. *Tattva-darśanāt*—NK takes (*bhidyante*) (*a*) *tattva-darśanāt* meaning *the bhūtas* are distinguished *through lack* of true knowledge". He who has realized Reality (*Tattva*) can realize the non-duality—the identity of the soul with the Universe.

10. By the fiat of his will of *Saṅkalpād evāsya pitaraḥ samuttiṣṭhanti*, quoting such śruti passages, NK states that His Will is enough for creation, no other material is necessary.

11. At the beginning of the Kalpa in Brahmā's region—NK.

12. NK quotes *Nīhāra-dhūmārka*, etc., (*Śve.* Upa 2-11) for comparison.

13. *bhavaha* in the NP is probably a mistake for *bhājana* in the Mbh. (*ibid*) vii. It is reasonable and within the experience of all that an empty vessel (*bhājana*) when filled with water makes sound, while "an abode without an outlet" is strange; so with *bhājana* as the emendation, the translation is "Just as an empty vessel without any aperture appears void of sound, but when with water, air comes in and creates a sound."

14. *Tathā salila-saṁruddhe-ghoṣavān*,

This (v. 52) also means : "Similarly when the infinite sky (void space) became full of water, and the wind penetrating through the ocean arose with a roar."

15. NK concludes that just as the creation of the Universe is mental (not real) in the case of god Mānasa, similarly we should also realize it to be unreal like a dream (*asmadādīnām api iyaṁ sṛṣṭiḥ svapnavad, etc.*).

16. *rakṣya* "to be protected" : is not a satisfactory reading in this context. *Mbh. Śānti* 184-1 reads "Brahma" which supplies the subject to *asṛjat* in the text).

17. The plain question is ; why *Mahābhūtas* (great elements) are also called *Bhūtas* (which is normally applied to creatures of different categories.

18. V. 60 in the NP appears defective due to the words *amitāni mahāṣṭāni* in 60a. The original Mbh. (*ibid*) verse 3a which is quoted in the NP reads:

amitānāṁ mahāśabdo yānti bhūtāni sambhavam

The epithet *mahā* is given to all things which belong to the category of 'immeasurables' or innumerables.

19. V.17 may alternately be translated thus:

In consequence of smell (pleasant or unpleasant—good or bad) and due to the perfumes of different kinds of incenses, trees recover their strength and blossom forth.

20. The Mbh. reads *Praṇīyate* for *Prīṇayate* of the NP. NK interprets: It is the vital breath called *Prāṇa* which enables a living being to move about; the vital breath named *Vyāna* gives him strength for exertions.

21. NK has given instances with a slightly different interpretation. Thus *nirhārī*: overpowering the smell of other things as the gum of Asafoetida used in articles of food.

Saṁhata— A composite mixture of many scents.

Snigdha—As one given out by boiled butter (when transformed into ghee).

Rūkṣa— Dry as of mustard oil.

22. *Aiśvaryeṇa*— Due to its quality of being all-pervasive like the Supreme Being —NK.

23. The NP v. 92 combines from the Mbh. vv. 40b, 41a, and omitting v. 41C, accepts v. 42a for 93a.

24. The text of v. 96 is defective as it combines Mbh (*ibid*) vv. 42b and 43a and NP V.97 combines Mbh. vv. 43b and 44a. Reconstructed according to the Mbh. the verses should be translated as follows: 96b-97a. The sound (which is the property of *Ākāśa* or space) is not heard, when different kinds of touch are inchaotive. The elements or constituents which mix up with other constituents in the body increase in strength.

te śabdādyutpādakā dhātavo dehārambhās tvagādi-golakā dhātubhiḥ prāṇendriyaiḥ āpyāyante ādita ārabhya saṁvardhyante / NK.

25. The reading *viṣamā gatiḥ* accepted by the NP is from the Bengali Mss of the Mbh. NK specifically states *viṣamā gatir iti gauḍa-pāṭhas tu prāmādikaḥ*. This reading shows that the author of the NP. copies a Ms. hailing from Bengal or he belonged to that part of the country and accepted the reading from the MS of the Mbh. used in that part.

26. Here ends ch. 184 of the Śānti of the Mbh. the next ch. (185) of the Mbh. is borrowed in the NP. vv. 2b onwards.

27. The *Mbh. Śānti* 185.5a (which is the same as NP v. 101a) reads *paricālyate* and NK interprets: The *Prāṇa* is the creature, the Supreme soul, the eternal *Puruṣa,* the mind...object of the sense. Thus the living being is made to move about by *Prāṇa* in every respect."

28. In *bāhuṣvagniḥ* etc. of the NP. *bāhu* is meaningless as the vital air called *Samāna* does not limit its activity to arms only, but covers the whole body, and secondly. the plural No. *bāhuṣu* implies more than two arms which means *Samāna Vāyu* does not function in two-armed beings. The Mbh. reading *dhātuṣu* for *bāhuṣu* is better. The mistake is repeated in v. 105 b where NP reads *rasān bāhūñś ca* where the proper reading should be *dhātūñś ca* as the breath *samāna* operates on all *dhātus* (constituents of the body) and not merely on (more than two) hands.

29. *Retas* in NP v.127 is obviously a blunder. For *retas* is irrelevant in the channel that extends from the mouth to the anus. That reading rendered the verse defective. The Mbh. (*ibid*) v. 107 which is borrowed by the NP reads *Srotas* and means "From this main channel many subsidiary channels or *Nāḍīs* spread out (like branches) all over the body."

NK. takes *Srotas* as "the passage of the vital wind" and its branches as *Nāḍīs*.

30. NK interprets : As a result of the rapid confluence of the (five) vital airs flowing through these arteries, the heat called gastric fire is generated and it causes digestion.

31. This shows that the NP. anticipated Harvey in physiology.

32. The gist of NK's long explanation: In all the physical and mental functions of the body, *Prāṇas*, etc. are the instrumental cause. When *Yoga* characterised by breath-control (*prāṇāyāma*) is practised, the eternal *Brahman* reveals itself resplendent. In the final analysis what remains is the *Brahman*.

CHAPTER FORTYTHREE[1]

The Traditional Duties of Brāhmaṇas

Bhāradvāja said:

1. If the wind is the lord of the Prāṇas and it is the wind alone that functions, breathes and speaks, there is no purpose served by the Jīva, (the individual soul is superfluous).

2. If the heat belongs to the fire, (the element called the Fire), if it is perceived through fire and if the fiery element digests (food, etc.) it, the Jīva, is futile.

3. When a creature dies, the so-called individual soul is not perceived leaving. Only the wind leaves him off and the heat is extinguished.

4. If however, the individual soul is identical with *Asu*[2] (i. e. Prāṇa, the vital wind) and if it has contact with the wind, it may be seen on a part with the zone of the wind along with the groups of Maruts.

5. Or if the contact be with it (the wind) and if it perishes thereby like a pot of water due to its being released (separated) from a great ocean.[3]

6. If anyone pours water into the well or places the lamp into the fire, it perishes immediately. Similarly, the individual soul too perishes instantaneously.[4]

7-8. The body consists of the five elements and (they say that) it is in this that the soul lives. Therefore, if one of the elements perishes all the others also must undoubtedly perish. If food (and beverages) are not taken in, the watery element perishes. The wind element perishes by means of the restraint of the breath. The (gastric) fire perishes by abstaining from taking food and if anything is taken to purge the belly.[5]

9. Through sickness, wounds and similar distress the earth element also gets shattered. If anyone of these elements is afflicted, the whole mass of the elements perishes.

10. If that (body constituted of five elements) perishes, what is it that the individual soul pursues? What is it that

the individual soul feels afflicted?* What does it hear or speak?

11. "When I am in the other world this cow will redeem me." A person thinks like this, offers the gift of a cow and then dies. But whom is it that the cow will redeem ?

12. When the cow, the giver (of that cow) and the acceptor—all these are dissolved here in this world, simultaneously, whence can there be the reunion of all of them ?

13. Whence can these be enlivened again—he who is swallowed up by birds, he who falls down from the top of a mountain and he who is consumed by fire ?

14. If the root of a tree is cut, it does not grow again. When a man is alive[6] all his parts function. But how will the dead come back again ?

15. All the individual souls had been created formerly and they revolve again and again. The dead ones perish even as the seeds perish one after the other.[7]

16. O Brāhmaṇa, this is the doubt that surges in my heart. O omniscient one, clarify it since I depend upon you (and have approached you for this).

Sanandana said:

17. O excellent sage, Bhṛgu the son of Brahmā who was asked thus by him spoke again to clear his doubts.

Bhṛgu said:

18. When the individual is killed or dies himself the *Prāṇas* cease to exist.[8] The living being (i.e. his soul) transmigrates to another body and this body decays and becomes shattered.

19. The *Jīva* is not dependent on the body. It does not perish when the body perishes. Just as the fire is seen (to be present) even after the sacrificial twigs are completely burned.

Bhāradvāja said:

20. (You say) that when they (the sacrificial twigs) perish the fire does not perish. But after the fuel has been used up the fire is not verily seen.

*NP "afflicted" but Mbh. "Does it know" (*Vedayate*) XII 10-186.

21. Hence, I understand that if fire is extinguished without further addition of fuel, it definitely perishes since, where it goes is not known. There is no proof of its existence.

Bhṛgu said:

22-25. (You say as follows:—) After the twigs have been used up the fire is not seen. I understand that the tranquil fire without fuel does perish since where it goes is not known. There is no proof of its existence. (Yet understand this.) Just as the fire is not perceived after the consumption of fuel as it has vanished into the ether, and so is without any base and as it is difficult to be perceived, so also, when the body is forsaken the *Jīva* remains like the ether (invisible). Since it is very subtle it does not perish,[9] undoubtedly in the same way as the fire. The fiery element sustains the *Prāṇa*. May that be understood as the *Jīva*.

26-27. The (gastric) fire that is sustained by the wind (i.e. the body temperature is sustained by respiration) perishes when the breath is curbed. When the fire of the physical body perishes the insentient body falls down and merges into the earth. Indeed, the ultimate goal of the mobile and immobile beings is the earth.

28-29. The wind follows (or merges into) the ether; the fiery element too follows it. Since all the three constitute one unit the set of two (viz. the earth and water) is established on the earth. Where there is the ether, the wind is present too. The fire is present where there is the wind. These must be known to be without forms but the embodied beings have forms.

Bhāradvāja said:

30. O sinless one, if the fire, the wind, the earth, the ether and the water are present in the embodied beings, what are the characteristics of the *Jīva*. Kindly explain this to me.

31. I wish to understand of what nature is the *Jīva* in the bodies of living beings which are constituted by a set of five things viz. the elements) and take delight in five things (e.g. taste, smell, etc.) and have five cognitive senses.

32. The body is a mass of flesh and blood, fat, bones and sinews. When it is shattered and split the *Jiva* is not perceived.

33. If the body is without a *Jiva* but it contains only the five elements, who experiences the pain in the course of mental and physical distress?

34. O sage, by means of his pair of ears, the *Jiva* hears what is uttered, but when the mind is preoccupied he does not hear it. Hence, the *Jiva* is futile.

35. What should be seen, everyone sees with the eyes in collaboration with the mind. When the mind is agitated, the eye does not perceive though it may look at things.

36. He does not see, or smell or hear, or speak or know the touch when he (the agent called *Jiva*) is under the influence of slumber.

37. Who is it that is delighted? Who is infuriated? Who bewails? Who is alarmed? Who shuns? Who wishes? Who meditates? Who is malicious? Who reads or utters words?

Bhṛgu replied:

38. The body holds one that is common to the five. It is the *Antarātman*[10] (the inner immanent soul). It is he who perceives the odour, taste, sound, touch, form and the *Guṇas* (attributes).

39. The *Antarātman* is present throughout the body, in the body consisting of five elements; it perceives the five *Guṇas*, it is this that experiences pleasure and pain always. Separated from it the body does not understand anything.

40. When there is no perception of colour, no touch and no heat in the fire within the body, the fire is tranquil. When the bodily fire (temperature) is cooled down, (the body) dies by being forsaken by *Jiva* (who does not die).

41. The whole of this (universe) (?) is full of water; it is the water that is the physical body of the embodied being. There the *Ātman* is *Brahmā* in all the living beings. He is the creator of the worlds. He is called *Mānasa*.[11]

42. That which rests in the physical body like the water-drop on the lotus-leaf is the *Ātman*. Know that the *Ātman* is conducive to the welfare of all worlds.

43. Know him as the indwelling soul (*Kṣetrajña*), the eternal well-wisher of the worlds. Know that the *Guṇas* (attributes) of the *Jiva* are *Sattva, Rajas* and *Tamas.*

44. Some say that insentience[12] is the attribute of the *Jiva.* But it is active and it activates everything. Those who know the *kṣetra* (the physical body) say that the Supreme *Ātman* has set the seven worlds in motion.

45. When the physical body is changed, there is no destruction of the *Jiva.* O sage, those who have not understood this, call this as untrue. The *Jiva* moves about in the world (only) after being covered by the body.[13] And its change of body takes place due to its fifth stage (death). (The other four being infancy, childhood, youth and old age).

46. Thus hidden in all the living beings, the *Ātman* always moves about. It is perceived through the subtle and excellent intellect[14] by the seers of the truth.

47. (Defective) The wise person continuously practising *Yoga* in the initial and final watches of the night and with his soul sanctified by assimilating pure food realizes the Supreme soul within his own soul.

48. By dint of the serenity and composure of the mind, and by giving up both auspicious and inauspicious *Karmans,* one should stabilise oneself in the *Ātman* and be delighted in the mind. He shall thereafter attain infinite bliss.

49. The mental fire in the bodies is called the *Jiva* (in the bodies). In the matter of decision regarding *Bhūtātman,* the creation of the lord of subjects[15] is as follows:

50. At the beginning (of creation) it was the Brāhmaṇas alone that *Brahmā* the Prajāpati created. They were evolved out of his own brilliance. Their lustre was like that of the Sun and fire.

51. Thereafter the Lord created the following things as conducive to the attainment of heaven, viz. truthfulness *Dharma* (virtue), the eternal Brahman (i. e. the *Vedas*), the conventional duties and purity both physical and mental.

52-53a. (Defective) Devas, Dānavas, Gandharvas, Daityas, Asuras and the great serpents, Yakṣas, Rākṣasas, Nāgas, Piśācas and human beings (were created). The human beings (were classified) into Brāhmaṇas, Kṣatriyas, Vaiśyas and Śūdras.[16]

Bhāradvāja said:

53b-54. (You say) that one *Varṇa*[17] (caste) in the four-fold division of men is different from the other. What is the criterion thereof? Sweat, urine, faecal matter, phlegm, bile and blood circulate within everyone. Then on what basis is the caste divided?

55. Among both the mobile and immobile beings there are innumerable groups and classes. Among these different *Varṇas* how is a particular *Varṇa* arrived at?

Bhṛgu said:

56. Originally, there was no distinction among the people. The whole universe formerly created by Brahmā was Brahmanical by nature. Though originally created as equals by Brahmā, it was as a result of their *Karmans* (acts) that people got divided into different castes.

57. Some of those Brāhmaṇas became fond of erotic enjoyments. They were furious by temperament. They were violent and zealous. They liked risky adventures. They forsook their original duties (of Brāhmaṇas), became red in complexion (i. e. full of Rajo-guṇa) and attained *Kṣatriya-hood.*

58. Those Brāhmaṇas, who maintained themselves by means of agriculture and lived by tending and rearing up cattle and did not practise original duties as Brāhmaṇas (grew) yellow (a mixture of *rajas* and *tamas*) and became *Vaiśyas.*

59. Those Brāhmaṇas who were engrossed in violence and untruthfulness, greedy and maintained themselves by means of all types of jobs (even forbidden to Brāhmaṇas) and were thus fallen from purity of conduct became dark (full of *Tamoguṇa*) and degenerated to the status of Śūdras.

60. Thus the (original) Brāhmaṇas affected adversely by these activities were changed into other castes. The power of austerities of those Brāhmaṇas who maintained their prescribed religious rituals and duties, does not perish.

61-62a. There are many sub-divisions of Brāhmaṇas in the different places, but all of them observe holy virtues, rites and restraints. They perpetually retain the Brahman (i. e. they study the Vedas regularly). Brahman (i.e. Vedas) had already been created formerly. Those who know them understand (everything else).

62b-c. There are many types of Piśācas, Rākṣasas, Pretas and Mleccha (outcaste) tribes. The creation by (Brahmā's) mind is verily intent on the religious rituals and duties.[18]

Bhāradvāja said:

63. O excellent Brāhmaṇa, how does one become a Brāhmaṇa or a Kṣatriya? O Brahmanical sage, how does one become a Vaiśya or a Śūdra? O excellent one among the fluent speakers, please explain it unto me.

Bhṛgu said:

64. One who is as follows is called a Brāhmaṇa. He should have been consecrated duly by means of post-natal purificatory rites and other holy rites as well and should himself be pure. He must possess the learning (recitation, etc.) of the Vedas. He must strictly adhere to the religious duties and rites prescribed for Brāhmaṇas.[19]

65. He must closely follow the rules of cleanliness both mental and physical and pure conduct. He must have soundly studied the different lores. He must be fond of his preceptors and elders. He must perpetually observe the holy vows and rites. He must be devoted to truthfulness. Such a person is verily called a Brāhmaṇa.

66. He in whom these qualities are seen is remembered as a Brāhmaṇa, viz. Truthfulness, charitable gifts, non maliciousness (absence of wickedness), kindness, mercy, sympathy and austerity.

67. One who is as follows, is called a Kṣatriya. He practises the duties assigned to a Kṣatriya, i.e. the military

profession). He practises studying the Vedas He must be interested in giving religious gifts and collecting taxes.*

68. Derivation of the word Vaiśya is as follows:— *viśati āśu iti Vaiśyaḥ.*[20] One who enters (worldly transactions) immediately is called a Vaiśya. Through the animals he is interested in taking to agricultural activities. He loves to donate charitable gifts and is pure. He is endowed with the study and the learning of the Vedas.

69. One who is always habituated to all kinds of diet, one who regularly performs all odd jobs, is impure, one who has forsaken the study of the Vedas and one who has no conventional duty is remembered as a Śūdra.

70. If a (born) Śūdra possesses all good characteristics and a (born) Brāhmaṇa does not possess the same that Śūdra is no longer a Śūdra and that Brāhmaṇa is no longer a Brāhmaṇa.

71. By every possible means restraint be put on covetousness and anger. This as well as self-control is the holiest of all wisdom.

72. Those two (covetousness and anger) attempt to destroy welfare. They must be avoided by all means. One shall save one's prosperity and glory from perpetual anger;[21] one shall save one's austerity (power of penance) from malice.

73. One should save one's learning from (the feeling of both) honour and dishonour and one should save oneself from errors and mistakes.

74. O Brāhmaṇa, he is a real renouncer and intelligent man, he whose every religious enterprise (e.g. sacrifice) is unfettered by longing expectations and he who has dedicated every thing (in his possession) to *Tyāga* (renunciation for the sake of others).

75. One should refrain from injuring or doing violence to all living beings; he should be friendly unto all. Renouncing all possessions and monetary gifts he should subdue his sense-organs intelligently.

---

*In my (Veṇk. Edt.) text, the reading is *Dānādānaratir* 'One who likes to give charitable gifts but not accepting them from others' (but collecting taxes from subjects).

76-78. One shall abide by that which causes no sorrow,[22] one that will afford him freedom from fear here and hereafter. The (Brāhmaṇa) should be perpetually engaged in austerities, self-control, restraint over the mind. He should be desirous of conquering what is not conquered. One should remain unattached to worldly affairs. What can be perceived by means of the sense organs is *Vyakta* (the manifest). That which is beyond the scope of the sense organs, and which can be grasped by inference from its symptoms and characteristic features should be known as *Avyakta* (unmanifest). If there is a nuclear conviction of reality one should continue to ponder more and more. When one is (thoroughly) convinced (about the truth)[23] he should steady the mind therein.

79. The mind shall be controlled through the *Prāṇa* (Breath-control) and the *Prāṇa* should be concentrated in the *Brahman*. One attains *Nirvāṇa* (extinction as a prelude to salvation) through Nirveda (complete detachment). One should not be worried or think of anything else.

80-81a. O Brāhmaṇa, it is verily by dispassion (and renunciation) that one gets (real) happiness. One should always be (striving) for purity and should be endowed with the norm of the conduct of the good.

81b-82a. Highest compassion for all beings—all these constitute the characteristic of twice-borns.[24] He (a twice-born) should observe Truthfulness as a sacred vow and should practise Penance, (mental and physical) purity. It is the truth that creates the subjects. The whole world is sustained by Truth. One goes to heaven only by truthfulness.[25]

82b-83. Falsehood is the feature of darkness; one is led downwards through darkness. Those who have been caught hold of by darkness, those who have been enveloped by darkness do not see the brilliant light (of heaven). They say that *Naraka* (hell) is darkness itself; it cannot be brilliant with light.

84. Both *Satya* (truth) and *Anṛta* (falsehood) is attained by the people roaming over the Earth. Even in that case, the predilection in the world should be thus towards Truth and falsehood.

85-86. Light and darkness indicate Dharma and Adharma as also happiness and misery. Wise, foresighted persons who observe what is created in the world affected by miseries and pleasures both physical and mental but both originating from or leading up to *Asukha* (i. e. unhappiness), do not become deluded. A clever man should (therefore) endeavour to get liberated from misery.[26]

87-88. Both here and hereafter pleasure is non-permanent. Just as the light of the moon eclipsed by Rāhu becomes faded and dim, so also the happiness of living beings, oppressed by darkness, perishes.

89. Happiness is said to be of two kinds, viz. the physical and the mental. Here, in this world verily all actions in regard to any object are said to be pursued for the sake of happiness. As to the other world there is nothing better than *Apavarga* (salvation). That alone is to be desired. It is a desirable quality. Its origin is caused by the endeavour for the same through virtuous activities. All the activities are aimed at the acquisition of happiness which is its purpose.

Bhāradvāja said :

89. It has been said by you that pleasures have the greatest status.

90. We do not accept this. Nor is it so in the case of sages who establish themselves in the Supreme.

91. This desirable special quality cannot be attained. They do not practise this. It is reported that Lord Brahmā, the creator of the three worlds, stands alone in austerity. He is a celibate. He does not entangle himself in erotic pleasure.

92. Moreover, Lord Viśveśvara, husband of Umā, controlled Kāma who attacked him by reducing him to bodilessness.

93-94 Hence, this is not accepted by noble-souled ones.[27] Nor am I convinced of this by you. It has been stated by you that women constitute the highest, ultimate happiness.[28] It is only a popular saying in the world. There are two types of benefit (or result). Happiness results from good deeds and misery otherwise.

Bhṛgu said :

95. Here it is being (thus) explained. Darkness (*Tamo-guṇa*) has manifested itself from *Anṛta* (falsehood). Those who are prevailed upon by darkness pursue only *Adharma* and not *Dharma*. Those who have been affected by anger, covetousness, delusion, violence, falsehood and similar vicious things do not attain happiness either in this world or in the other one. They are shattered and scattered through various kinds of sickness, pain and oppressions. They are afflicted by various distressing features such as capital punishment, imprisonment and tortures; they are overwhelmed by the distress and strain of hunger, thirst and tedium; they are subjected to various miseries of physical strain due to rain, gusts of wind, oppressing heat and biting cold; they are afflicted by various mental miseries caused by the death of or separation from kinsmen or the destruction of wealth; they are also dejected due to other causes such as old age, death, etc.

96. In the heaven there is neither physical nor mental pain; there is no old age or sin; it is always pleasure alone there; but here (in this world) both pleasure and pain are experienced.

97. They say that there is only misery in the hell, that the highest region (of the Lord) has pure happiness. The earth is the mother of all living beings; women are also of the same nature.

98-99. The male is lord of the progeny (begetter). They know that the semen virile is of the fiery element. Hence, he is the creator of the worlds of Dharma, of good conduct,[20] of well-performed penance, of self-study (of the Vedas) and of the performance of Homa. The sin is subdued through the sacrificial rites. There is excellent tranquility in the self-study of the Vedas.

100. They say that enjoyment of pleasures is due to charitable gifts; and that one shall attain heavenly pleasures through penance. They say that *Dāna* (charitable gift) is of

two types; that for the purpose of benefit here and that for the purpose of benefit in the other world.

101. Whatever is given to the good men is conducive to the pleasures in the other world; whatever is given as charitable gift to bad men is conducive to the pleasures in this world only. The benefit enjoyed (from charitable gifts) is in accordance with charitable gift offered.

Bhāradvāja enquired:

102. What is performance of holy rites? Who performs them? What are the characteristics of Dharma? Of how many types is Dharma? It behoves you to explain it.

Bhṛgu said:

103. The acquisition of the benefit of heavenly pleasures is only unto those learned men who are engrossed in carrying out their prescribed religious duties. He who is otherwise becomes deluded.

Bhāradvāja submitted:

104. It behoves you to explain to me here the respective conventional duties of the four stages of life ordained formerly by Brahmanical sages.[30]

Bhṛgu said:

105. Four *Āśramas* (stages of life) have been specified for the preservation of *Dharma*, even at the very outset, by Lord Brahmā who used to carry out what is beneficial to the worlds.

106. They mention that the residence in the house of the preceptor is the first *Āśrama*. The boy in this stage of life, properly controls his self by means of purificatory rites, consecratory rites, observances and holy vows. He performs the worship of the sun, the fire and the deities during the two *Sandhyās* (The Dawn and Dusk). He eschews all lethargy. He purifies his inner soul by means of obeisance to the preceptor, performance of the Vedic Studies and listening to (good discourses).

He takes his holy ablution thrice every day. He regularly practises celibacy, maintenance of holy sacrificial fires, service to the preceptor, begging for alms, etc.; he dedicates the alms so collected (to his teacher) and other activities to the inner soul. He abides by the words of the preceptor. He obediently carries out the behests of the preceptor. (He does not say anything against the preceptor.) He should be devoted to the study of the Vedas which he acquires, thanks to the grace of his preceptor. In this connection there is a Verse:-

107. If any Brāhmaṇa propitiates the preceptor and acquires the Vedas, he attains the benefit of residence in the heaven (and heavenly pleasures). All his mental desires will be accomplished.

They say that the second *Āśrama* is *Gārhasthya* (householdership).

108. We shall elucidate the characteristics of the conventional duties followed by the good of that period. The *Āśrama* of the householder is laid down in regard to those who practise good conduct, who have performed *Samāvartana* rites (conclusion of study and returned home) and who seek the benefits of joint-performance of holy rites.

109. In this stage (the aim) is the acquisition of *Dharma*, wealth and love. In view of the acquisition of the *Trivarga* (i.e. the above-mentioned three aims) he should earn wealth through non-despicable means. A householder should lead his particular stage of life by means of wealth earned by any of these means. He may earn wealth as a result of his pre-eminence achieved through recitation of the Vedas. Or he may earn wealth by means of any method open to a Brahminical sage. He may take wealth from the sea. He may take wealth acquired by good luck or by practice of observances.

110. They cite this stage as the root (support) of all stages (of life). The residents of the abode of the preceptor (i.e. Brāhmaṇas of religious students), Parivrājakas (i.e. Recluses and others such as those who observe the performance of holy rites and vows are also benefited through the house-holders through the alms given or oblations shared.[31]

111. The householders render service to the *Vānaprasthas* (the forest-dwelling hermits) also generally by supplying them

the articles (they require). Hence, these good men generally travel over the earth with the intention of visiting holy centres and sacred rivers. They continue their *Svādhyāya* (self study) also. While travelling, they take with them the wholesome cooked food they may require on the way.

112. The householders greet and welcome them. Without envy or jealousy they speak to them welcoming words. They offer them good seats and beds. They are hospitable to them and give them food to eat and render other good services.

113. In this context there is a verse. If any guest becomes disappointed and returns from anyone's house, he gives the house-owner all the sins and takes away his merits.

114. Through the performance of sacrifices and other rites (by a householder) the deities are pleased; the *Pitṛs* are pleased by the oblations and libations offered; the sages are pleased, thanks to the repeated recitations, listening and memorising of the *Vidyā* (Vedic passages, etc.) and god Prajāpati is pleased, thanks to the procreation of children.

115-116. In this context there are two verses. (Defective) (The Householders) entertain affection to all living beings like the ears and the speech unto the Vāyu[32] (?). The following are despicable (in a householder): Harassing (others), obstructing (others), using harsh words, disrespecting people, arrogance and egotism. The following is a penance common to all Āśramas, viz. nonviolence, truthfulness and absence of anger.

117 Again in the householder's life, one has the good fortune of having garlands, ornaments, good robes, oil bath, enjoyment, etc. every day; they can witness dances, they can hear and enjoy songs and instrumental music; they can have many things pleasing to the ears and cooling to the eyes; they can see beautiful women, they can enjoy the five varieties of food-stuffs, viz. *Bhakṣya* (that which is chewed and taken in), *Bhojya* (that which is swallowed), *Lehya* (lambatives), *Peya* (beverages) and *Coṣya* (articles of food squeezed and taken).

118. The householders can have the satisfaction of playing about as they please; they can attain erotic pleasures. He who can perpetually accomplish *Trivargas* (three aims in

life) in the *Aśrama* of a householder experiences all pleasures here and attains the goal of the elegent and virtuous men.[33]

119. If a householder maintains himself by gleaning, if he is engaged in performing his duties and if he has eschewed all enterprises leading to erotic pleasures—it is not difficult for him to attain heaven.

120. The *Vānaprasthas* too (Forest-dwelling hermits) pursue their virtuous activities. They visit holy centres, sacred rivers and cascades of water. In the forest full of deer, boars, buffaloes, tigers and wild elephants, they perform their austerities. They move about in those forests.

121-122. They have eschewed all dress and raiments, foodstuffs and mode of behaviour (suited to their former village life); their diet is confined to the medicinal herbs, fruits, roots and leaves; their food-intake is limited and restricted and consists of various products of the forest. They seat themselves on bare ground. They lie down on the earth, stone, sand, gravels or ashes; they cover their nakedness by means of Kuśa grass, hides or bark garments; they grow their hair, beard and moustaches as well as their nails; they take their ablutions (regularly) at the specified time; At the time prescribed for the performance of *Homa* they offer dry oblations; they take rest after sweeping the earlier offerings of sacrificial twigs, Kuśa grass, flowers, etc; their skins are cracked everywhere due to the exposure to chill or hot winds; their blood and flesh are dried up due to the performance of diverse vowed observances, Yogic activities[34] and they appear to have only skin and bones, yet they keep up their fortitude. By means of their inherent strength they uphold their bodies.

122. He who regularly maintains these rites ordained by the Brahminical sages shall, like fire, burn all his defects and conquer all invincible worlds.

123. I shall reiterate the conventional prescribed duties of the *Parivrājakas* (recluses). They eschew the sacrificial fires. They leave off wealth, property, wives and all attachment to worldly affairs. They take off their affectionate ties and renounce (everything) and become recluses. They view a lump of clay or a piece of gold or a stone equally; their attention is not diverted to those who are engaged in realising the three fold aims of life.

124. They observe enemies, friends and neutrals equally and impartially; they refrain from injuring either physically or mentally or verbally any type of living being whether an immobile, or a mammal, or a bird or a sweat-born insect; they do not have any fixed abode; they move about on the mountains, river banks, shades of trees and temples; they may go to cities or villages for temporary stay;[35] they never indulge in violence, anger, pride, greed, delusion, miserliness, arrogance, slandering or false prestige.

In this context there are three verses :

125-127. The contemplative sage (*muni*) who moves about as a *muni* (silent recluse) after granting freedom from fear to all living beings need not be afraid of any living being at any place. The recluse performs the *Agnihotra* in his own body; it is through his mouth that he consigns the *Haviṣ*-offerings obtained through begging for alms to propitiate the bodily fire. The Brāhmaṇa attains the other worlds through the fire of the funeral pyre. He who performs the duties of the *Mokṣāśrama* (*Sannyāsa*) as mentioned, should remain pure and keep his intellect properly conceived. As a fire that has no supply of fuel becomes calm, that Brāhmaṇa goes to the *Brahmaloka*.

CHAPTER FORTYTHREE

1. Chapter 43 in the NP is composed of the text of chs. 186, 187, 188, 189, 190, 191 and 192 of Mbh. Śānti Parva. As all the verses in these chapters are incorporated *en bloc* in the NP, when the text of the NP becomes unintelligible the Mbh. text is referred to and the reading in the Mbh. is suggested as the probable emendation. When NK differs his interpretation is also recorded.

2. *Vāsu* in the NP seems to be a misprint for *Vāyu* in the original (*Mbh. Śānti* 186.4). The verse then means: If life is composed of mere air and if it ends by the departure of the wind from the body, it will then mix up with another part of (the outer) atmosphere and would be visible like a whirlwind (*vātyācakravat*—NK).

3. The verse is obscure even if vv. 5 & 6 are taken together. NK however, treats them separately.

According to NK, v. 5 anticipates and replies the Digambara Jaina objection that the *Jīva* is always associated with eight types of Karmans and is never seen separate or independently distinct from them. NK is obviously not correct in limiting the *aṣṭa-karma-prakṛti* doctrine to the Digambaras only as the Śvetāmbaras (in fact all Jainas) hold it. NK reads *Saṁśleṣo yadi vātena* instead of NP's *yadi vā tena* (which is a bit obscure) The translation : "If the *Jīva*—the individual soul—be in contact with the assemblage (of *karmans*) dominated by the wind-element and if the *Jīva* be different from that assemblage, when the assemblage (of *karmans*) is destroyed like a vessel of water from which the dead-weight of stones is jettisoned it becomes free and floats in the sea."

Jainas compare the soul covered with Kārmic matter to a gourd plastered with clay, due to the weight of which it sinks down in water. But when the clay is washed off, the gourd naturally and automatically comes up and floats. So does the *Jīva*, free from Karmans, goes straight up to *Mokṣa*. The *Jīva*-gourd analogy of Jainas is better than the above Mbh. analogy.

4. Bhāradvāja, as a *Pūrva-pakṣin*, raises another objection. If as you say, *Jīva* (individual soul) be a portion of the *Brahman*, the *Jīva* gets extinguished in the *Brahman*, just as water poured into a well or a lamp (after being extinguished) becomes one with fire (*Saṅghāta-nāśe brahmāntargatasya jīvasya svarūpa-nāśaḥ* NK).

5. Mbh. (*ibid*) 186.8 reads *naśyate koṣṭha-bhedāt khaṁ* for *koṣṭhabhedārtham* of the NP. The Mbh. implies disapppearance of the element of space (*kham*) if excretions stop.

6. For *jīvānyasya pravartante*, Mbh. (*ibid*) v. 14 reads *bījānyasya pravartante* "It is seeds which put forth sprouts."

7. For *praṇaśyati* in the NP, Mbh: (*ibid*) v. 15 reads *Pravartate* "seeds

come forth from seeds". NK. explains: Semen virile is the seed of the body and not *adṛṣṭa* "the unseen" or *Karma.*

Here ends ch. 186 from the Mbh. *Śānti.*

8. For *na prāṇaḥ santi jīvasya* of the NP v. 18, Mbh. (*ibid*) ch. 187.1 reads *na praṇāśo sti jīvasya*: It means: there is no destruction of the individual soul and of whatever he has given (as gift) or of other acts.

9. For *na naśyate susūkṣmatvāt,* Mbh. (*ibid*) v. 6 reads *na gṛhyate* (the soul) cannot be seen (or inferred).

10. NK explains that it is the mind that is the 'seer' or 'experiencer'. When the mind is associated with sense-organs, one can see etc., but when, as in sleep or the *Samādhi* state, the mind is dissociated with the body, one does not see, etc.

11. According to NK 41b means : In those waters, it is the soul which manifests itself in the mind. That soul is god Brahmā, the creator of the world, who abides in all things.

12. The gross mis-print in the NP *acetana* for *Sacetana* in the Mbh. (*ibid*) v. 26 makes the verse selfcontradictory. The verse so emended means: they (the knowers of Reality) say that the soul is characterised by consciousness and exists with the attribute of life. (*Jīvaguṇa,* viz. the body, sense-organ and the mind—NK)

13. *dehāntaritaḥ* : Better : All that the Jiva does, is going from one body to another.

14. Viz. the realization of one's identification with the *Brahman*—NK.

15. *Or*: The *Jīva* is the element of fiery effulgence that abides in the mind. It is from the Lord that all this creation has come forth. This is the conclusion to be deduced after investigation into the origin of the soul and creatures.

Here ends ch. 187 of the *Mbh. Śānti.*

16. V.53a reads :

Brāhmaṇāḥ Kṣatriyā Vaiśyāḥ Śūdrāṇām asitas tathā

The line is defective as the first three words are in the nom. case (which is an enumeration of *Varṇas* or castes in continuation of the previous verse). And those words in the nom. case cannot be connected with *Śūdrāṇām asitas tathā.* Nor can these words be related with 53b which is an independent speech of Bhāradvāja. This is due to the mis-quotation in the NP of the *Mbh. Śānti* 188.4-5 which are as follows :

Brāhmaṇāḥ Kṣattriyā Vaiśyāḥ Śūdrāś ca dvija-sattama |
ye cānye bhūtasaṅghānāṁ varṇās tāṅś cāpi nirmame ||
Brāhmanāṇāṁ sito varṇaḥ Kṣattriyāṇām tu lohitaḥ |
Vaiśyānāṁ pītako varṇah śūdrāṇm asitas tathā ||

The NP quoted the 1st three words from 4a of the *Mbh.* and the last three words from 5b of the Mbh and composed its v. 53a. Hence the defectiveness.

The NP abounds in such misquotations to the despair of the translators who merely depend on the text of the NP as it is.

17. NK explains that the word *Varṇa* which means complexion or colour here represents certain attributes (*varṇena jātyā varṇaḥ sātvikatvādi bhidyate*).

18. This verse combines 18a and 20b from the Mbh. (*ibid*) ch. 188. NK interprets 20b (i.e. 62b and c in the NP) : The other creation is like the superimposition of the illusion of a serpent on a string and hence is called mental (*mānasī*). NK. takes *dharma* in the sense of *Yoga*. The mental creation rests upon *Yoga*.

Here ends chapter 188 in the *Mbh. Śānti.*

19. The duties of Brāhmaṇas are the everyday performance of ablution, *Sandhyā*, (twilight-prayer), *Japa*, *Homa* (fire worship), worship of deities, performance of Vaiśvadeva and hospitality—NK.

20. One who earns reputation by cattle-rearing, agriculture, commerce —NK.

21. *nityaṁ krodhāt* from the Mbh. is better, "one should always protect from anger," etc.

22. NK. takes *aśokaṁ sthānam* as the soul and interprets "One should be absorbed in the meditation of the *Ātman*."

23. *Visrambha*— that which can be relied on such as the words of the spiritual preceptor.

24. Here ends ch. 189 of the *Mbh. Śānti.*

25. The original (*Mbh. Śānti.* ch. 190) v.1 is a general statement: Truth is the Brahman. Truth is the Penance. The whole universe is upheld and sustained by Truth. It is through Truth (fulness) that one goes to heaven.

26. V. 85 in the NP is Mbh. (*ibid*) v. 4b and 6a and v. 86 is Mbh. v. 6b and 7a.

27. V. 93 in the NP is obscure : The Mbh. original is *tasmād brūmo na tu mahātmabhir ayam pratigṛhīto na tveṣām tāvad viśiṣṭo guṇa-viśeṣa iti* / Bhāradvāja objects: Hence we affirm that happiness is not acceptable to highsouled people. Nor does it appear to be a high attribute of the soul.

28. The text of the NP: *bhavatā tūktaṁ sukhānām paramāḥ striyaḥ* is strange as Bhṛgu in his speech made no reference to women as the ultimate happiness. The Mbh. original is : *bhagavatā tūktaṁ sukhānna param astīti* / '(I cannot believe in) what your worship stated. viz. there is nothing higher than happiness.'

29. Here (at the end of v.98), ch. 190 in the *Mbh. Śānti* ends. The NP, however, combines *Mbh. Śānti* 191. 1b and 2a in one verse, viz, 99 and this odd combination of Mbh. 2b and 3a into verse 100 etc. is carried on in the NP. I have, however, followed the text of the NP in translation.

30. The reading *brahmarṣi vihitāṁ purā*, though a faithful copy of the Mbh. (*ibid*) v. 7 is contradicted by Bhṛgu's reply : *pūrvam eva bhagavatā Brahmaṇā* and *Not brahmarṣiṇā*. The original reading in the Mbh. v. 7 should have been *Brahmaṇā vihitam* in view of consistency. That god Brahmā is the original Law-giver or ordainer of order is known to all.

31. *bhikṣā-bali-saṁvibhāgāḥ* : NK explains : *bhikṣā* (alms-giving) is to *atithis*, *bali* is the food offered on the ground, and *Saṁvibhāga* is the division of one's property among one's sons.

32. The obscurity in the meaning of these verses is due to the misprints in the text of the NP. The translation is an attempt to interpret rationally the printed text of the NP. The original of the NP verse in Mbh. (*ibid*) v. 14 is as follows :

vātsalyāt sarvabhūtebhyo vācyāḥ śrotra-sukhā giraḥ |
paritāpopaghātaśca pāruṣyaṁ cātra garhitam ||

"A person following *Gṛhastha-dharma* should speak to all creatures words full of affection and agreeable to the ears. It is censurable to give pain or inflict humiliation or mortification and harsh words."

33. Here ends ch. 191 of the *Mbh. Śānti.*

34. NK explains *niyama*—vowed observance such as sitting with fire on four sides under the sun (pañcāgnisādhana), *caryā*—activities such as pilgrimage to sacred places.

35. The NP has omitted the restriction on the duration of a stay in a town or a village. The Mbh. limits it to five nights (*pañca-rātrika*) in a big locality and one night in a village.

CHAPTER FORTYFOUR

A Discourse on Meditation

Bhāradvāja said:[1]

1. A world other than this is reported only, but is not perceived. I wish to know about it. It behoves your worship to recount it.[2]

Bhṛgu said :

2. On the northern side of the Himavān which is holy and endowed with all good qualities, there is a region which is holy, lovable and conducive to welfare. It is called the other world.[3]

3. There men do not commit sinful activities; they are pure and absolutely devoid of impurities. They have eschewed greed and delusion. They are perfectly harmless.

4. It is a land on a par with the heaven; all suspicious qualities are said to be present therein. Death occurs at the proper time; ailments do not touch (any one).

5. No one is covetous of other men's wives. The people are devoted to their own wives. No other man is ever killed there. No one is arrogant of his possessions.

6. There is no *Adharma* (sin), at all. Their knowledge being difinite, no doubt arises (in any one). The benefit of whatever is done is directly obtained there.

7. Some of the men here are endowed with vehicles, seats and (plenty) to eat. They live in palatial houses. They are surrounded by all desirable things. They are bedecked in gold ornaments.

8. In regard to some (it must be confessed that) they anyhow manage to remain alive. With great deal of hard labour, they retain their *Prāṇas* (vital breath).[4]

9. Here (in this world) some men are devoted to *Dharma*, and some men are absorbed in roguery. Some men are happy while some are miserable; some are indigent and others are affluent.

10. (In this world) there is hard labour, fear, strain, delusion and severe hunger. Here covetousness is seen and a passion that deludes all ignorant people.

11-12. The intelligent man who knows this, is not contaminated by sin.[5] The penance of those dwindles—those who resort to deceipt, fraud, stealth, censuring, enviousness, obstructing others, violence, back-biting and falsehood.

13. If a learned man were to pursue these, his penance never increases. Here the anxiety over pious and impious rites is of many kinds.

14. This is the *Karmabhūmi* (land of *Karmans* or holy rites). After performing suspicious and inauspicious acts here one attains corresponding results, viz. auspicious results due to auspicious activities and inauspicious results, otherwise.

15. Formerly, Prajāpati, Devas and the groups of sages had performed *Yajñas* and penances (here). Becoming purified (by the sacrificial acts and penances) they had attained *Brahmaloka.*

16-17. The northern section of the earth is the most auspicious and the holiest. The men who perform meritorius rites and feel regard for Yoga[6] are born here. Others are born in the species of animals and brutes, and when their span of life is exhausted, they get lost on the earth.

18. Those who are eagerly intent on devouring each other, those who are endowed with greed and delusion, move about (or are born) only here. They do not go to the northern quarter.

19. The learned men who worship their preceptors, those who strictly adhere to the vow of celibacy, do understand the path duly of all the worlds.

20. Thus the *Dharma* formulated by Brahmā (or proclaimed in the Veda) has been succinctly recounted by me. He who understands *Dharma* (righteousness) and *Adharma* of the world, is intelligent.

Bhāradvāja submitted :[7]

21. What is called *Adhyātma* (knowledge, etc, regarding the soul)? Of what nature is it and which is laid down by

Śāstras for every person. Elucidate to me, O sage (one whose richness is penance) that *Adhyātma* precisely (lit. as it actually is).

Bhṛgu explained :

22. O Brāhmaṇa sage, I shall explain what you ask about, namely the *Adhyātma*. It is conducive to happiness and welfare, O dear one.

23. Everything including the (knowledge about) creation and dissolution has been pointed out by preceptors. On knowing this, the man attains pleasure and happiness, even in this world.

24-26a. He will gain the benefit. It is conducive to the welfare of all living beings. The *Mahā Bhūtas* (elements) are the earth, wind, ether, water and the fifth one, fire. They are the source of the origin of and the ultimate place of dissolution of all living beings. They dissolve themselves unto him wherefrom they had been created. Just as the waves originate from and merge into the ocean, so also the living beings originate from the elements and merge into them.[8]

26b-28a. Just as the tortoise spreads out and withdraws its limbs so also the *Bhūtātman* (the Soul of all living beings or the creator) creates and withdraws the living beings or elements unto himself. The creator has made only five great elements for the constitution of) all living beings. But the individual soul does not see it, in proper perspective.

28b-30. The sound, ears and cavities in the body—these three have originated from ether. It is remembered that the three, viz. touch, *Ceṣṭā* (movement of the limbs) and the skin—are born of *Vāyu* (the wind element). Colour, eyes, and cooking (i.e. digestive process) — these constitute the three attributes of the fiery element. The tastes, moisture and the tongue—these three are remembered as the attributes of water element. That which is to be smelt (scents, etc.), the nose and the physical body—these three are the attributes of earth.

31-34. The *Mahā Bhūtas* are only five. The mind is said

to be the sixth. O resident of the Land of Bharata*, the sense-organs and the *Manas* (mind) have (thus) been known. The seventh, they say, is *Buddhi* (intellect). The *Kṣetrajña* (the individual Soul) is the eight. The ear is (created) for the purpose of hearing; the skin is for (the purpose of) touching; the tongue is for perceiving the taste and the nose is for perceiving smell. The mind creates doubts, the intellect decides; the *Kṣetrajña* is stationed like a witness. All that is above the soles of two feet, all that is behind and above are seen by him (the soul).

35. Know that the entire intervening space has been pervaded wholly by the omnipresent lord.[9] All the sense organs (mind and intelligence) have to be known (thus) by men in their entirety.

36a. The three *Bhāvas* (states) or *Guṇas*, viz., *Tamas*, *Rajas* and *Sattva* are dependent thereon (on the mind, etc.).

36b-37a. After understanding the intellect as well as the advent and departure of the living beings one slowly attains excellent tranquillity.

37b-38a. The *Buddhi* is quelled through the *Guṇas* and the *Indriyas* (sense-organs) through the intellect. The elements have the mind as constituting their sixth (member). If the *Buddhi* is absent how can there be *Guṇas*?[10]

38b-39a. In this way the entire creation, the mobile and immobile, is permeated by it. It (the creation) is born out of it and gets dissolved in it. Hence, it is so specified (in *Śāstras*).

39b-40. That through which one sees is the eye; that which hears is called *Śrotra* (the ear); they call what smells the *Ghrāṇa* (nose); one perceives taste through the torgue; one touches with the skin and feels the touch. That which is called the *Buddhi* undergoes modification at once.

41. When something is sought (by the Buddhi), it becomes the mind—The bases on which *Buddhi* rests are five, each

* The NP adopted the Mbh. (*ibid*) v. 12 along with the epithet of Yudhiṣṭhira, viz. Bhārata. Bhāradvāja was not a descendant of Bharata. Hence, this interpretation here, instead of the usual "O Scion of Bharata' intended in v. 12 of the Mbh.

functioning differently. (They are called *Indriyas*, the invisible principle *Buddhi* rests on them).

42. The *Buddhi* stationed in a person (as its basis) spreads over (is concerned with) the three *Bhāvas* viz. *Sattva*, *Rajas* and *Tamas*.

43. Sometimes it attains pleasure; sometimes it experiences sorrow and sometimes it feels neither happiness nor misery.

44. Thus the Buddhi occupies the three states (viz. the attributes) in the minds of men. Though identical with the *Bhāvas*, it sometimes transcends the three *Bhāvas*, through Yoga.

45. (Defective) Just as the ocean that is the lord of the rivers transgresses its boundary with its waves.[11]

45b-46a. That *Buddhi* which transcends the three *guṇas* or stages exists in the mind in a pure subtle state of existence (like the smell of garlic to the pot after washing—NK). The attribute *rajas* that propels them to action, soon pursues it. At time it makes all the senses function.[12]

47. *Sattva* is pleasure; *Rajas* is sorrow and *Tamas* is anger. Whatever state of mind there is in the world gets merged in one of these three.

48. Thus all the emotional conceptions and feelings of *Buddhi* (intellect) have been explained to you. All the sense organs must be conquered by intelligent men.

49. Three types of sensations (intelligence ?) are seen in all living beings, viz. that originating through *Sattva*, that which depends on *rajas* and on *tamas* for the origin.

50-51a. The attribute of *Sattva* produces happiness, of *Rajas* brings misery. When these two get up mixed with *Tamas*, then neither pleasure nor sorrow is produced (but it creates delusion.

51b-52a. If anything appeals to you and is pleasing physically and mentally, it shall be said that the *Sāttvika* emotion is present.

52b-53a. If anything provokes misery and is displeasing to the soul, O excellent sage, know that *Rajas* has begun to function.

53b-54a. If anything is deluding and confounding and

the object is not clear, is incomprehensible and is difficult to be conceived, understand it to be *Tamas*.

54b-55a. Ecstatic delight, pleasure, bliss, happiness and tranquillity of the mind—If these are present to a certain extent (though rarely) they are called *Sāttvika* attributes.

55b-56a. Dissatisfaction, distress, sorrow, greediness and impatience—these are the symptoms of the *Rajas Guṇa*. These are seen effected by the body.[13]

56b-57a. Dishonour, delusion, blunder, sleeping and lassitude—these various *Tamo-Guṇas* are present in men to a certain extent.

57b-58a. The mind is defective;[14] it wanders along many ways, is of the nature of seeking and entertaining doubts, if such mind is under one's control, one is happy here and hereafter.

58b-59a. Though both *Sattva* (*Guṇa*) and the *Kṣetrajña* (the individual soul) are subtle[15], the difference between them is that one (Intelligence) creates *guṇas*, while the other (the soul) does not.

59b-60. Just as *Maśaka* (gnats) and *Udumbara* (a fig) may be seen united with each other. Though united, they are distinct from each other, so also the *Guṇas* and the *Kṣetrajña* are by nature separate entities but they are seen united with one another.

61-62a. Just as the fish and water are separate entities, but are found to be in the state of union, the same is the state with reference to the Intelligence and the Soul. The attributes do not comprehend the *Ātman*, but he knows the attributes (*Guṇas*) thoroughly. The *Ātman* who is the witness of the *Guṇas*, regards them all as proceeding from himself.

62b-63a. Functioning through (five) senses[16], (the mind the sixth) and Intelligence as the seventh—all of which are (by themselves) inactive and without any consciousness, the *Ātman* discovers the objects (around it) like a (covered) lamp showing all objects by radiating rays through the apertures (in its cover).

63b-64. The *Sattva* (Intelligence) creates the *Guṇas* while the soul (*Kṣetrajña*) is a (mere) witness. That is the certain relation between *Sattva* and *Kṣetrajña* (from times immemorial). Neither *Sattva* nor *Kṣetrajña* have any support or refuge.

65-66a. The Intelligence (*Sattva*) creates the mind but never the *Guṇas*. When he (*Ātman*) properly controls their reins by means of the mind, then his soul becomes revealed (within himself), like a lamp burning within a pitcher.

66b-67a. The sage who eschews *Prākṛta* (ordinary) rites or acts and who is always delighted within his own *Ātman* becomes the soul of all living beings. He attains the excellent goal.

67b-68a. Just as an acquatic bird does not get wet (or is not besmeared or affected) with water, similarly, a person who is firm in (spiritual) wisdom, (and is free from any hallucination) moves about in living beings (without being attached to and affected by them.)

68b-69a. With the help of one's judgement and knowledge, one should behave in this world in this way, without bewailing or without being elated, but be equanimous and devoid of (even a trace) of jealousy.

69b-70a. A person who lives in his real state of being the *Ātman*, always creates the *Guṇas* even as a spider creating its threads. The *Guṇas* should be understood as the threads (emitted by the spider).

70b-72a. Some opine that the attributes (*Guṇas*) with regard to such men are not lost while some others say that they are lost. The first depend upon the *Śrutis* (*Pratyakṣa* the direct proof) which are not contradicting while the others—who advocate the loss, depend on *Smṛtis*. Pondering over both these one should decide for one's self which is correct.

72b-73a. In this way the hard insoluble knot in the heart which causes anxiety should be removed and one should dwell in happiness. With all one's doubts resolved one need not feel sorrow.

73b-74a. Just as men smeared with dust (or mud) obtains success (become pure) after plunging into full stream of water, similarly, men of dirty and unclean-hearts attain success by getting perfect knowledge.

74b-75. A person who sees only the other bank of a great river is tormented till he reaches the other side (mere sight of the other bank is not enough). But in the case of the knower of Reality, the mere knowledge of the Truth makes him happy. Persons who in their hearts realise that the soul is untouched by worldly objects (and is one) get that excellent knowledge.

76. Thus a man who realizes the advent and the departure of the living beings, ponders upon it slowly by means of his intellect and attains peace and tranquillity.

77. He who has understood the destructibility of the threefold goals (*Dharma*, *Artha* and *Kāma*) of life and investigating them (and following Yoga) mentally, discards them, becomes the real seer of Reality! (And having obtained bliss through self-realization), he becomes disinterested.

78. By persons who are not self-possessed, the soul is impossible to be realized through senses which are partially employed on diverse objects and which are very difficult to obtain[17] (to control—Mbh.).

79. After knowing this, one shall become enlightened. What else is the characteristic of an enlightened one ? Indeed after realising it, learned men consider themselves contented.

80. To the knower (of quality) what appears extremely frightful, to the unenlightened (e.g. the fear of a serpent which is really a rope) inspires no fear at all. There is no better state than *Mokṣa* (emancipation from *Saṁsāra*) to anyone. If there be superiority in qualities (in such persons), some difference in the gradation in reality may be seen, say the learned.

81. If a man performs holy rites without any specific aim or desire (in return) that act burns down what acts have been performed (by him) earlier. (Past acts being burnt down and present acts being desireless do not bring about undesirable results. But if such a knower continues to act how can these acts bring about *Mokṣa*?)

82. People of their own accord produce the world (they live in) and the duration of (their) life (in it). The above are (automatically) created while he is doing an act. Please see that even if he is ever subjected to a frightful state, he does not bewail the good actions.[18]

Bhāradvāja said:

83. Please explain the path of meditation unto me for the achievement of that region on knowing which, O Brāhmaṇa, a man is relieved from three types of distresses.

Bhṛgu said:

84. O Brāhmaṇa sage! I shall recount to you the four types of *Jñānayoga* (the path of knowledge), on realising which, great sages attain eternal *Siddhi.*

85. The great sages who are experts in Yoga and are gratified with their perfect knowledge and have fixed their hearts on Liberation from *Saṁsāra*, perform their Yogic meditation on proper lines.

86. Being freed from the blemishes of the worldly existence, they are liberated. With their liability to get a further birth being eliminated, they stabilise themselves in the pristine Soul-state.

87. (Defective) They are free from mutually clashing pairs such as pleasure, pain, always established in the *Sattva Guṇa*; they are liberated and they do not possess anything, They cultivate detachment that does not obstruct[19] and that is conducive to mental tranquility.

88. There, the sage should keep his extremely tormented and agitated mind concentrated by means of meditation. Withdrawing within him (as if in a lump) all his sense-organs, the sage should be seated (motion-less) like a log of wood.

89. He should not perceive any sound through his ears, nor feel any touch by means of his skin; he should not perceive any colour or feature through the eyes; nor should he have the taste of anything through his tongue.

90. Being immersed in meditation, the knower of reality should eschew all things to be smelt. The energetic Yogin does not covet these (five types of) objects which excite the senses.

91. Then the clever (devotee) shall withdraw into his mind the *Pañcavarga* (the group of five senses). He shall then enter into meditation (stabilising) erring mind alongwith the five sense organs.

92. The mind is a wanderer (in objects of senses, etc.) It consists of five gates (the cognitive senses). It is both powerful and weak[20], the wise Yogin should quickly[21] fix his mind into the path of meditation first, making it independent of any refuge.

93. At this time he should 'collect' the sense organs and the mind into one lump (and direct them to the path of meditation). Thus the first path of meditation has been explained by me.

94. The mind which is the sixth *aṅga* of the *Jīva*, when thus controlled, will throb like the streak of lightening in the clouds extending as far as the ocean.[22]

95. Just as a drop of water on the leaf (of a lotus) is very restless and moves all round, so also his mind moves about in the path of meditation.

96. For a moment the mind is a little attentive and becomes steady in path of meditation. Then it wanders into the path of the wind. The restless mind becomes flighty like the wind.

97. A person who knows the path of meditation should not be discouraged, should not mind the troubles undergone, should give up lethargy and malice and should again establish his mind in meditation.

98. Pondering, reflection, and discrimination[23] are produced in order (in the meditating Yogi). This is the first meditation of the sage endowed with trance.

99. If he is mentally distressed, he should console himself. The sage should not feel despondent. He should seek what is beneficial to himself.

100. A heap of dust, ashes or cowdung cannot be formed into a saturated paste by sprinkling with water all of a sudden.

101. It should be gradually made into paste, some part remaining dry in the beginning but later on made smooth. Thus everything will become drenched completely in the end.

102. In the same manner one must make the group of sense organs calm and tranquil. They must be withdrawn gradually. Then they will be subdued perfectly.

103. O leading sage! By stabilising one's mind and

five senses in the path of meditation first, a Yogī is able to subdue them completely by steadfast (practice in) Yoga.

104. Neither through manly effort nor through divine providence shall he attain that happiness which he attains by restraining the self (in Yoga).

105. Endowed with that bliss, he will find pleasure in the process of meditation. Thus the *Yogins* attain the blissful salvation (lit. with no ailments).

Sanandana said:

106. O Brāhmaṇa, thus instructed by Bhṛgu, the valorous Bhāradvāja, the extremely virtuous soul, was surprised. He worshipped Bhṛgu.

107. O learned one, thus the creation of the universe has been narrated unto you entirely. O excessively intelligent one, what else do you wish to hear?

CHAPTER FORTYFOUR

1. This is verse 7 in the *Mbh. Śānti.* ch. 192.

2. After a long discussion, NK. tries to show that this verse is an enquiry to show the path to God-realization (*śruti-yuktibhyāṁ jñāto'pi paramātmā na sākṣī kriyate iti tat-sākṣātkāropāyaṁ brūhīti prārthitaḥ Bhṛguḥ.*

3. NK treats the whole chapter as a continuous metaphor of a spiritual nature. Vyāsa (and here Nārada) describes an ideal place on this earth as the 'next' or 'excellent' world (*paralokaḥ*). But NK differs. He interprets: After the realization of the soul (*uttare*) near the Himālayas i.e. Meru (which stands for the nose) there is the excellent world just in the middle of the eyebrows, etc. NK cites a quotation from *mantra-śāstra* to 'prove' the identification of the nose and mount Meru, called also the Himalayas.

hema-rūpo bhruvor madhye merus tiṣṭhati parvataḥ /
tasyābhito mahī pārśve pañcāśatkoṭi-yojanā //

The Mbh. however, describes an ideal region on the earth. Hence, we have followed the plain meaning of these verses and not the esoteric significance of each point, as is done artificially by NK.

4. It is better to interpret as follows: In that region, some (ascetics) eat abstemiously just enough to keep themselves alive, while others with a great effort practise *Prāṇāyāma.*

5. V.11a is actually v. 16b in ch. 192 of the *Mbh. Śānti.* This appears unconnected with 11b and is obscure. But v. 16a and b in the Mbh. (*ibid*) clarifies it. That verse in the Mbh. means : (16a) Here various opinions prevail and are advocated by persons who did meritorious or sinful acts (16b=11a of NP). The intelligent man who knows all those opinions of both kinds (virtuous and sinful) is not contaminated by sin.

6. *Satkāram ṛcchanti—yoge ādaram ṛcchanti prāpnuvanti*—NK.

Here ends ch. 192 in the *Mbh. Śānti.*

7. The NP omitted ch. 193 and here ch. 194 from the *Śānti Parvan* (Mbh). is incorporated.

8. As usual, the printed Sk. text of the NP has separated in the original *ślokas* of the Mbh. in the unnatural way. Here v. 4 in the Mbh. (*ibid*) 194, consists of 3 lines. But the NP combined 4a and 4b into v. 23 and 4c and 5a of the Mbh. is given as v. 24. In this way the lines of the original *ślokas* in the Mbh. are found disarranged in the NP, in this chapter.

9. NK. explains : This whole body right from the soles of the feet, what is above and beneath the body and what is within and outside the body— all this is completely pervaded by him. Such is his omnipresence.

10. These are obscure verses in spite of (or because of ?) NK long comm. It appears that he supports Vijñānavāda. He means to say that nothing exists except as it exits in 'Ideas'. After using the arguments of the Advaita school, he sums up : "In the absence of *Buddhi* (Intelligence),

both the cause and products of *Buddhi* are destroyed. Hence the term *guṇa* implies attributes like *Sattva* etc., mind, sense-organs along with their objects.

11. V.45 appears defective as 45a is to be connected with 44b of which it is the illustration. The original Mbh. verse 24 is thus distributed over the two NP verses. The simile is unusual as the ocean according to poets, never crosses its boundary (though facts differ).

12. V. 45b and 46a form one verse (viz Mbh. *ibid*.25). Hence these lines are translated as forming one *Śloka*.

13. For *deha-hetubhiḥ* of the NP, Mbh. (*ibid*) v. 35 reads *hetvahetubhiḥ* (These are seen) with or without adequate causes for producing them.

14. For the obscure *dūṣaṇam* of the NP, Mbh. (*ibid*) v. 37 reads *dūragam*. NK interprets : (the mind) which is attached to things which are very difficult to obtain (*dūragam*) and which is capable of extending to a number of objects simultaneously (*bahudhā-gāmi*).

15. *Yasya* in the NP renders this sentence predicateless. For *yasya*, Mbh. (ibid) v. 38 reads *paśya*. Thus the translation : 'Notice the difference between Sattva (Intelligence —*buddhi-sattvam* NK).

16. Two printing mistakes in the NP, viz. *indriyastu* for *indriyais tu* and *pradīpavān* for *pradīpavat* render this verse obscure. I have accepted the correct readings from the Mbh. (*ibid*) v. 42 and translated accordingly.

17. For *durvāpeṣu* of the NP, Mbh. (*ibid*) v. 58 reads *durvāryaiḥ* 'difficult to control' I have followed NP.

18. The verse has become obscure in the NP due to faulty mixture of vv. 62 and 63 and misprints. The Mbh. reads:

Lokam āturam asūyate janas tasya taj janayatīha sarvataḥ
Loka ātura-janān virāvaśaṁs tat tadeva bahu paśya śocataḥ
tatra paśya kuśalān aśocato ye vidus tad ubhayam padaṁ satām

As NK explains : People reproach (*asūyate*) persons afflicted (with evil passions) which drive them to births of diverse kinds. Notice clearly how such afflicted persons suffer from loss of possession and those real learned persons who remain unaffected with grief. Those who know the gradual and instantaneous types of liberation, are the really wise ones.'

Here ends ch. 194 in the *Mbh. Śānti*.

19. The reading *asadgānya-vidhādīni* is obscure. The Mbh. reading (*Śānti* 195.4) is *asaṅgānya-vivādīni* is better. It means, they (live) in places detached from their relatives (wives, children, etc.) and where no disputant lives".

20. Mbh. (*ibid*) 9: *calācalam* 'constant in pursuing unstable objects (of senses)'.

21. Mbh. (*ibid*) reads *mano'ntara* and means : 'The yogin, in the cavity of his heart fixes etc.

22. Mbh. (*ibid*) 11 reads *samud-bhrānta*, 'capricious'.

23. *Vicāra*, *Vitarka* and *Viveka* are the different stages in the progress of Yoga. NK quotes from various works on Yoga in his long comm, to substantiate this.

CHAPTER FORTYFIVE

Exposition of Dharmas leading to Liberation

Sūta said:

1. O Brāhmaṇas! On hearing the words of Sanandana, based on the *Dharmas* leading to Liberation, Nārada who had understood the principles, again asked him about matters spiritual.

Nārada said:

2. O highly blessed one! The treatise on salvation expatiated upon by you, has been heard by me. Even after hearing it repeatedly, I am not fully satisfied.

3. O omniscient sage, please recount to me the *Mokṣa-dharma* (virtuous path leading to salvation) based on *sat* (the Reality), whereby the creature is liberated from the bondage of Nescience (*avidyā*).

Sanandana said:[1]

4. In this context, they cite the ancient mythological anecdote that narrates how Janaka, the Lord of Mithilā, attained salvation.

5. There was a king of Mithilā called Janadeva, in the Janaka dynasty. He was ever engrossed in reflecting upon the courses of conduct which would lead to the attainment of the Brahman which is super-physical and hence bodiless.*

6. Many preceptors propagating heresy and usual dwellers in cemeteries used to live in his house.** They being

---

* As the Comm. explains :
ūrdhva-deham aśarīram Brahma, tat-prāpti-kāraṇam aurdhva-dehikānām

** The text of the NP. is corrupt : It runs :
tasya śmaśānam ācāryā vasanti satataṁ gṛhe !

The original text in the Mbh. Śānti ch. 218.4 from which the passage in the NP. is borrowed is as under :

tasya sma śatam ācāryā vasanti satataṁ gṛhe

'A hundred preceptors always used to live in his palace'

propagators of heretic doctrines advised him on different courses of religious duties.

7. Basing himself on the study of the Vedas, he was not properly satisfied with the speculations of his preceptors regarding the nature of the soul, and in their doctrine of extinction (of the soul) after the dissolution of the body or of its rebirth after death.

8. On one occasion, a great sage called Pañca-śikha,[2] a son (disciple) of the sage Kapila, arrived at Mithilā during the course of his wandering all over the earth.

9. He had a thorough mastery over (lit. completed) the interpretation of Śāstras. He was an adept in arriving at a conclusion in the perfect knowledge of the principles of all Dharmas regarding renunciation. He was above *Dvandvas* (mutually clashing opposites like pleasure and pain). All his doubts were resolved.

10. They call him one of those sages who among men have finished their desires.* He sought eagerly and intensively after the very rare highest eternal bliss.

11. I think that the great sage whom the followers of the Sāṅkhya school call the greatest sage (*paramarṣi*) Kapila, the Prajāpati (Lord of all creatures) himself, reveals (everything) through that form (of Pañca-śikha).[3]

12. He was the foremost among the disciples of Āsuri whom they call 'long-lived' (*cirajīvin*). It was he who performed a holy sacrifice (of long duration—satra) for a thousand years in *Pañca-srotas*** (a land of five rivers?)

13 He came to *Pañca-srotas* and proclaimed to the huge assembly of the followers of Kapila, the real nature of the unmanifest abiding in the Puruṣa.

14. Āsuri[4] who possessed (was proficient in sacrificial

---

* The reading in the NP is *kāmād avasitam* which is defective. The chapter is bodily taken from *Mbh. Śānti.* ch. 218 where the original reading (in *Mbh. Śānti* 218.8) is *Kāmānāvṛtam*— "One who is not affected by desires."

** Sāṅkhyas use this term to imply 'the mind' which is said to have five currents. Thus this line may mean "He performed on the mental plane a sacrifice (i.e. meditation) that lasted for one thousand years."

mantras (*iṣṭimantreṇa* *) and had visualized his person *deha-darśana***) and realised through a great deal of penance the distinction between *Kṣetra* (the body) and *Kśetrajña* (the individual soul abiding in the body).

15. In that assembly of ascetics, Āsuri expounded that which is called the Eternal-Immutable, one-syllabled Brahman (*Om*) which appears in diverse forms.

16-17. Pañcaśikha was his disciple. He was nurtured by a woman with her breast milk. There was a certain Brāhmaṇa house-wife called Kapilī who adopted him as her son, and he used to suck her breasts. Hence, he came to be known as Kāpileya (the son of Kapilī). Thereafter, he attained the perfect and fixed *buddhi* (understanding in the Brahman).

18. It was the venerable Lord† himself who narrated to me the circumstances which led to (Pañcaśikha's) birth (adoption as a son of Kapilā) and his designation Kāpileya. His omniscience, however, was excellent and unsurpassed.

19. O sage! Janaka, the knower of *Dharmas*, accompanied by his ministers, knew him (Pañcaśikha) to be spiritually wise. Having come there, Pañcaśikha deluded and confused the hundred preceptors of Janaka by means of his logical reasoning.

20. Janaka became exceedingly attracted and attached to the school of thought of Pañcaśikha‡. Abandoning his hundred teachers, he (Janaka) followed closely behind him (Pañcaśikha).

21. To him (Janaka) who, according to prescription of religious duty, bowed down (to express his being Pañcaśikha's

---

* The original in *Mbh. ibid.* 13 is *iṣṭa-satreṇa saṁsiddho* "one who has accomplished the desired sacrificial session."

** This is an obvious misprint for *deva-darśanaḥ* in the original Mbh. text. It means 'one who has visualized God or attained divine vision.' The NP. reading *deha-darśanaḥ* is meaningless.

† The Mbh. comm. Nīlakaṇṭha (NL) guesses it to be either Mārkaṇḍeya or Sanatkumāra.

‡ Mbh. gives *Kāpileyānudarśanāt* for NP. *Kapileyānudarśanam.* According to Mbh. the verse means: By the intelligence and the school of thought of Kāpileya, Janaka became ..."

disciple), he expounded the highly auspicious (philosophy) which is called Sāṅkhya and which leads to the Supreme Liberation from Saṁsāra.

22. After expatiating on the sorrows attending upon birth, he set forth the sorrows in the performance of religious acts. After recounting the miseries inherent in *Karman*, he explained the sorrows of all the states of life.

23. He lectured upon Delusion for the sake of which there is contact with *Dharma* (and the religious acts prescribed by it) and the fruition of those acts—Delusion which is unreliable, destructible, unsteady and evanescent.

24. *The Pūrvapakṣin or the objector may argue*: When the destruction of body is seen and is the direct evidence witnessed by all people in the world, he who, out of his faith in the Sāṅkhya scriptures, argues that something called the soul is distinct from the body and survives the death of the body, is automatically defeated in his arguments.

25. The disputants maintain that the soul's death, or that which is called death is the extinction of the soul. Pain, old age and disease constitute the partial death of the soul. He who considers out of delusion that the soul being distinct from the body survives the death of the body holds an opinion which is unreasonable and untenable.

26. If that which is non-existent in the world is regarded as existent, it may be argued that the king who is regarded so, should never be subject to old age or death.

27. When the problem is about the very existence of an object (lit. whether an object is or is not in existence) and when that whose existence is predicated, presents dark characteristic (asaitlakṣana*) [or 'the indications of non-existence' (asatilakṣaṇe) as the Mbh reads] (under these circumstances) on what basis should people depend in deciding the affairs of life.

---

* The Mbh. reads *asatilakṣaṇe* (*ibid* verse 26) for *asita-lakṣaṇe* of the NP. In the NP. palpably a scribal error, as *asati* and *asita* in the Devanāgari script are easily confused.

28. Direct proof is the root (basis) of inference and scriptures* (*Kṛtāntaitihyayorapi*). The scriptures are contradictable by direct evidence *pratyakṣeṇa***). As to inference, its value as evidence is negligible.

29. Everywhere, in every topic, do not depend, simply on inference. There exists no entity called *Jiva* other than outside this body† according to the view of the *Nāstikas* (sceptics).

30.‡ The potentiality to produce leaves, fruits, roots, bark, etc. lies in the (small) seed of a banyan tree (*vaṭakaṇikāyām*). Substances, the nature of which is different from that of the causes which produce them, are seen in the following:) Milk and butter are produced from the grass and water consumed by a cow. Different kinds of substances when decomposed for some period in water sometimes produce alcoholic substances whose (inebriating) nature is quite different from that of those substances which produced the spirituous liquor (*ghṛtapākādhivāsanam*). In the same way from the semen (vital seed) is produced the body, its attributes alongwith intelligence, consciousness, mind and other possessions. Two pieces of wood produce fire by attrition. The *Sūryakānta* stone produces fire when it comes in contact with the rays of the sun.

---

* The NP. reads :

pratyakṣaṁ hyetayor mūlaṁ kṛtānta hyetayorapi

The Mbh. (*ibid* verse 27) reads:

Kṛtāntaitihyayorapi I have accepted it in translation.

** The NP. reads : *Pratyakṣo hyāgamo bhinnaḥ* which means "Direct Scriptural evidence is shattered or contradicted" I preferred the Mbh reading *Pratyakṣeṇāgamo bhinnaḥ* and translated it as above.

† The second line of this verse in the NP. is as follows :

anyo jīvaḥ śarīrasya nāstikānāṁ mate stitaḥ

The Mbh. (ibid v. 28b) reads : *nānyo jīvaḥ śarīrasya nāstikānāṁ mate sthitaḥ*. The omission of *nā* of *nānyo* in NP. attributes a totally different and contradictory view to the atheists. Hence I preferred the original reading in the Mbh. viz. *nānyo*.

‡ As this verse is the same as *Mbh.* (*ibid.* v. 29), I have followed the commentator Nīlakaṇṭha, as it is nothing but a series of keywords of different arguments which are grammatically loose. An explanatory translation is necessary in such cases. Hence the above translation.

Any piece of metal made red-hot in fire, when immersed in water, evaporates that water (*ambu-bhakṣaṇam*). Just as a load-stone moves iron, the mind controls the sense-organs.

31.* The *Nāstikas* are wrong for the disappearance of only the vital airs or animating force upon the physical body becoming lifeless and not the simultaneous disappearance of the body along with the departure or disappearance of the vital force, is the proof of the fact that the body and the soul are not identical but the soul and the body are distinct and different, and that the soul survives the body. As the dead body is seen even after the disappearance of the animating force, death means the departure from the physical body of something that is different from the body. The prayer (for getting something) to deities by those who deny the separate existence of the soul is another sound argument for, if deities who do not have gross material bodies can exist, why cannot the soul exist apart from and without the physical body? Another argument against the identity of the body and the soul: If one dies—the very occurrence of death would be an automatic end of all *Karmans* which cannot be accepted as there would be an end of inequalities in the world which is not the case.

32. Now the causes that have been mentioned and those that have material bodies, cannot be the causes of the non-material soul and his non-material accompaniment like perception, memory, etc. For the physical objects cannot by themselves be the causes for the creation of non-physical objects. (The causal relation of immaterial objects being produced by material objects is incomprehensible.)

33-34a.** Some say that there is rebirth and that it is

---

* The verse as printed in the NP. yields little sense due to corrupt readings. The *Mbh.* verse (*ibid*) v. 31 is as follows :

pretībhūte'tyayaś caiva devatādhyupayātanam /
mṛte karma-nivṛttis ca pramāṇam iti niścayaḥ //

The verse in the NP. is :

preta-bhūta-priyaś caiva devatā hyupayācanam /
mṛta-karma-nivṛttiṁ ca pramāṇam iti niścayaḥ //

I have translated the Mbh. verse the corrupt form of which is in the NP.

** The verse consists of 32a and 34b in the *Mbh.* (*ibid*) but the sentence is completed by adding 34b in the Mbh. (which is 34a in the NP.).

caused by Nescience, *Karmans* and strong desire or avidity. They (i.e. the Buddhists) maintain that when one mortal body is being destroyed, another immediately grows up from it. But, when it is consumed by the fire of knowledge the destruction of existence takes place.

34b-36a. It may be asked when the being that is thus born is a different one in respect of form, nature, birth, purposes connected with virtue, vice, etc., why should it then be regarded to have any identity with the being that existed? And if the being that is thus reborn be really different from what it was in the previous birth, what liking or satisfaction can a person have by acquisition of knowledge, learning and the power of asceticism, if all the acts performed by one are to be transferred for the accruing of benefit to another person* (in the next stage of life or existence, without the performer being the enjoyer or the beneficiary of the fruits of those acts.)

36b-37a. Even in this very birth, here, one may be forced to be miserable by the acts committed by another in some previous life or may become happy after being miserable. But proper conclusion should be drawn about 'the unseen' by observing what factually happens in this world.**

37b-38a. Just as upon the death of the body caused by heavy bludgeoning with pestles, a second body would not arise from the body that is deprived of life, it is totally a vain (false) knowledge,† if the very loss of the previous consciousness be regarded as the cause of the production of the second knowledge, for the end of the previous consciousness cannot

---

* *Sāmānyāt pratipadyate* in the NP. makes little sense. The reading in the *Mbh.* (*ibid*) v. 36 is *sarvam anyat pratipadyate* clearly states the Buddhistic position to which objections are raised.

** In this world we see that one is not affected by the good or evil acts of another. This direct evidence is enough to disprove the uncertainty of the doctrine of "the unseen" viz. whether the acts of Mr. X in the previous life can affect Mr. Y in the subsequent life when there is no identity between Mr. X of the previous birth and Mr. Y of the present birth.

Thus the Buddhist theory of momentariness stands refuted.

† Mbh. (*ibid*) v. 38 reads *Pṛthag jñānam*

act as the cause of a second consciousness arising out of the very end of the first.

38b-39a. Again the Buddhist doctrine of *Nirvāṇa* or *Sattva-saṅkṣaya* or extinction of life is open to the objection that *Nirvāṇa* will become a recurring phenomena like that of seasons or the year or the *Yuga* (lit. the Kali age), or heat or cold or disagreeable or agreeable objects. The Buddhist *Nirvāṇa* will not become an end of the cycle of births and deaths—the final emancipation from *Saṁsāra* like *Mokṣa* in Brahmanical scriptures.

39b-40a. If, in order to avoid these objections, the opponents i.e. the Buddhists advance the theory that the soul is permanent but every moment each new consciousness attaches itself to it we say: Just as the supports of a house get weakened in course of time leading to the total collapse of the structure, the permanent substance (the soul as posited by the opponents) by being overcome with old age and with death that results in destruction, will in course of time itself be weakened and destroyed. The soul according to Brahmanism is attributeless and hence immutable and eternal. But the Buddhist affirmance of attributes to the soul implies automatically its destructibility, and the permanence of the soul becomes untenable.

40b-41a. All the constituents of the body such as the senses, the mind,* the vital air, blood, flesh, bones become destroyed one after another, each of these entering its own substance (*dhātu*) or productive cause.

41b-42a. Here is the criticism of the Vedāntic concept of the soul. If the soul be the basis of consciousness, understanding and other attributes and yet is unconnected with any of these then all that is done in the world will be meaningless, especially the fruition of charity and other religious acts and all the injunctions of Śrutis prescribing these acts and all actions pertaining to the conduct of the world will have no meaning, (as the soul being aloof and unconnected with

* Sāṅkhyas believe in the destruction of the mind—Nl—(Nilakaṇṭha—the commentator on the *Mbh.*

understanding or mind, there is none to enjoy the fruits of meritorious acts and Vedic rites.

42b-43a. In this way many plausible hypotheses or speculations arise in the mind. But no criterion is seen to decide whether this particular view is right, while that speculation is not.

43b-44a. While reflecting on the pros and cons of these views, particular persons follow properly and closely particular views. The intelligence of these is settled and established on some like a tree and ultimately is lost therein.

44b-45. In this way, all creatures become miserable by actions good or evil. It is only the Vedas which bring them back to the right way, like conductors of elephants guiding their elephants.

46. *Many emaciated (weak-kneed) persons lick at (or wish for) objects which are full of happiness. But they are made to suffer a much larger lot of miseries. Being forced to and therefore having given up their coveted happiness (lit. piece of meat), they submit themselves to the power of death.

47. What is the use of relatives, friends, wives and property (possessions) to one who is definitely doomed to die and whose life is unsteady and momentary, and who, having abandoned all these in a moment, leaves this world never to return ?

48. The elements, viz. the earth, the ether, water, fire and even wind always protect and nourish the body. How can one cherish any affinity to this body when one observes

---

* A comparison between the NP. and Mbh. shows how the text of the NP. is incorrect and why one has to refer to the Mbh.

46a of NP. reads :

arthāṁs tathā hanti sukhāvahāṁśca
lihanta ete hanti bahavopaśuṣkāḥ /

Mbh. (*ibid*) 46a reads :

arthāṁs tathā'tyanta-sukhāvahāṁśca
lipsanta ete bahavo viśuṣkāḥ /

and reflects on this? There cannot be any pleasure with this body which is subject to destruction.

49. Having listened to these words of Pañcaśikha which (being based on the Vedas were free from confusion and deception and which were not connected with delusion as they did not extol *Karmakāṇḍa*), supremely salutary and dealing with the soul, king Janaka was wonderstruck and proposed to confront him with an argument (*Pūrva Pakṣa*-Nl.*)

*Janaka submitted***:

50. Venerable Sir, if, after departing from this body nobody is capable of retaining any consciousness or knowledge—if this be the case—what is the use of knowledge or ignorance? (We neither gain anything by possessing knowledge nor are we the loosers by being ignorant.

51. Look here, O excellent Brāhmaṇa, if everything is to end up in nothingness, if that be the nature of Liberation what avail are the observances of *Yama*, Niyama, etc. What special distinction is there in the fruits achieved by a careful or a careless person?

52. If Liberation means dissociation with pleasure-giving persons or objects like celestial damsels, or association with objects of destructible nature like life in heaven, what is the motivation for men to perform religious action or why after beginning the performance of an action, should men continue for attaining the desired goal.

Sanandana said:†

53. Reassuring with pacificatory words the king whose intelligence‡ was enveloped with ignorance, bewildered,

---

* Here ends chapter 218 in the *Mbh. Śāntiparvan.*

** Here Mbh. Śānti ch. 219 begins. In the NP. this being a continuation of I.45, the introductory verse of Bhīṣma is omitted. NP. I.45.50 corresponds to Mbh. (*ibid*) v. 2.

† In the Mbh. Śānti 219, Bhīṣma speaks this verse (no. 5).

‡ *Maticchatram* in NP. but *prati-chhanna* of the Mbh. is better.

mistaken and overanxious to know the truth, omniscient Pañcaśikha spoke to him.

Pañcaśikha said:

54-56a* In this *Mokṣa* (Liberation) stage there is no extinction. Nor is that any kind of existence easily conceivable. What we see here is an aggregate of body, senses and mind. The constituents of this aggregate exist independently, control mutually and thus go on functioning.

56b-57a. The ether, wind, heat (fire), water and the earth—the aggregate of these five makes up the body, but the body is not one homogeneous (whole or element).

57b-58. Sentience or intelligence, gastrie heat and the vital breaths—these three are called the aggregate of the organs of action. The effects of intelligence, viz. the sense-organs, the objects of senses, such as sight, sound, etc., the inherent power which makes them the sense-potencies or faculties whereby the senses perceive these objects, the mind, the effects of wind, viz., the vital breaths called *Prāṇa*, *Apāna*, etc. and the effects of gastric heat, viz., juices and humours generated in the digestive system—all these emanate from the above-mentioned three organs of actions.

59. Hearing, touch, taste (tongue), sight (eyes) and scent—these are the five senses which inherit their attributes from the mind which also is their cause.**

60. The mind which is the reflection or attribute of *Cit* has three states—pleasure, pain and absence of both pleasure and pain.

61† Sound, touch and form—these three form the bases

---

* The division of the lines of these verses corresponds to the original verses in the MBh. as the Mbh. verses give a complete sentence per verse.

** The reading in the Mbh. *Citta-pūrvaṁ gatā guṇāḥ* / is better than *Citta-purvaṁ-gamā guṇāḥ* in the NP. As NI. explains: *Cittam pūrvakāraṇam yasyā rtha-gaṇasya taṁ cittapūrvaṁ cittamātrotpādakaṁ gatāḥ prāptāḥ guṇāḥ guṇa-kārya-bhūtāḥ* /

† The text of this NP verse is confusing :
Śabdaḥ sparśaś ca rūpaṁ ca mūrtyarthameva te trayaḥ /
ete hyāmaraṇāt pañca saḍ-guṇā jñānasiddhaye //

of objects which they inhere. These five (?) good attributes last till death, for the achievement of knowledge.

62. Upon them—the senses—depends the accomplishment of fruits or the successful completion of *Karmans* which lead to heaven, as also the determination of the truth or essence of all the principles or the topics of spiritual enquiry. They (wise sages) affirm that the ascertainment of the truth is the highest (most potent) seed of Liberation as it leads to *Mokṣa* and that Intelligence (*buddhi*) leads to emancipation and as such it is called *avyaya*—indestructible and to Brahman and hence due to its power to lead to the Brahman which is *mahat*-great and omnipotent, the Intelligence is called Mahat*.

63. To a person who looks upon this aggregate of attributes viz. the physical body, senses and their objects as the *Ātman* (soul), there is unending misery as a result of incorrect knowledge and this misery never subsides.

64. Sorrow requires some basis or foundation to affect. What basis is there for misery or sorrow to affect those persons who consider worldly objects including their body as non-soul and are unattached to them, feeling that they (those objects) are neither 'me' nor 'mine'. Hence they never suffer any misery or sorrow.

65. For this a wise (honourable) person should listen to the excellent treatise on renunciation. When it is expounded, it will be conducive for your emancipation from Saṁsāra.

66. Renunciation of all acts—even of those prescribed in *Śāstras*, is enjoined for persons seeking *Mokṣa*. Those who have been taught and disciplined in the wrong way (by heretics) have always to bear a heavy burden of sorrows.

67. Vedic sacrifices and rites are advised, for the renunciation of wealth. *Vratas*—(religious observances and vows)

It means that so long as we live all these faculties are the cause leading to knowledge.

* *mokṣa-bījaṁ buddhir iti avyayaṁ mokṣadatvād avyayam iti cāhuḥ / mahad brahma tat-pradatvāt /*

are meant for the renunciation of enjoyments and pleasures. Performance of penance is laid down for the renunciation of pleasures. *Yoga* is advised for the renunciation of everything and that is the ultimate limit of renunciation.

68. The path of Yoga which will be enunciated now to you is the only one path shown by the learned for the renunciation of everything, in order to banish all miseries and sorrows.* But otherwise distress and sorrow is the lot of those who go astray from this path.

69. Having spoken of the five cognitive senses with the mind as the sixth—and all of which on the mental plane I shall now tell you the five conative organs for action with physical strength as the sixth.

70. The two hands should be known as organs of action and the feet as the organ of locomotion. The sexual organ is meant both for pleasure and continuance of the race. The anus is the organ for discharging faeces, excrements, etc. from the body.

71. The organ of speech is for the expression of particular sounds. The learned know that the mind is thus equipped with these five conative organs. In this manner one should cast off the mind, with intelligence (thus when the mind is shed off automatically, the conative organs are cast off or controlled, and by 'casting off' the Intelligence, its products, viz. cognitive senses are done away with).

72. In the act of audition three factors cause it, viz. the organ (ears), words or sound, and the mind. Similarly, three such factors exist in the perception of touch, of form, that of taste and of smell.

73. In this manner the five triads i.e. fifteen attributes (*guṇas*) are essential for the above-mentioned five kinds of perceptions. In consequence of these a person becomes aware of these triads (viz. particular organ, its function and the attending mind) about these perceptions.

---

* Nl. quotes Bhalla-viśākhins in support :
Tyāga eva hi sarveṣām mokṣa-sādhanam uttamam /
Renunciation is the best means for all to attain *Mokṣa*.

74. With reference to the perceptions of the mind—there are three categories pertaining to *guṇas* viz. *Sāttvika, Rājasa* and *Tāmasa.* Three categories of consciousness are running through them comprising everything — emotions, passions, feelings, etc.).

75. Rapturous delight, love, joy, happiness, tranquillity of the mind arising out of some cause or resulting from no apparent cause (due to gaining desired object or through renunciation these are the *Sāttvika* attributes of the mind.

76. Discontent, distress, sorrow, greed and non-for bearance whether due to some cause or without any cause—these are the indications of the attribute called *Rajas.*

77. Thoughtlessness, delusion, heedlessness, dreaminess and drowsiness (caused by anything)—these are the various *Tāmasa* attributes.*

78. A person who knows this understanding (knowledge) which leads to Liberation from *Saṁsāra* and who carefully seeks to realise the *Ātman*, is never soiled by undesirable fruits of *karmans* just as a leaf of lotus.**

79. When a person becomes liberated from the various kinds of strong bonds pertaining to one's children (subjects in the case of kings) as well as pertaining to gods, and when the person gives up (the sense of) pleasure and pain, he becomes emancipated and attains the highest end, becoming bereft of external signs (such as five vital breaths, mind, intelligence, etc.

80-81a. By understanding the implication of authoritative prescriptions of the Vedas and by practising the auspicious acts and virtues enjoined in the Veda and Āgamas, a person, transcending the fear of old age and death, lies at ease. When both merits and sins are shed off and fruits accruing therefrom to the body (*tanoḥ*) are destroyed, such persons being

---

* Here ends the 28th verse from the Mbh. Śānti 219. NP. 78 ff. correspond to vv. 44 of the Mbh. (ibid) Ch. 219.

** *Viṣasyeva* in NP. is a misprint for *bisasyeva* in the Mbh. ibid 44 as 'poison' is meaningless in the context.

unattached at first resort to the *Saguṇa Brahman* that is in the space of one's heart and then visualize the *Nirguṇa Brahman*.

81b-82a. Just as a spider* residing in his web made of threads woven by itself, becomes free by cessation of weaving out the thread, the same way a person who is released from *Saṁsāra* sheds off all miseries and they (the miseries) are shattered down and destroyed like a clump or sod of earth dashing against a rocky mountain (*adri*)**.

82b-83a. Just as the Ruru (a species of deer) casting off its old horns or a serpent casting off its slough, slips away without being noticed, similarly, a liberated person casts off his sorrow.

83b-84. Just as a bird, leaving off a tree (*drumaṁ*†) falling into the water flies up to a safer place, in the same manner this person gives up joys and sorrows and becoming liberated and dissociated from his subtle bodies, attains to the highest region (viz. *Mokṣa*).

85. Having listened to the discourse full of nectarine words delivered by Pañcaśikha himself the king Janadeva carefully pondered upon every point contained therein and ascertained the truth in it. Casting off his sorrow he lived joyfully merged in the supreme bliss.

86. It is reported that beholding his capital city enveloped in fire, it was exclaimed by the king of Mithilā himself: "In this burning city, nothing of *mine* is burning."[5]

87. O great sage ! He who reads this exposition on the ascertainment of (the means to) *Mokṣa* and continuously ponders over it, is not affected by calamities and sorrows and becomes emancipated as did the king of Mithilā, after this meeting with Pañcaśikha.

---

* The analogy of a silk-worm is better.

** *adim* in the NP is a printing mistake for *adrim* as *adi* is meaningless in that context.

† *matsyaṁ yathā va' pyudake patantam*/
in the NP. makes little sense. "How can a fish falling into the water" is to be connected with the bird. The Mbh. (Ibid) v. 83b gives *drumaṁ* instead of *matsyam*.

CHAPTER FORTYFIVE

1. From this follows the extract compiled from *Mbh. Śānti* 218. 2ff. Instead of *Bhīṣma uvāca* from the Mbh. here is *Sanandana uvāca*.

2. Pañca-śikha—An ancient teacher of the Sāṅkhya school. He belonged to Parāśara Gotra (*Mbh.* xii. 320.24). As a child he was breast-fed by Kapilā and hence was probably called Kāpileya. He was the disciple of Āsuri. He lived in Pañca-Srotas where he performed a sacrifice for 1000 years and came to be known as Pañca-Śikha. He visited the court of Janaka where he defeated the heretic teachers and king Janaka into a polemic contest. King Janaka respected him as his preceptor (*Mbh. Śānti* 218).

3. Being the disciple of Kapila's disciple Āsuri, he was comparable to Kapila (N1.).

4. Āsuri—The disciple of Kapila, the founder of the Sāṅkhya school of thought (Bh. P.I.3.10).

5. This saying is attributed to Janaka (when his capital Mithilā was shown to have caught fire) both in the Pāli Canon and Śvetāmbara Jain (Ardha Māgadhī) Canon. cf. *mihilāe dajjhamāṇīe ṇa me dajjhai kiṁ ca ṇa* in the *Uttarādhyayana* sūtra and

mithilāya dahyamānāya, na ma kiñci adahyatha in the *Mahājanaka jātaka* v. 249.

CHAPTER FORTYSIX

The Narration of Spiritual matters

Sūta said:

1. O Brāhmaṇas, on hearing that excellent spiritual discourse, the liberal-minded Nārada delightedly asked Sanandana again.

Nārada said :

2. O sage, O storehouse of mercy! I seek refuge in you. To me kindly relate those things whereby one may not experience the three types of distress such as the Ādhyātmika Ādhidaivika, etc.

*Sanandana said**[1]

3. O learned one, three types of miseries occur to one born here. They occur in the womb or in the course of the process of being born or in the old age.

4. The panacea (for all worldly ills) is the ultimate attainment of the lord, characterised by the state of happiness unexcelled in bliss.

5. Hence, effort to attain it (viz. God-realization) must be made by learned men. O great sage, the cause of attaining it is said to be both knowledge and activity.

6. Knowledge is said to be of two kinds: that which arises out of the Vedic texts and that which arises from discrimination. The *Śabdabrahman* is that which arises out of the *Āgamas*. The great Supreme *Brahman* is that which arises out of discrimination between Reality and illusion.

7. The excellent sage Manu too, after remembering the meaning of the Vedas says thus: May that be heard even as I recount it in an easily understandable manner.

8. "Two *Brahmans* are to be understood, viz., the

---

* VV.3-30 of this chapter are incorporated from VP. VI. 58-87.

Śabdabrahman and the Supreme *Brahman*. One who is an adept in the *Śabdabrahman* understands the great *Brahman*."[2]

9. The Ātharvaṇa Veda[3] also says—"Two *Vidyās* are to be known". The greatest *Vidyā* is the attainment of the Imperishable (*Brahman*). The other one is the lore of the *Ṛgveda*, etc.

10-11. Verily, wise sages see him who is unmanifest, unageing, devoid of longing, birthless and unchanging; who cannot be specifically pointed out, who is formless, devoid of hands and feet, powerful and omnipresent, eternal, causeless but the source of origin of living beings, who is pervaded and who pervades everything else.

12. That is the *Brahman*, the greatest abode. It must be meditated upon by those who seek salvation. It is the subtle one mentioned by the Vedic texts—the greatest region of Viṣṇu.

13. That same form of the greatest *Ātman* is expressed by the word *Bhagavat*. The word *Bhagavat* connotes it. It is so indicated in regard to the imperishable *Ātman*.

14. That whereby the reality of what has been thus described is factually realized, is the real perfect knowledge. The other consists of the Trinity of Vedas.

15. O Brāhmaṇa, though the *Brahman* is beyond the ken of *Śabdas* (sounds and words) the word *Bhagavat* is used formally in order to honour or to adore the same.

16. O holy lord, the word *Bhagavat* connotes the pure and Supreme *Brahman* called also Mahāvibhūti (One endowed with the highest Potency) and is the cause of all causes.

16A.* The syllable *bha* has two meanings (1) that which is to be known and (2) the knower**. O sage, similarly the syllable *ga* means the creator, the father of the *Āgamas*.

17. Six things are indicated by the term *Bhag* viz: perfect prosperity and glory, prowess renown, splendour, perfect knowledge and detachment.

18. In the *Bhūtātman* which is the soul of all, all the living

---

* Wrongly numbered 16 in the text.

** VP. VI. 5.73 reads : *sambharteti tathā bhartā*. The syllable *Bha* implies the cherisher and supporter of the universe. This reading is better as the syllable 'Bha' (acc. to VP.) is common to both the words : *Sambhartā* and *Bhartā*.

beings reside. Hence, the meaning of the word 'va' is the unchanging lord who abides in all living beings.

19. Thus O excellent one, the great word *Bhagavān* belongs to Vāsudeva who is the greatest *Brahman*. It does not refer to anyone else.

20. As a technical phrase the word indicates an object of worship. This word indicates Vāsudeva without being used in a secondary sense. When referring to other objects the word is used in a secondary sense.[4]

21. He who knows the origin, dissolution, the advent as well as the departure of the living beings and also he who knows *Vidyā* and *Avidyā*, should be expressed by the term *Bhagavān*.

22. Knowledge, power, strength, prosperity, virility and splendour, the entirety of all these are expressed by the word *Bhagavat*. Only the despicable qualities[5] are excluded.

23. All the living beings reside in the great *Ātman*. The lord is remembered as Vāsudeva, because he abides in the *Bhūtas*.

24. Formerly when requested, Keśidhvaja told Khāṇḍikya of the Janaka dynasty.[6] He factually explained the meaning of the epithet Vāsudeva, the Infinite.

25. He lives in the *Bhūtas* and the *Bhūtas* live in him. He is the creator and the protector of all worlds. Hence, Vāsudeva is a lord—the Governor.

26. O sage, he transcends the *Prakṛti* of all living beings, the aberrations and the faults such as the *Guṇas*, etc. He goes beyond all coverings. He is the *Ātman* of all, the space between the worlds is occupied by him.

27. He is endowed with all auspicious qualities and is of the nature of good qualities. (Defective).[7] He eschews the creation of the *Bhūtas* over-whelmed by too much of misery; he assumes a splendid form voluntarily in accordance with his Will. He achieves the welfare of the entire universe.

28. He is one sole repository of splendour, strength, prosperity, great enlightenment, virility and other qualities. He is greater than the greatest. In the lord of the finite and the infinite beings, there are no (such imperfections of Avidyā such as distress and others.

29. He is the lord called *Parameśvara*. He is of the form of *Vyasṭi* and *Samaṣṭi* (the Microcosm and Macrocosm); he is both of the unmanifest and manifest forms; he is the overlord of all, the knower of the entire creation, and he is omnipotent.

30. That whereby he is known is free of defects;[8] it is an extremely pure form devoid of impurities. It is seen and understood. That is the perfect knowledge, anything other than this is said to be *Ajñāna* (Ignorance).

31.* That Puruṣottama is seen by means of *Svādhyāya* (study of the Vedas) and *Saṁyama* (self-control i.e. Yoga), either of them being the cause of attaining him, is called *Brahma*.

32. One should practise Yoga after *Svādhyāya*; and one should commit to memory the prescribed Vedic texts after through Yoga.[9] The great *Ātman* is revealed through the accomplishment of *Svādhyāya* and Yoga.

33. *Svādhyāya* is the eye for visualising him. The other eye is Yoga. (The Lord) who is *Brahman* cannot be seen through the physical eye.

Nārada said:

34. O Holy lord, I wish to know that Yoga. Kindly elucidate that after knowing which I would be able to see the Supreme Ruler, the support of all.

Sanandana said:

35. I shall expound that Yoga, in the same manner as Keśidhvaja formerly explained it to the noble-souled Khāṇḍikya of Janaka race.

Nārada said:[10]

36. O holy lord, who was Khāṇḍikya? Who was Keśidhvaja? How did it happen that they had a dialogue in relation to Yoga.

Sanandana said:

37. Dharmadhvaja of Janaka family was the father. His son was Amitadhvaja. Kṛtadhvaja was his brother who was a king who always took delight in spiritual topics.

---

* VV. 31 ff of the NP. are the same as VP. VI. Ch. 6.

37a*. The blessed twice-born Keśidhvaja was the son of Kṛtadhvaja. The son of Amitadhvaja was named Khāṇḍikya of the Janaka dynasty.

38. Khāṇḍikya who followed the path of action, was banished from his kingdom, accompanied by his preceptor and the ministers. He had limited resources only.

39. After being exiled from the kingdom, he wandered, through the impassable forests. He (Keśidhvaja) performed many *Yajñas* and resorted to *Jñāna* also.

40-42. By resorting to the lore about Brahman, he wished to cross the ocean of death. O foremost one among the knowers of Yoga, once as he was performing a sacrifice, a fierce tiger killed his cow in the lonely forest. On knowing that the cow[11] was killed by a tiger, he asked the sacrificial priests about the atonement: "What shall be done in this context?" They replied —"We do not know. May Kaśeru be consulted."

43. O Nārada, on being asked by him, Kaśeru said—"O leading king! I do not know it. Please refer to Śunaka. He will know it, i.e. must be knowing it.

44-45. He went and asked him. O sage, he told the king,—"Neither Kaśeru, nor I, nor anyone in the world now knows it. Only your enemy Khāṇḍikya who was defeated by you, knows it. O sage, he said, "I shall go to my enemy in order to consult him."

46-48. If he kills me, the benefit of the *Yajña* becomes already acquired by me.[12] If on being asked, my enemy explains the atonement, O excellent sage, the Yoga will be unaffected." Saying thus, the king, clad in deer skin, rode in the chariot and went to the forest where Khāṇḍikya the king was present. On seeing his enemy coming, Khāṇḍikya said with his eyes reddened with anger. He kept his bow fully drawn.

Khāṇḍikya said:

49-52a. O, will you kill us with the deerskin for your coat of mail? You seem to know (i.e. think) "No one will

* Wrongly numbered 37 in the printed text.

strike me since I wear deer skin." O fool, tell me. Is there no deerskin on the back of the deer? I thought that sharp and fierce arrows discharged on them would be futile. I will now kill you. You will not be allowed to go alive. O evil-minded one, you are a desperado; my enemy who has taken away my kingdom.

Keśidhvaja said :

"O Khāṇḍikya, it is with a view to clear a doubt that I have come to you, and not to kill you. Considering this, leave off either your anger or the arrow."

52b-55. Thereafter, he (Khāṇḍikya) discussed the matter in private with his ministers and his preceptors and priests. Khāṇḍikya, the highly intelligent one, consulted everyone. The ministers advised him—"This enemy who has come under our control must be killed. If he is killed the entire earth will be under your control." Khāṇḍikya replied to all of them— "Undoubtedly it is so.

56. If he is killed the entire earth will be under my control. But the conquest of the other world will be his, while the whole of the earth may be mine.

57. If I don't kill him, the conquest of the other world is mine without the earth. The conquest of the other world lasts till infinity, while the conquest of the earth is of a short duration.

58. Hence, I will not kill him. I will tell him what he asks." Then Khāṇḍikya Janaka approached his enemy and said :—

59. "Whatever you have to ask me (freely) ask me. I shall tell you." Then, O sage, he told him about the slaughter of his sacrificial cow.

60. Then he asked him about the expiatory observance of this *Vrata*. O sage, he duly explained everything to Keśidhvaja.

61-62. All the expiatory rites ordained in the context were explained by him. After understanding the matter, and being permitted by the noble-souled one he went back to the sacrificial ground and performed the rites duly. After completing the sacrifice duly he took his ceremonial ablution (*Avabhṛtha*).

63-65a. Becoming contented, the king began to think— "All the sacrificial priests have been worshipped. All the members of the sacrificial assembly have been honoured. All the suppliants have been duly provided with the desired objects by me. Whatever was worth doing in this world has been performed by me. How is it that I feel in my mind as though some religious duty has not been finished?

65b-66a. While pondering over thus, the king remembered—" O, the requisite fees due to the preceptor have not been given to Khāṇḍikya by me."

66b-67a. The king thereupon got into his chariot again and went to the impassable forest region where Khāṇḍikya the devotee of Svayambhu, was staying.

67b-68a. On seeing him coming again, Khāṇḍikya took up his weapon. He stood ready with the intention to kill him. The king Keśidhvaja then told him.

68b-70. "O Khāṇḍikya, do not be angry. I have not come here to do any harm to you; know that I have come to requite my preceptor. In accordance with your instruction the sacrifice has been duly performed by me. I wish to give you the *Gurudakṣiṇā* (Preceptor's fees). Please choose it and tell me.

On being thus requested, the king again consulted his ministers.

71. "He is desirous of paying the fees of the preceptor. What shall be requested by me?" The ministers said to him— "He may be requested for the gift of the entire kingdom".

72. King Khāṇḍikya laughed and said— "The kingdom is being begged by contented people[13] whose soldiers have not undergone any stress or strain!

73-74a. The kingdom of the earth is of a short duration. How can it be requested for by people like me? This is it. You people are such advisors as advocate selfish interest. What is the truth underlying this? You are not clever enough to know it."[14]

74b. After saying this he went up near the king Keśidhvaja and said— "will you certainly give the preceptor's fees?" When he said 'Of course', Khāṇḍikya spoke to him.

76-77a. "You are truly an expert in the perfect knowledge of spiritual matters. If the preceptor's fee is proposed to be given to me by you, kindly explain to me that holy rite which is capable of subduing the distress."[15]

Keśidhvaja said :

77b-78a. Why was my thornless kingdom not requested for by you? There is nothing more pleasing to Kṣatriyas than the acquisition of a kingdom.

Khāṇḍikya said :

78b. O Keśidhvaja, you understand, why it (kingdom) has not been requested for by me ?

79-81. Learned men do not yearn much for the entire kingdom. It is the duty of the Kṣatriyas to protect the subjects. Those who are inimical to their own kingdom are to be killed in an honest straightforward war. It was my fault, since I had been weak. There was no harm done by you. This Avidyā will only be conducive to bondage though devoid of a direct onslaught. If I were to crave for the kingdom it is a desire for further births and their enjoyment.

82. Begging and importunity may not be defective in the case of others. They follow only Dharma. It is the considered opinion of good (wise) persons that begging is not conducive to the religious duties (binding on) Kṣattriyas.

83-84a. Hence, the kingdom that belongs to you and is embedded in Avidyā, is not requested for. Even the learned men whose minds are drawn towards *Mamatva* (sense of possession) yearn for a kingdom. Those who are inebriated due to the great intoxicating beverage of *Ahammāna* (egotistic self-esteem) (crave for kingdom) but not people like me.

Keśidhvaja said :

84b-85. By means of Vidyā, I am desirous of crossing (surmounting) death. I rule the kingdom and perform various sacrifices. By enjoyment of pleasures, the merit dwindles down, but fortunately your mind is richly endowed with the discriminating faculty.

86. Listen, O delighter of the Janaka family, to the form or nature of Avidyā. It is the misapprehension of the soul in objects which are not the soul. It is the mistaking of one's own what is not one's own.

87. This is the seed, the outcome of the tree of Nescience stationed in two types.[16] In the physical body consisting of the fine elements the embodied being is enveloped in delusory darkness.[17]

88-89. The man of crooked intellect has the deep conviction of 'I am this', with regard to the body severally composed of the five elements, viz. Ether, wind, fire, water and earth. Who will entertain the false conception that the body which is not the soul, is the soul? The objects of enjoyment such as the house, the field, etc. have indeed to be enjoyed through the body.[18]

90. Though the *Ātman* is not the body, even the intelligent man thinks 'This is mine'. It is thus that he feels in regard to sons and grandsons procreated by that body.

91. Even the learned man feels the sense of ownership in regard to the body which is non-Ātman. Every man performs every action for the enjoyment of the body.

92-93a. When the body itself is something other than the man, it is always interested in binding him. Just as the house made of the earth (a mud-house) is scrubbed, cleaned, and plastered with water and mud, similarly the physical body consisting of earth and other elements is maintained with smearing, etc. with mud and water.

93b-94a. If the body that consists of fivefold means of enjoyment is developed by the same fivefold means of enjoyment, what is it that the man can be proud of ?

94b-96a. The individual soul goes through the path of worldly existence in the course of many thousands of births. He is enveloped by the dust of *Vāsanās*, impressions of actions and experiences. He attains delusion and exhaustion. O gentle one, when the dust particles are washed off by means of hot water of perfect knowledge, the delusory exhaustion of the wayfarer in the path of worldly existence is subdued.

96b-97a. When delusion and exhaustion are subdued, the man's inner sense organ, the heart becomes clear.

Getting a support that cannot be excelled by anything else, he attains the highest bliss of Salvation.

97b-98a. The *Ātman* is of the nature of bliss. It is of the nature of perfect knowledge. It is free from impurities. Misery, ignorance and attributes that are their off-shoots belong to *Prakṛti* and not to the *Ātman*.

98b. Although water has no direct contact with fire, it has the indirect contact through the pot.

99-100. Just as a wise person carries on his functions of uttering sound, etc., similarly the *Ātman*, polluted with ego, etc. due to his contact with *Prakṛti* resorts to *dharmas* (attributes) connected with *Prakṛti*. When he sheds off the ego, he is immutable and changeless. The seed (root-cause) of *Avidyā* has thus been narrated to you by me.

101. There is nothing other than Yoga that is destructive of miseries.

CHAPTER FORTYSIX

1. Vv. 3-30 are a quotation from VP. VI.5.51-87.

2. Though both VP. (ibid) v. 64 and NP. attribute this verse to Manu, it is not found in the extant *Manusmṛti*. It is a quotation from *Maitrāyaṇī* Up. VI.22. The *Brahman* has two aspects : verbal and Real or Spiritual and for the realization of the latter, the mastery over the former is necessary.

3. This is a quotation from the *Muṇḍaka* Up. I.4.5. The *Muṇḍaka* belongs to the AV. and hence the quotation is called *Ātharvaṇī śruti*.

4. In other words, the term *Bhagavat* which is the general denomination of an adorable object is not used with reference to the Supreme in general but as a special significance. But when the term is used with reference to any other person or thing, it is used in the customary general meaning.

5. The three *guṇas* and their consequent *Kleśas* (miseries) which deserve to be eschewed are not found in *Bhāgavata*.

6. For the genealogy and mutual relationship of Keśidhvaja and Khāṇḍikya *vide* vv. 37-39 below.

7. The verse in the NP. contains defective wording. The original verse in the VP. (*ibid*) 84 is as follows :

Samasta-kalyāṇa-guṇātmako'sau
ava-śakti-leśāvṛta-bhūta-vargaḥ

He is one with and of the nature of all auspicious attibutes. He has permeated all created beings with but a small portion of His Power.

8. Instead of the confusing reading : *sa Jñāyate yena* of the NP. VP. (ibid) v. 87 reads *saṃjñāyate yena* and it gives better meaning as follows :

That whereby, the flawless, pure, Supreme, unsullied (by the contact of Prakṛti) and one (undivided) Brahman is properly known, revealed or realised is the real knowledge. What is other than this is ignorance.

Here ends chapter 5 of VP. VI.

9. Both the study of the Vedas and practice of Yoga are essential for God-realization. When a person is weary of the one, he should pursue the other. But the dictum in Yoga is that one should perform *Japa* (muttering the name of God or (*Mantra*) when tired of meditation and *vice-verse* :

japācchrāntaḥ punar dhyāyed
dhyānāc chrāntaḥ punar japet //

10. In VP.VI.6.6, it is Maitreya who speaks this verse and the reply of Parāśara in VP. VI.6.7 ff, is the same as given here by Sanandana in vv. 37 ff. These names do not occur in the Janaka dynasty in VP.IV.5 but are recorded by Bh.P.IX.13.19-21.

11. For *tasya dhenum* of the NP. *dharma-dhenum* in the VP. (ibid) v. 13 is better, as it is not any cow but the cow related to the sacrifice whose death needed atonement.

12. *Prāpta eva mayā yajñe* is obscure grammatically. VP (*ibid*) 18 *prapta eva mahā-yajño* is clear. Hence adopted in the translation.

13. VP. (*ibid*) 45 reads *Śatrubhiḥ* instead of *Kṛtibhiḥ* in the NP. that makes the clause form a part of the ministerial advice that the kingdom is obtained without military engagement.

14. Another interpretation : "Thus you are the people who tender advice in concerns of this worldly life. But you are not competent enough to advise on matters relating to the higher (spiritual) objects.

15. Here ends ch. 6 in VP. VI. Vv. 77 ff. of the NP. constitute VP. VI. ch. 7.

16. NP. V. 86b-87a constitutes VP. (ibid) v. 11 and the meaning becomes more consistent and clear as follows : "The erroneous notion to regard what is not self as the self and the notion in regarding what is not one's own as one's own, constitutes the double seed of the tree of Nescience.

17. Though this ch. in the NP. is taken from the VP. VI, the lining of the verses is different from the text of the VP. Thus VV. 88b and 89a constitute verse No 13 in the VP VI. 6 and when these are taken together as in the VP, the meaning is changed. Thus 88b-89a means : "Who will look upon the body as the soul when the soul abides indistinctly (apart) from the five elements constituting the body."

18. The lines of verses in the NP are re-arranged according to the VP. VI. 7 and briefly translated for the sake of comparison and noting the difference in the interpretation due to the changes in the lines of the VP. in the text of the NP.

(NP. VV. 89b-90a) What man of understanding would attribute to the incorporeal soul the enjoyments of the body like lands, houses, etc. and would call them his own ?

90b-91a. What learned person will entertain the idea of property, in sons and grandsons born of the body, when the body itself ceases to be the self.

91b-92a. It is for the enjoyment of the body that a man performs an act and to obtain its fruits in the next body. But that again results in the perpetuation of the bondage of the body (bodily existence).

92b-93a. Just as a house of clay is plasted with clay and water, so the body which is composed of the earth, is sustained by the earth (i e. food grown of the earth) and water.

93b-94a. The physical body which is constituted of five elements is nourished by things which are also made of those very elements. Under the circumstances, what did the soul enjoy ?

94b-95a. Wandering through the path of *Saṁsāra* for thousands of births, the soul enveloped in the dust (particles) of desires, attains nothing but exhaustion in the form of delusion.

95b-96a. When that dust is washed off by the hot water of real knowledge, the exhaustion of delusion of the traveller of Saṁsāra is removed.

96b-97a. When the fatigue caused by infatuation is relieved and the person gets internal peace, be attains the supreme salvation which is unparallelled and undisturbed.

97b-98a. The real nature of the soul is pure, constituted of bliss and knowledge. The attributes such as pain, ignorance and impurity belong to *Prakṛti* and not to the *Ātman*.

98b-100a. The water and fire do not come in contact but when the water is placed above the fire in a pot, it bubbles and manifests the properties of fire. Similarly, the soul though absolutely distinct from the Prakṛti and its attributes, and uncorrupted, assumes the attributes of the gross nature, when the soul in association with Prakṛti gets polluted by egotism and other properties.

100b-101. The seed of ignorance is as described by me. There is no panacea on these worldly miseries except the practice of Yoga.

CHAPTER FORTYSEVEN

Exposition of the way to realize the soul

Sanandana said :

1. On hearing these words of Keśidhvaja that consisted of an estimate of spiritual topics and that was like nector, Khāṇḍikya spoke again, urging him.

Khāṇḍikya said :[1]

2. O highly blessed one, O the most excellent one among the knowers of Yoga, recount details of Yoga. In this dynasty of Nimi, you alone are the person who have understood the topics in the Yogaśāstra.

Keśidhvaja said :

3. O Khāṇḍikya, even as I recount, may the nature of the Yoga be heard. A sage who is established in Yoga, does not fall off after attaining merger into the Brahman.

4. Mind alone is the cause of bondage and liberation of men. When addicted to the sensual objects, it is the cause of bondage. When it is devoid of objects, it is the cause of liberation.

5. A wise man possessing discriminative knowledge, should withdraw the mind from the sense-objects and through it for the sake of salvation meditate on the Brahman, the greatest Īśvara.

6. By means of the power of the *Atman* he should make the mind that is prone to aberration,[2] meditate on the *Brahman* by infusing it with the nature of Ātman, even as a magnet does it to a piece of iron.

7. The special movement of the mind that depends on the efforts of self is to conjoin to the *Brahman* and such union with the *Brahman* is called Yoga.

8. This includes the holy rites with special and peculiar characteristics. He who possesses Yoga is Yogin. He is called a *Mumukṣu* (one desirous of liberation).

9. At the outset, the Yogin who practises Yoga is called *Yuñjamāna*. He who is called *Viniṣpannasamādhi* (of accomplished meditation) is one, who has attained the greatest *Brahman*.

10. If due to defects and obstacles his mind is not[3] defiled, the former one attains salvation, thanks to the repeated practice in the course of many other births.

11. The latter one who is called *Viniṣpannasamādhi* (i.e. the knower of Brahman.) attains salvation in the very same birth. The Yogin attains everything ere long after burning the Karmans through the fire of Yoga.

12-14. A Yogin shall practise five *Yamas* (restraints) and five *Niyamas* (observances): Celibacy, non-violence, truthfulness, non-stealing and non-acceptance of monetary gifts (these are the *Yamas*). *Svādhyāya* (self-study of the Vedas), *Śauca* (purificatory rites), *Santoṣa* (contentment) *Tapas* (penance) and concentration of the mind on the great *Ātman*. He must keep his mind devoid of lusts. Thus the five *Yamas* and the five *Niyamas* have been recounted. If people practise these with specific desires, they yield special benefits; if people practise these without desires they yield salvation.

15. Thus the ascetic should practise the good postures. (like Bhadrāsana). He must be endowed with good qualities. He must perform the Yoga with what are called *Yamas* and *Niyamas*.

16. If what are called *Prāṇas* (vital airs) are restrained by practice, it should be known as *Prāṇāyāma*. It has two subdivisions: the *Sabīja* (with seed) and the *Abīja* (without seed).

17. When the two vital Airs—*Prāṇa* and *Apāna*, overpower each other (are merged together), by regulating them both by proper means, that is the third (variety of breath-control, viz., *Kumbhaka*).

18. O lord of the enemies, its form is as gross[4] as its *Ālambana* (support) the support of the *Ananta* (endless one) is obtained by the Yogin as he practises.

19. The knower of the Yogas shall curb the sense organs drawn towards their objects such as sound, etc. Being devoted to and insistent on *Pratyāhāra* (withdrawal of the mind from sense-objects), he should make the senses (withdrawn from sense objects but) merging in the mind.

20. If the sense-organs become steady, they become extremely submissive. If they are non-submissive, the Yogin cannot achieve Yoga.

21. After keeping the vital airs under control by means of *Prāṇāyāma* and the sense-organs by means of *Pratyāhāra*, the practitioner of Yoga shall make the mind stabilised in an auspicious support.

Khāṇḍikya said:

22. O highly blessed one, may it be mentioned to me, the auspicious support of the mind, by having which the mind dispels the outcome of defects entirely.

Keśidhvaja said:

23. O wise one, the support of the mind is twofold, that too based on the form. The form may be embodied or unembodied; it may be *Para* (greater) or *Apara* (smaller).

24. There are three types of *Bhāvanās* (conceptions). The form and the universe is said to be threefold: The first is called *Brahma bhāvanā*, the other is known as *Karma-bhāvanā* and the third is of the nature of both *Karma* and *Brahma*.

25. One *Bhāvanā* is of the nature of *Karman*, the other one is of the nature of the *Brahman*, and the third one is of the nature of both. Thus there are three types of *Bhāvabhāvanā* (conception).

26. O wise one, Sanaka and others are always endowed with the *Brahmabhāvanā*, while the others, Devas etc. the mobile and immobile beings — all these are endowed with *Karmabhāvanā*.

27. In *Hiraṇyagarbha* and others, the Bhāvanā is of the combined nature of the *Brahman and Karman*. In those invested with authority and with enlightenment, there is the Bhāvabhāvanā.

28. O king, in the eyes of those who differentiate regarding that this is the Universe, that other is some thing diffeent, when all the particularised *Karmans* and knowledge are not diminished completely.

29. That knowledge is termed *Brahman*, the knowledge where the differences have completely vanished which

is Existence alone, which is beyond the scope of words and which is self-produced.

30 That is the great form of Viṣṇu who is formless and unborn. The characteristics of the great *Ātman* are contrary to the diversity of the form of the entire Universe.

31. O king, since that (i.e. the greatest form of Viṣṇu) cannot be meditated upon by one who practises Yoga, the gross form of Hari that could be seen by means of the eyes should be meditated upon.

32-35. All these constitute the universe, viz.—Lord Hiraṇyagarbha, Vāsava (i.e. Indra), Prajāpati, Maruts, Vasus, Rudras, Bhāskaras (i.e. Ādityas), constellations, planets, Gandharvas, Yakṣas, Daityas, *Deva-Yonis* (all kinds of divine and semi-divine beings), human beings, animals, mountains, oceans, rivers, trees, in fact. O king, all living beings, all those causes of the *Bhūtas* namely those beginning with the *Pradhāna* and ending with the *Viśeṣas*, those who are sentient and non-sentient, the single-footed, the bipeds, the multi-footed, and the footless—all these are the embodied forms of Hari. They are of the nature of *Bhāvanās* of the three types.

36. All this universe, consisting of the mobile and immobile beings, is endowed with the potency of Viṣṇu of the form of the Supreme Brahman.

37. The greatest *Śakti* is said to be *Viṣṇu Śakti*; the other *Śakti* is called *Kṣetrajña* and the third *Śakti* is called *Avidyākarman*.

38-39. O king, the *Śakti* that is called *Kṣetrajña* is produced through *Karmans*. O highly intelligent one, in this worthless worldly existence, it is of the active nature. It attains the distresses of worldly existence. The individual soul is enveloped and concealed by this *Śakti*. Hence it is called *Kṣetrajña Śakti*.

40. O king, this is seen in all living beings in varying degrees. In lifeless ones, it is very little and in the immobile beings it exists a little more than that.

41. In the reptiles, it is more than in the immobile beings. It is very powerful in birds. The deer are more powerful than the birds and the beasts are superior to the deer in their strength.

42. Human beings are more powerful than beasts and men wield more power (among human beings). O king, superior to them are the Nāgas, Gandharvas, Yakṣas and other gods.

43-44. Indra is the most powerful among Devas and superior to him is Prajāpati. Hiraṇyagarbha is more powerful than he. O king, all these are his forms, since they are invested with his potency as though with the Ether.

45. O highly intelligent one, the second unembodied form of the Brahman called Viṣṇu is termed *sat* by the learned men. It is worthy of being meditated upon by the Yogins.

46. O king, it is there that all these potencies are founded. These are not the real forms of Hari. It is another and very great.

47. O lord of men, he assumes the forms of all potencies (*Śaktis*) having the activities of Devas, animals and human beings in his own sports.

48. His activities based on the Karmans (of other beings) are for helping the worlds. The activities of the incomprehensible Being are pervasive and very benevolent.*

49. O king, that form of the deity, the embodiment of the Universe must be meditated upon for the purification of the soul. It is destructive of all sins.

50. Just as the fire with shooting flames in collaboration with the wind burns down heaps of dry grass and wood, so also Viṣṇu, abiding in the minds of Yogins destroys all sins.

51. (Defective) Hence, this potency is the first and foremost of all potencies. The devotee shall keep it in the mind. If it is duly stabilised it should be known as one with pure characteristics (?)

52. It is the auspicious support of the *Ātman* that is present everywhere and is accompanied by the mind. It is

* The reading should be *atihitātmikā* and not *avihitātmikā* as in the printed text.

beyond the three *Bhāvabhāvanās* (emotional conceptions). O king, it is conducive to the salvation of the Yogins.

53. O tiger among men, all other supports of the mind, Devas and others with Karmans as their source of origin, are impure.

54. (Defective) One who has no desire for any of these supports shall meditate on the embodied form of the Lord. This is to be known as *Dhāraṇā* since the mind is concentrated there.

55. O ruler of men, may it be heard of what nature should Hari's form be, for being meditated upon. There cannot be a *Dhāraṇā* (retention) without a support.

56-60. The form shall be—one with beautiful and delighted face; with the eyes large like the petals of a lotus; fine cheeks with a wide and brilliant forehead; its earrings placed equally between ears and shoulders; the neck resembling a conch shell, with the chest marked with *Śrīvatsa*; the three folds in the skin in the curved umbilical region and the belly appearing beautiful; Viṣṇu may be conceived as having eight long arms or four arms, his thighs large and symmetrical, firm lotus-like hands and feet clad in pure yellow robes; bedecked in coronet, beautiful bracelets, armlets, etc. He is surrounded by a halo and is wielding the Śārṅga bow, a *Śaṅkha*, a mace and a sword. He is to be meditated thus as the Brahman also.

61. The Yogin shall identify himself with the deity, after concentrating his mind and meditate upon Viṣṇu, O king, until the *Dhāraṇā* becomes firmly fixed therein.

62. Whether the devotee is talking something or standing by or is engaged in some voluntary activity, the retention (*Dhāraṇā*) does not vanish from the mind. In that case he should consider that (i.e. *Dhāraṇā*) as achieved.

63. Thereafter, the sensible man shall meditate upon the Lord's form without *Śaṅkha*, *Gadā*, *Cakra*, Śārṅga (bow), etc., but it is tranquil with the rosary in the hands.

64. When this *Dhāraṇā* is more or less stabilised, one shall meditate upon the Lord's form without such ornaments as coronet, bracelets, etc.

65. Then the sensible man should mentally dwell on

that single limb; and subsequently he shall become engrossed in the one (Lord) that has the limbs.

66. At the perception of that form (there shall be) one obeisance and absence of desire for other objects. O king, his meditation is fulfilled by the first six *Aṅgas* (of meditation).

67. When his perception of the form of the deity without any fanciful conception becomes the outcome of mental meditation, it is called *Samādhi*.

68. O king, in regard to the thing to be achieved i.e. the great Brahman, that which makes the achievement possible is *Vijñāna* (perfect knowledge). That which is to be attained to is the *Ātman* whose *Bhāvanās* have been dispelled.

69. It is the perfect knowledge of the *Kṣetrajña* and the sense-organs therefore. After facilitating the achievement of the task of liberation, it has its purpose achieved and it recedes.

70. Then the devotee shall achieve the emotional identity with the great *Ātman*, he shall become non-different from him. The difference is caused by the ignorance about him.

71. When *Ajñāna*, the cause of differentiation, is utterly dispelled who will agree to this that the *Ātman* is different from the *Brahman* ?

72. O Khāṇḍikya, thus partly in detail and partly in brief, the Yoga has been recounted to you, since you have been asking me about it. What more can I do for you?

Khāṇḍikya said :

73. The excellent nature of the Yoga has been expounded by you. Everything has been done for me. Thanks to your instructions, the impurity in my mind has been entirely annihilated.

74. What has been called by me as 'Mine' is incorrect and not otherwise. Even by those who know what should be known, O king, it cannot be mentioned otherwise.

75. The feelings 'I' and 'My' are the outcome of *Avidyā* so also their utterance. The truth which is inexpressible is beyond the scope of words.

76. O Keśidhvaja, go, for the attainment of further welfare. Everything has been done for me by you since the

unchanging Yoga devoted to salvation has been explained to me.

Sanandana said :

77. Thereafter, having been worshipped duly by Khāṇḍikya, king Keśidhvaja returned to his capital duly worshipped by Khāṇḍikya, O Brāhmaṇa.

78. Khāṇḍikya made his son the king. With his mind, dedicated to Kṛṣṇa, he went to Viśālā for the achievement of mastery over Yoga.

79. He was endowed with the qualities of *Yama*, etc. He was solely engrossed in deep meditation. The king attained dissolution by merging himself into the pure *Brahman* called Viṣṇu.

80. For the sake of liberation and eager to dispel his *Karmans*, he enjoyed the sensual pleasures and performed holy rites without any desire in view.

81. O sage, by means of auspicious enjoyment of pleasures, he wiped off all sins and became free from impurities. He attained *Siddhi* that utterly quelled the three kinds of *Tāpa* (misery).

82. Thus everything that you had asked me has been recounted to you. What else shall I narrate to you for dispelling the three types of distress?

CHAPTER FORTYSEVEN

1. VV. 2 ff of this Purāṇa are the same as in the VP. VI. 7. 26 ff.

2. For 6a of the NP: *ātmabhāvaṁ nayet tena tad brahmadhyāpanaṁ manaḥ*, VP (*ibid*) 30a reads .. *nayatyenaṁ tad brahma dhyātum munim* and changes the meaning completely. For that Brahman attracts to itself the sage who meditates upon it and who is of the same nature, as the magnet attracts the iron.

3. NP 10a reads *dūṣyate nāsya mānasam* instead of *cāsya mānasam* in VP (*ibid*) 34a. But this *na* in the NP. makes the verse self-contradictory. Why should a yogi whose mind is not defined due to obstacles require many more births ? The reading *cāsya* for nāsya in the VP means : "Should the yogin's mind be vitiated by defects" etc.

4. For *ālambanavat sthūlam* of the NP 18a, VP *ālambanavataḥ sthūlam* (while the Yogi practises) his support (*ālambana*) is the gross form (*Hiraṇagarbha*) of the Lord.

CHAPTER FORTYEIGHT

The story of Bharata

Nārada said :

1. O blessed one, the antidote for the three types of distress has been heard by me. Still my mind is confused. It does not attain proper stability, easily.

2. O Brāhmaṇa, how can the sinful transgression against one's own self committed by wicked men, be tolerated by men? O bestower of honour, recount it to me.

Sūta said :

3. On hearing what has been spoken by Nārada, Sunandana, the son of Brahmā, remembered the activities of Bharata. With great delight he said :

Sanandana said :

4. In this context, I shall tell you the ancient traditional story on hearing which your confused mind shall attain great stability.

5. O excellent sage, formerly, there was a king named Bharata. He was the son of Ṛṣabha. This sub-continent is named Bharatakhaṇḍa after him.

6. After attaining the kingdom belonging to his father and grandfather in due succession, he protected it righteously. He delighted the subjects like their father.

7. He performed various kinds of sacrifices and worshipped Lord Viṣṇu, the embodiment of all Devas. He meditated upon him with the mind centering round him in the course of carrying out different activities.

8. He procreated sons. He was unattached to sensuous objects. The learned king left the kingdom and went to the hermitage of Pulastya and Pulaha.

9-10a. He went to the great holy centre Śālagrāma frequented by people desirous of liberation. O sage, he became an ascetic and performed the propitiation of Viṣṇu with great devotion, rendering service(unto the Lord) with things obtained by him.

10b-11a. O Nārada, every day in the morning he plunged into the pure clear water and prayed to the Sun with devotion muttering the Supreme syllable expressive of the Brahman (i.e. *Oṁ* or Gāyatrī).

11b-13a. He then returned to the hermitage. With great purity and devotional piety, he worshipped Vāsudeva the Lord of the universe with the materials of worship such as sacrificial twigs, Kuśa grass, clay, etc. brought by himself. He worshipped with fruits, flowers, leaves of Tulasī and clear water.

13b-14a. On one occasion, that highly blessed king took his ablution in the River Cakra. With great purity and attention he stayed in the water performing *Japa* for three *Muhūrtas*.

14b-15a. O Brāhmaṇa, a thirsty hind who was about to be delivered of a young one, came to the bank from the forest, in order to drink water.

15b-16a. As she had almost completed drinking the water, there arose the great roaring sound of a lion which was frightful to all living beings.

16b-17a. On hearing the roaring sound of the lion, the hind leapt to the bank of the river. While she was climbing the steep side of the bank, the foetus fell down into the river.

17b-18a. Bharata caught hold of the fawn that fell off from its mother's womb and was carried away by the forceful current and the waves of the river.

18b-19a. O leading sage, due to the misery on account of the fall of the foetus and the steep ascent, that hind fell down dead.

19b-22. On seeing the hind dead in the tragic circumstances, the royal saint took up the fawn and brought it to his hermitage. The king nurtured the young one of the hind day by day. O sage, nourished by him, it duly grew up. At first the fawn used to graze at the outskirts of the hermitage. Then it went to the forest, it went far into the forest but, afraid of tigers, it returned soon. After some time it used to go very far into the forest in the morning and return to the hermitage in the evening.

23-24a. Bharata kept it inside the hut in the hermitage during nights. His mind became highly involved with the deer-fawn that used to be near him or away from him by turns. O sage, his mind was not so much drawn towards Viṣṇu.

24b-25a. Remember that he had abandoned his kingdom and even sons; that he had eschewed all connections with his kinsmen. Still he had great affection (feeling of kinship) with the fawn.

25b-26. When the fawn was away from the hermitage for a long time, his mind was agitated by various doubts such as, "Has it been devoured by the wolves?" "Have tigers seized upon it ?" "Has it been struck down by the lion?" When the fawn was by his side his face was bright with delight and love.

27. As his mind was attracted by the feelings of 'my-ness', his *Samādhis* (trances and concentration) became disturbed often. After some time the king died.

28. At the time of passing away, he was looking at the fawn. Like a father by the son, he was looked at by the fawn with tears in its eyes.

29. O sage, since his mental fancy was of that nature, he was born as a deer—O excellent Brāhmaṇa. Since he had the faculty of remembering previous births, he became unenamoured of worldly existence.

30. He left off his mother (i.e. the mind) and went to Śālagrāma. He nourished himself by means of dry leaves and grass.

31. Thus he expiated for the evil action that had been the cause of his birth as a fawn. Having left off his body, he was born again as a Brāhmaṇa who had the faculty of remembering his previous births.

32. He was born in a leading, pure family of Yogins of good conduct. He was richly endowed with all knowledge. He was conversant with all principles and topics in the scriptural texts.

33-34. That excellent sage perceived his own *Ātman* beyond *Prakṛti*. O great sage, thanks to the knowledge of *Ātman* that he had acquired, that highly intelligent one saw Devas and others, nay, all living beings, without any difference. He was invested with the sacred thread, but he did not repeat the Vedic text as uttered by his preceptor.

35. He did not observe holy rites. He did not learn scriptural texts. When he was addressed many times, he made some stupid irrational statement.

36. Even that speech lacked in qualities of cultural refinement. It was often uttered in vulgar rustic language. O sage, accursed in body, he was always clad in dirty clothes.

37-40. Saliva oozed from the interstices of his teeth. He was always harassed by citizens. He used to remember the words of Hiraṇyagarbha (or Brahmā*) as follows: "Excess of respect affects the prosperity of Yoga. A Yogin dishonoured by the people achieves Yogic power. Hence, a Yogin should perform holy rites of good men without defiling them. He should so perform them that the people should begin to disrespect him and avoid associating with him." The highly intelligent one thus thought of the words of Hiraṇyagarbha, and showed himself to the public as one with sluggish features and of unsound mind. He regularly ate cakes made of Kulmāṣa grain, vegetables and fruits from the forests.

41-42a. He ate whatever he got and whenever it happened. When his father passed away, he was compelled to work in the fields by his brothers, nephews and other kinsmen.

42b-43a. All his limbs became stout, though he was fed on rotten food. He became a sluggish worker. With food for his wages, he helped the whole world.

43b-44a. (On seeing) him so unrefined but having the features and activities of a Brāhmaṇa, a charioteer of the Sauvīra[1] king considered him worthy of being taken as an unpaid labourer.

44b-45a. O Brāhmaṇa, that king was seated in a palanquin. He was thinking of going to the excellent hermitage of sage Kapila on the banks of Ikṣumatī river.[1]

45b-46. He wanted to ask the great sage Kapila who was well learned in the topic of virtues leading to salvation, as follows—"What is it that is conducive to the welfare of men in this

---

* An ancient teacher of Yoga-śāstra.

1. Variously identified with Eder (N. Gujarat), Upper Sindh, Multan (Alberuni)—N.L.De. accepts the last—De, p. 183.

world which is mostly full of miseries." On being urged by the words of the charioteer, he carried his palanquin.

47. O Brāhmaṇa, he, the sole receptacle of all knowledge, was taken as an unpaid labourer. He was one among other men who too were unpaid labourers.

48. Endowed with the faculty of remembering events of past lives, he bore the palanquin as he was desirous of wiping off his sins. He, the most excellent one among the intelligent men, slowly walked ahead gazing at the yoke of the palanquin.

49-50a. The other bearers walked quickly. On observing the irregular movement of the palanquin, the king said—"O palanquin-bearers! What is this? Go ahead at even step."

50b-51. Again the movement of the palanquin was irregular. The king laughed and asked them, "what is this? You are moving otherwise!" When the king (mildly rebuked) them many times, the palanquin-bearers said—"This fellow does not thus move quickly."

The king said:

52. "Are you tired? You have borne the palanquin only for a short distance. Are you not used to strenuous work? Aren't you seen a bulky fellow?"

The Brāhmaṇa said:

53. "I am not stout. Your palanquin has not been borne by me. I am not tired. I have no fatigue or trouble. O lord of the earth, the bearer is another one."

The king said:

54. "You are actually seen to be stout. The palanquin is still above you. Fatigue in carrying a load occurs to embodied beings (as they have to exert and carry the load).

The Brāhmaṇa said:

55. "O king, tell me what you have directly perceived. The qualifications of strong or weak may be added afterwards.

56. This is a false statement—"The palanquin is borne by you. The palanquin is still above you." All this is false, O Sir, listen to my words now.

57. The two feet are on the ground. The shanks rest on the pair of feet. The thighs are on the pair of shanks. The belly has the support of the pair of thighs and hips.

58. The chest, the arms and the shoulders rest on the belly. This palanquin is supported by the shoulders. How can it be said that I am the support?

59. The body designated as 'you' is stationed within the palanquin. "You are there. I am here". This is also a wrongly put statement.

60. O king, you, I, and the others are to be borne by the elements; the whole class of living beings (and the elements) are fallen in the current of the *Guṇas*.

61. O Lord of the earth, these—*sattva* and other *Guṇas* are subject to the control of *Karmans*. The *Karman* accumulated due to ignorance is present in all creatures

62. The *Ātman* is pure, imperishable and quiescent. It is devoid of *Guṇas*. It is beyond *Prakṛti*. The *Ātman* alone abides in all creatures but he has no increase (fatness) or decrease (slimness).

63. O king, when there is neither increase nor decrease, it was childish ignorance (that prompted you to say I am stout). On what basis was it uttered by you?

64-66. (Defective) This palanquin rests equally on the ground pair of feet, shanks, thighs, hips, belly and other things as well as on the shoulders. When the burden is equal, O king, the palanquin is not borne by you or the other creatures alone. A great burden originating from mountains, trees or houses nay, from the whole earth has to be borne by you and by me. As the Puruṣa has distinctness (separate existence) from the sense organs which are the products of Prakṛti what heavy load is to be borne by me, O King. O King the Puruṣa is separated from the sense organs produced from Prakṛti [?]

67. The material that constitutes this palanpuin is a conglomeration of all elements, grown large equally in regard to you, me or the entire world.

Sanandana said:

68. After saying this the Brāhmaṇa who was bearing the

palanquin became silent. Thereupon the king hurriedly got down to the ground and touched his feet.

The King said:—

69. O Brahmin, be pleased with me. Leave off the palanquin. May it be revealed to me who you are, in the guise of a low and degraded man.

70. I am eager to serve you. O learned one, may everything be mentioned by you, viz—who you are, whose son you are and what the reason for coming here is?

The Brahmin said:—

71-73. May it be heard, O king. It cannot be explained who I am. Everywhere the action of arrival is prompted by some utility [enjoyment of pleasures]. The enjoyment of pleasures and the experience of miseries is accomplished through the body, etc. A creature attains the body, etc. in order to experience the outcome of Dharma and Adharma, O king, everywhere, in the case of every creature the reason is Dharma or Adharma. Hence, how is it that the reason is being asked?

The king said:—

74. There is no doubt in this that Dharma or Adharma is the cause of all effects. The transmigration from one body to another is for experiencing pleasure or pain.

75. As to your statement that it cannot be said who am I in regard to the Ātman, I wish to state as follows.

76. O brahmin, How is it that it is not possible to say "I am he who exists. O twice-born, the word *Aham* (I) refers to the Ātman and not to the body.*

The Brahmin said:—

77. The word *Aham* refers to the body and not to the Ātman. The mistaken identity of the Ātman with the

* For *doṣāya* in this and the next verse read *dehāya*.

non-Ātman may be due to the secondary sense of the word (or the effect of hearing).

78-79. It is the tongue, teeth, lips and palate, O king that say *Aham* [I]. All of them must be meant by *Aham* [I] since all of them have been the cause of utterance. For what purpose does the tongue say of its own accord the word 'I'. Nor it is cogent to say *aham* means 'I am the tongue, I am the speech'. Is the utterance "I am" made through proper cause? Still it is not correct to say that I am the speech [?]

80. O king, the physical body characterised by the head, hands. etc. is separate from the Puruṣa. Hence, where shall I fix the term *Aham* ?

81. If there be any other person than I, O excellent king, I am not the body even if others wish to speak of it.

82. When, only one Puruṣa is present in all bodies it. is futile to say, "Who are you?' 'Who am I', etc.

83. "You are the king." "This is the palanquin." "We are the bearers going ahead." "This is your world". O king, it is not the reality to say thus.

84. A log of wood is obtained from a tree. From that this palanquin is fashioned out—this palanquin occupied by you. O king, is it termed as a tree or a log of wood?

85. The people do not say, "The great king is seated on the tree" when you are riding in the palanquin nor do they say that you are sitting on a log of wood.

86. The palanquin and the mass of log—each has its name and situation. O excellent king, may the palanquin that gives you delight be pondered over by you.

87. Similarly, the separate nature of the umbrella from the ribs may be considered. Wherefrom is the umbrella born?" This argument is applicable both to you and to me.

88. Man, woman, cow, goat, horse, elephant, bird, tree etc—it should be known that these are the terms given to bodies in the world, the bodies caused by Karmans.

89. The Being (Puruṣa) is neither a deva nor a man,

nor an animal nor a tree. O king, these are different shapes of physical bodies originating from Karmans.

90. O king, the object that is called a king in the world or the object that is called 'king's soldier' or any other object is not true. It is sheer imagination.

91. What is that object which perishes after sometime? O king, what is the object that is evolved after transformation?

92. You are the king for the whole world, son to your father, enemy to your enemy, husband to your queen, father to your son. O king what shall I say? Who are you?

93. Who are you? This head? Or, does the head belong to you? Who are you? this belly? Or does the belly belong to you? O lord of the earth, are you the foot, etc? Don't they belong to you?

94. You are separated from all limbs, O king, ponder carefully on the topic 'Who am I?'

95. When the real situation is this, how can what should be evolved out of separate foot etc. be conceived as 'By me' 'I' etc, O king [?]

CHAPTER FORTYNINE

*Exposition of the Virtuous Path to Liberation**

Sanandana said:

1. On hearing this speech, full of profound truth, the king respectfully bowed to him and submitted :

The king submitted :

2. Venerable Sir, what has been authoritatively stated by you certainly contains the ultimate truth, but on hearing it, the functioning of my mind is as it were whirling.

3. If this discriminative knowledge exists in remaining** beings, that which is superior to and beyond the ken of *Prakṛti* has been shown by you.

4-5. But the statements : "I do not bear the palanquin, the palanquin does not rest over me. The body whereby this palanquin is borne, is different from me. The propensity of creatures is due to influence the *guṇas* (attributes) and it is urged by activities (*Karmans*). (This being the case) what is there as mine (done by me) in it." This is what was spoken by you.†

6. O knower of the highest truth ! When such doctrines are heard by me, my mind which has become anxious to know the ultimate truth gets agitated and perplexed.

7. Even at the outset, I was out to go to the sage Kapila, O highly fortunate Brāhmaṇa, to enquire of him about the doubt "What is the most excellent thing in this life."

---

* This chapter is a combination of chapters 14, 15 and 16 of the II *Aṁśa* of VP. (*Viṣṇu* Purāṇa).

** VP reads : *yad aśeṣeṣu* for *yadi śeṣeṣu* of the NP. VP. means: The discriminative knowledge existing in all creatures is the Brahma (the great principle) itself, beyond the ken of *Prakṛti* (I have no doubt about it.)

† VP. (Ibid) v. 7, *Śaṁsa me* "Please explain to me".

8. But in the meanwhile such a statement has been made by you as makes my mind rush to you, for getting acquainted with the great objective in life.

9. It is reported that verily, the sage Kapila is the ray (portion) of Lord Viṣṇu, the pervader (embodiment) of all beings, who has incarnated for the dissipation of the delusion of the world.

10. Me-thinks really it is the venerable Lord Kapila himself, who with a desire for our welfare, has manifested himself to me in what has been spoken to me.

11. O twice-born one! Your honour is the veritable ocean with billows of all divine wisdom. Be pleased to explain to me what is the excellent-most welfare for the dissipation of my delusion.

The Brāhmaṇa replied :

12. You are asking again what is a welfare ? You are asking this in the real sense of the term.* O king, all ultimate truths are certainly conducive to welfare.**

13. To a person who, after propitiating deities, covets for wealth and property, desires to have sons or a kingdom, everyone of these is respectively the highest good.

14-15a. The association of the great Ātman of a person possessing discrimination is an excellence conducive to welfare. Excellent is the performance of sacrifice (and other rites) the fruit of which is obtaining the pleasures in the heaven. But the real excellent welfare lies in not coveting its fruit.

15b-16a. There are hundred and thousand types of welfares of this kind, but these are not the real objects in life. Listen from me what is the ultimate truth or welfare.

16b-17a. If wealth be the ultimate reality, why is it spent for the sake of *Dharma*? Or why is it utilised for obtaining desired objects ?

---

* VP. (II. 14.12A) reads *Paramārthaṁ nu pṛcchasi* for NP.'s *paramārthena*.

** VP. (*ibid*) 12b reads *Sreyāṁsyaparamārthāni*. The VP. verse means the opposite of the NP. verse above : "O king what are you again enquiring about—What is the most excellent thing or the ultimate truth? All such kinds of welfare are not the ultimate truths.

17b-18a. If a son be the highest object (worth coveting) then, O king, he himself becomes the highest object of another (i.e. of his father) and his father thus being the son of another (viz. that of his father), becomes the greatest object of another person.

18b-19a. Hence, in the world of mobile and immobile beings, the son (who is the product of his father) cannot be the highest object. Or, otherwise, the products of all causes would be the highest covetable objects.

19b-20a. If the acquisition of a kingdom (and such other forms of prosperities) in this world be the highest object, the Paramārtha sometimes becomes accomplished only to disappear or to be destroyed later on (as the highest objective is never thus lost, acquisition of kingdom cannot be with *Paramārtha*—the highest object.)

21b-22a. If in your opinion, the performance of sacrifices accomplished with the *mantras* of the *Ṛg*, *Yajur* and *Sāma Vedas*, be the highest object in life, may my say in the matter be listened to.

22b-23a. O king! The thing that is the product of the earth as its cause, partakes of the nature of its cause (i.e. becomes of the same material as its cause) and becomes made of clay.

23b-24a. In the same manner, the act (of sacrifice), the performance of which is accomplished with perishable objects like sacrificial sticks, clarified butter, *Kuśa* grass and such other things, is bound to be temporary and perishable.

24b-25a. But the ultimate truth (or the highest objective in life) is considered as imperishable by all the (spiritually) wise. There is absolutely no doubt that (the life in heaven, etc.) which has been attained by using perishable objects is certainly transient and perishable.

25b-26a. If it be my (your*) view that a religious act performed without the desire of getting its fruit in recompense, is the real *paramārtha* (the highest object or the truth),

* In the context, this (*tava*) is the correct reading.

(it is wrong for), it is only the means of Liberation (from *Saṁsāra* but the *paramārtha* is never the means (but the end).

26b-27a. If meditation over the soul (distinguishing it as different from the body) be called the highest truth, it (that meditation) is for the establishment of the discrimination between the soul and the non-soul. But *paramārtha* (the highest truth) is above such distinctions and differences. (Hence, such a meditation cannot be *paramārtha*).

27b-28a. If the merging of *paramārtha** (rather *paramātman* the Supreme Soul) and the individual soul is desired (accepted) as the highest truth, it is illusory and false, for one (different category or) matter cannot be substantially and completely merged with another kind of matter. (If the individual soul and the Supreme soul are essentially different, they can never merge. But the fact of the matter is that they are really one. And the highest Truth is the recognition of their essential oneness and *not* their combination or (merging).

28b-29a. Hence, O king, there is no doubt that all these are (different kinds of) welfares (but they are not the ultimate objectives—*paramārtha*). Listen from me, in brief, what is the highest objective or the truth.

29b-31a. O king! It is the soul (that is the ultimate end or the truth). It is one, all-pervading, uniform, pure, attributeless, transcendental to Prakṛti, devoid of birth, growth, etc., omnipresent, embodiment of knowledge, never related or un-relatable with unrealities like name, form, etc. in the past, present or the future.

31b-32a. The specific knowledge that He (i.e. the soul) is essentially one, though abiding in one's own body as

---

* This is a misprint for *Paramātman*, for there is the repetition of *Paramārtha* in the same line in the NP. which is meaningless. The line in NP is as follows :

Paramārthātmanor yogaḥ paramārtha itiṣyate /

VP. reads:

Paramātmātmanor yogaḥ paramārtha itiṣyate /

I follow the reading in the VP.

well as that of others, is the true knowledge. He who knows it* has the real knowledge.

32b-33. The diffusive wind, though one and pervades the whole of the flute, is distinguished as *Ṣaḍja* and other notes of the musical scale, when it passes through the different perforations (of the flute), the supreme soul, though one, has manifold forms arising as a consequence, of different external acts.

34-35a. He assumes** different forms like gods, etc., but he is not of such behaviour. Listen here, O king, what happened formerly and what was sung by Ṛbhu who wanted to awake (i.e. impart) enlightenment in the Brāhmaṇa Nidāgha.

35b-36. Ṛbhu was the son of the Supreme god Brahmā. He was innately endowed with the knowledge of true spiritual wisdom. He had formerly a disciple (called) Nidāgha, the son of Pulastya.

37-38a. With extreme delight, he imparted to him the whole of spiritual wisdom. Although he acquired the knowledge of reality, he had no inclination towards non-duality. Ṛbhu surmised this about Nidāgha, O king.‡

38b. O warrior ! It is reported that there was a city called Nāgara (VP. Vīranagara) on the bank of the river Devikā !§

39-40a. It was founded by Pulastya and was prosperous and very beautiful. O excellent king, in the beautiful grove adjoining the city, dwelt an expert in Yoga named Nidāgha who formerly became his (Ṛbhu's) disciple.

---

* VP. reads : *Dvaitino'tathya-darśinaḥ* / He who sees the duality (in the Soul and in the non-soul or in the individual and Supreme soul) has no correct vision (of the true knowledge).

** This line in the NP. viz.

devādibhedam adhyāste nāstyevācaraṇo hi saḥ /

is defective. The original line in the VP. (*ibid*) v. 33 is :

devādibhede'padhvaste nāstyevāvaraṇe hi saḥ /

When the difference in the investing form such as that of god, etc., is lost, there is then no distinction.

‡ Here ends ch. 14 in the VP. II.

§ The river Deeg, a tributary of the Ravi. —De, p. 55.

40b-41a. After a lapse of one thousand divine years, Ṛbhu went to his city (Vīranagara) with the intention of seeing his disciple.

41b-42a. When the (daily) sacrifice to Viśvedevas was over and he (Nidâgha) was standing at the door (waiting for a guest), he (Ṛbhu) was seen by Nidāgha who conducted him to his house.

42b-43a. After washing his hands and feet and when he was (comfortably) seated, Nidāgha respectfully requested: O excellent Brâhmaṇa, please take food.

Ṛbhu said :

43b-44a. O prominent Brāhmaṇa ! If I am to partake of food in your house, please mention the articles of food (to be served). I never like to take bad food.

Nidāgha replied :

44b-45a. O excellent Brāhmaṇa, you may partake of whatever food you like such as *saktu* (barley), gruel, fried cakes of meal, available in my house.

Ṛbhu said :

45b-46a. These are bad food-stuffs. Please give me such sweet food such as rice boiled with sugar, wheat, flour cakes (*Saṁyāva*), milk-pudding, sugar-cane juice (and such sweet dishes).

Nidāgha said to his wife :

46b-47a. O mistress of the house ! Prepare a sweet dish from whatever is the most delicious and sweet edible in the house.

47b-48a. When thus instructed, his wife, in compliance of her husband's commands, prepared sweet and delicious dishes.

48b-49a. Nidâgha who stood before him till the great sage had partaken of the sweet dishes, bowed him respectfully and enquired :

49b-51a. Are you well satisfied with the food? Has your mind felt contentment from the food partaken by you?

What is the place of your residence? Where do you propose to go? Be pleased to tell us from which place you have come?

Ṛbhu replied :

51b-52a. O Brāhmaṇa ! When a hungry person takes food, he does feel satisfied. How can I feel satisfaction, when I had no hunger ? How is it that you ask me about it?

52b-53. When the earthen element in the body is parched by the fire (element), hunger is engendered. Thirst is produced among men, when the moisture of the body is absorbed by the gastric fire. Hunger and thirst are the functions of the body with which I am not concerned.

54a. As there is no possibility of hunger (affecting me), I am ever satisfied.

54b-55a. Pleasure and satisfaction of the mind are the faculties of *Citta* (mind), O Brāhmaṇa. These are in no way related to the *Puruṣa* (soul).

55b-56. As to your three queries : "Where is your residence? Whither you go, or whence have you come?" Please listen to me. *Puruṣa* is omnipresent and pervades everything like the sky.

57. Hence is the query 'Whence', 'Where', 'Whither' about the *puruṣa* meaningful and rational ? I am neither going, nor coming, nor is my dwelling place in any place.

58a. Nor you are you; nor others others, nor I I.

58b-59a. If you are curious what explanation I offer for the distinction I made between sweetened and unsweetened food, listen to what I say, O excellent-most Brāhmaṇa.

59b-60. What is sweet becomes unsweet when it causes satiation and repulsion (when overeaten) and what is not sweet tastes sweet when a person (out of hunger) imagines it to be so. Does such a food exist there, which at first, in the middle and in the end is equally tasty?

61. Just as a house built of earth becomes reinforced when plastered with clay, similarly this body which is made of earth becomes strengthened with the particles of the earth which constitute articles of food.

62. Barley, wheat, pulse, butter, oil, milk, curds, raw sugar, fruit and the like consist of atoms of earth.

63. Hence, having realised that it is the mind which decides what is sweet and non-sweet, one should be equanimous in outlook with the notion of identity and this serene mind with this effect of identity is the only means of liberation.

64.* O king, having heard his (Ṛbhu's) speech implying the essence of the ultimate truth, the highly fortunate Nidāgha fell at his feet and spoke the following words :

65. Be gracious unto me, O Brāhmaṇa, please let it be disclosed who you are that have come for my good, as by listening to your words, my delusion has been dispelled.

Ṛbhu replied :

66. I am Ṛbhu, your spiritual preceptor who have come here to impart to you spiritual wisdom, O Brāhmaṇa ! I shall communicate to you enlightenment about the highest truth.

67. Know that the whole universe is only one. It is of undivided, entire nature of the Supreme spirit designated as Vāsudeva.

The Brāhmaṇa said :

68. "So be it," said Nidāgha. Then being worshipped with fervent devotion and due prostration at his feet by Nidāgha, the venerable Lord (Ṛbhu) went his way‡

69† Again after the expiration of another (divine) millenium, the spiritual preceptor (Ṛbhu) came to the same city (Vīranagara) for imparting spiritual knowledge to Nidāgha, O Lord of the people.

70-71. Then he saw sage Nidāgha on the outskirts of the city. While a king escorted with a large army and attendants was entering the city, his disciple Nidāgha was standing far afar, avoiding the crowd. His throat was parched with hunger, and he was returning from the forest with sacred sacrificial sticks (fuel) and kuśa grass.

---

* As VP. states vv. 63 & 64 are spoken by the Brāhmaṇa.

‡ Here ends ch. 15 of the VP. II.

† This is verse no. 1 of ch. 16 of the VP. (*ibid*) and it is preceded by (*Brāhmaṇa uvāca*).

72. Seeing Nidāgha there Ṛbhu approached him (and finding that he was not recognized by Nidāgha) saluted him and asked him, "Why are you standing here in such a lonely place, O Brāhmaṇa?"

Nidāgha replied :

73. O Brāhmaṇa! There is such a huge crowd of people, as this king is desirous of entering this beautiful town. Hence I am standing here.

Ṛbhu asked :

74. O excellent Brāhmaṇa ! I believe you to be well informed. Please tell me which is the king here and who are the other persons ?

Nidāgha replied :

75. He who is riding the stately elephant that is in rut and huge like a mountain peak, is the king and the others are his attendants.

Ṛbhu said :

76. Both the king and the elephant are seen by me simultaneously. But you have seen them separately with their special features.*

77. Explain to me, therefore, what is the difference between them, as I wish to know which is the elephant here and who is the king, O highly fortunate one.

Nidāgha replied :

78. That which is under is the elephant and he who is above it (the elephant) is the king. O Brāhmaṇa, do you not know the relation between that which is borne and that which bears.

Ṛbhu requested :

79. O Brāhmaṇa ! Please enlighten me so that I can

---

* NP reads *nirviśeṣeṇa* for VP *na viśeṣeṇa* "without specific characteristics distinguishing them".

understand what is that which is called the *underneath* (the lower section) and what is it that is *above* (the upper section).

The Brāhmaṇa narrated :

80. As soon as he spoke this, Nidāgha jumped upon Ṛbhu and said : Please listen to my reply to what you are enquiring about.

81. I am above like the king and you are underneath like an elephant. This practical demonstration is given by me for your understanding, O Brāhmaṇa.

Ṛbhu asked :

82. O excellent Brāhmaṇa! If you are sitting as if you are a king and if I am the elephant, please let me know which of us is you and which is I.

The Brāhmaṇa said :

83. As soon as Nidāgha heard these words, he instantly bowed down to his feet and said, Venerable Sir, you are Ṛbhu, my spiritual preceptor.

84. The mind of no other person is so much consecrated by the concept of non-duality as that of my spiritual preceptor. I, therefore, presume that you are my preceptor who have come to me for imparting instruction.

Ṛbhu replied :

85. Due to the service rendered by you previously and out of deep love, your teacher called Ṛbhu has come to impart him spiritual instruction.

86. O highly intelligent one! The entire range of the philosophy of non-dualism which is the epitome of the highest truth—the essence of which is the non-duality of all—has been succinctly communicated to you.

The Brāhmaṇa said :

87. After saying this, the preceptor Ṛbhu imparted to him the lore, (the non-dualistic philosophy). Impressed by that advice, Nidāgha became devoted to non-dualistic philosophy.

88. He saw all creatures as being non-distinct from his *Ātman*. And thus (in due course) the Brāhmaṇa got the highest liberation into the form of the *Brahman*.

89. In the same way, O knower of the *dharma* you also be equal to your friends and enemies. Acquiring the knowledge of the soul, identify yourself with the soul who is all pervading.

90. Just as the sky, though one, appears diversified as white, blue, etc., so is the soul though one, looked upon as different by persons with erroneous visions.

91. That one which abides here in all things is the Immutable Viṣṇu. There is none other than He. He is I, you and all others. He is the embodiment of the Universe. Give up the error of differentiation.

Sanandana said :

92. The king when thus enlightened, became truthful of vision, eschewed the notion of distinct existence. While the Brāhmaṇa, who, due to the recollection of his previous births, had obtained the perfect knowledge, and in this very life, attained Emancipation (from *Saṁsāra* and had not to take another birth).

93. O prominent sage! The highest truth pertaining to the soul which has been elucidated to you is efficacious to grant Liberation to Brāhmaṇas, Kṣatriyas and Vaiśyas who ever listen to it.

94. I have explained to you as and what has been asked by you, O Brāhmaṇa! This is the pure knowledge about the *Brahman*. What else shall I explain to you ?

CHAPTER FIFTY

The arrangement of notes and syllables

Sūta said :

1. On hearing these words of Sanandana, sage Nārada spoke to his brother Sanandana, as though not fully satisfied.

Nārada said :

2. Venerable Sir! Everything of whatever has been asked by me, has been narrated by your worship. But despite hearing the stories of Hari repeatedly, my mind does not feel satisfied.

3. It is heard that Śuka, the son of Vyāsa, was a great knower of Dharma. He became disgusted (with the world) both internally and externally. He attained very great *Siddhi* (spiritual accomplishment).

4. O Brāhmaṇa, without the service rendered to the great ones, no man can gain perfect knowledge. How did, then, the infant son of Vyāsa attain perfect knowledge?

5. I am eagerly listening. Kindly recount to me the secret of his birth as well as his activities. O highly blessed one, you are the knower of the scripture on salvation.

Sanandana said :

6. O Brāhmaṇa, listen. I shall narrate to you the origin of Śuka succinctly. O sage, on hearing it, a man becomes the knower of reality of the Brahman.

7. It is not through the ageing years or greying hairs, riches or kinsmen that the sages performed their Dharma (and gained esteem). A person who is *Anūcāna* (so well-versed in the Vedas and their Aṅgas that he can both repeat them and teach them) is a great man unto us.

Nārada said :

8. O bestower of honour, O Brāhmaṇa, how does a person become an *Anūcāna*. Please narrate to me that achievement. I am eager to hear of it.

Sanandana said :

9. O Nārada, listen. I shall recount to you the characteristics of an *Anūcāna*. On knowing them, a man becomes well conversant with the Vedas along with their *Aṅgas* (ancillary subjects.).

10. *Śikṣā* (the science dealing with laws of euphony, phonetics), *Kalpa* (treatise on rituals and ceremonials), *Vyākaraṇa* (Grammar), *Nirukta* (Etymology and Semantics), *Jyotiṣa* (Astronomy) and *Chandas* (Prosody)—the learned men know that these are the six ancillaries of the Veda.

11. The *Ṛgveda*, the *Yajurveda*, the *Sāmaveda*, and the *Atharvaveda*—these are the four Vedas mentioned while ascertaining Dharma.

12. The excellent Brāhmaṇa who learns the Vedas alongwith the Aṅgas, from his preceptor becomes an *Anūcāna* and not otherwise, even (by studying independently) through crores of books.

Nārada said :

13. Mention the characteristics of ancillaries as well as those of the Vedas in details. Among us, O bestower of honour, you are the greatest scholar of these (Vedas) alongwith their *aṅgas*.

Sanandana said :

14. O Brāhmaṇa, this unparalleled burden of problems has been placed on me by you. I shall, however, succinctly narrate the quintessence of these definitely.

15. *Svara* (Note or Accent) is glorified as the most important item in the *Śikṣā* by sages and *Brāhmaṇas* well-versed in the Vedas. I shall describe that to you. Listen.

16. In the authentic treatise of the Science of *Svaras* (notes), it is enjoined that the *Svarāntaras* (the type of the interval of the *Svaras*—notes) viz. *Arcika*, *Gāthika* and *Sāmika*[1] are to be employed for specific purposes.

17. The *Svara* with one interval is used in *Ṛgveda mantras*, the Svara with two intervals is used in the *Gāthās* (religious Verses) and the *Svara* with three intervals is used in

the *Sāman* hymns. One should know that this much is the interval in regard to the notes in these).

18. Those who make use of the *aṅgas* of the *Ṛk*, *Sāman*, and *Yajus* in the *Yajñas* without the thorough knowledge of *Śikṣā* will be committing the blunder of *Visvara* (wrong intonation.).

19.* A mantra uttered with a defective accent or deficient in *Svara* and badly pronounced *Varṇa* (syllable) does not convey the proper meaning. It is like a *Vāgvajra* (thunderbolt in the form of words). It injures the house-holder (on whose behalf the *Yajña* is performed) just as the compound word *Indraśatru* (the *Bahuvrīhi* compound was used instead of Genitive *Tatpuruṣa*) when there was the wrong utterance of *Svara*.[2]

20. In the treatises (of *Śikṣā*) the bases of pronunciation is the chest, throat and head. These are called *Savanas* or *Sāmans* with half the intervals.

21. *Uras* (chest) has seven *Vivāras* (expansions) so also the *Kaṇṭha* (throat) and the *Śiras* (the head). You are incapable of clearly understanding. Such is the rule regarding the Exposition.

22. The first *Svara* (viz. *Ārcika*) is to be used in chanting the *Kaṭha* (*Kāṭhaka*) *Saṁhitā*, the *Saṁhitā* called *Taittira* (i.e. the *Taittirīya Saṁhitā* of the Black Yajurveda), the *Ṛgveda* and *Sāma-Veda Saṁhitās*.

23. The *Ṛgveda* continues (i.e. is chanted) in the second (i.e. *Gāthika*) and the third (viz. *Sāmika*) *Svaras* as well. From the material point of view, the *Svara* is (*classified as*) *Ucca* (high pitched) *Madhyama*, (the middle one) and *Saṅghāta* (combined or a vowel with its consonant).

-4. (Out of the seven *Svaras*) The Āhvarakas[3] use the third, first and *Kruṣṭa* (loud, sixth) *Svaras*, the chanters of the *Taittirīya Saṁhitā* use the four *Svaras* beginning from the second and ending with the fifth.

25. O great sage, the Sāma-singers use (in chanting) the first, second, third, fourth, the fifth *Mandra* and the sixth (*Kruṣṭa*).[4]

---

* Cf. *Pāṇinīya Śikṣā* v. 52. and *Nāradīya śikśā* I.1.5.

26. The second and first of these *svaras* are associated with **Tāṇḍya-Brāhmaṇa* and its school *Bhāllavi*. These are the *Svaras* of the chanters of *Śatapatha Brāhmaṇa* and the *Vājasaniya*—the *Saṁhitā* of the white *Yajurveda*.

27. These(*Svaras*)are especially laid down(for the above), although (all) *Svaras* are common to all the Vedas.

28.‡ I shall now explain to you the functions of the *Svaras* in the *Sāma-Veda*. The ancillary (viz. *Sāma-veda Śikṣā*) though brief is profound in meaning.

29. The characteristics of *Tāna* (the protracted tone or a key-tone in music), *Rāga*† (a musical mode or order of sounds), *Svaras*, *Grāmas* (Gamuts or scale in music) and *Mūrchanās* (or *mūrchā* a melody**) which are sacred, sanctifying and meritorious, have been already[a] expounded to you.

30a. The education of the twice-born castes is characterised by the (study of) the *Ṛgveda*, *Yajurveda* and *Sāmaveda*.

30b-31a. *Svaras* are seven, *grāmas* are three and *Mūrchanās* are twentyone. *Tānas* are fortynine—all these constitute the *svara-maṇḍala*.

31b-32a. Ṣaḍja (*Sā*), Ṛṣabha (*Re*), Gandhāra (*Ga*), Madhyama (*Ma*), Pañcama (*Pa*), Dhaivata (*Dha*) and Niṣāda (*Ni*) is the seventh *Svara*.[c]

---

* *Nāṇḍi-bhāllavinau*. Out of this *Nāṇḍi* is an obvious misprint for *Tāṇḍi*—as in the Devanāgari—script *ta* and *na* are often mistaken for each other, *Bhāllavi* is the name of the school of that (*Tāṇḍa*) *Brāhmaṇa*, *vide* MW p. 754.

‡ After completing the general discussion about the use of *svaras* (*Svara-sañcāra*) in Vedas, the NP. deals with the *Svara-Sañcāra* in the *Sāma-veda*.

§ According to Bharata (*Nāṭya-Śāstra*) *Bhairava*, *Kauśika*, *Hindola*, *Dīpaka*, *Śrī* and *Megha* are the primary *Rāgas*. Other writers give different names. Each *Rāga* has "female consort" or a *Rāgiṇī* and their union gives rise to several musical modes.

** This is a gradual rise (*crescendo*) and fall in the volume of *Svaras*.
Kramāt svarāṇām saptānām ārohaścāvarohaṇaṁ sa mūrchetyucyate.
Quoted in Apte—*Sk. Dict.*

a. This is a misplaced quotation, for the description of this is not yet given. Many verses from this chapter are quotations from a common source (*Nāradīya śikṣā*) of the NP. and Nārada's *Saṅgīta Makaranda*.

b. It is hazardous for a translator to combine such lines as 30b & 31a as constituting one verse in the absence of MS evidence but such a combination gives the complete sense syntactically.

c. Cf. Bharata—NS (Nāṭya-Śāstra) 28.31.

32b. Grāmas (scales is Music) are said to be three, viz. *Ṣaḍja*, *Madhyama* and *Gāndhāra*.

33. *Ṣaḍja* is born of the earth (*Bhū-loka*), *Madhyama* from *Bhuvar-loka* (the ether, the atmosphere just above the earth) and Gandhāra from the heaven (or the firmament) —These are the three abodes of *Grāmas*.

34a. It is remembered (by ancients) that *Grāmas* and *Rāgas* are due to the particular (combinations of) *Svaras*.

34b-35a. In the case of Sāma-singers, twenty *Tānas* (protracted tones) are in the *Madhyama-grāma*, fourteen are in the *Ṣaḍja-grāma* and fifteen are in the *Gandhāra* (Grāma) (Thus 20+14+15=49 are distributed in three *Grāmas*).

35b-36a. The seven *Mūrcchanās* 'Modes' or regulated rise and fall) of the Devas are *Nadī*, *Viśālā*, *Sumukhī*, *Citrā*, *Citravatī*, *Mukhā* and *Balā*.

36b-37a. The seven *Mūrcchanās* of the *Pitṛs* are *Āpyāyinī*, *Viśvabhṛtā*, *Candrā*, *Hemā*, *Kapardinī*, *Maitrī* and *Bārhatī*.

37b-39. The seven *Mūrchanās* pertaining to sages (*Ṛṣis*) should be known as follows: *Uttara-Mandrā* in the *Svara* called *Ṣaḍja*, *Abhirūhatā* in *Ṛṣabha*, *Aśvakrāntā* in *Gandhāra* is remembered as the third *Mūrcchanā*, *Sauvira* verily in *Madhyama* (the *Svara* Ma,), *Hṛṣikā* in the *Svara* called *Pañcama*, the *Mūrchanā* called *Uttarā* should be known in *Dhaivata* and *Rajanī* in the *Svara* *Niṣāda*.

40. The Gandharvas depend upon the seven Mūrcchanās of Devas. Undoubtedly the Yakṣas depend upon the seven Mūrcchanās of Pitṛs.

41-43a. The seven Mūrcchanās of sages are remembered as *Laukika* (worldly, popular). The Ṣaḍja note pleases Devas, the *Ṛṣabha* note pleases sages, the Gandhāra note pleases Pitṛs, the Madhyama note pleases Gandharvas, the Pañcama note pleases Devas, sages, and *Pitṛs*, the *Niṣāda* note pleases Yakṣas and the *Dhaivata* pleases the whole multitude of living.

43b. The good qualities of music are ten viz., the *Guṇas* (good qualities) such as : *Rakta*, *Pūrṇa*, *Alaṁkṛta*, *Prasanna*, *Vyakta*, *Vikruṣṭa*, *Ślakṣṇa*, *Sama*, *Śukumāra* and *Madhura*.

[*Rakta* (lovely, charming) : the harmonious mingling of the notes of the flute and the lute and (the voice of the singer) is called *Rakta*.

Pūrṇa (complete) : So called as it complements (*Svara* and *Śruti* (a division of the octavo) as well as the 'filling in' of the metre and the syllable.

Alaṅkṛta (Bedecked): Properly emanating from the regions of the heart, the head (i.e. the upper part of the palate) and the throat. i. e. lowering down or raising up the *Svara* from the throat region.

Prasanna (Easily intelligible): That which is free from inhibitions, choking and hesitation (confident, uninterrupted).

The Vyakta (clear) : That which correctly renders the following grammatical subtleties, viz., the *Pada* (the word), the meaning, the base, the alteration, the augment, the *Kṛt* and *Taddhita* suffixes, the compound, the root, the *Nipāta* (the exceptional and the irregular forms and particles), the preposition, the vowels, the gender, the gloss, the *Vārttika* (an explanatory rule)*, the meanings of the cases and the numbers.

The Vikruṣṭa (Distinct) : That which is uttered loudly with the clear pronunciation of words and syllables is called *Vikruṣṭa*.

The Ślakṣṇa (soft, bland): Accomplishment and presentation (of song) with rapid and quick accentuations (like *ucca*, *nīca*, *pluta* and their combination), dalliance, beating of time, etc.

The *Sama* (the equanimous): The simultaneous applying together of Svaras in the proper place (in the rise and fall of *Svaras*.)

The Sukumāra (the gentle, tender) that which is accompanied by soft words, letters, notes and the cooling[5] sound is called *Sukumāra*.

The Madhura (sweet) that which is rich in the qualities of pleasing and jingling words and syllables occurring naturally is called *Madhura*.]

---

* It is a supplementary rule which explains the meaning of that which is said, of that which is left unsaid and of that which has been imperfectly said e.g. Kātyāyana's *Vārttika* on Pāṇini.

A (good) song is endowed with all these ten qualities.

In this context the following verses are cited:

44-45. There are fourteen defects[5] in music (song), viz., *Śaṅkita* (hesitant) *Bhīṣaṇa* (terrible), *Bhita* (frightened), *Udghuṣṭa* (pronounced loudly), *Anunāsika* (nasally produced) *Kākasvara* (shrill tone as that of a crow), *Mūrdhagata* (undue cerebralization) (or *Ūrdhvagata*—that has gone too high up), *Sthānavivarjita,** Non-observance of the places of articulation), *Visvara* (Discordant), *Virasa* (unpleasant or disagreeable), *Viśliṣṭa,* (disjoined), *Viṣamāhata* (odd and non-sensical), *Vyākula* (Agitated or bewildered) and *Tālahīna* (out of tune).

46. The preceptors wish for the quality of *Sama* ; the scholars wish for the quality of *Padaccheda* (i. e. *Vyāpta* mentioned above); women wish for the *Madhura* (sweet) quality and the other people wish for *Vikruṣṭa* (a loud song) with clear pronunciation of words or letters.

47-48. The *Ṣaḍja* note has the lustre of the petals of the lotus; the *Ṛṣabha* note, the reddish yellow colour like that of the parrot; *Gāndhāra* note is gold-coloured; the *Madhyama* note is white like the *Kunda* flower, the *Pañcama* note is of black colour; they know that *Dhaivata* is yellow in colour; and the *Niṣāda* has all the colours — these are the colours of the *Svaras.*

49-50. The *Pañcama,* the *Madhyama* and the *Ṣaḍja*—these notes are remembered as *Brāhmaṇas.* Both the *Ṛṣabha* and the *Dhaivata* notes are *Kṣatriyas.* The notes *Gāndhāra* and *Niṣāda* are partially *Vaiśyas* and partially *Śūdras* undoubtedly because they are fallen.

51. That scale of notes should be known as *Ṣāḍja* in which the *Svara Ṛṣabha* is devoid of *Mūrchanā,* Pañcama is combined with *Dhaivata* and falls in the *Madhyama Rāga* along with *Niṣāda.*

52. If the *Pañcama* note ceases, the *Gāndhāra* becomes the internal note, and the *Ṛṣabha* is accompanied by *Niṣāda,* know that *Pañcama* also like this (i.e. *Ṣāḍja*).

53. It is called *Madhyama Grāma* when *Dhaivata* is weak, *Gāndhāra* rules (i.e. becomes dominant) and the *Niṣāda* has *Gatāgata* (comes and goes).

54. It is called *Ṣaḍja Grāma* when *Niṣāda* is *Īṣatspṛṣṭa* (i.e. slightly touched or intoned); the *Gāndhāra* is predominant and the *Dhaivata* is tremulous.

55. It should be known as the *Kaiśika* (*Rāga*) based on *Pañcama* (*Pa*) and with proper support, where a low sweet tone (*Kākali*) is perceived accompanied by *Āntara-Svara* (internal note).

56. After associating *Kaiśika* through all the *Svaras* all round, if (it is commenced from) there is *Nyāsa* (fixation) in the *Madhyama* note, it is called *Kaiśika Madhyama*.

57. When *Kākali* is seen and there is the importance (predominance) of *Pañcama*, Kāśyapa calls that Kaiśika-rāga as originating from *Madhyamagrāma*.

58. The word *Gandharva* represents all the constituents or parts of musicology: Intelligent persons know that the letter *Ga* stands for vocal music, the letter *Dha* means playing on the musical instrument, and the letter *va* symbolizes the musical instruments.

59-60. [These verses give the correspondence between the notes of the flute and those of *Sāma* (singing) :] What is the first note of the *Sāma*-singers is the *Madhyama* of the flute, what is the second (of *Sāma*) is remembered as *Gāndhāra* [of the flute] and the third is *Ṛṣabha*, the fourth is called *Ṣaḍja* while the fifth will be *Dhaivata* and the sixth should be known as *Niṣāda* while the seventh is *Pañcama*.

61. The peacock gives out the *Ṣaḍja* note and the bulls bellow the *Ṛṣabha* note; goats and sheep bleat the *Gāndhāra* note; and the *Krauñca* bird (heron or curlew) chirps the *Madhyama* note.

62. During the (spring) season when flowers bloom, the cuckoo coos the *Pañcama* note. The horse neighs the *Dhaivata* note and the elephant trumpets the *Niṣāda* note.

63. The *Ṣaḍja* note originates from the throat; the *Ṛṣabha* note is remembered as one produced from the head (or the upper palate), the *Gāndhāra* note is a nasal one and the *Madhyama* note originates from the cardiac region.

64. The *Pañcama* note originates from the cardiac region, the head and the throat. One should know that *Dhaivata*

originates from the forehead and the *Niṣāda* is born from all the joints.

65. *Ṣaḍja* note is so called because it originates from six organs, viz. — the nose, the throat, the cardiac region, the palate, the tongue and the teeth.*

66. The wind originating from the umbilical region and striking against the throat and the head sounds like the bellowing of a bull. Hence it is called *Ṛṣabha*.

67. The wind originating from the umbilical region and striking against the throat and the head blows (as if) wafting sweet fragrance. For that reason the note is called *Gāndhāra*.

68. The wind originating from the umbilical region and striking against the thigh[6] and the heart comes back to the umbilical region. Stationed in the middle (of all the notes) the note is called *Madhyama*.

69. The wind originating from the umbilical region and striking against cardiac region, cavity of the heart, throat and the head produces the *Pañcama* note, since it originates from five places or organs.

70. Excepting *Dhaivata* and *Niṣāda*, all the other five notes are known as originating from five organs.

71. As the notes are found abiding in five places, it is maintained (as produced ?) in all places. The note sung by the Fire-god is *Ṣaḍja* and that sung by Brahmā is *Ṛṣabha*.

72. *Gāndhāra* was sung by Soma (the moon) and the *Madhyama* note by *Viṣṇu*. Understand that the *Pañcama* note was sung by you alone (i.e. Nārada).

73-75. The notes *Dhaivata* and *Niṣāda* were sung by Tumburu. It is said by the learned men that the deity of *Ṣaḍja*, the first note is Brahmā. The deity of *Ṛṣabha* is *Hutāśana* (the fire-god) since its lustre is warm and brilliant. When this note of *Gāndhāra* is presented, cows are satisfied. Hence it is so called. Undoubtedly on hearing this note, the cows stand still. The deity of the *Pañcama* note is Soma. It is remembered as *Brahmarāṭ* (Royal Brahman).

76-78. On attaining *Grāma* (?) its increase and decrease is like that of the moon. Since this note over-reaches all the notes

* Cf. *Nārada Śikṣā*. 1-57

previously originating, this note is called *Dhaivata*. Since all the other notes sit down (i.e. are submerged) the (last) note is called *Niṣāda*. It excels and dominates all the other notes, as its deity is Āditya (the Sun).

79. In the sphere of music there are two types of *Viṇā* (lute), viz. the *Dāravi* (wooden) and the *Gātraviṇā*. The *Gātraviṇā* is used for singing *Sāmans*. Listen to its characteristics. That in which the singers of *Sāmans* sing is called *Gātraviṇā*.

80-82. It is accompanied by the manifestation of the note; it is 'coloured' by the thumb and the other fingers. The hands should be placed controlled above the knees and kept together. (The student) should imitate the teacher and his mind should not be elsewhere. At the outset, the *Praṇava* is uttered and the (seven) *Vyāhṛtis* (utterances *Bhūḥ*, *Bhuvaḥ*, etc.).

83. The *Sāvitrī mantra* is then chanted. Then only the regular song is begun. The sphere of Svaras must be fixed up after spreading out all the fingers.

84. One shall not touch the thumb with the (other) fingers nor the fingers with the thumb. The fingers shall not be kept separated from one another leaving much space in the middle. Nor should he touch it at its root.

85-86. He shall touch it always with the tip of the thumb at the middle joint. In order to differentiate the *Mātrās*, two *Mātrās* and the extended (span of time), the knower of the division shall point out two *Mātrās* by means of the fingers of the left hand, where three lines are seen, one shall specify the *Siddhi* (*sandhi* ?) therein.

87. (Where the lines are seen) shall be known as the *Parvan* (joint) and the remaining portion is called *Antara*. In the *Sāmans* one shall make the interval as much as that between the joints. In the Ṛks (Mantras of RV.) one shall make the interval as much as that between two gingelly seeds. (?)

88. The sensible man shall place the *Svaras* in the middle *Parvans* (joints) closely knit with one another. He shall not shake any of the limbs even slightly.

89-91. (Defective) The learned singer shall dust his hand with the earth-particles below (?) He shall remain steady, calm, and fearless and utter the syllables. He shall withdraw all his sense organs like the tortoise its limbs. His eyes shall be fixed and the mind concentrated. Just as the lightning is seen in the middle of the clouds, like a thread in a necklace of jewels, similarly should the padas be distinct just as the shearers of the hair pass the scissors over it silently. As he utters the letters (of the Mantra) he shall keep the nose held with the hand like (holding) the cow's ear.

92. Fixing the eye to the tip of the hands, he should ponder over the meaning of the holy scripture. He should duly express the sentence by means of the hand and mouth.

93. He shall conclude the letters in the same manner as he utters it. (No different system be introduced in the same mantra). And the beating of time should be synchronous with the song, nor should he tremble (?). [There should be no omissions or additions nor should he tremble]

94-96a. He must sing the Sāmans with the quality of *Sama* (smoothly) like the flying movement of the *Śyena* (falcon) in the air. Just as the path of the fish moving about in the water is not observed, just as the movement of the birds in the sky is not visible, so also the *Śruti* (a division in the octave) of the note (is not noticeable). Just as the clarified butter present in the curds, or the fire latent in the firewood is obtainable only with effort so also the *Śruti* is latent in the *Svara*.

96b-97a. He shall make the transit from one *Svara* to another, the joining of notes, not very intense (strained), or manifest. He shall make it even, gradual, its continuity being uninterrupted like the subtle and imperceptible change from the sunshine to shadow.

97b-98a. This verse gives six defects or mistakes in the 'Protraction' (*Karṣaṇa*)[7] of the tones and advises to avoid them. They are as follows: (4) The 'non-arrival' (*anāgata*) stage is before the beginning of the second note, the completion of the first *svara* is the *atikrānta* stage. The first note should not be 'pulled or protracted' in both the stages. He should not interrupt the first *mātrā* for this. It will be *Viṣamāhata*. He should not pass on to the next *Svara*, with tremulous note (as if trembling.) During the period of *karsaṇa*, the note should not be extended beyond three *mātrās*. He should give up the *asthitānta*. He should stabilise in the next *Svara* for a period of three *mātrās* only (not of two *mātrās*).

98b-99a. If a note swerves from its place of origin or goes far beyond its place of origin, the singers of *Sāman* call it *Visvara* (discordant) and the players on the *Viṇā* (lute) call it *Virakta* (unsymphonic).

99b-100a. For the purpose of practice, one shall adopt *Druta Vṛtti* (quick movement), for the performance one shall adopt the middle movement and for the purpose of instructing the disciples one shall adopt the slow movement.

100b-101a. In this way, the learned Brāhmaṇa who has mastered the treatise of *Sāma-gāna* (singing of Sāmans) according to the scientific method of study, should impart injunctions in the *Śikṣā* texts to pupils with the movement of his hands.

101b-103a. The place (of origin) of the *kruṣṭa* (Seventh or Fifth Svara) is in the head, of the first *Svara* (*Ṣaḍja*) in the forehead, of the second (*Ṛṣabha*) Svara in between the eye-brows, of the third (*Gāndhāra*) in both the ears, of the fourth (*Madhyama*) in the throat, and of the *Mandra* (*Pañcama*) in the tongue. And the place of *Niṣāda* called *atisvara* is located at the heart (chest cavity).

103-105. *Kruṣṭa* Svara (seventh and fifth) should be placed upon (and thus as if 'fixed') on the tip of the thumb. The place of the first *svara* is the thumb. The *Gāndhāra* is located in the index finger, the *Ṛṣabha* in the middle finger, the *Ṣaḍja* in the ring-finger and the *Dhaivata* in the small finger. The *Niṣāda* should be indicated below at the beginning of the small finger. As it is not completely distinct from the *Mandra*, it is called *aparva* (अपर्व); as it is not separately (audible and) grasped it is called *asaṁjña* (undesignated). And due to its continuity by nature ? (or non-relation with gender, number etc.) it is called *Avyaya* (indeclinable).

106-109a. When *Mandra* becomes lower it is called (*Parisvāra Niṣāda*). Deities live by (depend for their life on) the *Kruṣṭa Svara* and human beings by the first (*Ṣaḍja*), the animal world by the second (*Ṛṣabha*), Gandharvas and Apsaras by the third, the oviparous beings (like birds) and *Pitṛs* (manes) live by the fourth (*Madhyama*). Piśācas (goblins), Asuras and Rākṣasas subsist upon the *Mandra* while the (lower) mobile and immobile world lives upon the low *Atisvara* (*Niṣāda*). In this way all the created beings are sustained in life by the *Svaras* of the *Sāman*.

109b-110a. A person who is not an expert in the *Śrutis* (the divisions of the Octave) known as *Diptā*, *Āyatā*, *Karuṇā*, *Mṛdu* and *Madhyamā* (terms explained below) does not* deserve to be called a preceptor.

110b-111a. The *Śruti* of the five *Svaras* viz. *Mandra* (*Pañcama*) second, fourth, *atisvara* (sixth) and the third (*Gāndhāra*) is called *Diptā* while that of the seventh *Svara* is *karuṇā*.

111b-112a. The Śrutis known as *Mṛdu*, *Madhyamā* and *Āyatā* are in the second Svara. I shall now separately deal with their distinctive characteristics.

112b. When based on the third *svara*, it is the *Āyatā Śruti* of the second *svara*, while when it is based on the fourth *svara* (*viparyaya*), it is the *Mṛdu Śruti* of that *Svara*.

113a. When *Śruti* depends (entirely) on its own *Svara* and does not shift or change to another *Svara* it is the *Madhyamā Śruti*. It is after duly considering (and examining) these that the *Sāma* notes are to be applied (sung).

113b-115a. The *Śruti* which is established in the *Kruṣṭa* note ends up finally and settles on the *Dvitiya*. *Ṛṣabha* note is called *Diptā* but if it does so with *Prathama* (*Ṣaḍja*), it is regarded as *Mṛdu* (soft *Śruti*). It is also called *Mṛdu śruti*, if it finally settles on the *Caturtha* (*Madhyama*) *svara*, but if it does so with *mandra svara* it is called *Diptā*. The *Śruti* which may be settled or established on any *svara* at the time of completion of *Sāma*-singing, becomes *Diptā*.

115b-116a. After the completion of the note (*Svara*), *Śrutis* like *Āyatā* should not be used. Even after completing the note but before the end of the musical concert *Śruti* should not be used in between two *Svaras*. (A *Śruti* is to be used in *pluta*-prolongated *Svara*) but not when a short or a long syllable is to be sung. Nor where the note called *Ghuṭa* is sung.

* This single *na* in the text is to be taken with both the clauses.

116b-117a. Where there are two *gatis* (viz. '*ā*', '*i*' *Bhāva* and '*ā*','*u*' *Bhāva* of palatal vowel *i*,) and the *sandhi* of the final syllable of a word with sibilants *ś*,*ṣ* and *s*—in these five 'places', the note is called *ghuṭi*. (Here no *Śruti* is allowed).

117b-118a. In *Śrutis* where the note (*Svara*) or the interval between *svaras* is not completed and the notes, viz. short, long and *ghuṭa*—are all devoid of *Śrutis*, *Śruti* is not to be sung. In this position the *svaras* by themselves act as *Śrutis*.

118b-119a. (In places other than *Sāman*) know that the *Śruti* called *Dīptā* is in the *Udātta* (highly or acutely accented *Svara*.) Learned persons know that the *Dīptā Śruti* is in the *Svarita* (mixed tone lying between high and low) tone. *Mṛdu* (soft) *Śruti* should be recognised in the *Anudātta* (the grave) accent or which is not raised or accented as *Udātta*) *Svara*. In the Gandharva method of singing (where *Śrutis* are absent) *Svaras* are to be used like *Śrutis*. The grandeur and sublimity of *Śrutis* lies in tones (*svara*).

119b-120a. The kinds of *svaras* are five—*udātta*, *anudātta*, *svarita*, *pracaya* (*svarita* followed by *svarita*) and *Nighāta* (*svarita* preceding *pracaya* is affected. This affected *svarita* is *Nighāta*).

120b-121a. Henceforth, I shall explain to you the three svaras connected with *Ṛks* (*ārcika Svara*). They are *udātta* (the acute accent, the highly accented *svara*), *anudātta* (the grave accent), and the third *svara*, *svarita* (mixed tone or accent lying between *udātta* and *anudātta*.)

121b-122a. If the *svara* which is called *udātta* is beyond *svarita*, that is called *Pracaya* by experts (in that science). There is no other variety of *svara* elsewhere.

122b-123a. The accent or *Svara* called *svarita* is remembered as of two kinds : (1) *varṇa-svara* and (2) *atīta-svara*. In the same manner, a *varṇa* (a syllable) which requires a period one *mātrā* (*mātṛka*) to pronounce becomes long (of more than one *mātrā*) after *uccarita* (articulation).

123b-124a. That *svara* should be known of seven types by having a look at the desinence. What it is, where it is and how it is should be understood by its (actual) use in the word.

124b-125a. The seven notes should be applied (for hearing) to the right ear. This science (of Phonetics-*Śikṣā*) has been composed by *ācāryas* (learned preceptors) with a view to serve the interests of their sons and pupils.

125b. There is no tone (*svara*) louder than the *Udātta* and no tone lower than the low (*Anudātta*).

126-127a.* What is the position of *svāra* — the particular form of the *svāra* which came to be designated as Svara. The common (*Sādhāraṇa*) *Svara* between *Udātta* and *Anudātta* is known by the teachers of the *Sikṣā Śāstra* under the designation *svāra*.

127b-128a. In the *Udātta* are found *Niṣāda* and *Gāndhāra* and in the *Anudātta, the svaras Ṛṣabha* and *Dhaivata* and *Ṣaḍja*, Madhyama and Pañcama have *svarita* as their source.

128b-129a. That after which comes the sound 'k' and 'kh' as well as that which employs the sibilant sound called *Jihvā-mūliya* ≍ (viz. ≍*k*, ≍*kh*,) should be regarded as *Mātrā*. By its very nature it is *kalā* as well. (This should be applicable to the sounds *upadhmānīya* i.e. ≍ *p*, ≍ *ph*.)

129b-131a. There are seven *Svāras*: *Jātya Kṣaipra*, *Abhinihita*, *Tairavyañjana*, *Tiro-virāma*, *Praśliṣṭa*, and the seventh *Apāda-vṛtta*. Now I shall describe the separate, distinct characteristics of these. After defining them I shall give specific illustrations of these.

131b-132a. The syllable (or letter-*akṣara*) which is accompanied with -*y*- or-*v*- sound and becomes *Svarita* and has no *Udātta svara* in front of it (i.e. following it) is called the *Jātya svāra*.

132b-133a. When an *Udātta* (acutely accented) *i* or *u* has a Sandhi with an *anudātta* (grave accented) *a*- in the initial position of word and thus become *svarita* (a mixed tone between high and low tones) *y* or *v*, it should be regarded as the characteristic *Kṣaipra Śvāra*.

* In Prātiśākhyas, the term Svāra is used for *Svarita* (the circumflex accent). They record the following seven varieties of Svāra : *Kṣaipra Nitya, Pratihata, Abhinihata, Praśliṣṭa, Pada-vṛtta*, and *Tairo-vyañjana* (All with slight difference in terminology are explained in the NP. below). Cf. *Taittirīya Prātiśākhya* XX. 1-7.

133b-134a. The *Anudātta* that comes after an *Udātta* *e* or *o* and gets disappeared (lost in previous *-e* or *-o*) is called *abhinihita svāra.*[8]

134b-135a. If in *Chandas* (Vedic literature), there be a *Svarita* vowel preceded by an *Udātta* that *bahu-svāra* (*svarita* that is optionally found everywhere) is called *Tairavyañjana*[9] (or rather *Tairo*-Vyañjana according to Prātiśākhyas).

135b-136a. When a *Svarita* vowel comes after *Avagraha* (separation of a compound word into its component elements as shown in the Vedic *Pada pāṭha*) and if the *Avagaha* be acute-accented (Udātta), it is called *Tiro-virāma* (or *Tairo-virāma*)[10] of the *Prātiśākhyas*).

136b-137a. Where an acute-accented (*Udātta*) *i* is seen combined with a grave-accented (Anudātta) *i*, regard it as *Praśliṣṭa Svara*.

137b-138a. The Śāstric treatise gives the following characteristic of *Padānta-vṛtta*: If the vowel is acutely accented, and its combination with the previous *Pada* (word) becomes separate (For example: *ka iṁ veda*/ RV. VIII.33.7).

138b-140a. The illustration of *Jātya*[11] *svāra* is : *sajātyena* (RV.VIII.20.21). The *Kṣaipra Svāra* is in *Śrutyagre* (prob. a misprint). In *te manvata* (RV.IV. 1.16) is the *Abhinihita svāra*. The *Tairavyañjana svāra* is in *ūtaye* (i.e. *u*+*ūtaye*). In *Viṣkaṣita* (Viṣkabhita ?) there is *Tirovirāma*. The *praśliṣṭa svāra* is in *hi i govarṇa* (?). The *Pādavṛtta* vowel is in *ka iṁ veda*, (RV. VIII.33.7).

These are the seven *svāras*.

140b-141a. With the exception of *Jātya svaras*, the syllable which follows upon an acute accented syllable is the characteristic of *Svarita* (the circumflex accent between the acute-*udātta* and the grave-*anudātta* accents).

141b-142a. If the above-mentioned four *svāras* are *udātta* or if they precede an *anudātta*, from the scientific point of view it creates vibrations (the wording of the text *kaṁsaṁpuṁsphuti* is confusing). The example of it is *juhvògniḥ*.

142b-143a. When the previous *pada* (word) ends in *-i* and is followed by *-u* the intelligent man should clearly understand it to be a short vibration (the larynx vibrating for a short while).

143b-144a. If a *pada* with two *ukāras* (*u* vowels) follows a *pada* (a word) ending in *-i*, one should know that there is a long vibration in *-i*. Here the example is *Śāgdhūsū* (some misprint and hence obscurity in the illustration).

144b-145a. It should be known that in the diphthongs (*e, ai, o and au*) there are three long vibrants (*kampas*). For example *manyā yathā*(?), *na Indrābhyām*. The rest are declared as short ones.

145b-146a. If there be any *Anudātta* affix after many *Udāttas*, it should be regarded as *Śiva-Kampa* (in the second and third *Udātta*) if the *pratyaya* is *Udātta*.

146b-147a. Where two (three, four) syllables are *Udātta* and they are followed by an *Anudātta* or *Udātta*, learned people know that the previous and the syllables preceding it are *Udātta*.

147b-148a. There is no reduplication of *r* or *h*. Nor are the second and fourth letters of different classes of consonants (i.e. *kh -gh, th-dh-* etc) geminated.

148b-149a. The fourth letter be combined with the third and the second with the first and the first, middle and end letters of a class (such as *k, g,* and *ṅ*) may be geminated.

149b-150a. If in a conjunct consonant, the non-final letter (e.g. *k* , *kh, g, gh,*) is followed by the nasal, then *yama*[12] of its own *varṇas* intervenes and becomes the same as the previous syllable.

150b-151a. Seeing the nasals (last letter of each of the five classes) conjoined with the sibilants *ś, ṣ,* and *s-* or with semi-vowels (*y, v, r,* and *l*), *yama* (sounds) recede like travellers on seeing high-waymen.

151b-152a. (When in Vedic recitation) the third and the fourth letter (of the five classes of consonants) is a conjunct, the *pada* is to begin from the fourth. If the second letter or the third letter is conjoined with *-h*, the latter word is to begin with *-h*.

152b-153a. The nasal (utterance) the (*upadhmānīya* (≍*p* or ≍*ph*) the phonetic element substituted for a *visarga* followed by *p* and *ph* and the *jihvāmūlīya* (⌣ *k* or ⌣ *kh*) : the phonetic element into which a *visarga* is changed when followed by -k or -kh) seldom form a part of a word; it is not repeated (twice) in the word. If the previous syllable or letter be a conjunct with *r* or *h*, the following letter is doubled.

153b-154a. Where the conjunct has a circumflex accent (or the accent intervenes between *udātta* and *anudātta* or vice-versa), the *svarita* should be placed at the beginning of the next *aṅga* (*parāṅga* is the consonant which begins the next *pada*).

154b-155a. When after being separated from the conjunct the consonant that appears freed (and separate) from the next consecutive word, it should be regarded as *pūrvāṅga*. And the consonant which begins the next word is *parāṅga*.

155b-156a. The latter part (letter) of the conjunct (should be accented as it) is the main factor (a leader) of the conjunct (as that is a 'resting-place' of the *svara*). The previous member of the conjunct consonant is *svarita* (but should be pronounced without an accent.)

156b-157a. *Anusvāra*, end of the *pada* (word) affix, gemination (due to the repetition of the same letter at the beginning of the next word), the consonant *r*, and *svara-bhakti* (vowel-separation, insertion of a consonant (glide) sound in a conjunct with *r* or *l* e.g. *Tryambakaṁ* (*yajāmahe*) is pronounced as *Triyambakam*—all these are included under *pūrvāṅga*.

157b-158a. At the beginning of a word, or in the middle, in (pronouncing) conjunct consonants and *avagraha*, *ya* should be known as a geminated-*ya* (*yy* -). It is remembered that in other places it is simply a *ya*.

158b-159a. With the exception of the unseparated conjuncts of *r* and *h* in the initial and final positions in words and -*ry*-, other letters or syllables are not duplicated.

159b-c. A conjunct consonant is (metrically) *guru* (of two mātrās). A consonant conjoined with a nasal or a *visarga* are obviously *guru*. The rest are atomic (*laghu*- of one mātrā).

For example *hri*, *goḥ*. In this, the first is a conjunct consonant while the second is accompanied by a *Visarga*. The *gurutva* (heaviness) of a vowel followed by a conjunct consonant or a *visarga* is obvious.

160. The *Udātta* (acute accent) remains as acute (i.e. the acutely accented vowel remains as it is.). What is *Svarita* (circumflex accent) becomes *anudātta* (grave accent) in the body of the word. The anudātta vowel remains unchanged. The *pracaya** type of accent becomes anudātta (accentless).

161. The (following) words (occurring in different *mantras*) such as *Agniḥ, Sutaḥ, Mitram* (a friend), *Idam, Vayam, Ayā, Vahā, Priyam, Dūtam, Ghṛtam, Citta m* and *Abhi*—are *anudātta*.

162. The (recitation of) Śruti starts with an unaccented syllable (*anudātta* vowel) in words like *Akka* (*Arka*?), *Suta, Yajña, Kalaśa, Śata* and *Pavitra*.

163. In words like *Hāri, Varuṇa, Vareṇya, Dhārā* and *Puruṣa*, the vowel with *r* is *svarita* (circumflex). In the word *Nara*, the vowel with *r* is always *Svarita* except in the case of *Viśvānara* which- *na-* is *svarita*.

164. In the two *Mantras* pertaining to Varuṇa: viz. *ud uttamaṁ tvaṁ Varuṇa* (RV. I. 24. 15) the *Va* of Varuṇa is *svarita* and not *ru* (despite the *r*-element).

In the *Mantras* (1) *uru-dhārām araṁkṛtam* (RV. VIII. 1. 10) and (2) *uru dharesva dohate* (misprint for *uru-dhareva dohate* RV. VIII. 93. 3), in the words *dhārā dhā* is svarita and not the syllable with *r* (An exception to the rule in v. 163.) In these examples the syllable whether of one *mātrā* (short) or two *mātrās* (long), the first half *mātrā* is udātta and the rest is anudātta.[13]

Where a *dvi-svara* (dissyllabic, containing two vowels) is used, the short vowel should be pronounced as long.

165. In the *Kampa, ut-svarita* and *Abhigita* (terms explained already) the short-vowel should be protracted. (As to the duration of a *mātrā*, according to one authority) a *mātrā*

---

* *Pracaya* is a specific feature or quality (*Dharma*) of the *Anudātta* accent, when a vowel, accented grave, is preceded by a *Svarita* (Circumflex accent and is followed by another grave-accented vowel. The grave accented vowels which are not followed by an acute or circumflex (accented) vowels are neither distinctly circumflex nor distinctly grave. They are uttered slightly like acute. e.g. Imam *me* Gaṅge Yamune Sarasva*ti* (*me, ti* herein are uttered thus).

extends upto the twinkling of the eye while the others hold that the duration is that of a flash of lightning.

166. While it is opined by some others that duration of a *mātrā* is the time required to pronounce the vowel *ṛ* (the reading *ṛksvara* is a bit confusing as literally it means 'a vowel in a *ṚK-mantra*').

167. A compound may be dissolved but the members of the compound should retain their original form in the Saṁhitā. For that initial syllable[14] (?) that *Svara* is known as the end of the member of the compound.

168a*. (Everywhere the words *putra, mitra, sakhi, ahi, Śatakratu, Āditya, Viprajātaveda. Satpati, Gopati, Vṛtrahā, samudra* deserve to be dissolved (when members of a compound).

In cases of *svarayupuvo* (?) *Devayavaḥ* (*Devayuvaḥ*), *Aritam* (*Aratim*?), *Devatātape* (? *Devatātaye*), *Cikitiḥ, dha Caiva*(?), the learned persons do not dissolve the compound.

168b-169a**. According to my view four *vivṛtis* (rather *vivṛtti*—separation of two vowels which were euphonically combined into one) should be known according to the order of the letters. Listen to their names from me.

169b-170. When the first *pada* has a short vowel which is followed by a long vowel (like a calf followed by the mother cow), the *Vivṛtti* is called *Vatsānusṛtā*, but the *vivṛtti* in which the previous *pada* ends in a long vowel followed by a short vowel in the latter *pada*, is called *Vatsānusāriṇi*. When vowels in

---

* The text gives the above portion in brackets. Hence this matter is bracketted here. It is included under v. no. 168, although the printed text gives it no number.

** 168b ff : These verses describe the pause (technically called *Virāma* in Prātiśākhya works) which is to be taken (at the end of the word or at the end of the first member of the compound (which is shown split up in the *Padapāṭha*) or inside a word or at the end of the word or at the end of a vowel when it is followed by another vowel. The *Taittirīya Prātiśākhya* (XXII. 13) gives four kinds of such pauses : (1) *Ṛg-virāma*—pause at the end of a foot or a verse and the duration of the pause in three *mātrās*. (2) *Pada-virāma* pause of two *mātrās* between two words and e.g. *iṣe tvā ūrje tvā*. (3) A pause of one *mātrā* between two words the preceding one ending in a vowel, and the following one beginning with a vowel but the vowels are not euphonically combined e.g. *sa idhānaḥ*. (4) A pause of half a *mātrā* between two vowels inside a word e.g. *dra-ugam*.

both the *padas* are short, it is called *Pākavatī*, while vowels in both the *Padas* are long, that *vivṛtti* is called *pipilikā*.

The difference in time or duration between these *vivṛttis* is of one *mātrā*.*

171. According to some other teachers, the duration between these two is half, while according to others it is just atomic (*aṇumātrikam*).

172. When *ṁ* (*makāra*) is followed by affixes beginning with the consonant *r*, *ś*, *ṣ*, and *s*, the *m* is changed into *anusvāra*. If followed by *-y*, *-v-* (*p-v-* in the print of text is wrong) and *l-*, it becomes *para-savarṇa*, while before *sparśa varṇa* contact consonants viz. *ka-varga*, *ca-varga*, *ta-varga* etc., it is changed to the last (nasalised) consonant.

173. When the preceding word ends in *-n* and is followed by a vowel beginning the next word, the vowel preceding *-n* in the previous word is coloured (affected and changed into nasalized pronunciation) and hence it is called 'coloured' *rakta* (e. g. *mahān asi mahā̃ ३ asi*).

174. If the preceding word ends in *-n* and is followed by *y-*, *v-* and *h-* (in the following word,) half the *mātrā* of the vowel preceding *-n* is slightly (atom-like) coloured (i.e. nasalised).

175. If the previous word ends in a conjunct of *n* and is followed by another word it is changed into four forms. Sometimes it becomes *r* (*repha*), sometimes it colours (slightly nasalises) the syllable, sometimes it is dropped and sometimes it becomes an *anusvāra*.

176. The colour (*raṅga*) is emanated from the heart and resembles the sound produced by a bell-metal. It is soft and of two *mātrās* in duration, as illustrated in the pronunciation of *dadhvān*. (In other words, *raṅga* is the nasalisation of a vowel)

---

* Some *Śikṣā* treatises say that the duration between these different *Vivṛttis* should be one *mātrā*, one half *mātrā*, three-fourth *mātrā* and one fourth *mātrā* respectively. But the duration between two words of a compound-word split up in the *Pada-pāṭha* should be one *mātrā*.

177. Just as a woman from Saurāṣṭra pronounces (the nasalized vowel in) Arñ, the same way *raṅga* of nasalized vowel be produced.[15] This is my opinion, O Nārada.

178. The four classes of words [viz. *Nāma* (substantives), *Ākhyāta* (verbs), *Upasarga* (prepositions) and *Nipāta* (particles)] end in the ten syllables viz. *g*, *ḍ*, *d*, *b*, *ṅ*, *ṇ*, *n*, *m*, *ṣ*, and *s*. These are declared as word endings.

179. The vowel (accent) may be acute, grave or circumflex, consonants have to follow the *svara* (they have no independent accentual status.)

180. Authoritative preceptors have declared the prominence of only three accents of *svaras*. Consonants are like beads while vowels are the thread (which weaves and holds them together).

181. Just as a powerful monarch snatches away (and annexes) the kingdom of a weak king, similarly the (accented) vowel, being powerful, takes possession of the weak consonants.

182. *O-bhāva* (i.e. *O,-u-bhāva* in the NP is a misprint), *vivṛtti*, *ś*, *ṣ*, *s*, r, (*repha*) and the special pronunciation of the *Visarga* before *k-*, *kh-* and *p-*, *ph-* (specially known as *jihvā-mūlīya* and *upadhmānīya*. These eight are the transformations of sibilants.

183. The interval between two vowels placed near each other in Saṁhitā[16] should be regarded as *visarga* or is changed to a palatal.

184. If in a penultimate diphthong (like *e*, *o*, *ai* and *au*) *y* or *v* is dropped, there is the consonantal vīvṛtti, विवृत्ति and the *pratisaṁhitā* of vowels.

185. Where the pause is on a sibilant (and under exceptional cases) there is -v- in the *Sandhi* (Saṁbhāvaḥ ?), that *vivṛtti* or hiatus should be called vowel-hiatus (*svara-vivṛtti*).

186. If the vowel *o* of the previous *pada* is to be linked up (*prasandhāna*[17]), then the next pada begins with *ṛ* (e. g. *vāyo ṛ-*). And this 'link up' should be regarded as vowel-ending. What is different from this is the 'link-up' (*Prasandhāna*) of sibilants.

187-188. If the first or the last letter of a class (e. g. *t-*, *n-* of the dental class) are at the end of a *pada* and is followed by sibilants, *ś*, *ṣ* and s, it is changed to the second position. When they are combined with sibilants as the second member of the conjunct, the first member of the conjunct consonant, even if it be the first letter(like *t*, *k*, *p*) of a class is to be shown (pronounced) as the second letter (such as *th*, *kh*, *ph*) but should not be recognised or represented as actually the second letter e. g. *Mat-sya*, *K-ṣura*, *Ap-saras* (their pronunciation will have some aspiratory tinge like *th*, *kh*, or *ph* but for all purposes they are *t*, *k*, and *p*).

189. In ordinary metrics, to understand the metre, etc. of a verse (*śloka*) there are three causes: (1) *Chandomāna*, (2) *Vṛtta* (the metre) and (3) the end of the *pāda* (*Pādānta*). But Vedic *mantras* (Ṛcs) have been composed in their own respective metres (like *Gāyatrī*, *Jagatī*, *Triṣṭubh*); the metrical feet of ordinary metres are governed by the number of letters and their being of one or two *mātrās*.

190. The *r*-element present in the vowel *ṛ* or in *Svarabhakti* should be indicated as a separate syllable (for calculation of *mātrās* or *Akṣaras*. But in *Svarabhakti* the letter (without the *repha*, -*r*- element) should be calculated alongwith the affix.

191. In the letter *ṛ*, the consonantal *r* is distinctly apprehended and its nature as a vowel (vowel form) is clearly perceived. If the *r* is not conjoined with a sibilant, know it to be *laghu* (short, of one mātrā only).

192. If the vowel *ṛ*, is combined with a sibilant and is compressed[18] in pronunciation, the syllable should be regarded as a *guru* (heavy i.e. of two mātrās). Here the illustration is (the form) *Tṛcam*. Here *ṛ* is short.

193. There is no doubt that in the following five instances, the (vowel) *ṛ* is short (the illustrations are: *Ṛṣabha*, *Gṛhita*, *Bṛhaspati*, *Pṛthivī* and *Nir-ṛti*).

194. In case of words with conjuncts beginning with *ś*, *ṣ*, *s*, *h*, and *r* in the initial position, there is internal *svarabhakti* (in the same word without insertion of *i*, or *u* as a glide), when it is being conjoined with another word.

195. *Svarabhakti* is of two types—one characterised by *ṛ*, the vowel and the other by *r*, the consonant. These are known as *Svarodā* and *Vyañjanodā* (respectively) by contemplative grammarians.

196. The learned ones know that the *svarabhakti* in the case of sibilants (*ś*, *ṣ*, and *s*) is (vowel-born) *svarodayā* and open

(*vivṛta*), while that with *h* is *vyañjanodayā* (consonant-born) and closed (*saṁvṛta*).

197. A person resorting to *svarabhakti* should avoid three defects viz. *Svarabhakti* with *i*, *u* and a faulty (pronunciation).

198. The following syllables are not regarded as *Laghu* (short, of the duration of one *Mātrā*) : 1. That which is followed by a conjunct consonant; (2) or which is followed by *ch*; (3) or is combined with a *Visarga*; (4) or which possesses two mātrās (= is long) or (5) is at the end of a foot (word) or (6) be combined with an *Anusvāra* or (7) ends in *ghuṭ* (the first five case affixes).

199. The metre (viz. *Āryā*) whose first and third foot consists of twelve *mātrās*, the second contains eighteen and the last consists of fifteen *mātrās* only. This characteristic has been spoken of (the *Āryā*). That (metre) which is different from this is *Vipulā*.

200. If a syllable is short (*laghu*) and if it is not followed by a conjunct consonant, it is still *laghu* (of one *mātrā* only). If a short (vowelled) syllable is followed by a conjunct consonant or if it itself is long, it should be regarded as *guru* (heavy or long of two *mātrās*).

201-202a. Where *Vivṛtti* is found in front of the vowel, it should be regarded as a *guru* vowel, there is no (prevalence of) *Kṣaipra* (or *kṣipra-sandhi*)[19].

202b-203. There are eight kinds or types of *svaras* of a pada: *Antodātta*, *Ādyudātta*, *Udātta*, *Anudātta*, *Nica-Svarita*, *Madhyodātta*, *Svarita*, *Dvirudātta*. These are the eight designations of those *padas*.

204. (Now follow the illustrations of the above Padas);

(1) *Agnir vṛtrāṇe*—(RV. VI. 16. 34). Here *Agniḥ* is *Antodātta*.

(2) *Somaḥ pavate* (RV. IX. 96. 5 also VS. 7. 21). Here Soma is *Ādyudātta*.

(3) *Pra vo yahvam* (RV. I. 36. 1). In this *pra* is udātta while *vaḥ* is Anudātta.

(4) (Balaṁ nyubjam) Vīryam (Sāma Veda I. 95). Here *Vīryam* is *Nica-svarita*.

(5) *Vidhema haviṣā* (AV. I. 31. 1). Here *Haviṣā* is *Madhyodātta.*

(6) Bhūr, Bhuvaḥ, *Svar-*(*Ait. Br.* 5. 31.4. etc.). Here *svaḥ* is *svarita.*

(7) *Vanaspatiḥ* (AV. XII. 3. 15). Here both *va* and *spa* are Udātta. This is an instance of *Dvirudātta.*

(8) Tāmyat (?). This is Madhyodātta. Nipātas are Anudātta. In prepositions, Svarita follows the initial vowel. There are two Anudāttas in Ākhyātas (conjugations ?). The *dhārya* letter after the *svarita* e.g. *nihotā satsi.* Here *Satsi* is a *dhārya* letter, as it follows the *svarita* in o *tā* which are the *pracaya** *sthānas.* There is the previous Svarita, becomes toned down to a grave accent.

205. A wise reciter should tone down the *svara* to a grave accent wherever *pracaya* is seen. Where there is merely a soft circumflex accent, there is no need to tone it down.

206. The duty of a preceptor is of five types—*Mukha* (mouth, *Nyāsa, Karaṇa, Pratijñā* and *Uccāraṇa.* It is said here that utterance with a vow (*sapratijña uccāraṇa*) or positive vocal utterance is creditable.

Those (castes) to whom the science of *Śikṣā* is not available (or who are not eligible for the same), the affirmative assertion (backed by a tradition of *gurus*) is to be resorted to. For *Karaṇa* (phonetic treatise) is of the form of the affirmative teachings (of traditional *gurus*).

207. O Nārada! You, Tumburu, Vasiṣṭha, Viśvāvasu and other Gandharvas are not able to comprehend the entire lore of Sāma-singing due to the niceties and subtleties of the Svara-śāstra.

208. You should always take care of your gastric fire (i.e. digestive capacity). Take in wholesome (?) food which contributes to it). When food is digested, one should wake up at dawn and meditate on the Brahman.

209. It is desired (prescribed) that after autumnal equinox, to vernal equinox, one should get up early at dawn for the study (and recitation of the Vedas).

---

* *Vide* note on *Pracaya.* p. 623.

210. Getting up early in the morning, one should silently chew the tooth-brush twig of (any of) the following trees: Mango, Palāśa (Butea frondosa), Bilva (Aegle Marmelos), Apāmārga (Achyranthes Aspera), Śirīṣa (Acacia Sirissa).

211. The following trees too are holy: Khadira, Kadamba, Karavīra, and Karañja. All thorny and milk-exuding trees are holy and conducive to fame.

212. By using these for the purification of the mouth, sweetness in tone and subtlety of tone in generated. He is able to utter every syllable clearly and distinctly as recognised by the ancient teacher Audavati (a misprint in the text for Audavraji—the ancient sage and scholar of Vedic grammar, who revised the original text of the *Ṛk-tantra-Prātiśākhya* of the Sāma Veda).

213. The student should always take in *Triphalā* (the three Myrobalans) along with salt. This increases digestive power and intellect, heightens the clarity of tones and distinctness in the utterance of letters (syllables).

214. After performing the necessary morning duties (like brushing the teeth, taking bath, which is necessary for the care of the gastric fire, he should purify himself by taking in honey (*Dhūma* in the printed text is probably a misprint for *Madhu*) and ghee, and then start the recitation.

215. It is the general rule in all branches of the Veda that one should start recitation in a low tone. After reciting seven Mantras in a low tone, one should then utter in the desirable (or prescribed) tone.

216. At dawn, one should not strain his voice as would obstruct the normal breathing. For such obstructions in breathing cause wrong intonation (*Vaisvarya*). Not merely that, it certainly spoils the sweetness of vowels and consonants.

217. Just as there is no absolvement to a person eating forbidden food coming from an evil source, as in the case of saving the life of a person (bitten by a poisonous serpent) from the poison of the venomous serpent in the form of the sin of wrong pronunciation in this case), similarly a person who imbibes the fruitless (lit. burnt) teaching (of Vedas etc.) with wrong pronunciation, accentuation etc., of syllables from a

bad (incompetent) teacher (*Ku-tirtha*) cannot escape the sin of distorted pronunciation, etc. learnt from that sinful teacher (like serpent-poison spread within the body).

218. The Vedas, coming from (i.e. taught by) a good teacher well-rehearsed and well-established in good intonation—when orally recited shine beautifully.

219. A person with frightful appearance, protruding lips, pronouncing all syllables through the nose or with a choked voice or tongue-tied (due to difficulty in the movements of the tongue) is not eligible to utter Mantras.

220. A person exercising control over his mind and one who has concentrated it and whose teeth and lips are shapely, becomes pure after performing his bath, avoids singing (or sing-song manner) should pronounce the syllables of the Mantras (clearly).

221. The following five types of persons cannot grasp a new lore:—A fierce person, a stubborn or arrogant one, an idle person, a sick person and one with unsteady (scattered) mind.

222. One should acquire learning slowly, should hoard wealth slowly (i.e. saving even small amounts); one should climb a mountain slowly (by degrees); one should travel on foot slowly (not more than a Yojana at a stretch).

223. An ant walking slowly and steadily covers even a thousand Yojanas. But Garuḍa, if he does not move at all, cannot cover the distance of even a single foot.

224. A (person whose) speech is affected by sins (or defects) does not deserve to utter the text of the Vedas just as a clever (intelligent) beautiful maiden does not deserve to hold a conversation with a deaf person.

225. He who recites the Vedas in a low mumbling voice as though he is afraid, remains always in doubt about thousands of its forms.

226. Studies carried on with the help of books only and not under (i. e. near) a preceptor, do not shine in the assembly of learned men like a woman impregnated (out of wedlock) by a paramour (from point of social status).

227. Having observed how even a heap of collyrium disappears (by its daily use) and how ant-hills become accumulated in a high, huge heaps (by slow but continuous additions of particles of earth by ants), one must utilise every day by engaging one's self in religious gifts, studies and religious acts.

228. That a very big ant-hill is built up by insects (ants) with very small particles of earth is not due to the (immense) physical power (of the ants). Sheer hard work is its cause.

229. If a lore is studied (repeatedly) for thousands of times and taught to pupils for hundreds of times, it (automatically) comes to the tip of the tongue like water flowing from a higher level to a lower level.

230. Just as horses of noble breed go to sleep for the half part of half the night (i.e. for three hours only), similarly sleep does not (nay should not) occupy the eyes of students for a long period.

231. A student should not be late for studies by spending a long time for his meals. Nor should he be enmeshed in temptations about women. A person desirous of mastering a lore should traverse (fig. study) long and fast like eagles and swans flying over seas.

232. A person who is afraid of (i.e. does not mix with) crowds of men and shuns the formation of company of friends as if it were a hell, and protects himself against association with women as if they were ogresses—only such a person attains mastery over learning.

233. Dishonest persons do not get wealth (or learning); nor do cowards or persons whose heads are swollen with pride; nor can people afraid of public criticism or who put off their work (out of procrastination) can earn money or learn a lore.

234. Just as a person digging with a spade or pick-axe (reaches the water-level in the bowels of the earth and) gets water, so, a student, bent on rendering service to the teacher, obtains learning possessed by the teacher.

235. Learning can be obtained either by rendering service to the teacher or by paying sumptuous amount of money (as the fee) or by exchange of one type of lore for another (by

imparting one's expertise in a particular field for learning the special technique of another field). Otherwise learning cannot be mastered.

236. Even if one masters a lore by dint of his intellectual gifts, even without serving a teacher, it does not yield fruit to him like a barren young woman.

237. O Nārada! In this way, I have briefly indicated to you the treatise on *Śikṣā* by just pointing out to its direction. By understanding this first accessory to the Veda, one becomes eligible to be absorbed in the *Brahman*.

CHAPTER FIFTY

1. It is not understood why Niṣāda (*Atisvāra*) is omitted. Cf. *Tait. Prātiśākhya* XXIII. 12.

2. *Ārcika* (pertaining to Ṛks), *Gāthika* (pertaining to Gāthās) and *Sāmika* (pertaining to Sāma-singing).

3. This refers to the wrong pronunciation of *Indra-Śatru* in *svāhendra-śatrur vardhasva* (TS. II. 5.2.1), by vṛtra's father.

4. N. of a school, Taittirīya Prātiśākhya —MW, p. 163.

5. *Kuharaṇa* also means indistinct pronunciation in low tone. Cf. *Naradīya Ṣikṣā* I 3.11-12.

6. Probably a misprint for *urasi* (on the chest)

7. Cf. *Nāradīya śikṣā* I.7.19.

8. *Abhinihita* is a *sandhi* or euphonic combination in which the vowel *a*, as a first or second member, is absorbed into the other member. e.g. *rathebhyaḥ+agne=rathebhyo'gne* or *dāśuṣe+agne=dāśuṣe'gne*. Here *a-* of *agni* is absorbed in the preceding *-o* and *-e*. —*A Dict. of Sk. grammar*, p. 34.
Here the term is used with reference to the absorbed vowel. *-a*.

9. Here the definition in the NP does not explain why *Vyañjanā* is associated with this vowel. The fact is that this is a kind of *svarita* or circumflex-accented vowel which follows the acute-accented vowel, with the intervention of a consonant between the acute-accented vowel and the circumflex vowel which (vowel) was originally grave, e.g. *īḍe, havye*. Here the vowel—*e* is a *Tairo-vyañjana-svarita*. cf. *Svaro vyañjana-yutas tairo-vyanjanaḥ—Vājasaneyi Prātiśākhya* I. 117.

10. Tairo-virāma is a kind of *svarita*, a vowel with a circumflex accent which follows an acute-accented vowel characterised by an *Avagraha*, i.e. coming at the end of the first member of compound e.g. *gopatāviti go'patau*. Here the vowel *a* of *pa* which follows the (') *avagraha* is called *Tairo-virāma-svarita.—A Dict. of Sk. gram*, p. 178.

11. *Jātya* is a variety of *svarita* or circumflex accent, e.g. *svaḥ nyak*. Cf. *Ṛk Prātiśākhya* IV.4.

12. *yama* is a twin letter available in pronunciation before a nasal letter and similar to it, when the nasal consonant is preceded by any one of the four consonants of the five classes. The *S. K.* on Pāṇ. VIII.1.1 explains it as a transitional sound intervening between a non-nasal and the following nasal as a counterpart of the non-nasal. e.g. Aggniḥ, ghghnanti, cakhkhnatuḥ,

13. Pan. I. 2.32 S.K. explains *āditaḥ*=the first half of the *mātrā* should be understood as Udātta and the latter half as Anudātta.

14. *Yetīkṣarādikaraṇam* is a bit obscure.

15. Cf. Pāṇinīya Śikṣā, V. No. 26

16. Cf. *Saṁhitāyāṁ yat svarayor antaraṁ tad vivṛtti*-saṁjñaṁ syāt—Uvvaṭa on Śaunaka's *Ṛk-prātiśākhya II*.1 This interval is one *mātrā* according to

the *Taittirīya Prātiṣākhya* XXII. 13 but is of only one half *Mātrā* according to *Ṛk. Tantra*-35.

17. *Prasandhāna*—this term means repeating a word in the krama-pāṭha and joining it with the following word e.g. RV.I. 1 to be recited thus: *iḷe purohitam, purohitam yajñasya.* But in this verse, "joining or linking up" is implied.

18. When in pronunciation of vowels and consonants a fault is caused by the compression or contraction of the place of utterance, it is called *Pīḍana* cf. *vyañjanānām atiprayatnenoccāraṇam pīḍanam.*

Ṛk-Prātiśākhya XIV.5

19. According to *Prātiśākhyas*, a euphonic combination of the vowel *i, u, ṛ, ḷ,* with a following dissimilar vowel. The name *kṣipra* (quick, short) is given to this *Sandhi* as the vowel, short or long which is turned into a consonant, becomes very short.

CHAPTER FIFTYONE

The Treatise on Rituals (Kalpa) [1]

1. O leading sage, henceforth I shall recount to you the treatise on rituals, on understanding which a man becomes efficient in holy rites.

2. There are five *Kalpas*, viz., (1) *Nakṣatra Kalpa* (i.e. *Kalpa* pertaining to the constellations), (2) *Veda Kalpa*, (3) *Saṁhitā Kalpa*, (4) the fourth *Kalpa* is that of Āṅgiras and the (5) fifth one is *Śānti Kalpa*.

3. The narration precisely and in detail of the presiding deities of the constellations is indicated in the *Nakṣatra Kalpa*. The same thing should be known here also.

4. O leading sage, the injunction regarding the Ṛks etc. for the purpose of the achievement of the *Puruṣārthas*, viz. virtue, wealth, love and liberation, has been mentioned in detail in the *Veda Kalpa*.

5. The sages (seers of the *mantras*), the metres and the deities of the *Sūkta- mantras* have been specified in the *Saṁhitā Kalpa*, by the sages who have seen the Reality.

6. In the *Āṅgirasa Kalpa* the *ṣaṭkarmans*[2] have been specified by the self-born deity (Brahmā) by way of enjoining black magic and spells.

7. O excellent sage, the modes of subduing the evil portents of divine, earthly and atmospheric origin are separately mentioned in the *Śānti Kalpa*.

8. These characteristics are succinctly mentioned in the context of defining *Kalpa*. The special characteristics of these are separate in other *Śākhās* or *Branches**.

9. Since all these are of utility in the *Gṛhya Kalpa* (i.e. the *Kalpa* pertaining to the duties of a householder), I shall recount them to you, O excellent Brāhmaṇa. Listen attentively.

---

* *Śaṅkha* in the NP. is probably a misprint for *Śākhā* as 'the conch-shell' is inexplicable in this context.

10. The *Oṁkāra* (the syllable Om) and the word *Atha*—these two words formerly pierced through the throat of god Brahmā and came out (were uttered). Hence these two are auspicious ones.

11. He who has completed the rites mentioned and wishes to do the subsequent ones, shall utter the word *Atha*. It is sought for the purpose of endless benefits.

12. Kuśa grass which is spread (in a particular way) is extolled for the rite of sprinkling water (in the prescribed way) round the fire. In the desired holy rite, the number (of kuśa grass-blades) should not be less or more, lest it should be fruitless.

13. The rite of *Parisamūhana* is enjoined as a preventive action against worms, germs, insects, etc. that crawl and move about on the surface of the Earth.

14. O Brāhmaṇa, the three (parallel) lines that are enjoined, should be made equal. It has been laid down that they should not be made smaller or larger.

15. O Nārada, the fat of the demons Madhu and Kaiṭabha has spread over the Earth. So, it should be smeared over the cowdung.

16. It has been mentioned that the cowdung of certain types of cows should not be used in the holy rite of *Yajña*—viz. the barren cow, the wicked or defiled cow, the cow with afflicted limbs and the cow whose calf is dead.

17. O Brāhmaṇa, the rite of *Proddharaṇa* (i.e. sprinkling of water upwards) is intended for the purpose of eradicating such terrible beings as moths, etc. that always roam about in the atmosphere.

18. One should scrape or scratch the ground with the *Sruvā* (sacrificial ladle or spoon) or the Kuśa grass. It has been enjoined by Brahmā for the achievement of *Asthikaṇṭaka** (bones and thorns?)

---

* NP. reads : *asthi-Kaṇṭaka-siddhyartham*. Hence this strange translation. I suggest °*Śuddhyartham* for °*siddhyartham*, as the *emendation*. The emendation will mean : "For the purification of bones, thorns etc." In the Devanāgari script, such slips (*si-* for *śu-*) are possible.

19. The waters represent all the groups of Devas and Manes (*Pitṛs*). O Brāhmaṇa, hence the sprinkling (the altar) with water has been laid down by sages who are experts in injunctions.

20. It is mentioned that the sacrificial fire should be brought by women endowed with *Saubhāgya* (good fortune) (i.e. woman having her husband and sons alive) in an auspicious earthen pot. The fire should be placed in the earthen pot sprinkled with water.

21. On observing the wastage (i.e. disappearance by being stolen away by demons) of the nectar, the fire latent in the sacrificial twigs has been placed on the altar by Brahmā and all other deities (for its protection).

22. O Nārada, Dānavas and others are standing (in readiness to create trouble) to the south of the *Yajña*. For the sake of protection from them, one should establish god Brahmā in that direction.

23. The vessels (intended for consecration and cooking) and all other vessels must be placed in the north; the *Yajamāna* (the householder on whose behalf the *Yajña* is being performed) sits to the West. O Nārada, all the Brāhmaṇas sit to the east.

24. The maxim (or situation) is that whether in playing dice, business transactions or performance of sacrifice, if the performer be unconcerned or has an indifferent attitude, that activity goes to ruin.

25. The Brahmā and the Ācārya must be appointed from one's own Śākhā (branch of Veda) in the course of the rite of *Yajña*. There is no restriction in the case of the Ṛtviks. They should be invited and honoured according to availability.

26. The two *Pavitras* (the Kuśa grass twisted into a ring like loop with a tail) must be three *Aṅgulas* in length. The *Prokṣiṇi* (the vessel containing the holy water) must be four *Aṅgulas* in length. The *Ājyasthāli* (the vessel holding ghee) shall be three *Aṅgulas* in length and the *Carusthāli* (the vessel in which the *Caru* i.e. food offering is kept) must be six *Aṅgulas* in length.

27. The *Upayamana* (the Kuśa grass used to place down fire) shall be two *Aṅgulas* long; the *Sammārjana* (that used for

sweeping) shall be one *Aṅgula* in length. The *Sruvā* (sacrificial ladle) is enjoined to be six *Aṅgulas* long and *Srucā* (sacrificial spoon) is said to be three and a half *Aṅgulas* long.

28. The sacrificial twigs are a span in length, the *Pūrṇapātra* (vessel filled with water) is six *Aṅgulas* in length. The *Praṇītā* vessel eight *Aṅgulas* in length is placed to the north of the *Prokṣiṇī* vessel.

29. Whatever sacred water is there in the world as rivers and oceans, is present in the *Praṇītā* vessel. Hence it should be filled with water.

30. O Brāhmaṇa, the *Vedikā* (sacrificial altar) is said to be naked and devoid of garments (otherwise). Hence a wise man shall clothe it by means of the Darbha grass.

31. The *Pavitra* consists of three cutters, viz. the thunderbolt of Indra; the discus of Viṣṇu and the trident of Vāmadeva in the form of the *Darbhas*.

32. The sprinkling must be done from the water taken from the *Praṇītā* vessel. Thereby the holy rite becomes the yielder of great merit. It is glorified as very sacred.

33. The *Ājyasthālī* (the vessel holding ghee) shall be made with a *Pala* weight of metal. The earthen pot shaped by the potter's wheel is remembered to be demoniac (in character).

34-38. The vessel *Sthālī*, etc. shaped by means of the hand is said to be divine. The auspiciousness or inauspiciousness of all rites depends on *Sruvā*. In order to make it sanctified it is warmed in the fire. When it is held at the tip there is no widowhood (?), if it is held in the middle deficiency of progeny (or death of children is the result); if it is held at the root, the *Hotṛ* dies. Hence it should be held after considering all this. The following six deities resort to the *Sruvā* at the interval of each *aṅgula* **viz**:- Agni, the sun, the moon. Viriñci (i.e. Brahmā), the wind god and Yama. Agni may lead to the destruction of objects of pleasure; the sun may cause sickness; the moon does not yield any special result; Viriñci is the bestower of all desired objects; the wind god is said to be the bestower of prosperity and Yama is considered to be the bestower of death. (Hence the *sruva* should be held at the fourth or fifth *aṅgula*).

39. The *Sammārjana* and the *Upayamana* are to be made

with Kuśa blades of grass. The former one may be of all* the branches (?) and the other of five branches (or blades of *darbha* grass).

40. In order to make *Sruvā* and *Sruk*, it should be known that the trees, *Śrīparṇi*, *Śami*, *Khadira*. *Vikaṅkaṭa* and *Palāśa* are used.

41. A *Śruvā*, a *Hasta* (24 *Aṅgulas* or about 18 inches) long is commendable, and a *Sruk* of thirteen Aṅgulas is also commendable. This is laid down for the Brāhmaṇas. In the case of others, it should be one *Aṅgula* shorter.

42. O Nārada, it is laid down (in *Smṛtis*) that the sprinkling of the vessels is for the destruction of defects (defilement) due to the glances of Śūdras, the fallen ones and donkeys and other beings (at them).

43. If the vessel is not filled up completely, there may be a loop hole in the *Yajña*. O Brāhmaṇa, if it is filled (completely), the *Yajña* becomes full.

44. Learned persons have known that eight *muṣṭis* (a particular measure of capacity-'handfuls') make a *Kuñci* (*kiñcit* is a misprint), four *kuñcis* make a *Puṣkala*[2] (a particular measure of capacity), four *Puṣkalas* make one *Pūrṇa-pātra* (a full vessel).

45. When the time for *Homa* has arrived, one shall not offer any seat anywhere. If it is offered, the fire may be excited and may give a terrible curse.

46. Two *Āghāras* (sprinklings or oblations of ghee) are said to be the two nostrils, the two oblations of *Ājya*, two eyes, this is said to be the face of Prajāpati and the waist is (formed out) of the *Vyāhṛtis*.

47. The head, the hands and the feet—these five are said to be of the *homa* called Pañca-vāruṇa (?). O Brāhmaṇa, what is *Sviṣṭakṛta* (offering belonging to Agni) and the *Pūrṇāhuti* (the final offering) are the two ears.

48-51. The physical body of the Fire god should be

‡ Probably the reading should have been *sapta* instead *sarva* as seven *darbha* blades are used for the former.

conceived as follows*:—It has two faces, one heart, four ears, two noses, two heads, six eyes, tawny colour, and seven tongues. It has three hands on the left side and four hands on the right side. In the four right hands it holds the *Sruk*, *Sruvā*, *Akṣamālā* (rosary) and *Śakti* (javelin). It has three girdles, three feet, a vessel for ghee and two chowries. Agni is seated on a ram. It has four horns and the lustre of the morning sun. It has a sacred thread and it is bedecked in earrings and has matted hair. One shall perform the rite of *Homa* after conceiving the physical body of Agni thus.*

52. The Brāhmaṇa who performs the Homa rite by using (mere) hand for oblating milk, curds, ghee and any fried object becomes the slayer of a Brāhmaṇa.

53. The food that a man eats, his deities also eat; (but) for the prosperous achievement of all desired objects, the gingelly seeds must be used more in the *Havis* offered.

54. In the course of *Homas*, three *Mudrās* (ritualistic gestures or symbolic representations by certain positions of fingers, etc.) should be shown, viz. what is designated as the hind, the she-swan, and the sow. While magic spells and incantations are used, the *mudrā* called the sow should be used and during the auspicious rites, the gestures of the hind and the she-swan shall be used.

55. The ritualistic gesture called the (female) swine shall be by means of all the fingers; that of the she-swan shall be without the (use of the small finger); the *mudrā* called 'the hind' shall be by means of the three fingers, viz. the middle, the ring finger and the thumb.

56. One shall perform the *Homa* with gingelly seeds along with curds, honey and ghee the magnitude being the same as (mentioned) before, grasping these with all the five fingers.

57. In all auspicious rites the Kuśa grass-blades should be held closely to the ring finger.

---

* Cf. RV. IV. 58.3 and the description of the fire god in the *Smṛti* or *Paurāṇic* verses in the *Vaiśvadeva* of Ṛgvedins.

Vināyaka-Kalpa

58. Vināyaka (god Gaṇeśa) has been appointed as the controlling head of *Gaṇas* (like Puṣpadanta and others—Mit. = *Mitākṣarā** for creating as also in warding off impediments in acts (conducive to the attainment of *Puruṣārthas*), by gods Rudra, Brahmā and Viṣṇu.

59-61a. Understand the symptoms of a person who is haunted (lit. caught hold of) by Vināyaka: In dreams (he sees that) he is carried away by (a stream of) water or is drowned in deep water; he sees men with shaven heads and clothes reddish (blue *Mit.*) colour, (in dream that) he is riding carnivorous birds (like vultures) and beasts of prey (like tigers). He sees that he is surruonded by Caṇḍālas, donkeys and camels. (He feels that) while he is going he is hotly pursued by enemies (to attack him).

61b-63a. Such a person's mind becomes distracted or agitated; all his efforts (at success) become fruitless; without any reason, he becomes dispirited. Even though born in a royal family (and endowed with bravery, learning and such other qualities -*Mit.*); a maiden (though possessing beauty, good family-background etc.) does not get a spouse and a married woman does not become pregnant. A learned Vedic Scholar does not get preceptorship and a student (though endowed with discipline and other virtues) gets no study facility or tuition. A merchant gets no profit nor a husbandman gets profit in his agricultural activities.

63b-c. (For the propitiation of Vināyaka for pacification of troubles) on a meritorious day (with a favourable constellation) such a person's ablution as per due formalities should be performed with the viscous pulp of white mustard seeds (after extracting oil), while benedictory *mantras* are being recited by (learned) Brāhmaṇas** (*who should perform puṇyāhavācana-Mt.*).

---

* This is a famous commentary on the *Yājñavalkya Smṛti*. It was the paramount authority on the Hindu Law in British Courts and even after, before the Hindu Code Bill. Its author, Vijñāneśvara (A.D. 1070-1100) being such an authority I follow his interpretations, as this and the next Kalpa are borrowed from the *Yāj. Smr.* by the *NP*.

** NP. 63c is a combination of the 1st part of *Yāj.* I. 277b and the latter half of *Yāj.* I. 278 b.

64. Clay must be taken from (five places, viz.) the stables of horses, elephants, an ant-hill, from the confluence of two rivers and from a deep lake. *Rocana* (yellow pigment), scents, Guggulu (gum-resin), etc., must be thrown quickly* (into the water).

65. (Defective) Water must be brought from the deep lake in four pots of the same colour. The *Bhadrāsana* (the honoured holy seat) must be placed on a red-coloured hide of a bull (when the haunted person is thus seated. Brāhmaṇas should recite *Svasti* mantras.

66. (After recitation of *Svasti mantras*, *Suvāsinis*—women whose husband and sons are alive—should pour water over the haunted person from the pitcher kept to the eastern side of the *Bhadrāsana* while the following *Mantra* is being uttered).

"I sprinkle you with waters endowed with innumerable potencies, flowing in hundred(s) of streams, sanctified by sages (like Manu). May the purificatory waters sanctify you."

67. (Water from the second pitcher placed to the south should be poured with the following *Mantra*): "May king Varuṇa bless you with fortune. May the sun, Bṛhaspati, Indra, Vāyu, (each of them) confer auspicious blessings on you. The seven sages have bestowed blessings on you."

68. (Incantation while pouring the third pitcher): "May the water goddess destroy for ever whatever is inauspicious (and unlucky) in your hair on the head (*Mit.*) the parting of the hair, the forehead, ears and eyes."

69. (The fourth pitcher is to be poured while reciting the previous three *mantras*—After water from the fourth pitcher is poured) holding in the left hand blades of Kuśa grass, mustard oil should be oblated (poured over) the head (of the haunted person) with a ladle (spoon) made of Indian fig tree, when the person is thus bathed.

70-71a. (While pouring the mustard oil as oblations the following names of Vināyaka preceded by *Oṁ* and followed by *Svāhā* should be uttered per oblation as follows: *Oṁ Mitāya Svāhā, Oṁ Sammitāya Svāhā, Oṁ Śatāya Svāhā, Oṁ Kaṭaṅkaṭāya*

* For *āśu* of NP., Yāj-1.279 reads *apsu*.

Svāhā, Oṁ Kūṣmāṇḍāya Svāhā, Oṁ Rājaputrāya Svāhā. (Then in fire *Caru* oblations be given with these very *Mantras* and the remaining portion of the *Caru* should be oblated with *bali-Mantras* to Indra, Agni, Yama, Nirṛti, Varuṇa, Vāyu, Soma, Īśāna, Brahmā and Ananta using each name in the dative case followed by *namaḥ* 'Bow to,' as follows *Oṁ Indrāya namaḥ*, etc.

71b-75. As an offering (*Naivedya*) the following articles are to be presented to Vināyaka (and his mother—Pārvatī*) :— rice once beaten (half-polished), boiled rice mixed with powder of sesamum seeds, fish both raw and cooked, flesh both raw and cooked, flowers of variegated colours, incense, three kinds of spirituous liquor, radish, *Puris*, *Apūpa* (baked or boiled pies), garland of *Voṭa* (*Vaḍe*—in Marathi), boiled rice mixed with curds, milk pudding, flour-cake with raw sugar or jaggery along with *laḍḍus* (*Mit.*).

He should then bow them down with head (with the Mantras as follows**

The remainings of this offerings should be placed in a winnowing basket which is spread over with *Darbha* grass, and should place that *Bali* where four roads meet (with the following invocation†

After offering *Arghya* (with water, flowers, etc.), he should again offer *Dūrvā* -grass and mustard-flowers filling the cavity of his folded and joined hands (*añjali*).

76. (He should then pray)

"Be pleased to bestow on me beautiful form and features, renown, fortune, sons, wealth and grant me all desired objects."

---

* I am following *Mitākṣarā* on *Yāj.* in interpretation. The Mantras for bowing are :

(a) *tatpuruṣāya vidmahe / vakra-tuṇḍāya dhīmahī / tan no dantī pracodayāt //*

(b) *subhagāyai vidmahe / kāma-mālinyai dhīmahī / tan no gaurī pracodayāt. /*

** *Mit.* quotes the *Mantras* which may briefly be translated here : "May Devas, Ādityas, Vasus Marut-gods, Aśvinī-kumāras, Rudras, Suparṇas, serpents, planets, Asuras, Yātudhānas, Piśācas (Goblins), reptiles, Mātṛ-devatās, (divine mothers), female evil spirits, Yakṣas, Vetālas, Yoginis, Pūtanās (goddesses of epidemics), spirits causing yawning etc.), Siddhas, Gandharvas, Vidyādharas, men, guardians of quarters, protectors of different worlds, Vināyaka-godlings creating impediments accept this offering.

O great sages beginning with Brahmā, the promulgators of peace ! May there be no trouble or impediment or sin or enemies to me. May goblins and departed spirits be statisfied and bring us happiness."

77. After worshipping Durgā, the consort of Śiva, he should worship Śiva, the Lord of Umā, by means of incense, lights, food-offerings, scents, fragrant garlands and unguents.

78. Thereafter the worshipper should wear white garments, garlands of white flowers and apply (sandalpaste like white) unguents to his body. He should feed the Brāhmaṇas and give a pair of clothes to the preceptor (who conducted this worship with full knowledge).

79. After performing the worship of Vināyaka the person desirous of wealth, peace, nourishment, prosperity, longevity and virility should worship the planets.

The rite conducive to
Pacification of Planets

80. The nine planets are to be installed in the following order, viz. the Sun, Moon, Mars, Mercury, Jupiter, Venus, Saturn, Rāhu and Ketu.

81. For attaining auspiciousness, the replica or representation of the planets should be made of what follows respectively:* copper, crystal (silver in NP), red-sandalwood, two in gold and silver (gold in NP), iron, lead and bell-metal.

82a. Or they may be painted on the canvas-cloth in their respective colours or they may be represented by means of esoteric diagrams with coloured powders or pastes.

82b-83. (The procedure of worshipping planets). Each planet should be worshipped by offering cloths, scents, or unguents and flowers according to the complexion of the planets. They should also be offered scents, *Bali* (food-offerings), incense and *Guggulu* (a particular fragrant gum resin). For each (presiding) deity (of the planets). (oblation of) *Caru* (and *Samidhs*) be offered (in the fire) with the following (nine) *mantras*.

* v. 81 is defective as the objects are duplicated and do not make up the number 9 required for the planets. Thus NP reads :
tāmrakād rajatād rakta-candanāt svarṇakād api |
hemno rajatādayasaḥ sīsāt kāryā śubhāptaye ||
Here *rajata* 'silver' and gold (*svarṇaka* & *heman*) are repeated twice. The original verse (*Yāj.* I. 297) is accepted for translation.

84-85. The following are (the *Pratikas* of) *Mantras* of the planets (1) *Ā kṛṣṇena* (RV.I.33.2), (2) *Imaṁ devā* (VS.9. 40), (3) *Agnir mūrdhā* (RV.VIII.44.16), (4) *Udbudhyasva* (VS.15. 54), (5) * *Yad aryaḥ* (RV.2.13.15), (6) *Annāt parisrutaḥ*, (7) *Śan no devīḥ* (RV.X.9.4), (8) *Kāṇḍāt* (VS. 13. 20), (9) Ketuṁ kṛṇvann aketave (RV.1.6.3) (?).

86. The sacrificial sticks (special to each planet) are as follows: the sun-plant (*arka*), ***palāśa*** (tree), ***khadira*** (*Acacia catechu*), ***Apāmārga*** (the Achyranthes Aspera) the ***pippala***, *Udumbara* (the Indian fig. tree), *Dūrvā* and *Kuśa* grass.

87. To each of the planet one hundred eight or twenty eight sacrificial sticks (that of the sun-plant for the sun, the *palāśa* twigs for the moon, etc.) smeared with honey or ghee or curds or milk should be oblated.

88-89. The *Naivedya* offered should consist of the following articles: rice cooked with jaggery, milk-pudding, *haviṣya* (food partakable to sages), Ṣaṣṭikā grains cooked in milk, cooked rice with curds, *Havis* (rice cooked in milk) *Cūrṇa* (rice mixed with sesame), rice mixed with flesh (*Mit.*), boiled rice of various colours (due to its various components). These articles should be offered (to each planet) in due order. The wise person should give meal to Brāhmaṇas according to his (financial) ability and the availability of the foodstuffs. The food etc. should be offered after duly honouring them (by washing their feet, etc.).

90. The following is the prescribed religious fee (*Dakṣiṇā*) for the planets (respectively); a cow, a conch, a (strong) bull, gold, (yellow) cloth, (a white) horse, a black (tawny?), coloured cow, iron (a weapon), a goat.

91. The different articles (offered as Dakṣiṇā) should be a *Pala* in weight. At the time of monetary gifts this should be said, "O Brahmaṇa, boon has been granted by these: Being worshipped (bless) them."**

---

* the *mantra* should be *Bṛhaspate ati yad aryo* (RV. 2.13.15)

** The text in Yāj : "A boon has been granted to these planets by god Brahmā." "Ye planets, when worshipped you worship (reciprocally) the worshippers (by removing their calamaties and conferring blessing on them) Yāj. I.307.

92. "Wealth, nobility, rise in position of leading men are controlled by planets. The existence and the nonexistence of the universe depends on the planets. Hence, planets are highly adorable."

93-94. The performance of worship every day of Lord sun with red-sandal, etc.) as well as that of god Skanda and the great god Gaṇapati leads to accomplishments of desires, fruits of one's religious acts and unsurpassed affluence.

95. If a person begins to worship planets without performance of *Mātṛ-yāga* (a sacrifice in propitiation of divine Mothers), the Mothers get angry with him and create impediments.

96-97. Those who seek auspiciousness should perform *Vasordhārā* (a particular libation of ghee at the *Agni-cayana*) by means of holy mantras of Vasu. Gaurī and other holy mothers should be propitiated by them on auspicious occasion.

98. The mothers are sixteen in number viz.—Gaurī, Padmā, Śacī, Medhā, Sāvitrī, Vijayā, Jayā, Devasenā, Svadhā, Svāhā, Mātṛkā, Vaidhṛti, Dhṛti, Puṣṭi, Dṛṣṭi and Tuṣṭi—these sixteen should be worshipped on the occasions or for the sake of prosperity alongwith the *Ātmadevatā* (the family deity). They are even superior to Gaṇeśa.

99-100. All the necessary items in the worship should be followed: viz. the invocation, offering of *pādya* and Arghya, ablution, sandal paste, *Akṣatas* (raw rice grains), flowers, incense, burning light, fruits, *Naivedya*, *Ācamanīya*, betel leaves, areca nut, showing of lights (*Nīrājanā*) and *Dakṣiṇā*. All these must be offered for their satisfaction.

*The Pitṛ-Kalpa (Śrāddha)

101-102. I shall now explain to you the *Pitṛ-Kalpa* which increases wealth and progeny. The following are the occasions for the performance of *Śrāddha*.: The new moon day; the *Aṣṭakā* days**, *Vṛddhi* (prosperous occasions like the birth of a son),

---

* The NP has borrowed this section from the *Śrāddha-Prakaraṇa* of the *Yāj. Smṛti* I. 217 ff. The printed text has the lines of the *Yāj.* disarranged with printing mistakes in addition. Please vide *Supra* ch. 28 and notes, as the topic of *Śrāddha* is treated there.

** The 8th day in the dark half in the months covered in the seasons Hemanta and Śiśira—Āśvalāyana.

the dark half of the month, the two *Ayanas* (southern and northern transits of the sun), availability of suitable Brāhmaṇas (as detailed in the next verse—*Mit.*), equinoxial transits of the sun, (the first point of Aries or Libra into which the sun enters at the vernal or autumnal equinox), *Vyatīpāta* (a particular evil *yoga** or time) *Gajacchāyā* (a particular day**), the solar and lunar eclipses and whenever one feels inclined to perform a Śrāddha.

103-106a. The following Brāhmaṇas are regarded as the "wealth or assets to Śrāddha,† (*Brāhmaṇa-sampadaḥ* mentioned in the above verse): proficient in (recitation and teaching) all the Vedas, *Śrotriya* (well-versed in the Vedas), the knower of the meaning of the Vedic texts, a middle-aged person—*Mit.*, the knower of the meaning of the Veda-mantras, one expert in teaching and observing the vow of the *Jyeṣṭha-sāma* portion of the *Sāma-veda*,†† the expert (as described above) in the *tri-madhu* and *tri-suparṇa* hymns, ‡sister's son, a *Ṛtvik* (a priest officiating at a sacrifice), a son-in-law, the father-in-law, or the maternal uncle who can perform a sacrifice, the knower of the *Triṇāciketa hymns*, a grandson (through a daughter), the disciples, kinsmen and relatives‡, performers of prescribed karmans, practitioners of austerities, keepers of five (sacrificial) fires, strict followers of the vow of celibacy and those who carefully serve their parents.

---

* *Vyatīpāta*—the day of new moon when it falls on Sunday and the moon is with certain constellation such as Śravaṇa, Dhaniṣṭhā, Ārdrā.
Śravaṇāśvi Dhaniṣṭhā'rdrā nāga-daivatamastake /
Yadīmā ravivāreṇa Vyatīpātaḥ sa ucyate //
(*Bṛhan-manu* quoted in SKD. IV. 531.

** A particular constellation (MW. 342). But SKD II. 290 quotes from *Kṛtya-cintāmaṇi* :
kṛṣṇa-pakṣe trayodaśyām Maghāsvinduḥ kare raviḥ /
yadā tadā gaja-cchāyā śrāddhe puṇyair avāpyate //

† Vide Manu III. 150-169. Cf. Supra 28.6-10 and notes.

†† *Jyeṣṭha-sāma, sāma-viśeṣas tad-adhyayanāṅga-vratam ca tad-vratācaraṇena yas tad adhīte—Mit* on I. Yāj 219

‡ The list from "sister's son to relatives" is for the 2nd preference, if the Brāhmaṇas enumerated in the previous verse are not available—*Mit.* on Yāj I. 220.

106b-109a. The following (Brāhmaṇas) are despicable (and should not be invited for *Śrāddha*)*:

One affected with heinous diseases (like leprosy), one possessing a surplus limb or deficient in a limb, a squint-eyed person, a son of a remarried widow, a religious student who violates the vow of celibacy, a bastard, one of deformed nails or of conspicuously black teeth, a salaried teacher, a eunuch, a (false) accuser of girls (a girl-teaser or outrager of the modesty of girls), one accused of serious crimes, a traitor of friends, a backbiter or slanderer, one who sells (sacrificial) Soma, one who marries or takes up *Agnihotra* before his elder brother, one who abandons his parents or preceptor, one maintaining himself on the earnings of unchaste women, the son of a Śūdra, the husband of a divorced woman, a thief, a person fallen from holy rites.

109b-110a. The house-holder himself remaining self-controlled and pure, should invite Brāhmaṇas on the previous day** itself. The invited Brāhmaṇas too must control themselves mentally, verbally and physically.

110b-111a. He should welcome and honour the Brāhmaṇas as they come in the afternoon (on the *muhūrta* called *Kutapa-Mit.*). After they have sipped water as *Ācamana* he with a *Pavitra* (of Darbha grass) in his hand (fingers), should seat them in their respective seats.

111b-112a. In the rites pertaining to deities he may have (invited) as many Brāhmaṇas as he can afford. In the rites concerning *Pitṛs*, he must have odd number of Brāhmaṇas. He should seat them on a ground purified (by smearing with cow-dung *Mit.*) covered and sloping to the south.

112b-113a. The two Brāhmaṇas representing deities should be seated with their faces to the east. And each of the Brāhmaṇas representing *Pitṛs* should be made to face the north (or one Brāhmaṇa for Devas and one for *Pitṛs* may do). In the case of the Śrāddha of the maternal grandfather, the procedure of Brāhmaṇas representing gods etc. is the same.

---

* Cf. *Supra* 21.11-18 & notes.

** Cf. Manu III. 187 : *vide Pd. P. Sṛṣṭi* 9.85.88. and the *Matsya* 16.17-20, also *S. Śrāddha*, P. 406.

113b-114a. He (the householder) gives them water for washing their hands and even number of Kuśa-grass (blades) for the purpose of a seat. When so permitted by Brāhmaṇas, he should invoke the gods with the Ṛk verse *Viśvedevas** (RV. I. 3. 7).

114b-116a. After scattering the barley grains in a vessel along with the *Pavitra*, he should pour water with the Mantra *Śanno devī* (RV.X. 9. 4). Repeating the Mantra *Yavo'si* (VS. 5. 26; TS. I. 3. 11), he should scatter barley grains. He should then pour the *arghya* water** into the hands, repeating the Mantra *Yā divyā* (TB. 2. 7. 15. 4). After giving water, serving food, with a lamp lighted, applying fragrant sandals and flower-garlands (he should give them water to wash hands).

116b-117. He should then change† his sacred thread, hang towards the left part of the body over the right shoulder (when he deals with rites concerning *Pitṛs*—manes) offering Kuśa grass (blades) twice in number to the Brāhmaṇas representing *Pitṛs*, he should invite his fathers (i.e. father, grand-father and great-grand-father) with the mantra *Uśantas tvā nidhīmahi* (RV. X. 16. 12, AV. 18. 1). After inviting the *Pitṛs*, he should, with the permission (of the Brāhmaṇas—representatives of *Pitṛs*) perform the *Japa* (undertone recitation) of the mantra *Ā yantu naḥ pitaraḥ* (*Mit.*)

118-119a. The rites to be performed with barley may be performed with gingelly seeds. Offering *Arghya* along with barley grains put in their vessel according to the ritual he will repeat the mantra *Pitṛbhyas sthānam asi* (*Yāj. Smṛ.* I. 234,) and place the vessel with (its) face downwards.

119b-120a. Wishing to perform *Agnau-Karaṇa* (offering into sacrificial fire), he takes cooked rice soaked in ghee and formally requests the permission (to offer oblations). If the Brāhmaṇas say "Do so" and permit him he oblates them formally into the fire‡ as in *Pitṛ-yajña*.

* The *Smārta Mantra—āgacchantu mahābhāgāḥ* etc.—is also recited.

** The NP reads *haste Pādyaṁ viniḥkṣipet* The oddity of pouring water meant for washing feet into the hands being obvious, the *Yāj.* reading (which is the original one) *hasteṣvarghyaṁ vinikṣipet* is accepted.

† NP reads *sapradakṣiṇam* but the original text and the actual practice of *Śrāddha* shows that the reading *apradakṣiṇam* in the *Yāj.* I. 232 is correct.

‡ In practice, now-a-days, these are offered in the hand of Brāhmaṇa in stead of in fire. This is sanctioned by Manu.
Agnyabhāve tu viprasya pāṇāvevopapādayet (quoted by *Mit.*)

120b-121a. After the Homa is over, he will carefully (with great concentration) place the remaining food into vessels. Those vessels may be of whatever material available, but particularly silver vessels are recommended.

121b-122a. After keeping food into the pots, the pots are invoked with the mantra *Pṛthivī te pātram* (*Mānava-Śrauta-sūtra* II. 9. 2.) and make the *Brāhmaṇa* place his thumb on the food with the Mantra *Idaṁ viṣṇur vicakrame* (RV. I. 22. 17).

122b-125a. He shall then repeat the *Gāyatrī* along with the *Vyāhṛtis* and the three Ṛks beginning with *Madhu vātā* etc. (RV. I. 90. 6-8). After the *Japa* he must say, "All of you, take food at your leisure". They also shall take food with restricted speech. (The householder) shall serve them the desirable food and ghee. He shall not be angry. He shall not be in a hurry. Till they are satisfied (the food is offered). (While they take food) he shall repeat the *Japa* as before. He shall formally ask them "Are you satisfied ?" He shall then take the formal permission regarding the leavings of food etc. He shall then take the cooked rice and strew them on the ground. Water shall be offered once for each.

125b-126a. Taking all the strewn food along with the gingelly seeds he shall stand facing the south. He shall place the *Piṇḍas* near the *Ucchiṣṭa* (leavings of the food) as in the case of *Pitṛyajña*. To the maternal grandfather also, the *Śrāddha* offered is like this. He shall then offer water as *Ācamana*. He should then request them to give the benediction *Svasti* and they say it. He should then request them to bless him with benediction. He should pour water on their hands and they utter that blessing.

126b-128. After giving *Dakṣiṇā* according to his ability, he should seek their permission to say *Svadhā*; when so permitted by them he should utter the word *Svadhā* with reference to the concerned *Pitṛs* on his father's and mother's side. Then water should be sprinkled on the ground.

129a. He shall say then "May the *Viśve devas* be pleased." When the Brāhmaṇas say this, he shall repeat it.

129b-130a. He should then pray to Brāhmaṇas: "May donors flourish and multiply in our family. May Vedas increase (by recitation, teaching etc.); May my race flourish. May not our faith in Śrāddha and other religious rites dwindle. May we have abundant (gold etc.) to give."

130b-131a. After saying such pleasing words, he should (go round them and) bid them adieu. He should repeat the mantra *Vāje vāje* (RV. I.10.7?) and with delighted heart take leave of *Pitṛs* with due formalities.

131b-132a. The *Arghya-pātra* in which *Arghya* water given to the Brāhmaṇas was poured, should be placed with its face upwards and the Brāhmaṇas be formally let go (after being blessed by them).

132b-133a. After accompanying the departing Brāhmaṇas to the border (of the village), he should circumambulate them clock-wise and returning, he should eat the food partaken of by his *Pitṛs*. On the night of the *Śrāddha* he (alongwith the invited Brāhmaṇas) should observe celibacy.

133b-134a. Thus repeating the circumambulation, he shall perform *Nāndi* and other *Yajñas* to the *Pitṛs* during the occasions of prosperity. The *Piṇḍas* must be made of barley grains and mixed with curds and *Karkandhu* (the fruit of the Jujube tree).

134b-135a. The *Ekoddiṣṭa* (*śrāddha* with a single Brāhmaṇa) consists of one *Arghya* and one *Pavitra*. It is devoid of *devas*.

135b-136a. It has neither the *Āvāhana* (invocation) nor the *Agnaukaraṇa* (consigning of cooked food into the fire). The circumambulation is anticlockwise. (Here the difference between the two *Śrāddhas* is :) Here *akṣayyasthāne upatiṣṭhatām* should be uttered (instead of *akṣayyodaka* etc). At the time of bidding goodbye to the Brāhmaṇas, after reciting *Vāje vāje* he should request with the words *abhiramyatām* (please do enjoy) and they would say *abhiratāḥ* (enjoyed). (This is to be performed at mid-day-*Mit.*).

136b-137. He shall have four vessels made filled with gingelly seeds and scented water. For the purpose of *Arghya*, water shall be poured into the vessels of the *Pitṛs* from the vessel of the Preta (the dead one). At that time the two *mantras* beginning with *Ye Samānāḥ* (VS. 19.45) etc. shall be repeated. He shall perform the other rites as before.

138-140a. This rite of *Ekoddiṣṭa* and *Sapiṇḍikaraṇa* is for women also. If the *Sapiṇḍikaraṇa* is performed after a year, the food along with the water pot shall be given to a Brāhmaṇa for a year(?). Every month, this rite shall be performed on the day of death. The rite is performed every year, and month as well as on the eleventh day.

140b-141a. The *Piṇḍas* shall be given to the cows, goats or Brāhmaṇas or consigned to fire or water. While the Brāhmaṇas are present at the place of the meal, the leavings of food of the Brāhmaṇas shall not be swept.

141b-142a. The *Pitṛs* are delighted for a month with *Haviṣyānna* (cooked rice soaked in ghee) and for a year with milk pudding. The meat of the following shall be offered in the different months, viz—fish, deer, ram, birds, goats, *Pṛṣat* deer, *Eṇa* deer, Ruru deer, boar and hare. If these are offered the Pitāmahas are satisfied.*

142b-145a. If a person staying at Gayā (or at any highly sacred place like Prayāga, Naimiṣa,—*Mit.*) gives i.e. performs *Srāddha* with the flesh of a rhinoceros, a kind of fish called Mahāsalka,** honey, food suitable to sages, flesh of a red-coloured goat, *Mahāśāka* (i.e. Kālāśāka or *Narcā* in Hindi), white goat, he attains eternal benefit (or bliss). That is particularly so, if it is performed on the 13th day of the dark half of Bhādrapada when the constellation Maghā is on that day.

145b-148a. A person who offers *Śrāddha* from the 1st day of the dark half of Bhādrapada upto the new moon day (with the exception of the fourteenth day which is reserved for those killed with a weapon in battle, etc.) forever gets (as a fruit of performance of *Śrāddha* on that particular *tithi* as follows): a (beautiful) girl (of good character and characteristics),

---

* The Mitākṣarā clarifies that it is *haviṣyānna* (rice boiled in milk) that should represent each kind of flesh for *Śrāddha*.

** *Mahākalpa* in the NP is most probably a misprint as this is a list of food-stuffs).

(intelligent, handsome) sons-in-law, small beasts like sheep, good-mannered sons, success in gambling, (Harvest in) agriculture, profit in commerce, two-hoofed animals like cows, one-hoofed animals like horses, sons with the brilliance of Vedic studies, etc., gold and silver (also other metals like lead, zinc), leadership in one's caste, fulfilment of all desires (of heaven etc.) The (*ekoddiṣṭa*) *Śrāddha* on the fourteenth day of the dark half of *Bhādrapada* is (reserved) for persons who die of being struck with weapons.

148b-152a. If a person, full of faith, deep reverence, devoid of arrogance and jealousy performs a *Śrāddha* with due formalities on every *Nakṣatra* (constellation) beginning from *Kṛttikā* (the Pleiades) and ending with *Bharaṇī* will attain the following desired objects : the heaven, progeny, exuberance of Ātmic (spiritual) powers, bravery or fearlessness, fertile fields, physical strength, a (virtuous) son, prominent social status (in one's community), popularity, affluence in wealth etc., prominence, auspiciousness, unchallenged command, commerce, agriculture, cows, etc. health, fame, absence of sorrow (due to bereavement of a dear person), attainment of the highest (*Brahman*) region, money, gold, etc. (mastery over) the Vedas, effectiveness of medicines, metals (except gold and silver), cows, he and she-goats and longevity.

152b-154a. The deities presiding over and propitiated in *Śrāddha* such as Vasus, Rudras, sons of Aditi (devas) and *Pitṛs* when satisfied by propitiation through *Śrāddha* give pleasure to the manes of the performer but these grandsires of human beings bestow longevity, progeny, wealth, learning, heaven, emancipation from Saṁsāra, all pleasure and (even) a kingdom.

154b-155a. In this way are narrated a few special features or particulars of the *Kalpādhyāya*. The details should be known in Vedic *tantras* and other *purāṇas*.

155b-157. He shall attain auspicious goal here and hereafter. The man who devoutly listens to this chapter on *Kalpa* during the holy rites pertaining to the Devas and the *Pitṛs* obtains the benefit of the holy rites pertaining to Devas and *Pitṛs*. He obtains wealth, learning, renown, and sons here and the highest goal hereafter.

158. Henceforth, I shall recount to you the treatise on Grammar which is called the face of the Vedas. I shall recount it succinctly. Listen attentively.

CHAPTER FIFTYONE

1. *Kalpa* deals with Vedic rituals. According to the topic discussed, it was classified as *śrauta*, *Gṛhya* and *Dharma* sūtras. The NP. divides them under: (1) the Veda, (2) Saṁhitā (3) Aṅgiras, (4) Śānti, and (5) Nakṣatra Kalpa. NP. borrows mostly from Yāj. Smr. in this chapter.

2. These are measures of capacity. vide SKD III p. 203 where *Āpastamba Śrauta Sūtra* is quoted.

CHAPTER FIFTYTWO

*Exposition of Grammar**

Sanandana said:

1. O Nārada, I shall now explain to you in brief *Vyākaraṇa* (grammar) by means of (illustrations of) readymade forms (inductively?); grammar is regarded as the mouth of the Veda.

2. Words are either *Subantas* (substantives) or *Tiṅantas* (verbs). O Brāhmaṇa, the seven cases are covered by *Sup*-terminations. The (inflexions) *Su*, *Au*, *Jas* constitute the *Prathamā* (the first i.e. the Nominative) case. It consists of the *Prātipadika* (the noun in its uninflected state before case-terminations are applied).

3. A significant form of a word, not being a verbal root (*Dhātu*) or an affix (*Pratyaya*) or a word ending in an affix is called *Prātipadika* (crude-form or Nominal base)[1]. The Nom. (Nominative) case-affix is employed when the sense is that of addressing (*Sambodhana*)[2] or where there is the additional sense of gender only or to denote the subject.

4. *Am*, *Au*, *Śas* are the inflections of the Accusative case. That which is done (by the agent) is *Karma* (object). In the object, the Accusative case is used.[3] And also when a word is joined by (i.e. governed by) the word *Antarā* or *Antareṇa* it takes the second case-affix[4] (i.e. of the objective case).

5. *Ṭā*, *Bhyām*, *Bhis* are the terminations of the third (Instrumental) case. In denoting the agent or the instrument the third (Instrumental) case-affix is employed)[5]. That

---

* As stated in the Introduction, the presentation of Sk. Grammar in the NP is popular but unsystematic, as he gives a number of examples without discussing the rules. But vv 2-24 show that the NP has given a number of Pāṇini's *sūtras* in a verse form, *vide* the *Kāraka Prakaraṇa* and the annotations on these verses. It appears that this section was written after the 7th cent. *A.D.* that is after Pāṇini regained his popularity by Bhartṛhari's *Vākyapadīya* and such other works.

wherewith something is done is the instrument and he who does it is the agent (*Kartā*).

6. The desinences of the Dative case are *Ṅe*, *Bhyām*, *Bhyas* and they are to be used with *Sampradāna Kāraka*. The person to whom something is desired to be given, something is owed[1] or something appeals (or is liked) is called the *Sampradāna*.

7. *Ṅasi*, *Bhyām*, *Bhyas* are the terminations of the fifth (Ablative) case. They are to be used in the *Apādāna Kāraka*. *Apādāna* is that from which something moves away, gets separated or is taken away.

8. The terminations for the sixth (Genitive) case are *Ṅas*, *Os* and *Ām*. It is mainly used when the relationship of possession or ownership is indicated. *Ṅi*, *Os*, *Sup* are the terminations of the seventh or, Locative case. It shows *Adhi-Karaṇa*.

9. O prominent Brāhmaṇa! it (the term *Adhikaraṇa*) is used in the sense of *Ādhāra*[7]. Verbs implying protection govern the Ablative case. That which is desired or that which is abhorred are called Apādānakas (and they take the Ablative case).

10-11. The ablative case is used when the preposition *Pari*, *Apa*, *Āṅ*, *Itara* and *Ṛte*[8] are used as *Karma-pravacanīya*[9] and with words denoting quarters. The *karma-pravacanīyas* govern the accusative case also. The words *Prati*, *Pari and Anu*[10] are *Karma-pravacanīya* when used in the sense of (1) 'sign', 'in the direction of', (2) 'mere statement of a circumstance or as regards (*ittham bhūta*), and the word *Abhi* in the above sense of 'in the direction of', 'as regards' but *not* when it means division or 'share of'[11]. *Anu* is used in the sense of *Saha*. In the sense of *hīna*[12] (inferior, subordinate to) and *Upa*[13]. They are used as *Karma-pravacanīyas* (governing instrumental).

12. In the case of roots implying motion, the place to which the motion is desired or directed take the termination of the second (Accusative) or the fourth (Dative) case[14]. In denoting the indirect object, which is not an animal, of the verb *manya* ($\sqrt{man}$ + *ya*) 'to think'. The Dative case is (optionally) employed, when contempt is to be shown[15].

13. The Dative case is used with words *Namaḥ* (Bow to), *Svasti* (peace and bliss), *Svāhā*, *Svadhā* (to be uttered in

offering oblations to gods and manes respectively), *alaṁ* 'a match for' and *Vaṣaṭ*[16] (a mystic term in sacrifices). This case termination is used when the crude-form (base) ends in an affix denoting 'condition' or having the force of the infinitive of purpose (which has—*tum* as the affix)[17].

14. The instrumental case is used with *Saha*[18] (accompanied by), in an attribute pointing to the physical defect of a person[19]. While indicating time, abstract notion both the Locative as well as the Genitive case is used.

15. The Genitive and Locative case terminations are used when they are conjoined with words *Svāmin* 'master', *Īśvara* 'Lord', *Adhipati* 'Sovereign ruler', *Sākṣi* 'witness', *dāyāda* 'an heir', *Sūtaka* (*Prasūta* in the *Sūtra*) 'born'[20] and with words specificating an individual from the class (*nirdhāraṇa*)[21]. But only the Genitive in *Hetuprayoga*[22] i.e. after a noun implying the cause of an action, when the word *hetu* is used only with such a word (e.g. *annasya hetor vasati*. 'He dwells for the sake of food' and not the Instrumental.

16. The Genitive case is used with objects of verbs connoting memory, attempting or exerting for or doing violence to or with a word denoting an agent and the object when it is used alongwith a word ending in a *Kṛt* affix[23].

17a-b. The terminations of the Genitive are not used to express the agent or the object, when the word is formed by a past participle (in *kta* and *ktavatu*[24]. In the case-ending beginning with *Sup*, etc., the alternative uses should be known.

17c. In case of roots (of 1st, 2nd conjugations) like *Bhū*, *Vā*, which end in (i.e. take the inflexions) *Tiṅ*. There are ten *Lakāras*[25] (tenses and moods) for conjugation.

18-19. *Tip*, *Tas*, *Anti* are the inflexion of the *Prathama*[21] *Puruṣa* (but in modern Sk. grammar it is called the 'third') person. *Sip*, *Thas*, *Tha* are the inflections of the *Madhyama Puruṣa* (called the 'second person' in modern Sk. grammar). *Mip*, *Vas*, *Mas* are the terminations of the *Uttama Puruṣa* (designated 'first person' by modern Sk. grammarians). The above terminations are in the *Parasmaipada*.

In the *Ātmanepada* set of roots, the terminations of the third person are *Te*, *Āte* and *Ante*. Those of the second person are *Se*, *Āthe* and *Dhve*; and those of the First person are *E*, *Vahe* and *Mahe*. It should be known that there are other substitutes for these terminations in *Liṅ* and other tenses and moods.

20. When a substantive is used it is called the 'third person.' When the word *Yuṣmad* ('you' or 'thou') is used it is called the 'second person', and when the word *Asmad* ('I' or 'we') is used it is called the 'first person'.

21-22. *Bhū* and others (i.e. other roots of different conjugations) are called *Dhātus*. Those ending in *San* and other suffixes are (also) called *Dhātus*. In the present tense *Laṭ* is used. In the past Tense (not of the present day), and with the use of the particle *Mā sma*, the *Laṅ* (Past Imperfect) is used. In expressing benediction, *Loṭ* is used. To denote injunction, permission, etc. as well as in giving blessings *Liṅ* (the Potential mood) is used. These are the twofold uses of *Liṅ*, O Sage.

23. In the past not witnessed by the speaker personally, *Liṭ* (Perfect) is used. In the future (not of today), *Luṭ* (I future) is used after the roots.

24. In denoting the past, *Luṇ* (the Aorist) is used. In case of *Atipatti* (lapse or non-occurable condition) *Lṛṅ* (लृङ्) (conditional mood) is used.

Now understand the ready made examples beginning with *Saṁhitās* (sandhis).

25-30.	Daṇḍa	+	Agram	=	Daṇḍāgram
	Dadhi	+	Idam	=	Dadhīdam
	Madhu	+	Udakam	=	Madhūdakam
	Pitṛ	+	Ṛṣabha[27]	=	Pitṛṣabha
	Hotṛ	+	Ḷkāra	=	Hotṛkāra
	Sa	+	Iyam	=	Seyaṃ
	Lāṅgala	+	Īṣā	=	Lāṅgalīṣā
	Manas	+	Īṣā	=	Manīṣā.
	Gaṅgā	+	Udakam	=	Gaṅgodakam
	Tava	+	Ḷkāra	=	Tavalkāra
	Ṛṇa	+	Ṛṇam	=	Ṛṇārṇam
	Śita	+	Ārta	=	Śitārta
	Sa	+	Indra	=	Sendra

Sa + Oṅkāra = Sauṅkāra*
Vadhū + Āsanam = Vadhvāsanam
Pitṛ + Artha = Pitrartha
Nai + Aka = Nāyaka
Lo + Aṇa = Lavaṇa
Te + Ādyāḥ = *Ta ādyāḥ*
Viṣṇo + E = Viṣṇave
Hi + Atra = Hyatra
Tasmai + Argho = Tasmā argho
Gurau + Adhaḥ = Gurā adhaḥ
Hare + Ava = Hare'va
Viṣṇo + Ava = Viṣṇo'va
Iti + Eṣa = Ityeṣa
Amī + Aghāḥ = Amī aghā.

From this onwards O excellent sage, the words remain as before i.e. without any Sandhi or phonetic change.

Śaurī + Etau = Śaurī Etau
Viṣṇū + Imau = Viṣṇū Imau
Durge + Amū = Durge Amū
No + Arjuna = No Arjuna
Ā + Evam = Ā Evam

Absence of phonetic change only upto this.

Ṣaṭ + Atra = Ṣaḍatra
Ṣaṭ + Mātaraḥ = Ṣaṇmātaraḥ
Vāk + (Ś) Chūraḥ = Vākcchūraḥ
Vāk + Hari = Vāgghari
Hariḥ + Śete = Hariśśete
Vibhuḥ + Cintyaḥ = Vibhuścintyaḥ
Tat + Śeṣa = Taccheṣa.
Yat + Cara = Yaccara
Praśnaḥ + Tvatha = Praśnastvatha
Hariḥ + Ṣaṣṭhaḥ = Hariṣṣaṣṭhaḥ
Kṛṣṇaḥ + Ṭīkate = Kṛṣṇaṣṭīkate

31. Bhavān+Ṣaṣṭhaḥ Ṣaṭ+Santaḥ and Ṣaṭ+Te (in these three cases no phonetic change)

---

* If *Saukāra* be the reading, it will be from *Sa+Okāra*.

	Tat	+	Lepaḥ	=	Tallepaḥ
	Cakrin	+	Chindhi	=	Cakrimśchindhi
	Bhavān	+	Śauriḥ	=	Bhavāñchauriḥ or Bhavāñśauriḥ (two forms)
32-34.	Samyaṅ	+	Ananta	=	Samyaṅṅananta
	Aṅga	+	Chāyā	=	Aṅgacchāyā

O excellent sage, Kṛṣṇam+namāmi 'I salute Kṛṣṇa'. (Here 'M' becomes *Anusvāra*) = Kṛṣṇaṁ namāmi. Similarly, in *Tejāṁsi* and *Maṁsyāte*. In Gaṅgā, the *Anusvāra* becomes 'Ṅ' (the gutteral nasal letter).

Hariḥ	+	Chettṛ	=	Hariśchettṛ.
Amaraḥ	+	Śivaḥ	=	Amaraśśivaḥ.
Rāmaḥ	+	Kāmya	=	Rāmaḥ⌣kāmya

(Here the *Visarga* becomes *Jihvāmūliya*).

Kṛpaḥ	+	Pūjyaḥ	=	Kṛpa⌣Pūjyaḥ

(Here the *Visarga* becomes Upadhmānīya or simply Hariḥ Pūjyaḥ, Arcyaḥ+Eva = Arcya eva.)

Rāmaḥ	+	Dṛṣṭaḥ	=	Rāmo dṛṣṭaḥ
Abalāḥ	+	Atra	=	Abalā atra

Suptāḥ + Iṣṭāḥ + Imāḥ + Yataḥ = Suptā Iṣṭā Imā Yataḥ

Viṣṇuḥ	+	Namyaḥ	=	Visnurnamyaḥ
Raviḥ	+	Ayam	=	Ravirayam
Gīr	+	Phalam	=	Gī⌣phalam (*Upadhmānīya*).
Prātaḥ	+	Acyutaḥ	=	Prātaracyutaḥ
Bhaktaiḥ	+	Vandyaḥ	=	Bhaktairvandyaḥ
Api	+	Antarātmā	=	Apyantarātmā
Bhoḥ	+	Bhoḥ	=	Bho Bho
Eṣaḥ	+	Hariḥ	=	Eṣa Hariḥ
Eṣaḥ	+	Śārṅgin	=	Eṣa śārṅgin
Saḥ+Eṣaḥ	+	Rāmaḥ	=	Saiṣa rāmaḥ

Thus the *Saṁhitā* (*Sandhi*, close proximity) has been narrated.

35. This verse gives the declension of Rāma (Masc. Noun ending in—*a*) in all the cases :

Rāmeṇā[28] bhihitaṁ karomi satatam
Rāmaṁ bhaje sādaram /

Rāmeṇā' pahṛtaṁ samasta-duritam,
Rāmāya tubhyaṁ namaḥ /
Rāmān muktirabhīpsitā mama sadā
Rāmasya dāso'smyaham /
Rāme rañjatu me manaḥ suviśadaṁ
he *Rāma* tubhyaṁ namaḥ / /

(1) Rāma does those things that benefit all;
(2) I always respectfully worship Rāma
(3) all sins are removed by Rāma
(4) Obeisance to you, Rāma
(5) Liberation is always sought for from Rāma by me.
(6) I am the servant unto Rāma.
(7) May my mind be clear and take delight in Rāma;
(8) O Rāma, obeisance to you.

36-37a. All the words (ending in vowels) are (to be declined like this) Gopāḥ, *Sakhi* becomes *Sakhā* (friend); Pati (lord), Hari; Suśrīḥ (one with good glory); Bhānu (the Sun); Svayaṁbhū (the self-born), Kartṛ (the Agent); Rāḥ (*Rai* means 'wealth'); Gauḥ (bull); Nauḥ (boat).

37b-39. Words ending in consonants: Anaḍvān (bullock); Godhuk (one who milks cows), (liṭ. one who licks), Dve (two); Trayaḥ (three); Catvāraḥ (four); Rājā (king); Pānthāḥ (way); Daṇḍī (one with a staff); Brahmahā (a slayer of a Brahmin), Pañca (five), Aṣṭa and Aṣṭau (eight); O sage (these are all examples of consonant ending words). (The following too are words ending in consonants): Samrāṭ (Emperor); (the next two words are defective); Pratyaṅ (the individual soul); Pumān (man); Mahān (great); Dhīman (Intelligent); Vidvān (learned); Pipāṭhīḥ (one who desires to read); Doḥ (the arm); Uśanā (the preceptor of the demons). All these above words are in the masculine (and are typical of nouns ending in different consonants.)

40[29]-45. The following are feminine words ending in vowels and consonants viz.: Rādhā; Sarvā (all); Gati (goal, gait); Gopī (cowherdess); Strī (a woman); Śrī (glory); Dhenu (cow); Vadhū (bride); Svasā (sister); Go (gauḥ) (cow); Nauḥ (boat), Upānat[30] (shoe); Dyauḥ (heaven); Glauḥ (moon);—Kṣut (hunger); Kakubh (the quarters) Saṁvit (knowledge) ; Ruk (lustre); Viṭ (excrement); Bhāḥ (splendour). All the above words are feminine. (Then the neuter nouns) : Tapas (penance) ; Kulam (family); Somapam (that which imbibes Soma juice) ; Akṣi (eye); Grāmaṇi (leading in the village); Ambu (water) ; Khalapu (that which sweeps); Kartṛ (that which does*).

Svanaḍut (that which has good bull); Vimaladyu (a non-cloudy bright day); Vāḥ (water) ; Catvāri (four) ; Idam (this) ; Etat (this) Brahman; Ahaḥ (day) ; Daṇḍī (having a stick); Asṛk (blood). There are some words beginning with *Tyad***. The different forms of *Go+Añc*[31] are Gavāk, Gavāṅ, Goak, Go-aṅ and Goṅ; Tiryak (animal); Yakṛt (spleen); Śakṛt (ordure); Dadat (that which gives) ; Bhavat (that which takes place); Pacat (that which cooks); Tudat (that which inflicts pain) ; Dīvyat (that which shines); Dhanus (bow) ; Pipāṭhīḥ (that which reads) ; Payas (milk, water) ; Adas (this) ; Supumāṁsi (those which have good men) ; I shall mention a few qualities, objects, and actions of the three *liṅgas* (genders); Śukla (bright clean) ; Kīlālapāḥ (goblins); Śuci (white); Grāmaṇī (leader of the village); Sudhīḥ (intelligent); Paṭuḥ (clever); Svayambhūḥ (self-born) ; Kartā (Agent), Mātā (mother), Pitā (father), Nā (Nṛ).

46-47a. (Defective***)

47b-49. Sarva (all); Viśva (all); Ubhaya (both); Ubhau (both); Anya (other); Antara (interval); Itara (other); Uttara (higher); Uttama (highest, excellent); Nema (half, part); Asama (unequal), Sama; Īṣa (one possessing strength); Purvottara (north-east); Dakṣiṇa (southern) Uttarādhara (northwest) ; Apara (another) ; Catura (clever) Yāvat (As much [relative]) ; Yuṣmad (you) ; Asmad (we); Prathama (first) ; Carama (last); Alpa (little) ; Ardhaka (half).

50. (Defective) and the Avyayas (indeclinables) (?)

---

* Two words after this viz. *Cātiri* and *Vātinu* appear defective. Are They *ca—atiri* and *Vā—atinu* (non-navigable).

** The *tyadādi* group consists of *tyad, tad, yad, etad* etc.

*** Probably the following words in V. 46: *Satya, anāyuṣ, apuṁsa, mata, bhramara, dīrgha-pāt..agarha...svarṇa, bahu* (47a *unintelligible*).

51. In the sense of 'child' or 'Progeny' Taddhita suffix* is used. The examples are :— Pāṇḍavas (sons of Pāṇḍu); Śraidhara (son of Śrīdhara i.e. Viṣṇu); Gārgya[32] (descendant of Garga); Nāḍāyana[33] (Descendant of Naḍa); Ātreya[34] (son of Atri); Gāṅgeya (son of Gaṅgā); Paitṛṣvasrīya (son of father's sister).

52. In the sense of "Deity", "that which belongs to", the example is Aindra (that which belongs to Indra, that the deity of which is Indra); Brāhma means belonging to Brahmā; these two refer to *Havis* and *Bali* (offerings and oblations). When the object and the agent (of a verb) are united with the action (Taddhita suffix is used as in the case of) *Dhaureya* (one worthy of bearing burden) and *Kauṅkuma* (pertaining to saffron).

53. In the sense of 'born of', Taddhita suffix is used and the example is Kānīna (born of a virgin); the word Kṣatriya (one who protects from wound), Vaidika (one who follows the injunctions of the Vedas). Here the suffix—*Aka* is used. 'Cora' itself is 'Caura'. Here the suffix *aṇ* is used in the same meaning. Both Cora and Caura mean 'thief' The usage, 'he sees the face like the moon" is for the purpose of equality.

54. In the sense of an abstract noun the suffixes—*Tvam* etc. are used. Examples are Brāhmaṇatva, Brāhmaṇatā and Brāhmaṇya (all mean Brahminhood). The word *Goman* means "one who has cows", similarly, Dhanin and Dhanavān mean "one who has wealth". In the sense of magnitude Kiyān (How much) is used.

55. The words Tundila and Śraddhā-lu are derived after the suffixes have been added in the sense of "that which has occurred." 'Tundila' (one who has protuberant belly) and 'Sraddhālu' means "one who has faith", Dantura (one who has long projecting teeth). In the following cases the Taddhita suffix-'*In*' is in the sense of 'it exists', 'possessing' Sragvin (one who has garlands), Tapasvin (one who performs penance), Medhāvin (one who has excellent intellect), Māyāvin one who has Māyā (deception).

---

* Though we can trace the examples in these verses to Pāṇini, the treatment is not systematic in the NP. *vide* : Intro.

56. The words Vācāla and Vācāṭa are used to indicate 'one who speaks many despicable things', the suffixes Kalpa and Deśīya are used in the sense of 'a little short of'.

57-58. Kavikalpa and Kavideśya mean "one who is almost a poet". The word Paṭujātīya is used in indicating similitude. In indicating contempt the suffix *Pāśa* is used. 'Vaidyapāśa', means 'one who is not worthy of being a physician'. The word Vaidyarūpa means 'a praiseworthy physician'. O sage, the word 'Dṛṣṭa-cara' is used in the sense of 'what it was formerly!' In the sense of abundancy, etc., the suffix 'Maya' is used e.g. Annamaya (full of cooked food), Mṛṇmaya (mostly of clay) and Strīmaya (abounding in women).

59. The word Lajjita means 'one in whom bashfulness has occurred'. O Nārada, in indicating excess Śreyān and Śreṣṭha are used. They mean very excellent and most excellent; Kṛṣṇatara (blacker); Śuklatama (whitest). From the pronoun Kim (what) indeclinables are derived! [They are :]

60-62. Kiṁtarām, Atitarām (too much), Abhihyuccaistarām (highly, etc.). To indicate the measure some suffixes are used. Jānudaghnam, Jānudvayasam and Jānumātram (upto the knee). To specify one among many, we say 'Katara' (which of the two?). In order to specify the ordinals there are suffixes : Dvitīya (second), Tṛtīya (third), Cāturtha (fourth), Ṣaṣṭha (sixth), Pañcama (fifth) Ekādaśa (eleventh). O Nārada, Katipaya, Katitha and Kati mean; 'How many?'

63. Viṁśa and Viṁśatitama both mean 'twentieth'. Similarly 'Śata-tama' and other words. O leading sage, in order to indicate divisions of number there are suffixes as for example : Dvidhā, Dvedhā, Dvaidhā (in two ways).

64. In indicating frequencies, suffixes are used e.g. Pañcakṛtvaḥ (five times): Dviḥ (twice), Triḥ (three times) Bahuśaḥ (many times). Dvitayam and Dvayam mean the same. So also Tritayam and Trayam.

65. Suffix—rā is used in signifying dimunitive forms Kuṭīra (a small hut); Śamīra (a small fruit, legume) Śuṇḍāra (a small trunk of the elephant), Straiṇa (belonging to women) Pauṣṇa (belonging to the sun). Tundibha (one who has the umbilical region 'protruding'; Vṛndāraka (Deva); Kṛṣīvala (farmer).

66. Malina (dirty); Vikaṭa (hideous); Gomi (an owner of cattle); Bhaurikī (treasurer), Utkaṭa (exceedingly manifest); Avaṭīṭa and Avanāṭa both mean flat-nosed. Nibiḍa (dense, compact); Ikṣuśākinam (having sugarcane as crop?).

67. Nibirīsama (compact, crooked nosed), Iṣukārī, Vitto, *Vidyat, Cana** (?), Vidyācuñcu (celebrated for learning); Bahutitham (many days); Parvata (mountain), Sṛṅgiṇaḥ (of one which has peaks).

68-69. Svāmin (owner); Viṣamarūpyam (?), Upatyakā (a land at the foot of a mountain); Adhityakā (a table land) Cilla (the Bengal kite); Cipiṭa (flat-nosed); Cikva[35] (?) Vātūla (affected by wind, crazy); Kutapa (the eight Muhurta of the day); Valla (covering); Himelu (competent to endure snow). Kahodā[36] (?), Copaḍa[37] (cream MW-402), Urṇāyu (ram, woollen blanket); Marutta (a king of the solar race); Ekākin (alone); Carmaṇvatī (name of a river).

70. Jyotsnā (moonlight); Tamisrā (night); Ṣṭhīvat (spittle); Kakṣīvardyamaṇuatī (?);[38] Āsandī (a small couch) Cakrīvan (An ass) Tūṣṇīka (Taciturn, silent); Jalpaka (garrulous); (Reading *Jalpaketyapi*).

71. O Nārada, to the words Kam and Śam seven terminations are added in the sense of possession. They are VA, Bha, Yus, Ti, Tu, Ta and Ya and the new words formed are Kamva, Kambha, Kaṁyus, Kaṁti, Kaṁtu, Kaṁtaḥ, Kamyaḥ, as well as Śamva, Śambha, Śaṁyu, Śamti, Śamtu, Śaṁta and Śaṁyah.

Similarly, Ahaṁyu (an arrogant fellow), Śubhaṁyu (one endowed with auspiciousness).

Conjugation

72-73. The forms of the roots of different conjugational classes in the different tenses and moods are given in the third person singular:

I conj. : *Bhavati* (is), *Babhūva* (was), *Bhavitā* and *Bhaviṣyati* (will be), *Bhavatu* (let it be), *Abhavat* (was), *Bhavet* (should be), *Bhūyāt* (may it be), *Abhūt* (was), *Abhaviṣyat* (if it had been).

II conj. : *Atti* (eats), *Jaghāsa* (ate), *Attā* and *Atsyati* (will eat), *Attu* (let him eat), *Ādat* (ate), *Adyāt* (twice) (should eat, may eat), *Aghāsat* (ate), *Ātsyat* (if it had eaten).

* Probably, the word is *Vidyā-caṇa* (well-known for learning).

74-76. III conj.: *Juhoti* (performs a *Homa*), *Jahāva* and *Juhavāñcakāra* (performed the *Homa*), *Hotā*, *Hoṣyati* (will perform the *Homa*) *Juhotu* (let him perform the *Homa*), *Ajuhot* (he performed the *Homa*), *Juhuyāt* (he should perform the *Homa*), *Hūyāt* (May he perform the *Homa*), *Ahauṣit* (He performed the *Homa*); *Ahoṣyat* (if he had performed the Homa).

IV conj. : *Divyati* (he gambles) *Dideva* (he gambled), *Devitā*, *Deviṣyati* (he will gamble) (*Divyatu* omitted in the text), *Adīvyat* (he gambled), *Dīvyet* (he should gamble), *Divyāt* (may he gamble) *Adevīt* (he gambled), *Adeviṣyat* (if he had gambled).

V conj.: *Sunoti* (he distils), *Suṣāva* (he distilled), *Sotā* and *Soṣyati* (he will distil), *Sunotu* (Let him distil) *Asunot* (he distilled), *Sunuyāt* (he should distil), *Sūyāt* (may he distil), *Asāvit* (he distilled), *Asoṣyat* (if he had distilled).

VI conj. : *Tudati* (he inflicts pain) *Tutoda* (he inflicted pain); *Tottā*, *Totsyati* (he will inflict pain), *Tudatu* (let him inflict pain), *Atudat* (he inflicted pain), *Tudet* (he should inflict pain), *Tudyāt* (may he inflict pain), *Atautsīt* (he inflicted pain), *Atotsyat* (if he had inflicted pain).

VII conj. : *Ruṇaddhi* (he impedes), *Rurodha* (he impeded) *Roddhā*, *Rotsyati* (he will impede), *Ruṇaddhu* (let him impede) *Aruṇat* (he impeded), *Rundhyāt* (he should impede) (This is omitted in text). *Rudhyāt* (may he impede), *Arautsīt* (and the alternative form *Arudhat* which is omitted in the text) (he impeded) *Arotsyat* (if he had impeded).

77-79. VIII conj. : *Tanoti* (he spreads or stretches) *Tatāna* (he stretched), *Tanitā*, *Taniṣyati* (he will stretch), *Tanotu* (let him stretch), *Atanot* (he stretched), *Tanuyāt* (he should stretch), *Tanyāt* (may he stretch—omitted in the text), *Atanīt* and *Atānīt* (he stretched) *Ataniṣyat* (if he had stretched).

IX conj. : *Krīṇāti* (he buys) *Cikrāya* (he bought), *Kretā*, *Kreṣyati* (he will buy), *Krīṇātu* (let him buy) *Akrīṇat* (he bought), *Krīṇīyāt* (he should buy), *Krīyāt* (may he buy), *Akraiṣīt* (he bought), *Akreṣyat* (if he had bought).

X conj. : *Corayati* (he steals), *Corayāmāsa* (he stole), *Corayitā* and *Corayiṣyati* (he will steal), *Corayatu* (let him steal), *Acorayat* (he stole), *Corayet* (he should steal) *Coryāt* (may he steal), *Acūcurat* (he stole), *Acoriṣyat* (? *Acorayiṣyat*) (if he had stolen).

Thus there are ten *Gaṇas* or conjugational classes.

The causal form is *Bhāvayati* (causes something to be), the desiderative form is *Bubhūṣati* (desires to become). As the frequentative form, O sage (we have) *Bobhūyate* (again and again he becomes).

80-81. In the *Yaṅluk* (i.e. where *Yaṅ* termination is omitted) the form is *Bobhaviti*. O Nārada, in order to denote wish or emulating action. *Putrīyati* is the form meaning 'desires a son for himself' or 'behaves like a son'. O Brāhmaṇa know that a root with an *Anudātta Ātmanepada* (low tone) or letter '*N*' as its '*IT*' (i.e. indicatory mark) takes *Ātmanepada* terminations. When the duty is interchanged it takes *Ātmanepada* (as for example *vyatilunite*, 'he reaps the harvest' (though it is some one else's duty). The root *Viś* - after the preposition *Ni* takes *Ātmanepada* terminations. Where the *Ātmanepada* does not have access, the *Parasmaipada* terminations are used by grammarians.

82-85. If the root has a *Svarita* or *Ṇ* for its indicatory mark, it takes both padas (but when the fruit of the action goes to the agent, it takes the *Ātmanepada* terminations). In the impersonal passive, *Yak* termination is used. O sage, in order to indicate the excellence and facility in the action, the activity of the agent is not taken into consideration. Then the other *Kārakas* too take up the term *Kartṛ* (agent), as in the use *Asiḥ Sādhu Chinatti* (the knife cuts well), *Sthālī Pacati* (the vessel cooks). If the root is transitive, the terminations are added to both the impersonal and the passive bases (?) Hence the use *Odanaḥ pacyate* (the rice is cooked). If the root is intransitive it is impersonal and active only. O sage, if the action and the fruit of the action are in one and the same person, it is intransitive.

86-88* If they (i.e. action and the fruit to the action) are stationed in different substantives, the root is said to be

---

* cf. *gauṇe karmaṇi duhyādeḥ pradhāne nī-hṛ-kṛṣvahām /*
buddhi-bhakṣārthayoḥ śabda-karmakāṇām nijecchayā //
prayojya-karmaṇyanyeṣāṁ ṇyantānāṁ tādayo matāḥ /
Kārikā quoted in *Siddhānta Kaumudī* on Pān. 7.1.69.

transitive. When roots that take two objects are to be changed into passive, the secondary object is turned into the nominative in the case of roots *Duh*, *Yāc* etc. (e.g. *Gauḥ Duhyate Payaḥ*). But in regard to the roots *Ni*, *Hṛ*, *Kṛṣ*, and *Vah*, the main object is turned into the nominative in the passive (e.g. *Ajā grāmaṁ Niyate* "The goat is taken to the village"). But in the case of roots of the sense of knowledge or eating, any of the two objects may be turned into the nominative (e.g. *Bhojyate māṇavakam odanaḥ* or *Bhojyate māṇavakaḥ odanam*). (In the case of causal roots, (the object so caused) the *Prayojyakarman* is changed into the nominative. (*Devadattaḥ grāmaṁ gamyate*—Devadatta is made to go to the village). The *tiṅ* terminations are remembered in the receptacle of the fruit as well as the action. The action is important in the case of the fruit. The meaning of the *Tiṅ* is an attribute.

89-90 The *Kṛtya* suffixes are used in the impersonal and passive forms. The *Kṛt* suffixes are used in the active forms. Example for a *Kṛtya* suffix is *Edhitavyam* and *Edhanīyam*. The Agent and the *Kārakas* etc. are cited in the event of the past (?). *Gamya* etc. are indicated in the future sense and the remaining is considered applicable in the present. (?)

Compounds

91-92. Examples of compound words are given now: *Adhistri* and *Yathāśakti* are examples of *Avyayībhāva*. Examples of *Tatpuruṣa** are *Rāmāśrita*, *Dhānyārthī* (one seeking grains) *Yūpadāru* (wood intended for sacrificial post) *Vyāghrabhī* (fear from tigers) *Rājapuruṣa* (A king's officer) and *Akṣaśauṇḍa* (clever at the dice). Now *Dvigu* is explained: *Pañca-gava* "an aggregate of five cows", *Daśagrāmī* (collection of ten villages), *Triphalā* (the three myrobalans). The last word is conventionally used in this sense.

93. When the two words constituting a compound are equally important and have the same meaning it is called *Karmadhāraya*. Examples are *Nilotpala* (blue lotus) *Mahāṣaṣṭhī*

---

* These examples are according to cases e.g. *Rāmaṁ āśritaḥ Rāmāśritaḥ* is the accusative (Dvitiyā) Tatpuruṣa and illustrates Pan. 2.1.14, while the last *akṣeṣu śauṇḍaḥ akṣa-śauṇḍaḥ*, a locative (*Saptamī*) Tatpuruṣa is an illustration of Pan. 2.1.40.

(A form of Durgā in Tantras). The example for *Nañtatpuruṣa* is *abrāhmaṇaḥ* (non-Brahmin). *Kumbhakāra* (potter). —This is an example of a *Kṛt Samāsa.*

94. O Brāhmaṇa, the examples for a *Bahuvrihi* compound where the meaning refers to another word (as its qualifying adjunct) are: *Prāptodaka* (where the water has reached), it qualifies *Grāma* (village) *Pañcagu* (one ‥ ɔ has five cows *Rūpavadbhāryaḥ* (one whose wife is beautiful), *Madhyāhnaḥ* (middle of the day), *Sasutādikaḥ* (one who is accompained by sons and others).

95. The particle *Ca* has two meanings viz. *Samuccaya* aggregate, assemblage) and *Anvācaya* (secondary statement). The example for the former is *Gurum ca Īśaṁca Bhajasva* (worship the preceptor and God). The example for the latter is *Bhikṣām aṭa, gāṁ ca ānaya* (Go begging and also bring a cow).

96. Example for *Itaretarayoga Dvandva* is *Rāmakṛṣṇau* (i.e. Rama and Kṛsṇa). As a *Samāhāra* (collection the form is Rāmakṛṣṇam). O Brāhmaṇa, only the Brahman is worshipped. As it is devoid of *Dvandvas* (clashing opposites).

CHAPTER FIFTYTWO

1. NP. 3 is an echo-*verbatim* reproduction of Pāṇ. (Pāṇini) 1.2.45 & 2.3.46. Thus Pāṇ. 1.2.45 is :
Arthavad-a-dhātur apratyayaḥ prā tipadikam
NP. 3b
Arthavat prātipadikaṁ dhātu-pratyaya-varjitam

2. Pāṇ. 2.3.47.
3. Pāṇ. 2.3.2.
4. Pāṇ. 2.3-4.
5. Pāṇ 2.3.18.
6. Pāṇ. 1.4.35, 1.4.33.
7. Pāṇ. 1.4.45, 2.3.36.
8. Pāṇ. 2.3.29, 1.4.88, 2.3.10.
9. When certain prepositions, particles or adverbs are not connected with a verb, yet they govern a noun in particular cases they are called *Karma-pravacanīya* e.g. ā : *ā mukteḥ saṁsāraḥ* 'the *saṁsāra* lasts till *Mokṣa*'; *anu* : *Japam anu prāvarṣata* 'It rained heavily after the performance of *Japa*.'
10. Pāṇ. 1.4.90.
11. Pāṇ. 1.4.91.
12. Pāṇ. 1.4.85-86.
13. Pāṇ. 1.4.87.
14. Pāṇ 2.3.12. The *Sūtra* further clarifies that the cases are used in denoting the 'object' when actual motion is meant and the object is not a word expressing 'path'.
15. Pāṇ. 2.3.17.
16. Pāṇ. 2.3.16.
17. Pāṇ. 2.3.15.
18. The original *sūtra* is *Saha-yukte' pradhāne* 2.3.19 which means : when the sense is that the word in the Instrumental case is not the principal but the accompaniment of the principal thing or person. For example : *putreṇa Sahāgataḥ pitā* 'the father has come with the son. The same rule holds about the synonyms of *Saha* such as *Sāka, Sārdha.* —*Siddhānta Kaumudī.*
19. Pāṇ. 2.3.20 For example : *pādena Khañjaḥ* 'Lame foot'.
20. Pāṇ. 2.3.39.
21. Pāṇ. 2.3.41.
22. Pāṇ. 2.3.26.
23. Pāṇ. 2.3.65.
24. After these the Instrumental case must be employed to denote the agent and the Accusative case to denote the object. For example, *Viṣṇunā hatā daityāḥ* or *Daityān hatavān Viṣṇuḥ* 'Viṣṇu killed demons'. This Sūtra (2.3.69) debars the Genitive which would have been applicable under Pāṇ. 2.3.65. The NP. however, partially quotes Pāṇ. 2.3.69 which includes

affixes ending in-*U*, -*Uka*, -*Tṛn*, and those having the sense of *Khal*.

25. The *Lakāras* are as follows : *Laṭ* (Present), *Liṭ* (Perfect) *Luṭ* (First Future), *Lṛṭ* (Second Future), *Leṭ* (Vedic Subjunctive), *Loṭ* (Imperative). *Laṅ* (Imperfect), *Liṅ* (Potential), *Luṅ* (Aorist), *Lṛṅ* (Conditional).

26. Old traditional Sanskrit grammarians use the term *Prathama Puruṣa, Madhyama Puruṣa and Uttama Puruṣa* for what European and (imitating them) Indian grammarians designate as the 'third person', the 'second Person' and 'the first person'. *In translating the following verses I use the modern terminology though the NP uses the old traditional terms.*

27. But Bhaṭṭoji Dikṣita on Pāṇ. 6.1.101 clarifies that ṛ+ṛ will be either ṛ or ṛ thus Hotṛ+Ṛkāra will also be Hotṛkāra. The NP.'s *Pitrarṣabha* is doubtful. The v.l. Pitṛṣabha is better.

28. Here Nom. sg. *Rāmaḥ* is necessary as there is duplication of the Instrumental case in the verse and the nom. goes unrepresented. An emendation like *Rāmaḥ sarvahitaṁ karoti* 'Rama does things beneficial to all, may be suggested. The italicised words contain the declension of Rāma (Masc. Noun ending in—a) in the sg. no.

29. V. 40 illustrates Pāṇini's sūtras for declension of feminine nouns ending in vowels e.g. 7.1.18, 7.3.114, etc.

30. Pāṇ. 8.2.34.

31. *Gavāc* (he who honours cows or who drives cows) has the following bases according to the meaning—the traditional verse quoted in the *Siddhānta Kaumudī* on Pāṇ. 8.2.68 records the following bases : Go-añca, Gavāñca, Go'ñca, Goac, Gavāc and Go'c.

32. Pāṇ. 4.1.105.

33. Pāṇ. 4.199.

34. Vide Vārttika Pāṇ. 4.1.110.

35. If *Cikka* (Areca nut).

36. N. of a man with the patronym Kauṣitaki—MW-266.

37. a Deśya word.

38. *Kakṣīvat* for *Kakṣyā-vat*—*Kāśikā* on Pan. 8.2.12. A Vedic seer of many Sūktas. But the next word—untraced, possibly carmaṇvat.

CHAPTER FIFTY THREE

*The Exposition of Nirukta**

Sanandana continued :

1. I shall now delineate to you the excellent accessory of the Veda, called Nirukta. It is said to be of five kinds and pertains to Vedic conjugations or verbal formations.

2. Therein at some places is found epenthesis, in other cases is seen metathesis, at some places is found modification of the syllable, at other places, (we get) haplology.

3. O Nārada, where due to the change or loss of a syllable, light is thrown on the special connotation of the root, it is called *Saṁyoga*.

4. (Now follow the illustrations of these processes :) By addition of a syllable, the word *Haṁsa* ($<\sqrt{}$ *han* —) 'a swan' is formed[1] (by the addition of *sa*). The word *Siṁha*[2] 'a lion' is formed by metathesis, *gūḍhotmā* (*gūḍha* + *ātmā*) is formed due to change of syllable (here the vowel *ā* is changed to *u*) while in *pṛṣodara* (*pṛṣat* + *Udara*) there is a loss of a letter (*t*).

5. The fifth kind of modification should be known in words like *bhramara* ' a bumble bee' (from √*bhram* + *ara* by the *uṇādi sūtra artikamibhramicami* etc., cf. √*kam* — $>$ *kamara*, √cam — $>$ *camara*)

In the Vedic (language) there are changes or options in the formations of words etc. Here is the example of Punarvasū. (In the Vedas, the two stars *Punarvasū* may optionally be singular and connote a dual vide, Pāṇ. I. 2. 61).

6. The form *nabhasvat* (*nabhas* +*vat* 'like the sky' vaporous', retains $\frac{1}{2}$ *S* though followed by — *vat* (vide the *Vārttika*- '*nabho 'ṅgiromanuṣāṁ vatyupasaṅkhyānam* on Pāṇ. I. 4. 9 or by the *Vārttika Vṛṣaṇvasvaśvayoḥ***/. The form *Vṛṣaṇśva* retains $\frac{1}{2}$ *n* $\frac{1}{2}$ even

---

*Being a technical and difficult subject, an explanation is added in the translation itself as mere literal translation would be unintelligible.

**वृषण्वस्वश्वयोः ।

though the derivation is *vṛṣā aśvo yasya saḥ*, (whereas in classical Sk. it would be *Vṛṣāśva*. Sometimes the *Parasmaipada* is used in stead of the *Ātmanepada* (In Classical Sk., the prepositions or proverbs like *pra* -, *ā* -precede the verb and are called *gati*). But in the Vedic, these *pre*-positions are used after the verbs (as *post*-positions). They are called *gatis* (e.g. *haribhyām yāhyoka ā* RV. VII. 32.4) Here *ā-yāhi* is the verb but *ā-* is placed separately after the verb in the Vedic.

7. (In the Vedic) there is a change in the cases. For example, *dadhnā juhoti*, 'He offers oblations of curds (into the fire)'. Here the word *dadhi* is in the Instrumental case in stead of the Acc. case. But as per Pāṇ.II.3.3. the object of the verb √*hu* — 'to sacrifice' takes the terminations of the Instr, as well as of the Acc. case.

The Aorist form of *abhi* + *ut* + √*sad* — is *abhyutsādayāmaka* (instead of Cl. Sk—Classical Sanskrit—*abhyudasiṣadat*) in the Vedic (as per Pāṇ. III.1.42), and *dhvanayit* (<√*dhvan* 'to sound') as per Pāṇ. III.1.51 (in Cl. Sk. *adidhvanat* is found. But in RV.I.162.15 we find : *mā tvā'gnir dhvanayit*). These are the prominent instances. The forms like *niṣṭarkya* (> *nis* +√*kṛt* — 'to cut') and others are similar[3] And also formations like *gṛbhāya* and others. Here √ *gṛbh* + *śāyac* √ *gṛbhāya*, the —h in *grah* 'to seize' is √ transformed to bh i.e. √*grah* -< √*gṛbh* —in Vedic (vide Pāṇ. III.1.84 and S. K. on it.[4] e.g. *gṛbhāya jihvayā madhu* (RV.VIII.17.5).

8. Due to optional formations (in the Vedic) the writers on this science desire (accept) changes in declension, conjugation, *Padas* (*Parsmaipada* and *Ātmanepada*,) gender, person, tense, consonants, vowels, causatives and *yaṅ* (the intensive suffix—*ya*).

9. The verse lists the following peculiar Vedic forms :

rātri : *rātri* + *ṅip* in the Vedic as per Pāṇ. IV.1.31 for class. Sk. *rātri* 'a night'.

Vibhvi : fem. of *vibhu* as per Pāṇ. IV 1.47 we get *vibhu*+*ṅiṣ* (i.e. the affix—*i*) in forming the feminine.

Kadrū : As per Pāṇ. IV.1.71 the feminine affix—*Ūṅ* (—*Ū*) comes after the words *Kadrū* 'tawny' (and *kamaṇḍalu* 'water bowl').

āviṣṭya : As per *Vārttika* on the above sūtra the affix—*tyap* is added to the word *āvis* in the Veda e.g. *āviṣṭyo vardhate* /

Vājasaneyinaḥ : As per Pāṇ. IV.3.10.6 the affix—*ṇini* comes in the sense of "enunciated by him", after the word Śaunaka e.g. (*Śaunakinaḥ* "who study the *chandas* as per Śaunaka." Similarly, *Vājasaneya* + *ṇini* = Vājasaneyin : who studies the Veda as per Vājasaneya.

10. The following Vedic forms are explained as below: *Karṇebhiḥ* : Instr. Pl. of *Karṇa* "an ear". The termination —*ebhiḥ* instead of the usual —*ais* as per *bahulaṁ chandasi* (Pāṇ. II.4.76.).

yaśobhagya : (*yaśo-bhāgya*— in the printed text of the NP is not correct) is dissolved as follows : *yaśas tad eva bhagaḥ* : This Karmadhāraya compound has *bhaga* changed to *bhagya* by the addition of the suffix—*yat* as per Pāṇ. IV.4.131,32.

yaśobhagya and others include forms like *veśobhagya*. *caturakṣaram* indicates four-lettered formulas like *āśrāvaya astu śrauṣaṭ*.[5]

devāsaḥ : The Nom. pl. of *deva* 'a god' (vide Pāṇ. VII.1.50) *sarva-devatāti* : *sarva-deva* + *tātil* (pleonastic) e.g. *savitā naḥ suvatu sarvatātim* / —RV.X.36.14 *tvāvat* 'like you'. Here, as in *asmad* & *yuṣmad*, the affix—*vatup* showing similarity is added.

11. The following forms are formed thus :

ubhayāvinam : Here the possessive affix *vini* (i.e. *vin*) is added (optionally) as per Pāṇ. V.2.122 and the final—*a* in *Ubhaya* is lengthened as per *Vārttika* : *Chandovit prakaraṇe dīrghaś ceti vaktavyam* /

Pralayādyāḥ is prob. a misprint.

Tṛcam : *tri* — *Ṛc* (a Sūkta with three *Ṛks*). This form is derived, thus : *tri* > *tṛ* by *Saṁprasāraṇa* + *C* < *Tṛc*.

*apaspṛdhethām**

avyāt—**as in *vasubhir no avyāt ayo asman mukhas tathā* / If *ayo* be a misprint for *āpo*, the quotation in the NP is probably :

**apaspṛdhethām*—Imp. 2nd p. dual of *apa*+√*spardh* 'to challenge'). As per Pāṇ. VI.1.36, the reduplication of the root, vocalisation of *ra* and the elision of *a* irregularly is accepted in the Vedic.

***avyāt*—As per Pāṇ. VI.1.116, the *e* or *o* retain their original form in the middle of Vedic verse in the case of *avyāt* (*avadyāt*, *avakramuḥ*, etc.) though 'a' in these has -a '*v*' & 'y' following it.

āpo asmān mātaraḥ śundhyantu / ṚV X.7.10 and the form is as per Pāṇ VI.1.118, the short *a* is retained after *āpo* (also *'uṣāṇo, Vṛṣṇo* etc.)

12. The following forms are derived thus :

Sagarbhyaḥ : 'a brother of the whole blood, by the same father and mother'. Here *sa* = *samāna* 'common' but the affix—*yaṅ* (—*ya*) is as per Pāṇ. IV.4.114.

sthāpadi or *asthāpadi* (a misprint prob. for *aṣṭāpadi* ?)

Ṛtvyam 'seasonal' *ṛtau bhavaṁ*. This formation from *ṛtu* is as per Pāṇ. VI.4.175 the final —*u* is changed to —*va* (similarly *vāstva* < *vāstu*)

Rajiṣṭha : *ṛju* > *iṣṭha* 'the most straight-forward & delicate' vide Pāṇ. VI.4.162 for the change of *ṛ* > *ra*— before the affixes — *iyas*, — *iṣṭha*

tri-pañcakam :— *triṇi pañcakāni yatra Bahuvrīhi comp.*

Hiraṇyaya—'golden, abounding in gold'

Hiraṇya + *ya* (*mayaṭ*)

Hiraṇyayena is a part of the *mantra hiraṇyayena savitā rathena* (RV.I.35.2)

naram—(misprint ? otherwise no Vedic speciality)

parame vyoman : instead of *Vyomni*, the Loc. sg. term is dropped as per *supāṁ suluk* /

13. The explanation of the following irregular forms :

urviyā (Sk. *uru-ṇā*) But —*yā* is affixed instead of —*ṇā*, as per *Vārttika*—*iyāḍiyāji* etc. on Pāṇ. VII. 1.39.

svaprayā—(?) Is it a misprint for *svapnayā* ?

vāravadhvāt—(?) Is it a misprint for *vārayadhvāt* ?

Aduha (?) The root √*duh* is obvious but the special formation—not clear.

Vadhi (?) The Vedic special form is *Vadhim* & not *Vadhi*. We have in RV. I.165.8, X.28.7 the form *Vadhim* from √*Vadh*. The Cl. Sk. form would be *avadhiṣam*.

yajadhvainam < *yajadhvam* + *enam*. These are joined after dropping — m of °*dhvam*.

Emasi — irregular for *imaḥ* by Pāṇ. VII.1.46.

snātvi (as in *svinnaḥ snātvi malād iva* — AV. VI.115. 3, VS.20.20). Also —*tvi* for Class. Sk. —*tvā* vide Pāṇ. VIII.1.49 (cf. pītvī < √pā — to drink)

gatvā pacāsthabhiḥ : Out of this *asthabhiḥ* may be a

misprint for *aṣṭhabhiḥ*, Instr. pl. of *asthin*. The rest is anybody's guess. (possibly *gatvāya cāsthabhiḥ* /).

14. (The following irregular forms are explained). Gonām — Gen. Pl. of *go* 'a cow'—Pāṇ. VII. 1.57

Aparihvarataḥ As per Pāṇ. VII 2.31 √ *hru* is substituted for √*hvar* (*Bhvādi* 978) before a participial affix.

cāturi or *āturi* (?) prob. a misprint.

Grasita ppp. of √*gras* — (Cl. Sk. *grasta*) treated as *seṭ* (cf. *skabhita*) vide Pāṇ. VII.2.34.

Paśya — Nothing special.

Dadhat as in *dadhad ratnāni dāśuṣe* RV.IV.15.3. It is the Ved. subjunctive of √*dhā*.

Babhūtha—Perfect 2nd p. sg. of √*bhū* in Vedic, vide Pāṇ. VII.2.64.

Pramiṇānti is prob. a misprint for *pramiṇanti* for classical SK *pramiṇanti* — *mi* — is shortened to— *mi* — as per Pāṇ. VII.1.81

Avīvṛdhat — Aor — 3rd p. sg. of √*vṛdh* — As per Pāṇ. VII. 4.8., in Vedic (*Chandas*), *ṛ* is substituted invariably for penultimate *ṝ* or *ṛ* of a causative stem in the Reduplicative Aorist.

15. (The following forms are derived as follows :) *mitrayu* 'friendly-minded'. As per Pāṇ. VII.4.35, rules of lengthening or the substitution of —*ī* for the final vowel of the stem before the affix *Kyac* is not applicable in the Vedic.

Durasyu—*duṣṭa ivā'carati* & 'Wishing to do harm'. As per Pāṇ. VII.4.36, *duṣṭa* becomes *duras* — before the affix—*kyac*. [The NP. gives *durasvā* which is prob. a mis-print).

hātvā: Abs. of √*hā* 'to abandon' √*hā*. >√*hi* (hi) optionally in Vedic (Pāṇ. VII.4.44).

Sudhita : 'well-placed' ppp. of *Su* —√dhā. Pāṇ. VII.4.45 sanctions √*dhā* >ppp —*dhita* in *Sudhita*, *Vasudhita*, *nemadhita*.

Dadharti should have been *dādharti*. As per Pāṇ. VII.4.65, in Vedic the Caus. Aor. 3 p. sg. of √*dhṛ* becomes *dādharti* cf. *dardharti*, *dardharṣi* sanctioned in the same Sūtra.

Svavadbhih : Instr. pl. of *Svavas*. As per *Vārt*. on Pāṇ. VII.4.45, —*t* is substituted for —*s* in the case of *Svavas*. 'He whose protection is good (derived from Su— √*av*) 'to protect well'.

Sasūva. — Perf.— 3 p. sg. of √*sū* 'to give birth to' Formation as per Pāṇ. VII.4.74.

Dhiṣva — Imp. II p. sg. of √*dhā* — as per Pāṇ. VII 4.45 (but Cl. Sk. form is *dhatsva*).

16. (the following forms are explained thus :)

praprāya as in *praprāyam agniḥ* (RV.VII.8.4) shows the reduplication of the prefix *pra* — as per Pāṇ. VIII.1.6 Pāṇini sanctions *pra*, *sam*, *upa* and *ut* as *pādapūraṇas* (the completers of the foot of a verse).

Harivate — Here *v* is substituted for *m* of the affix — *mat*, as the stem Hari ends in —*i*. Pāṇ. VIII.2. 15 sanctions this change for stems ending in —*i* —*ī* or *ṛ*.

Akṣaṇvataḥ (a misprint for *akṣaṇvantaḥ*) vide RV. X. 71.7 (*akṣaṇvantaḥ karṇavantaḥ sakhāyaḥ*) /

A— kṣaṇ — vat 'not injuring'. As per Pāṇ. VIII.2.16. The augment— *nuṭ* is added to the possessive affix, after stems ending in — *an*.

Supathi — tara : *Supathin* + *tara* *> *Supathi-tara* (as per Pāṇ. VIII.2.7) and —*n ṇuṭ* is augmented to *tara* by Pāṇ. VIII.2.17.

Rathī-tari : '*rathin — tari* >*rathi* (Pāṇ. VIII.2.7) & lengthened to -*rathī* + *tarī* as per *Vārttika* on VIII.2.17. *nasat* (? Is it *nasatta* <*na* — √ *sad* for Pāṇ. VIII. 2.61 sanctions *nasatta* and *niṣatta*.

Amnar : The original word is *amnas* 'unawares'. According to Pāṇ. VIII.2.70, it becomes *amnar* before Sandhi e.g. *amnareva*.

Bhuvaratho : Pāṇ. VIII.2.71. states that in *Chandas* —*ru* or —*ra* replace the final of the word *Bhuvas*.

17. (the special formations recorded in this verse)

Brūhyādeḥ : Acc. to Pāṇ. VIII.2.91 the first syllable of *brūhi*, *preṣya*, *śrauṣaṭ*, *vauṣaṭ*, and *āvaha* is *pluta* or prolated. Thus we say : *agnaye 'nubrū3hi* / (By the next Sūtra) both the syllables become prolated or *Pluta* as in '*O3śrā3vaya*) ' when the *Adhvaryu* (the chief sacrificial) priest gives order to the Āgnidhra priest (who is to kindle the fire.).

Dāśvān — p.pf. from √*daś* — 'to honour' √*daś* + *Kvasu* but here the reduplication and the augment —*i*— are prohibited as per Pāṇ. VI.1.12.

Svatavān — nom. sg. of *sva-tavas* 'inherently powerful'. This formation takes place in case of *yāpau* but *yāpau* is obscure, (a misprint probably for *Pāyu* ?)

Tribhiṣṭvam <*tribhis* + *tvam*; As per Pāṇ. VII.3.103—*S* coming within the (Vedic) metrical foot is changed —*Ṣ* before the *t* — of *tvam* and of *tatakṣuḥ*.

nṛbhiṣṭutaḥ < *nṛbhis* + *stutaḥ*. Here ending —*s* of *nṛbhis* is changed to —*ṣ*— as per Pāṇ. VIII.3.105 the cerebralization of *st* — > *ṣṭ* — in *ṣṭutaḥ* and *stoma* in *go-ṣṭoma* (< *go* + *stoma*) is allowed.

18-19. (The following forms are derived as explained below).

Abhiṣuṇaḥ — As per Pāṇ. VIII. 3.107, the *s* — > *ṣ* — of the particle — *ṣu* is permissible when it stands in the beginning of a second word and preceded by a word ending in *i* etc. (in the Vedic) e.g. *madhusthānam* : *madhuṣṭhānam*.

Ṛtāvāha — obscure. Is it a misprint for *Ṛtāṣāha*, mentioned by Pāṇ. in *Saheḥ pṛtanartābhyāṁ ca* ? (Pāṇ. VIII.3.109).

nyaṣīdat — Here — *s* — > —*ṣ* — in this form (though — *s* is preceded by *ā*) is permissible as per Pāṇ. VIII.3.119.

Nṛmaṇāḥ — As per Pāṇ. VIII.4.26, in the Vedic *na* of a second term is changed to *ṇa* when preceded by ṛ — even though there is a hiatus (*Avagraha*) between the two terms.

Optionals are of four types : sometimes it shows a tendency to add, sometimes to withhold, sometimes both are optional and sometimes a new substitute is added. Such is the word formation in the Vedic.

√ *bhū* (I. conj.), √ Vā (II conj). — These are the *dhātus* (roots indicating different conjugations). They are remembered as being *Parasmaipadī*.

20*. Thirty-six roots (*dhātus*) beginning with √*edh* — 'to prosper'— are *Udātta* (of acute accent) and *Ātmanepadī*.

---

*verses from 20 onwards are based on *Pāṇinīya dhātupāṭha* and the verses are practically quotations from it. For example, after listing 36 *dhātus* from *edh*—'to prosper' to √*katth*—'to boast', Pāṇ. Dhātupāṭha remarks :

edhādaya udāttā anudāttetaḥ ātmanebhāṣāḥ. And after listing 37 (No. 38 to 74) *dhātus* from √*at* 'to move constantly' to √*śundh*—' to purify or to get purified', the Dhātupāṭha concludes : *atādaya udātta udāttetaḥ parasmai-bhāṣāḥ*. NP. repeats or paraphrases in verse these remarks of Pāṇini's-Dhātupāṭha.

And thirtyeight *dhātus* beginning with √ *at* :- 'to go constantly' or 'to obtain' are *Parasmaipadī*.

21. Fortytwo *dhātus* beginning with √*śi*-, √kṛ-, are spoken of as belonging to Ātmanepada. Fifty *dhātus* beginning with √*phakk*- 'to move slowly' are laid down as *udāttet* i.e. *Parasmai-padī*.

22. Twentyone roots beginning with √*varc* — 'to shine' are spoken as *Anudāttet* or *Ātmanepadī*, while the group of fortytwo *dhātus* beginning with √*gup*- 'to protect' are said to be *udāttet* (*parasmaipadī*).

23. Grammarians have stated that ten Dhātus beginning with √*ghiṇ*—'to take, to grasp' (cf. Pkt. √*geṇha*-) are *anudāttet* (*Ātm. pada*)[6] while twenty-seven roots[7] beginning with √*aṇ*- ('to breathe' are also *Udāttet* (Parasmaipada).

24. Grammarians have regarded thirty-four[8] *Dhātus* beginning with √*ay*[9] — 'to go' as *Anudāttet* (Ātm. pada), while seventy-two (in all) Dhātus[10] with √*mavy*[11] 'to bind' as its first are *Parasmai-padīs*.

25. √*dhāv* — 'to run' is declared as the only root which is *svaritet* while fiftytwo *Dhātus* beginning with √*kṣudh*[12] — 'to be hungry' are spoken as *Anudāttet* (*Ātm. padī*).

26. Eighty *Dhātus* [13]beginning with √*ghuṣ* — 'to make noise', 'to proclaim' are regarded as Udāttet (Parasmaipada) while twenty-two *Dhātus*[14] from √*dyut* — 'to shine' are considered as *Anudāttet* (Ātm. pada).

27. In the group beginning with √*ghaṭ* — the thirteen roots are spoken as *ṣit*[15] and Anudāttet (Ātm. pada). Thereafter fiftytwo[16] *dhātus* from √*Jval* —'to burn' are regarded as *Udāttet* (*Parasmaipadī*).

28. √*rāj* — to shine is both *Udātta* and *Svarita*.[17] While the three roots √*bhrāj*, √*bhrāś*, √*bhlāś*, are spoken as Anudātta (Ātm. pada), while Dhātus from √*syam* — 'to shout' No. 851) onwards are *Udāttet* (*Parasmaipadī*).

29. There only one Dhātu √*sah* — 'to bear' (recorded as √*ṣah* in the Dhātupāṭha is Anudāttet and √*ram* — 'to play' is *Ātm. padī*. Thereafter three *dhātus* beginning with √ṣad (or √*sad*—) are *udāttet*, while four Dhātus e.g. √*kuc* — and others are *Parasmaipadī*.

30. Thereafter thirtyfive *Dhātus* beginning with √*hikk*-

—'to make an indistinct sound' (Dhātupāṭha — ibid Nos. 886—921 upto √*guh* — 'to conceal) are *Svaritet* or both the Padas.[18] Similarly √*Śri* — 'to serve' and the four roots √*bhṛ*-, √*hṛ*—, √*dhṛ*— and √nī—are also *Svaritet*.

31. Fortysix Dhātus[19] from √*dhe*—'to drink' are said to be *Parasmaipadi*, while eighteen[20] *dhātus* from √smi 'to smile' are opined to be *Ātm. padi*.

32. Three roots beginning with √*Pū* 'to purify (Dhātu nos. 991-993) are described as *Anudāttet* (*Ātm. padi*). √*hṛ*— 'to take away' is Parasmai-padī, while the three roots √*gup*— 'to protect' (nos. 995-998) are Ātm. padī.

33. √*rabh* —, √*labh*—, √*svaj*—, √*had*—) these four roots are *Anudāttet*, while √*Kṣvid*—'to be wet' is *Udāttet* and fifteen roots from √*skambh*—(Dhātupāṭha records √*skand*—) are Parasmaipadī.

34. √*kit* — 'to desire' is Udāttet (Parasmaipadī) while √dān— ('to cut' ' and √Śaṇ— to shine are *Ubhaya-padi* (i.e. are found both Par. & Ātm. pd). Nine roots beginning with √*pac* — 'to cook' (Dhātu nos. 1021-1029 from √*pac* — to √*vah* — 'in Pāṇ. Dhātupāṭha) are Svaritet. They are regarded as Parasmaipadī, (and Ātm. pd) as well.

35. Three more dhātus are *Svaritet*—. √*Vad*— and √*vac* — both meaning 'to speak' are Parasmaipadī. In this way, one thousand and six are said to be the roots of the group of *Dhātus* beginning with √*bhū* (i.e. of the 1st conjugation).

DHĀTUS OF THE 2ND CONJUGATION

36. √*ad** — 'to eat' and √*han* — 'to kill or to go' are spoken of as belonging to Parasmaipada). And the four Dhātus beginning with √*dviṣ* 'to hate' (i.e. Dhātu Nos. 3-6 of *Pāṇ. Dhātupāṭha*) are regarded as *Svaritet* (both Par. *pada* and *Ātm. pd.*).

37. Here the Dhātu √*cakṣ* 'to speak' is regarded as *Ātm. pd.***, while thirteen roots from √ *ir*— 'to go' (Nos. 8-20 in *Pāṇ. Dhātupāṭha*) are *Anudāttet* (*Ātm. pd*).

---

*√*vad* is a misprint as this conjugation is called *adādi* and as such √*ad*— & not √*vad* (of the 1st conj.) can be the original.

**the Dhātupāṭha states *udātto anudātted atmanepadi* /

38. O sage ! grammarians have proclaimed √*sū* — to give birth to and √*śī* — 'to sleep' as Ātmane-padīs, while seven Dhātus beginning with √*ṣū* (it should be √*yu* as per *Dhātupāṭha*).

39. O lord of sages ! Only one root viz. √ūrṇu 'to cover' is said to be *svarita* (i.e. both Par. pd & Ātm. pd), while three *dhātus* beginning with √*ghu* (a misprint for √*dyu* as evidenced in the *Dhātu-pāṭha* — Dhatu No. 30) are spoken as *Parasmaipadis*.*

40. O Nārada ! √*stu* — 'to praise' is the only root pronounced and remembered /as *Par. pd.* by the grammarians.

41. Eighteen Dhātus beginning with √*rā* 'to give' (prob. from √yā 'to go' to √vac 'to speak', in the Dhātupāṭha) are Par. pd. O Nārada ! Only √*i* — 'to study' (*adhyayane*) is declared as Ātm. pd.).

42. Four Dhātus from √*vid* — 'to know' to √*rud* — 'to weep', nos. 54-57 in the *Dhātupāṭha* are considered as *Par. padi* √svap — 'to sleep' is pointed as Par. pd.

43. √*Śvas* — 'to breathe' etc. (*syamādayaḥ* in the NP. is probably a misprint as per series of roots in the Dhātupāṭha) have been told by me as Parasmai-padī. √*dīdhī* 'to shine' and √*vevī*— 'to go' (rarely used in Cl. Sk.) are Ātmanepadī, O sage.

44. Three roots beginning from √*pṛth* — (prob. a misprint for √*prath*— 1st conj. are Ātm. and the *Pāṇ. Dhātupāṭha* reads: '68 √*ṣasa*, 69 √*sasti svapne*, 70 √*vaśa kāntau*' as the three Dhātus in the serial list of roots of 2nd conj. are proclaimed as *Udāttet* (Par. pd)**. *Carkarita**** is a term for any intensive formed without the syllable *ya* like *carkarīti* < √*kṛ*—. √*hnu* — 'to cover' is declared as Anudātta, O excellent sage.

45. Thus seventythree roots have been said to be included in the 2nd conjugation (*adādi gaṇa*).

(Now begins the list of the 3rd conjugation—*juhotyādayaḥ*)

---

*Pāṇ. Dhātupāṭha. 2nd conj. enumerates four dhātus viz. √*dyu-*, √*su-*, √*ku* and √*stu*. NP. records the first-three in this verse and relegates √*stu* to the next (no. 40) verse.

***Ṣasādaya udāttā udāttetaḥ parasmai bhāṣāḥ—Pāṇ. Dhātupāṭha.*

***This is listed as *Dhātu* No. 71 in the *Dhātupāṭha*.

DHĀTUS OF THE III CONJUGATION

The four roots from √dā (√*hu* ?) are regarded as parasmaipadi.[21]

47. √*bhṛ* is *svaritet* (both Par. pd & Ātm. pd) & '*ohāk*' (√*hā* 'to abandon') is *udāttet*. √*mā* 'to measure' and √*hā* — 'to go' are Anudāttet. √dā — to give — √ dhā 'to hold', 'to contain' are symbolised as '*it*' indicating their being *svarita* (both Par. pad and Ātm. pad).

47. Three roots beginning with *vānitir* (prob. a misprint for *ṇijir* in the *Dhātupāṭha*) are spoken of as *Svarita* (both Par. pd and Atm. pd.), while twelve *dhātus* from √*ghṛ*—to besprinkle' are regarded as Parasmaipadīs.

48a. Thus twentytwo roots have been mentioned in the 3rd conjugation (*hvādika gaṇa*).

DHĀTUS OF THE IV CONJUGATION

48b. Twentyfive *Dhātus* beginning with √*div.*—'to shine' have been spoken of as being Parasmaipadī.

49. O Nārada ! There are two Ātmanepadi *Dhātus* viz. √*sū*—'to give birth to' and √*dū*. 'to trouble'. The seven Dhātus beginning with √*pū*—are regarded as Ātmanepadī.

50. O Brāhmaṇa ! Roots beginning with √*dī*— 'to perish' 'to die' are known here as Ātmanepadī, while the four Dhātus beginning with √*so*—'to kill' are Parasmaipadī.

51. O sage ! Fifteen roots beginning with √*jan*— 'to be born' (Dhātus from 43-49) are Ātmanepadī while the five *dhātus* beginning with √*mṛṣ*—'to bear' 'to endure' are *svaritet* (both Par. pd. & Ātm. pd.)

52. Eleven *dhātus* from √*pad*— 'to go' (Root Nos. 63-74) are considered as Ātm. padīs [22]while eight Dhātus from √*radh* 'to hurt', 'to injure', are known as Parasmaipadī.[23]

53. Fortysix Dhātus from √*śam* — 'to pacify' are spoken of as *Udāttet* (*Par. pd*). Thus one hundred and forty *Dhātus* are regarded as belonging to the *divādi gaṇa* (IV conjugation).

DHĀTUS OF THE V CONJUGATION (SVĀDI GAṆA)

55. Nine roots beginning with √*su* — 'to extract *soma* juice' are described as being *svaritet* (both Par. & Ātm. pd),

while seven roots such as *dunoti* (√*du* — to trouble) are Parasmaipadīs.

56-57a. The two roots √*aś* — 'to pervade' and √*stigh*— — 'to mount over' are known as *Anudāttet* (*Ātm. pd.*), while fourteen Dhātus beginning with √*tik*—'to go', 'to assail' are Parasmaipadī here. O excellent Brāhmaṇa ! Thirty two *dhātus* are spoken of as constituting the *svādika gaṇa* (V conjugation).[24]

DHĀTUS OF THE VI CONJUGATION (TUDĀDI GAṆA)

57b. O excellent sage ! Six *dhātus*[25] beginning with √*tud*— 'to trouble' are said to be *svaritet* (both Par. pd. & Ātm. pd.)

58. √ṛṣ — 'to go' is *udāttet* (Par-pd.), while nine roots from √*juṣ*—'to be pleased' are Ātm. pd., and one hundred and five Dhātus[26] beginning from √*vraśc* — 'to cut' are declared as *Udāttet*.

59. O chief of sages ! Only one *Dhātu* √*gur* — 'to make exertion' is declared as *Udāttet*. Four roots beginning with √*nu* — 'to praise are considered as Parasmaipadī.

60. The *Dhātu* √*ku*—'to sound' is spoken of as *Anudāttet* (Ātm. pd.). Here ends the *Kuṭādi gaṇa*. √*pṛ*— 'to be active' and √*mṛ*— 'to die' are Ātmanepadīs, while six Dhātus from √*pi-*, √*ri*— 'to move 'to go' are Parasmaipadīs.

61. Two roots viz. √*dṛ*. — 'to honour', and √*dhṛ*—'to exist, to live' are spoken of as Ātmanepadīs, while sixteen Dhātus from √*pracch* — 'to ask' are Parasmaipadīs.

62. Thereafter, O sage, six roots beginning with √*mil*— 'to join' are spoken of as *svaritet* (both Par. pd. and Ātm. pd.) And Three Dhātus beginning with √*Kṛt*—'to cut' are Parasmaipadīs.

63a. Thus there are one hundred and fifty seven *dhātus* in the VI conjugation (*tudādi gaṇa*).

ROOTS OF THE VII CONJUGATION

63b. Nine roots beginning with √*rudh* — 'to obstruct are *svaritet* (both Par. and Ātm. pd.), *Kṛti* (Veṣṭane) is parpadī.

64. Three *Dhātus* from √*indh*—to kindle (& √*khid* — & √*vid*) are said to be *Anudāttet* (Ātm. pd.) (Twelve Dhātus from) √*śiṣ* — 'to leave as remainder', √*piṣ*— 'to reduce to powder' are *udāttet*. In this way, there are twentyfive roots in the VII conjugation (*rudhādi gaṇa*).

DHĀTUS OF THE VIII CONJUGATION (TANĀDI GAṆA)

65. Seven Dhātus[27] beginning with √*tan*— 'to spread' are proclaimed as being *Svarita* (both Par. & Ātm. padīs) √*van* — 'to beg', 'to request' and √*man* — 'to think' are Atmanepadi and √*kṛ*— (technically called *ḍukṛñ*) 'to do' is *Svarita* (both Par. and Ātm. Pd.).

66a. In this way, ten *dhātus* have been proclaimed as belonging to the eighth conjugation.

DHĀTUS OF THE IX CONJUGATION (KRYĀDI GAṆA)

66b-67. Seven Dhātus[28] beginning with √*krī*—'to buy' belong to both the Padas. Four dhātus beginning with √*stambh* and which are used (by Pāṇini) in the Sūtras are Parasmaipadī. O chief of sages, twenty two *dhātus* from √*krudh*— 'to get angry' (This is obviously a misprint for √'knūñ' as stated in the Dhātupāṭha) are Udāttet (*Par. pd.*)

68. √Vṛ — 'to select' is Ātmanepadī. Twenty-one Dhātus from √*Śranth* —'to loosen' are Parasmaipadī while √*grah*— 'to take' is *svaritet* (both Par. padī & Ātm. padī).

69a. In this way fiftytwo roots[29] have been enumerated in the IX conjugation by the learned.

DHĀTUS OF THE X CONJUGATION: (CURĀDI GAṆA)

69B. One hundred and thirtysix Dhātus beginning from √*cur* — 'to steal' belong to (both) parasmaipada and Ātmanepada.

70. O sage ! Eighteen (but actually thirtynine roots from 140 √*cit* — to 178 √*kusm*—) Dhātus are Ātmanepadī. O sage ! Roots from √*carc* — 'to study' upto √*dhṛṣ* (Dhātu nos. 318) are declared as belonging to both Parasmaipada and Ātmanepada.

71. Fortyeight Dhātus from √*kath* — (Dhātus 319-365)

—known as *adantas*, and ten Dhātus beginning from √*pad*— (i.e. Dhātus 366-375) are Ātmanepadī.

72. Here eight roots beginning from √*Sūtr* — 'to cover' are spoken as belonging to both *Parasmaipada* and *Ātmanepada* by the wise. In the sense of a root (verb) the *prātipadika* gets the affix *ṇic* (—*i*) and is formed in most cases like the application of the —*iṣṭha*.

73-74. This affix —*i* is in the sense 'does for the sake of' or 'tells the other'. In the sense of causative, this *ṇic* is added. Eight roots beginning with √*Citra* (root no. 385 onwards) upto √*Saṅgrāma* (root no. 390) are spoken as *Anudāttet* by the learned grammarians. Sixteen Dhātus from √*Stoma* 'to praise, are the illustrations of *adanta dhātus*.

75. The meaning of "optionally" (*bahulam etan nidarśanam*—as stated in the *Gaṇa-pāṭha*) is that it includes all the remaining *dhātus* irrespective of their use in (Pāṇini's) Sūtras, *laukika* Sanskrit and the Chāndasa (Vedic) language. All dhātus belong to all conjugations and have different meanings.

76. In addition to these roots, *dhātus* ending in the affixes beginning with —*san* (i.e. the twelve affixes viz. —*san*, —*kyac*, —*kāmyac*, —*kyaṅ*, —*kyaṣ*, —*ācāra-kvip*, —*ṇic*, — *yaṅ*, —*yak*, —*āya*, —*iyaṅ* and —*niṅ*.) are also called roots, and also Denominatives (e.g. *Garuḍāyate* — acts like a Garuḍa). In this way innumerable number of Dhātus are formed here. O Nārada. Here it is explained in a nutshell. The details are given in the relevant treatises.

77. In Dhātus ending in the vowels, all Dhātus with the exception of those ending in —*ū* and —*ṛ* and the roots √*yu*- √*ru* √*kṣṇu*, √*śī*, √*snu*, √*nu*, √*kṣu*, √*śvi*, √*ḍī*, √*śri*, √*Vṛ* (of both Padas)— are regarded as *Anudātta* or *Aniṭ*.

78. The following is the list of one hundred and two Dhātus ending in consonants which are *Anudātta* or *Aniṭ*. √*śakḷ*, √*pac*, √*muc*, √*ric*, √*vac*, √*vic*, √*sic*, √*pracch*, √*tyaj*, √*nij*, √*bhaj*, √*bhañj*, √*bhuj*, √*bhrasj*, √*masj*, √*yaj*, √*yuj*, √*ruj*, √*rañj*, *vi* √ *ji*, √*svañj*, √*sañj*, √*sṛj*

79. √*ad*, √*kṣud*, √*khid*, √*chid*, √*tud*, √*nud*, √*pad*, (4th conj), √*bhid*, √*vid*, *vi*-√*nad*, √*śad*, √*sad*, √*svid*, √*skand*, √*had*, √*krudh*, √*budh*,

80. √*bandh*, √*yudh*, √*rudh*, √*rādh*, √*vyadh*, √*śudh*,

√*sādh*, √*sidh*, √*man* (IV conj.), √*han*, √*āp*, √*kṣip*, √*chup*, √*tap*, √*tip*, √*tṛp*, √*dṛp*.

81. √*lip*, √*lup*, √*vap*, √*śap*, √*svap*, √*sṛp*, √*yabh*, √*rabh*, √*labh*, √*gam*, √*nam*, √*yam*, √*ram*, (not *rabhiḥ* i.e. √*rabh*— as in the text of the NP.), √*kruś*, √*daṁs*, √*diś*, √*dṛś*, √*mṛś*, √*riś*, √*ruś*, √*liś*, √*viś*, √*spṛś*, √*kṛṣ*.

82. √*tviṣ*, √*tuṣ*, √*duṣ*, √*puṣ*, (IV conj.) √*piṣ*, √*viṣ*, √*śiṣ*, √*śuṣ*, √*śliṣ*, √*ghas*, (= *ad*), √*vas*, √*dah*, √*dih*, √*duh*, √*nah*, √*mih*, √*ruh*, (√*lih*, √*vah*.)

83b-85. *Ca* and others are called *Nipātas*.[30] The 'pre'-positions like *pra*—are known as *gatis* (*gavayaḥ* in the NP should have been *gatayaḥ*); words which have been created in different quarters, regions and periods have a number of connotations. And, O Brāhmaṇa , they are characterised by all genders. Here *Gaṇapāṭha*, *Sūtrapāṭha* Dhātupāṭha *Anunāsika Pāṭha* are called *Pārāyaṇa*.

O Nārada ! All words whether *laukika* (current) or Vedic — are permanent and imperishable.

86a. The vocabulary collected by grammarians is hence intended for recitation.

86b.-88. The formation of the (already formed, permanent) words is briefly explained by (the study of) its original form (the noun base or root), terminations, substitutes, the augment, etc.

In this manner a bit of *Nirukta* has been briefly related to you. Who is capable of recounting it in its entirety, as it is infinite (limitless), O Nārada ?

CHAPTER FIFTYTHREE

1. *Hantīti haṁsaḥ.*

2. √*hiṁs* 'to kill' : *hiṁs—a* =*hiṁs* a & metathesis by Pāṇ. VI. 3. 109. Bhaṭṭoji Dīkṣita quotes this very verse in the NP. to elucidate the above sūtra of Pāṇini. If Bhattoji Dīkṣita is not presumed to have consulted the NP. both S.K. (*Sīddhānta Kaumudī*) and the NP. used a common source.

3. As a matter of fact though the form *niṣṭarkya* is sanctioned by Pāṇ. III.1.123 the formation is extremely irregular.

nis +√*kṛt* + *ya* (*ṇyat* instead of the regular *kyap*) and the root √*kṛt* becomes √*tṛk* and we get *niṣṭarkya.*

4. As a matter of fact the change—*bh*>—h is accepted by modern linguists and Vedic √ gṛbh-->class. Sk √*gṛh. grah*—is more natural linguistically.

5. In the Vedic, the following seventeen letters are implied in *akṣarasamūha* (collection of letters viz. *āśrāvaya* (4 letters), *astu śrauṣaṭ* (4 letters), *ye yajāmahe* (5 letters), *yaja* (2 letters) and *vaṣaṭ* (2 letters) =17 letters in all.

6. *vide* Dhātu Nos. 435-444 (both inclusive) in the Dhātupāṭha (conj. I).

7. *Vide* Dhātu Nos. 445-474. (*ibid*).

8. *vide* Dhātu Nos. 475-508 (*ibid*).

9. *amādayaḥ* is a misprint in the NP.

10. *vide* Dhātu Nos. 509-601 (*ibid*).

11. Dhātu Nos. 602.

12. The *Dhātupāṭha* records √*dhukṣ*—to be kindled and not √*kṣudh*— vide the group from *dhātu* Nos. 603-653.

13. *vide, ibid* Dhātu nos. 654-741.

14. *vide, ibid* Dhātu nos. 742-763.

15. *ṣit*—an affix attached to roots to show the verb-activity. The *Gaṇa sūtra* in the Dhātupāṭha includes the roots from √*ghaṭ*— to √tvar (nos. 764-776) as *ṣit* for the purpose of adding the *Kṛt*. affix — *a* e.g. *ghaṭā, vyathā, tvarā.*

16. *vide, ibid* Dhātu Nos. (806-846 ?)

17. ,, ,, Dhātu No. 847.

18. *A Dict.* of *Sk. Grammar* (GOS 134, 1961) p. 409.

19. *vide*—Dhātupāṭha (ibid) Dhātu Nos. 927-972.

20. *vide ibid Dhātu* nos. 973-990.

21. The text of this line is as follows :

dādayo dhātavo vedāḥ parasmai-padino matāḥ / The 3rd conjugation is called *juhotyādi* i.e. √*hu dānādanayoḥ* is implied in *dādayo.* V. 46a shows that here in v. 45b dhātus √hu √bhi, √*hrī* and √pṛ are implied, the number 'four' seems to be implied in *Vedāḥ.*

22. √rādh—'to prosper' is also found in the 5th & 10th conjugation (*Svādi-curādike*).

23. Thirteen roots from √*rādh* to √*sidh* in Pāṇ. Dhātupāṭha) are *udāttet* (*tudādya*) in the NP. is a mistake & Pāṇ. Dhātupāṭha does not support it).

24. Actually the Dhātupāṭha gives 35 *dhātus*.

25. Viz. from √*tud*—'to trouble' to √kṛṣ. 'to plough', to draw.'

26. Viz. from No. 12 √Vraśc to No. 115 √*bhṛd*—to plunge', in Pāṇ. Dātupāṭha.

27. i.e. Dhātus from (1) √*tan*—to (7) √*ghṛṇ*—

28. viz. Dhātus from (1) √*krī*—to (7) √*yu*—'to join' or 'to bind'.

29. Pāṇiniya Dhātupāṭha lists sixty one roots in this conjugation.

30. Pāṇini gives no definition of a *Nipāta*, but states a number of particles with no gender, number or sense beginning with *ca* : *cādayo'sattve* /

CHAPTER FIFTYFOUR

Mathematics and Astronomy

Sanandana said :

1. I shall now set out the auxiliary (of the Veda) called *Jyotiṣa* which had been enunciated by Brahmā in days of yore and through the mere knowledge of which men can attain the fulfilment of their ordained duties.

2. O Brāhmaṇa ! the science of *Jyotiṣa*, which has been expounded in four lakhs of verses, falls into three sections, devoted, respectively, to mathematics and astronomy (*Gaṇita*), horoscopy (*Jātaka*) and natural astrology (*Saṁhitā*).

3-4a. *Topics of Mathematics and astronomy.* In the *Gaṇita* section have been set out the arithmetical operations (*vv.*12b-59); computation of the mean and true positions of Planets (*vv.* 60-127); 'the questions' (on time, place and direction)[1] (*vv.* 128-53a); lunar and solar eclipses, (*vv.* 153b-65a); the diagrammatic representation thereof,[2] (gnomonic) shadow, (*vv.* 165b-67a); elevation of the lunar horns (*vv.* 167b-69), (planetary) conjunction (*vv.*170-73) and the (*vyati-*)*pātas*[3] (*vv.*174-87).

4b. *Topics of Horoscopy.* In the *Jātaka* section are treated — the signs (*rāśi*) (of the zodiac), their divisions (and properties); Nature of the planets (and their properties; (Manifold inferior) births;

5. Conception; Birth; Early death; Longevity; Order of divisions (and subdivisions in one's life): Vocations; Eight emplacements, (being those of the 7 planets and the *lagna*, in the horoscopic chart); 'Royal' planetary combinations; 'Atmospheric' planetary combinations;

6. 'Lunar' planetary combinations; 'Ascetic' planetary combinations; Effect of the planets occupying the different signs; Effect of planets aspecting one another; Effect of the planets being in the several 'houses'; Effect of mutual associa-

tion (of planets); Miscellaneous matters (relating to the association of planets) :

7. Malefic combination (of planets; Female horoscopy; Death; Reconstruction of lost horoscopes; and Effects of decanates.

8. *Topics of Natural astrology.* The contents of the *Saṁhitā* section are: Effects of the motion of the planets (across the different signs) (*vv.* 1-108); *Abdalakṣaṇa* (Characteristics of the year) (*vv.* 109-33a); *Tithi* (Lunar day) (*vv.*133b-56a); *Vāra* (Weekday) (*vv.* 156b-67a); *Nakṣatra* (Asterism) (*vv.* 167b-211a); *Yoga*[4] (*vv.* 211b-19a); *Tithyartha* or *Karaṇa*[5] (*vv.* 219b-23).

9. (*Auspicious moment Muhūrta*) (*vv.*224-2a); *Upagraha* (Secondary atmospheric phenomena) (*vv.* 230-50a); (*Saṅkrānti* (Sun's transit into a sign) (*vv.* 250b-70); *Gocara* (Current motion of the planets) (*vv.* 271-82); *Candra-Tārābala* (Astrological strength of the Moon and of the Asterisms) (*vv.* 283-89); *Sarvalagna* (Rising of the signs) (*vv.* 290-312a); *Ārtava* (First menstruation) (*vv.* 312b-17).

10. *Ādhāna* (Conception) (*vv.*318-19); *Puṁsavana* (Rite for the birth of a male child) (*vv.* 320-25); *Jāta-Nāma-karma* (Birth rites and Naming Ceremony) (*vv.* 326- 30a); *Annabhukti* (*Annaprāśana*, First feeding) (*vv.* 330b-34); *Caula* (Tonsure) (*vv.* 335-43a); *Aṅkurārpaṇa* (Auspicious sowing) (*vv.* 343b- 47); *Mauñjībandhana* (and *Upanayana*, Tying the girdle and commencing studies) (*vv.*348-79), *Kṣurikābandhana*, (Girding the sword) (*vv.* 380-91a).

11. *Samāvartana* (Return from studies) (*vv.* 391b-94a); *Vivāha* (Marriage) (*vv.* 394b-523); *Pratiṣṭhā* (Installation of deities in temples) (*vv.* 524-39a); *Sadma* (Building of human residences) (*vv.*539b-619); *Yātrā* (Travel for pilgrimage, war etc.) (*vv.*620-712): *Praveśana* (Return home) (*vv.* 713-20); *Sadyovṛṣṭi* (Immediate rain) (*vv.* 721-39a); *Kūrma-vibhāga* (Division of the globe) (*vv.*739b-45); and *Utpāta* (Portentuous phenomena) (*vv.* 646-56a). I shall be setting out all these briefly.

MATHEMATICS

12b-14a. *Notational places.* *Eka* (one), *daśa* (ten), *śata* (hundred), *sahasra* (thousand), *ayuta* (ten thousand), *lakṣa* (lakh), *prayuta* (ten lakhs/million), *koṭi* (crore), *arbuda*, *abja*, *kharva*, *nikharva*, *mahāpadma*, *śaṅku*, *jaladhi*, *antya*, *madhya*, *parārdha*—these are the names (of the notational places), each succeeding one being ten times (the preceding).

14b. *Addition and subtraction.* Addition and subtraction (of numbers) can be done either in a forward or in a backward manner.[6]

15a. *Multiplication.* In multiplication, the multiplicand (*guṇya*) is multiplied up to its last digit (by the multiplier) (and the products added together).[7]

15b. *Division.* O sage ! In division that is the quotient (*phala*) which when multiplied by the divisor is completely subtractable (from the dividend).

16a. *Square.* The product of a number multiplied by itself is called *varga* (square); the learned call it also (by the term) *kṛti*.

16b-18a. *Square root.* (Mark off the odd digits of the number whose square root is required.) Having subtracted the (greatest possible) square from the last odd place, keep that 'root' apart. Double that 'root' and divide the remainder and place the quotient alongside the previously obtained 'root'. Subtract, O Brāhmaṇa, the square of that and again divide as before by the (newly formed) 'root'. O great sage, by repeating as above (till all the digits are completed) the square root is obtained.

18b-21a. *Cube and cube root.* The product of the multiplication thrice of the same number is called its *ghana* (cube). The method to derive the cube root (*pada*) is as follows : The first place (unit's digit of the number whose cube root is required) is termed 'odd'; the next two digits (*i.e.*, the tens and hundreds) are termed 'even.' (Mark off the digits of the number into groups of three digits each in this manner, each group having one 'odd' and two 'even-s'). Subtract from the last (group having an) odd place the (greatest possible) cube; that is the cube root (*mūla*) (of that group). Divide (the next) even place with thrice the square of the (previous) cube root and place the quotient alongside the previous cube root. Square the new quotient and multiply it by three and by the last cube root and subtract it (from the next even place). Subtract, the cube (of the new cube root-digit) from the next odd place. Repeat the process and the cube root of the number is obtained.

21b. *Fractions.* Two fractions are reduced to a common denominator when their numerators and denominators are multiplied by the denominator of one by that of the other.

22. *Fractions of fractions.* O sage ! Enquirers into science should understand that in fractions of fractions (*bhāga-prabhāga*), the products of their numerators and of their denominators give the correct figures (of the numerator and denominator of the resultant fraction).

23-24a. *Associated and dissociated fractions.* Associated fractions (*bhāgānubandha*) and dissociated fractions (*bhāgāpavāha*) are those in which a number is increased or decreased (by a fraction of its own). Here, multiply the whole number by the denominator (*talasthahāra*), ascertain whether the fraction is positive or negative and accordingly add to or subtract from it the numerator.

24b. *Addition and subtraction of fractions.* O sage ! (Addition and subtraction of fractions are effected by) adding together or subtracting one from the other their numerators (after reducing the fractions) to a common denominator.

25a. *Denominator of an integer.* When a denominator is not attached to a number, take 1 as its denominator.

25b-26. *Multiplication and division of fractions.* The product of the multiplication of two fractions is obtained by dividing the product of the numerators by the product of the denominators. In the division of two fractions, the numerator and denominator of the divisor are inverted and the process of multiplication applied.

27. *Square etc. of fractions.* For the square, cube, square root and cube root of fractions, calculate the respective squares etc. of the numerator and of the denominator. These for zero are always zero.

28-29. *Inverse operations.* When the result (of certain operations) is 'given' (*dṛśya*) and the original number is to be found (*rāśiprasiddhaye*), calculate taking the denominator as the numerator and the numerator as the denominator, the square as the square root and the square root as the square, minus as plus and plus as minus. However, in such cases of inverse operation where a part (of an item) has been added to or subtracted from it, the denominator to which the numerator has been added to or subtracted from should be taken as the denominator, and the denominator as such should be taken as the numerator; the rest (of the calculations are to be done) as before.

30. *Operations with assumed numbers* (*Iṣṭakarma*). When an intended number (*uddiṣṭa-rāśi*) has been multiplied, divided, has a part of its taken away from it or added to it (and the result is *dṛṣṭa* 'known'), the intended number can be found by multiplying that result by an assumed number and dividing by the resultant (obtained by subjecting the assumed number to all the said operations).

31. *Operations with sums and differences.* The difference (of two numbers) when added to or subtracted from the sum (of those two numbers) and (the result) divided by two, will give the two numbers.[8] (This operation is called) *Saṅkrama.* The difference of the squares (of two numbers) will give their sum.[9] (And from the said sum and difference), the individual numbers (can be found as stated above).

32-34. *Methods to get perfect squares based on any assumed number* (*vargakarma*). Multiply the square of an assumed number by 8 (*gaja*), subtract 1, halve it and divide by the assumed number. This would be one (number). Square this number and add 1. This would be another such number.[10]

Or, 1 divided by twice the assumed number and the assumed number added is one (number). The other number is 1. The sum or difference of these two numbers reduced by one would be the squares of the two (desired) numbers.

Or, multiply the square of the square and the cube of the assumed number and add 1 to the first. The two desired numbers are obtained. These are according to the methods to be adopted in arithmetic (*vyakta-gaṇita*) and algebra (*avyakta-gaṇita*).

35-36. *Operation involving the addition of a quantity to squares.* When a resultant (*dṛṣṭa*) is obtained by adding to or subtracting from a square its root multiplied by a multiplicand, that resultant should be added to the square of half the multiplicand and the root of the result calculated. To this result half the multiplicand is added (when *guṇaghanamūla* had been subtracted) and subtracted (when the *guṇaghanamūla* had been added) and the result squared. (This would give the required number). (This is called) *Guṇa-(Karma)*.

When, however, the resultant (*dṛśya*) is less or more by a part of the (required) number, the resultant and the root are to be appropriately reduced or increased and using them the required number is calculated as before.

37. *Rule of three* (In a *Trairāśika*) the *Pramāṇa* (argument) and *Icchā* (requisition) are to be of the same denomination and (are to be placed) at the beginning and at the end. *Phala* (fruit) (which would be of a different denomination) would be placed in the middle. *Phala* multiplied by *Icchā* and divided by *Pramāṇa* (*ādya*) will yield the *Icchā-phala*. In the Inverse (rule of three), (the method is) reversed.

38. *Rule of five etc.* In *Pañcarāśika* etc. the *pramāṇa* side and the *phala* side are properly set down. By dividing the product of the larger number (of quantities) by the product of the smaller number (of quantities) the result is obtained.

39a. *Capital and interest.* Capital is obtained through calculation with an assumed number (*iṣṭakarma-vidhi*, see verse 30, above). That subtracted from the composite amount (of capital and interest) will give the interest (*kalāntara*).

39b-40a. Rate multiplied by time, and the interest multiplied by the invested time are to be calculated and kept independently. Each divided by their sum and multiplied by the composite amount, would yield results which are respectively the capital and the interest.

40b-41a. (In the matter of the loan of different amounts for different periods, the individual income is identical), while arranging the sides (as in *Pañcarāśika* etc., see above, verse 38), if the product of the smaller number of quantities and the months be greater than the product of the larger number of quantities, the interest divided by the total number of months, would give the rate.

41b. (In the case of investments by different people making up the capital), the investment by each (*kṣepa*) multiplied by the total income (*miśra*) and divided by the total investment (*kṣepayoga*), would give the (proportionate) income (*phala*).

42a. *Time for filling a tank.* (When different pipes individually take different times to fill a tank, in order to find the time required to fill the tank if all the pipes are opened together), divide the denominators by the numerators of the individual fractions of time taken by each to fill the tank), find the sum (of the new fractions obtained) and (with that sum) divide 1. The time to fill (the tank) is obtained.

42b-43. *Geometrical progression* (*Guṇottaraśreḍhi*). The sum of the series in geometrical progression (*mānaṁ guṇottare*) (is found thus): when the number of terms (*gaccha*) is odd, reduce it by 1 and multiply; when it is even, halve it and square. (Continue the process) till the number ends. Then, beginning from the last term (*gacchānta*) perform backwards (*vyasta*) the operations of multiplication (*guṇa*) and squaring (*varga*) (in continuation). From the result subtract 1, divide the remainder by 'guṇaka-1' and multiply by the first member of the series (*prāg-ghna*).[11]

44-45a. *Triangles and quadrilaterals.* In the case of plane figures (*kṣetra*), like triangles and quadrilaterals (*tri-caturaśraka*), the following apply; The hypotenuse (*karṇa*) is the square root of the sum of the squares of the base (*bhuja*) and altitude (*koṭi*). The base would be the square root of the difference between the squares of the hypotenuse and the altitude. And, the altitude would be the square root of the difference between the squares of the hypotenuse and the base.[12]

45b-46a. (The rational sides of a right angled triangle, as calculated from any two numbers would be : (1) The square of the difference of two (natural) numbers added to twice the product of the numbers, which is equal to the sums of their squares; (ii) the product of the sums and differences of the two numbers, which is equal to the difference of their squares, and (iii) twice the product of the numbers.[13]

46b. *Circumference of a circle.* O sage, the diameter of a circle multiplied by 22 (*ākṛti*) and divided by 7 (*adri*) will give the circumference of a circle.[14]

47-48. *Relation of Sine, Reversed sine and Diameter.* Experts in trigonometry say: Reversed sine (*śara*) is given by multiplying together the sum and difference of the sine (*jyā*) and the diameter (*vyāsa*), finding the square root thereof and halving the result. The sine (*jyā*) is given by (diameter-*minus*-reversed sine) multiplied by the reversed sine, finding its root and doubling it. And, the diameter is obtained by squaring half sine, dividing it by the reversed sine and adding to the result the reversed sine.[15]

49-50a. *Sine of an arc.* Let the (circumference *minus* arc) multiplied by the circumference be called 'First' (*prāg*). One fourth the square/of the circumference is multiplied by 5 and the 'First' subtracted therefrom. With the result divide (Diameter 'First'). O brāhmaṇa ! the result obtained would be the sine (*jyā*) (of the relevant arc).[16]

50b-51a. *Arc from sine.* One fourth the sine is multiplied by the square of the circumference and divided by four times the diameter to which the sine is added. The result is subtracted from one fourth the square of the circumference and the square root (of the same is calculated). Thus, when subtracted from half the circumference, gives the arc.[17]

51b-52a. *Measure of corn heaped up in a cone.*

When coarse, medium and fine grain are heaped, the heights (*vedha*) (of the cones so formed) would, respectively, be one-ninth (*aṅka*) one-tenth (*āśā*) and one-eleventh (*iśa*) of the respective circumferences. The measure of the grain in cubic cubits (*ghana-kara*) would be given by the square of one-sixth (*aṅga*) multiplied by the height.[18]

52b-53a. *Measure of water in a tank.* The length of the (stretch of) water multiplied by its breadth and height in inches and divided by 3100 (*khakhendurāma*) will give the volume of water in *droṇa* measures.[19]

54b-55a. *Measure of rubble.* The height, breadth and length, in inches, O brāhmaṇa, of a heap of rubble, multiplied together and divided by 1150 (*kha-akṣa-iśa*) would give its volume in *droṇa* measures.

55b-56a. *Measure of metal.* In the case of metal pieces, the length, breadth and height, in inches, multiplied together and divided by 585 (*bāṇa-ibha-mārgaṇa*) should be declared to be the volume of the heap in *droṇa* measures.

56b-57. *Gnomon and the lighted lamp.* O sage ! the gnomon[20] multiplied by the distance between the lamp and the gnomon and divided by the height of the lamp less the gnomon, gives the gnomonic shadow.[21]

Again, the gnomon multiplied by the distance between the gnomon and the lamp and divided by the gnomonic shadow, gives the height of the lamp.[22]

58. The height of the lamp-*minus*-gnomon multiplied by the gnomonic shadow and divided by the gnomon will give the distance between the lamp and the gnomon.[23]

58b-59a. *Two gnomons and the lighted lamp.* The distance between the shadow tips multiplied by the shadow and divided by the difference between the shadows gives the base (*bhūmi* of the relevant shadow).[24]

59. The base multiplied by the gnomon, and divided by the shadow gives the height of the lamp by the rule of three.[25]

ASTRONOMY

Mean Planets (Madhya-graha)

60. (Operational) mathematics has been set out concisely, as above. Now, shall be set out in brief, (the computation of) the mean planets etc. according to (astronomical) mathematics.

61-62a. *The aeon (yuga).* O brāhmaṇa ! The measure of the (great) aeon (*mahā-yuga, caturyuga*) is said to be 43,20,000 (*khacatuṣka-rada-arṇava*) (*divine*) years.[26] Four tenths of it is said to be the *kṛta-yuga*; three tenths form the *Tretā-yuga*; two tenths the *Dvāpara-yuga*; and one tenth the *Kali-yuga.*

62b. Seventyone *yugas* plus one *kṛta-yuga* period form (the time duration of) one Manu.[27]

63. O foremost among brāhmaṇas ! fourteen Manus occur during the day-time of God Brahmā. That much period, again, O foremost among brāhmaṇas ! is said to be His night.

64. O Nārada ! the years that have gone by from the beginning of creation by God Brahmā might be consolidated and the computation of planets could be commenced

from that beginning. Alternatively, the computation could be done from the beginning of any desired *yuga.*

65. *Revolutions of the planets.* The number of eastward revolutions (*bhagaṇa*) in a *yuga* (*i.e., mahā-yuga*) or (*caturyuga*), of the Sun, Mercury (Budha) and Venus (Śukra) and of the *śighrocca*[28] of Mars, Saturn and Jupiter is 43,20,000.

66. The number of revolutions of the Moon is 5,77,53,336; that of Mars is 22,96,832.

67. The number of revolutions of the *śighrocca* of Mercury (*Budha*) is 1,79,37,060. The revolutions of Jupiter are 3,64,220.

68. The number of revolutions of the *śighrocca* of Venus is 70,22,376. The revolutions of Saturn are 1,46,568.

69. The number of revolutions of the Moon's *mandocca* (apogee) is 4,88,203 and the retrograde revolutions of the Moon's ascending node (*pāta*) are 2,32,238.

70. *Terrestrial and Lunar days.*[29] The time from sunrise to sunrise is a terrestrial civil day (*bhūmi-sāvana-vāsara*). The number of terrestrial days in a (*mahā-yuga*) is 1,57,79,17,828. The number of lunar days (*tithi-s*) in the *yuga* is 1,60,30,00,080.

71. *Additive months*[30] *and Subtractive days.*[31] (In a *mahā-yuga*) there are 15,93,336 additive months (*adhimāsa*) and 2,50,82,252 subtractive days (*tithi-kṣaya*).

72. *Solar months*[32] *and lunar months.*[33] There are (in a *mahā-yuga*) 5,18,40,000 solar months (*ravi-māsa*), and the number of lunar months is 5,34,33,336.

73-74. *Mandoccas or Apogees of the planets.*[34] The number of eastward revolutions of the Sun's apogee (*Śūrya-mandocca*) in a *Kalpa* period is 387; that of Mars 204; that of Mercury 368, that of Jupiter 900; that of Venus 535; and that of Saturn 39.

74b-76a. *Pātas or Nodes of the planets.*[35] Now, to the retrograde (*vāma*) revolutions of the nodes (of the planets) in a *Kalpa*: Of Mars it is 214, of Mercury 488, of Jupiter 174, of Venus 903 and of Saturn 662.

76b-79. *Ahargaṇa or number of days from the epoch.*[36] The (solar) years, called *bhagaṇa* that have elapsed in the current *yuga* are converted into (solar) months (by multiplying them by 12) and added to the (lunar) months *Madhu*, (*Caitra*)—Śukla (bright fortnight). etc. which have elapsed (in the current year), and the result is written down separately (in two places). It is then multiplied by the number of additive months (in a *yuga*) and divided by the number of solar months (in a *yuga*). The quotient got (which will be the elapsed additive months) is added to the result (in months) got before and converted into days (by multiplying by 30). The number of days elapsed (in the current month) is added to it and the result written down in two places. (In one place) it is multiplied by the subtractive days (*tithikṣaya*) (in the *Yuga*) and divided by the number of lunar days (in the *Yuga*). The quotient obtained would be the elapsed subtractive days. These (elapsed subtractive days) are subtracted from the result (kept as above, in the second place). The result would be the number of elapsed terrestrial days (from the commencement of the *yuga*) to the previous midnight at Laṅkā.[37]

79b-80a. *Lords of the day etc.* The Lords of the current day, month and year are reckoned, as counted from the Sun. Thus, (the *ahargaṇa*) divided by 7 and (the remainder) counted from Sunday will give the name of the Lord of the day. (Again, the *ahargaṇa*) is divided by the number of days in a month and that in a year (*viz.*, 30 and 360); the quotients are then multiplied, respectively, by 2 and 3, and the products increased by 1. The results are divided by 7 and the remainders counted from the Sun will give the Lords of the present month and year, respectively.

81b-82a. *Mean planets.* The number of revolutions of a planet (in a *Mahāyuga*) multiplied by the (currently) elapsed terrestrial days and divided by the number of terrestrial days (in the *yuga*) will give the elapsed revolutions of the planet (in signs, degrees etc.).

82b-83a. *Mean apogees and nodes.* In the same manner, can be computed the mean positions of the apogees with direct motion, mentioned before. The nodes, too, (should be computed) similarly, but the results have to be subtracted from the circle (*cakra*, 180° or 12 signs) because of their retrograde motion).

83b-84a. *Measurements of the Earth.* The diameter of the Earth is 1600 *yojanas*.[38] The square there is to be multiplied by 10, and the square root of the product will give the circumference of the Earth.

84b. The Earth's circumference multiplied by the sine colatitude (*lambajyā*) (of a given place) and divided by the radius (*trijivā*)[39] is the exact circumference of the Earth at that place.

85-86a. *Deśāntara correction to due terrestrial longitude.* The *Deśāntara* (*i.e.*, the distance of the place, in *yojanas*, along the said local circumference, from Zero or Laṅkā-Ujjain meridian) is multiplied by the daily motion of the planet (in minutes) and divided by the local circumference of the Earth. The quotient, which would be in minutes (*kalā*), should be subtracted from the mean planet (at Laṅkā, *vide* verse 81b-82a, above) if the place is east of the meridian, and added if it is to the west of the meridian. The result would be the mean position of the planet at the given place.

86b-87a. *The central meridian.* On the central meridian, which extends from the capital of the demons (Laṅkā) to the divine mountain (Meru), are (the cities of) Avantikā (Ujjain), Rohitaka and the one near the 'Tank' (Kurukṣetra).

87b-88a. *Beginning of the weekday* (*Vārapravṛtti*). A weekday (at a place) commences (at midnight at that place, which would be) midnight (at Laṅkā meridian, vide verse 79) to which the *deśāntara-nāḍis* (time-difference due to terrestrial longitude) are added (if the place is) to the east and subtracted from (if the place is) to the west (of the meridian).

88b-89a. *Mean-position of a planet at any time.* The desired time in *nāḍi-s* (after the local midnight as calculated above) multiplied by the mean daily motion of the planet and divided by 60 gives a result in terms of minutes. This, when added (to the mean position at midnight) if the time taken after midnight and subtracted from it before midnight, will give the position (of the planet) at the desired time.

89b-91a. *Vikṣepa or Celestial latitude of the Moon and the planets.*[40] The Moon is deflected by its node towards north and south from the limit of its declination, the maximum deviation being 1/80 of a circle (i.e. 4°30'). Jupiter (is similarly deflected) by twice one-ninth (*i.e.*, 2/9) thereof (*i.e.*, of the deflection of the Moon (*i. e.*, 2/9 of 4°30' = 1°), Mars thrice (*i.e.*,

3/9 of 4°30 = 1° 30') and Mercury, Venus and Saturn are deflected four times (*i.e.*, 4/9 of 4°30' = 2°).

TRUE PLANETS (SPHUṬA-GRAHA)

91b-93a. *Primary Sines.* The eighth part of the minutes contained in a sign (*rāśi*) is the first sine (*jyārdha*).[41] That divided by itself, the quotient subtracted from the sine and the remainder added to the sine will give the second sine. In the same manner, divide, successively, the sines found by the first sine, subtract (the sum of) the quotients from the divisor and add the remainder to the previous sine. The result will be the next sine. Thus the 24 sines are to be calculated successively.[42]

93b-94a. *Krānti or declination.* The sine of Maximum declination (*Parama-apakramajyā*) is 1397.[43] When any sine is multiplied by this and divided by *trijivā* (sine 90°, *i.e.*, 3438), the arc of the result would be the declination (of the planet required).

94b-95a. *Sines re. planetary positions.* When (the longitude of) the planet is subtracted from that of its *mandocca* (higher apsis of the equation of the centre) or from its *śighrocca* (higher apsis of the equation of conjunction), the remainder is its *kendra* anamoly); the *pada* (quadrant) (of the *kendra* is noted, and from that) its base-sine (*bhuja-jyā*) and perpendicular-sine (*koṭi-jyā*) are found.[44]

95b-96a. In an odd (*viṣama*) quadrant the base-sine is reckoned from the part gone by (*gata*) and the perpendicular-sine from the part yet to be covered (*gamya*). In an even quadrant (*sama*), the base-sine is reckoned from the part yet to be covered and the perpendicular-sine from the part gone by.

96b-98a. *Derivation of sines of arcs.* (To derive the sine of any arc, *e.g.*, the kendra-*minus*-planet, convert the arc) to minutes and divide by 225 (*tattva-locana*); the result would be the number of the preceding tabular sine (*jyā-piṇḍaka*). Multiply the remainder (in minutes) by the difference of the preceding and following tabular sines and divide by 225 (*tattva-locana*). The quotient obtained is added to the preceding tabular sine; the result would give the sine (of the arc taken).

The same procedure is to be adopted also for versed sines (*utkramajyā*).

100b-101a.[45] *Derivation of arcs from sines.* Subtract from the given sine the next less tabular sine; multiply the remainder by 225 (*tattvāśvi*) and divide by the difference between the next lower and next higher tabular sines. Add the quotient to the product of the serial number of the next less sine and 225. The result would be the arc (of the sine taken).

101b-103a. *Manda-paridhi* (*Epicycle of the apsis or the equation of the centre*). The number of degrees of the Sun's *mandaparidhi* is 14, and that of the Moon 32, at the end of the even quadrants; at the end of the odd quadrants, they are 20 minutes less (in each case).

(In the case of the other planets, they are), at the end of even quadrants, 75 for Mars, 30 (for Mercury), 33 (for Jupiter), 12 (for Venus) and 49 (for Saturn). At the end of the odd quadrants, (they are) 72 for Mars, 28 (for Mercury), 32 for Jupiter, 11 (for Venus) and 48 (for Saturn).

103b-105a. *Śighraparidhi or Epicycles of the equation of conjunction.* The *Śighraparidhis* at the end of the even quadrants are 235 for Mars, 133 (for Mercury), 70 (for Jupiter), 202 (for Venus) and 39 (for Saturn). At the end of the odd quadrants they are 232 for Mars, 132 (for Mercury), 72 (for Jupiter) 260 (for Venus) and 40 (for Saturn).

105b-106a. *Sphuṭaparidhi or corrected epicycle.* The base-sine (*bhujajyā*) should be multiplied by the difference of the epicycles at the odd and even quadrants and divided by the Radius (*trijyā*) and the result, (which would be in minutes), should be applied to the even epicycle (*Yugma-vṛtta*): (these minutes are) additive if the even epicycle is less than the odd epicycle and subtractive otherwise. The corrected (*sphuṭa*) epicycle (is thus obtained).

106b-107a. *Mandaphala or Equation of the centre.* The base-sine (*bhujajyā*) and perpendicular sine (*koṭijyā*) should be multiplied by the corrected epicycle and divided by the number of degrees in a circle (360). (The result would be the corresponding *bhujāphala* and *koṭiphala*, respectively, in minutes). The arc corresponding to the base-sine (*bhujajyā*) would be the equation of the centre (*mandaphala*) in minutes etc.

107b-108. *Śighraphala or Equation of conjunction.* When the *kendra* is in the half-orbit beginning with capricorn (*makarādi*), the result from the perpendicular-sine (*koṭi-phala*) of the distance from the conjunction (*kendra*) is to be added to Radius (*trijīvā*) and subtracted when in that beginning with Cancer (*karkyādi*). The square of this sum or difference is added to the result from the base-sine (*bhujāphala*). The square root of their sum is called *calakarṇa* (variable hypotenuse).

110b-111.[46] The result from the base-sine (*bhujāphala*) is multiplied by radius and divided by the variable hypotenuse (*calakarṇa*). The arc corresponding to the quotient is in minutes and will be the equation of conjunction (*śaighrya-phala*). This (the *Śaighryaphala*) is to be employed in the first and fourth process of correction for Mars and other planets.

112. *Computation of True planets.* For the Sun and the Moon, *mandakarṇa* alone is required. That for Mars etc. is now stated: (First) that for conjunction, then that for the apsis, again that for apsis and for conjunction—the four in succession (half the corrections being applied of the first two and the entire correction of the last two).

113. When the *kendra* is in the half or bit beginning with Aries (*Ajādi*) the equation is additive (*dhana*) for all planets, both in the correction for conjunction and for the apsis; they are all subtractive in the half orbit beginning with Libra (*Tulādi*).

114. *Bhujāntara correction for the equation of time.* The daily motion (*bhukti*) of a planet multiplied by the sun's result from the base-sine and divided by the number of minutes in a circle (*bhacakra*). The result, which would be in minutes, is applied to the True planet got (verses 112-13 above) in the same direction as (the equation applied to) the Sun.

115-16. *Mean daily motion.* The equation of a planet's daily motion is to be calculated like that for the Mean planet in the process for the apsis. The daily motion is multiplied by the difference of the tabular sines corresponding to the base-sine (*doriyāntara*) of anamoly and then divided by 225 (*tattvanetra*). The result is multiplied by the corresponding epicycle of the apsis (*mandaparidhi*) and divided by the number of degrees in a circle (*bhagaṇa*); (the result) is additive when in the half-orbit beginning with cancer, and subtractive when in the half-orbit beginning with Capricorn.

117-18. Subtract the daily motion of the planet corrected for the apsis from the daily motion of its conjunction (*śighra*). Multiply the remainder by the difference between the last hypotenuse (*antya-karṇa*) and the radius and divide by the variable hypotenuse (*calakarṇa*), verses 107b-108). The result is to be added to the daily motion when the hypotenuse is greater than the radius and subtractive when it is less; (in the latter case, if the result) is greater (than the daily motion) subtract the latter from it; the remainder will be the retrograde (*vakra*) daily motion (of the planet).

119-120a. *Retrogression of planets.* Mars and other planets would (commence to be in retrograde motion (*vakri*) when the degrees of their *kendra* in the fourth process (verse 112) are, respectively, (Mars) 164, (Mercury) 144, (Jupiter) 130, (Venus) 163 and (Saturn) 115. They cease to be retrograde from when the degrees (of their *kendras*) are equal to the above-said numbers subtracted from (the degrees in) a circle.

120b-121a. *Length of day and night.* Sine declination (*krāntijyā*) multiplied by the equinoctial shadow (*viṣuvadbhā*)[47] and divided by 12 is the Earth-sine (*kṣitijyā*).[48] This multiplied by Radius (*trijyā*) and divided by the 'day-radius' (*dina-vyāsa*)[49] (gives the sine of the ascensional difference, *cara*). The corres-pondic arc (in minutes) would be the ascensional difference in *prāṇas*[50] (*cārāsavaḥ*).

121b-122. The said arc added to and subtracted from the fourth part of the day and night, separately, will give the duration of half day and half night respectively, when the declination is north (*udak-krānti*). The reverse would be the case when the declination is south (*yāmya-krānti*). Double these (half days and nights) would give (the lengths of) the day and night, respectively.

123. *Position of a planet in an asterism,*[51] (Since 27 *nakṣatra-s* or *bham-s* or asterisms make up the full ecliptic of 360°), the extent in it of one asterism (*bha-bhoga*) is 800 minutes (or 13° 20'). (And, since the Moon gains in longitude over the Sun one circle or 360° in 30 lunar days or *tithis*), the extent of a *tithi* (*tithi-bhoga*) is 720 minutes. The asterisms crossed by a

planet is got by dividing the longitude of the True planet by 800. (The remainder divided) by the daily motion of the planet will give the days etc. (traversed by the planet in the next asterism).

124. *Yoga at a given time.*[52] The sum of the true longitudes of the Sun and the Moon at the required time, reduced to minutes, if divided by 800, will give the number of *Yogas* which have elapsed. The portion gone (*gata*) and to go (*gamya*) in the current *Yoga* multiplied by 60 and divided by the sum of the daily motion of the Sun and the Moon will give the corresponding *nāḍikās* thereof.

125. *Tithi at a desired time.* Subtract the longitude of the Sun in minutes from the longitude of the Moon in minutes and divide by the extent of a *tithi* (*tithibhoga*, 720'); the result will be the *tithis* elapsed. The *nāḍis* gone or to go in the current *tithi* at the desired time are derived by multiplying the remainder by 60 and dividing by the difference between the daily motion of the Sun and Moon at the desired time.

126-127. *The Karaṇa at the desired time.*[53] The *tithis* elapsed after the first half of the first *tithi* of the bright fortnight are multiplied by two and divided by seven (*nāga*). The remainder, counted as Bava, Bālava, Kaulaka, Taitila, Gara, Vaṇij and Viṣṭi, would give the elapsed *karaṇas*. The *karaṇas* from the latter half of the fourteenth *tithi* of the dark fortnight (to the first half of the first *tithi*, of the bright fortnght) are *Śakuni*, *Nāga*, *Catuṣpāt* and *Kiṁstughna*.

ON DIRECTION, PLACE AND TIME

128. *Setting the gnomon.* On a stone slab, levelled with water, or on hard level plaster, describe a circle with any radius measured in gnonomonic digits.

129-131. At its centre fix the gnomon, of twelve digits of the measure of the gnomonic digits used above. Mark the two points where the (gnomonic) shadow meets the circumference of the circle, before and after noon; these two points are to be called the west and east points, (respectively). Midway between them, draw, (using a pair of compasses), by means of a fish-figure (*timi*), a north-south line. Also, Midway between the north and south directions, draw, by means of a fish-figure, an east-west line. In the same manner, by means of fish-figures (*matsya*), draw the intermediate directions between the four cardinal directions.

132. Draw a square circumscribing (the circle), along with the (eight) lines emanating from the centre. Any given shadow is reckoned by the digits of its base-sine (*bhujā-sūtra*) projected on the square.

133. *Prime vertical etc.* The east-west line is called the prime vertical (*sama-maṇḍala*); it is termed also the equatorial horizon (six o'clock circle, *unmaṇḍala*) and equinoctial circle (celestial equator, *viṣuvanmaṇḍala*).

134. *Agrā* (*Amplitude*). (In the circle) draw another east-west line through the extremity of the equinoctial shadow (*viṣuvadbhā*); the interval between any given shadow and the line of the equinoctial shadow is termed the amplitude (*agrā*).

135. The square root of the sum of the squares of the gnomon and of the shadow is the hypotenuse (*karṇa*). If, from the square of the latter, the square of the gnomon be subtracted, the square root of the remainder is the shadow; the gnomon is found by the converse process.

136. *Precession of the equinoxes* (*Ayanacalana*), *at any desired time.* In a *Yuga*, the circle of asterisms librates eastward thirty score (*i.e.*, 600) times. This (number) multiplied by the terrestrial days elapsed (at the desired time) and divided by the number of days in a *Yuga* gives the elapsed liberations, (signs, degrees) etc.

137. Derive the sine (of the *ayana-sphuṭa* thus got), multiply it by three and divide by ten. The result will be the amount of the precession of the equinoxes (at the desired time). The longitude of the planets should be corrected (by adding to or subtracting from the longitudes) the said precession. It is from this (corrected longitude of the planets) that their declination (*krānti*), gnomonic shadow (*chāyā*), ascensional difference (*cara*) etc. are to be calculated.

138. *Latitude and co-latitude from shadow.* The radius multiplied separately by the gnomon (12) and the equinoctial shadow (*chāyā*) and divided by the equinoctial hypotenuse

(*viṣuvatkarṇa*)[54] will give the cosine and sine, respectively, of the latitude. The arcs of these sines will be the co-latitude and latitude. These two will always be inclined to the south.

139. *Zenith distance of the Sun.* The Zenith distance of the Sun (at any time) would be the sum of the latitude of the place and the Sun's declination, when both are in the same direction; and, their difference when in opposite directions. From the Zenith distance, its sine and cosine are to be found.

140. *The shadow and its hypotenuse from Zenith distance.* The sine (of the Zenith distance, found as above) and the Radius[55] multiplied by the length of the gnomon in digits (*i.e.*, 12) and divided by the cosine (of the Zenith distance), give, respectively, the shadow of the gnomon and its hypotenuse at midday (*ahardala*).

141. *Sun's declination and longitude from latitude of a place and zenith distance.* Find the difference between the degrees of the latitude (of the place) and those of the Sun's zenith distance at noon when both are in the same direction and their sum, otherwise. The sun's declination (apakrama) would be detained.

141b-143a. Multiply sine declination by the Radius and divide by the maximum declination of the Sun (*i.e.*, 1397 minutes). (Taking the quotient as the sine) find its arc. This arc will be the longitude of the Sun (in the first quarter of the ecliptic) beginning with Aries. When the Sun is (in the second quarter) beginning with Cancer, subtract (the arc) from 6 signs (*cakrārdha*). When (in the third quarter beginning with Libra), add (the arc) to 6 signs (*bhārdha*). When (in the fourth quarter) beginning with Capricorn subtract (the arc) from 12 signs (*cakra*); in each case, the result will be) the true longitude (*sphuṭa*) of the Sun at midday.

143b. *Mean Sun.* Apply to this the equation of the apsis (*mandaphala*) repeatedly in the opposite sign and the Sun's mean longitude will be got.

144. *Ahorātrāsu of a planet.* The diurnal motion (in minutes) of any planet (on any day) is to be multiplied by the number of *prāṇas* (*asus* or respirations, of time) contained in the rising periods of the sign (*rāśi*) occupied by the planet and

divided by 1800. The quotient added to the number of *prāṇas* in a circle is termed the day-night duration in *prāṇas* of the planet (on that day).

145-146. *Right ascensions of the Signs at Laṅkā.* (Towards finding the right ascensions of the ends of the first three signs, Aries, Taurus and Gemini, find the declinations of the said ends), multiply the day-radius of three signs (*tribhadyukarṇārdha*) and divide by their own respective day-radii (*svāhorātrārdha*), in order, the sines of one, of two and of three signs. The quotients when converted into arc and subtracted, each from the one following, give, beginning with Aries, the times of rising (in *prāṇas*) (of the three signs) at Laṅkā. They are, respectively, 1670, 1795 and 1935.

147a. *Right ascensions at any place.* The above, diminished each by its portion of ascensional difference (*carakhaṇḍa*), as calculated for a place, give the times of rising at that place.

147b-148a. For the three signs beginning with Cancer, invert the times of rising at Laṅkā and add the portions of ascensional difference of the respective signs inverted. The above six, in inverse order, will be the times for the other six commencing with Libra.

148b-149a. *Udaya-Lagna* (*rising point of the ecliptic*) *at any time.* The ascensional equivalents of the parts of the sign (occupied by the planet) which are gone (*bhukta*) and to come (*bhogya*) are to be calculated from the longitude of the Sun at the given time. They will be given by the number of degrees traversed and to be traversed, multiplied by the ascensional equivalent (*udayāsavaḥ*) of the sign and divided by 30.

149b-150a. From the desired time in *nāḍikās* (as reckoned from sunrise) reduced to *prāṇas,* subtract the equivalent in *prāṇas* of the part of the sign to come, and also the ascensional equivalents of the further signs, in succession. In the same manner, subtract the equivalents of the part which has gone by and of the signs which have to go, in inverse order.

150b-151a. If there be a remainder, multiply by 30 and divide by the equivalent of the unsubtracted sign; subtract or add the quotient, appropriately, to the whole signs. The result would be the point of the ecliptic at the horizon at that time.

151b-152a. *Madhyalagna* (*Point of the ecliptic at the meridian*). From the east or west hour-angle of the Sun in *nāḍis* (*nata-nāḍi*), calculate as above using the equivalents in right ascension (*laṅkodayāsavaḥ*) and apply the result as an additive or subtractive equation to the Sun's longitude. The point of the ecliptic upon the meridian (*Madhya-lagna*) at that moment would result.

152b-153-a. *Time from Lagna.* (In order to find the instant when a given point of the ecliptic would be upon the horizon), add together the ascensional equivalents, in *prāṇas*, of : (1) the part of the sign to be traversed by the given point (on the ecliptic) if it is less (than the longitude of the Sun), (2) of the part traversed if it is greater (than the longitude of the Sun), and (3) of the intervening signs. The sum (in *prāṇas*) will give the instant (for the given *lagna*).

SOLAR AND LUNAR ECLIPSES

153b-154a. *Possibility of a lunar eclipse.* (Compute the True Sun, Moon and Node at the syzygies). If sine (Sun-minus-Node) is less than 14 (Indra), there is a possibility of an eclipse. The said sine in minutes is to be multiplied by 11 (Śiva) and divided by 7 (śaila). The result is called *Śara* in digits (*aṅgulas*), and would be directed towards the hemisphere in which (Sun-minus-Node) lies.

154b. *Eclipser and the eclipsed.* (In the solar eclipse, which occurs only at new moon), the Moon obscures the Sun; and in the lunar eclipse, (which occurs only at full moon), the shadow of the Earth obscures the Moon.

154b-155a. Half the (angular) diameters of the eclipsed and the eclipser minus the *śara* is called *channa* (*ka*), (the eclipsed portion, reckoned in digits).[56] Subtract, (if possible), the eclipsed body from the *channa*; the result would be *kha-cchanna* (empty space eclipse).

155b-156b. *Computation of the lunar eclipse.* Half the angular diameters is to be added to the *śara*, the sum multiplied by ten and divided by *channa.* The square root (of the product) is found and a sixth of it is subtracted from it and divided by the angular diameter of the Moon (*glau-vapuḥ*). The result will give the half-duration of the eclipse (*sthityardha*) in *ghaṭikā* etc.

156b-158a. The *sthityardha* (is placed at two places). Sine Sun-minus-Node in degrees is doubled and the number taken as *palas*. They are subtracted from or added to the *sthityardha* if Sun-minus-Node is less than 6 signs or 12 signs, respectively, and vice versa if otherwise. The results got would be the true *sthityardha* (as reckoned) from the commencement and completion of the eclipse. The eclipsed portion (in digits) multiplied by 20 (*nakha*) and divided by the angular diameter of the eclipsed body will give the results called *Vi(ṁ)śopaka-s*.

158b-159. *Computation of the solar eclipse.* (In the solar eclipse), the mid-eclipse occurs at the moment of conjunction. Calculate the *tribhona-lagna* (rising point of the ecliptic-minus-three signs) of the Sun for the moment of conjunction (*parvānta*) and keep it apart. (For the *tribhona-lagna*) calculate the parallax in latitude in degrees (*natāṁśa*) by combining, appropriately, the declination (*krānti*) and latitude (*akṣa*). Divide it by 22 and square the result. If the square is less than 2, halve it and add to the square; if the square is more than 2, subtract 2 from it, halve the result and add to the square. The result thus got is added to 12 and the sum is called 'divisor' (*hara*).

160. Find the difference between *tribhona-lagna* and the Sun, reduce it by a tenth thereof, multiply by 14 (*purandara*) and divide by the 'divisor' (found in verse 159). The result would be the *lambana* (parallax in longitude, in *nāḍikās*). If *tribhona-lagna* is more than 12 (arka), the *lambana* is positive and, if otherwise, negative.

161. The *lambana-nāḍikās* are multiplied by 13 (viśva); the result is to be reckoned in terms of minutes and added to or subtracted from Sun-minus-Node appropriately and (from its sine) its *śara* is determined (*vide* verse 154a). The *lambana* therefrom is multiplied by six. After appropriate addition and subtraction thereof, re. *tribhona-lagna*, the *natāṁśas* are again calculated.

162-163a. A tenth part of these *natāṁśas* are subtracted

from 18 and the result multiplied by the said tenth part. The product is subtracted from 18 minutes and divided by 6. The result will give parallax in longitude (*nati*) in the same direction of the (previous) *natāṁśas*. Appropriate application of this subtractively or additively in accordance with opposite directions or the same direction of the two, will render the *śara* accurate.

163b-165a. Using the said *śara*, the (exact) eclipsed portion (*channa*) and half duration of the eclipse are to be found (as before). The half-duration is multiplied by 6; the result, which would be in degrees, is kept at two places and the *tribhona-lagna* subtracted from or added to it, respectively, and the *lambana* calculated from the two, as before. The results being appropriately applied, the exact (first and second) half durations are obtained. These subtracted from and added to, as the case may be to the mid-eclipse (*madhya-kāla*), will give the exact times of the commencement and the conclusion of the eclipse.

MISCELLANEOUS MATTERS

165b-166a. *Heliacal visibility of the planets*[57]. The *kālāṁśa*-(degrees of time) of the planets beginning with the Moon are : 12 (Moon), 17 (Mars), 13 (Mercury), 11 (Jupiter), 9 (Venus) and 15 (Saturn). The heliacal setting and rising of these planets occur, respectively, at times got by subtracting (the *kālāṁśas*) from sunrise and by adding them to sunset.

166b-167a. *Shadow of a planet.* Consider the reflection of a planet (in water or in a mirror) and ascertain the ocular altitude (*dṛgaucyaṁ lambam*). The distance between the foot of the gnomon and the spot of the reflection, multiplied by 12 (*ravi*) and divided by the ocular altitude, will give the measure of the shadow of the planet (in digits).

167b-168. *Elongation of the Moon's horns.* At sunset (on the desired day) the *tithi* and its divisions (*nāḍikā, vināḍikā* etc.) gone and to go are accurately determined. The *tithis* are multiplied by 16 and the square of the *tithis* subtracted therefrom. The result is multiplied by the equinoctial shadow (*akṣabhā*) and divided by 15. The direction of the result is taken as north and corrected appropriately with the declination (in minutes) of the Sun and also by *śara* of the Moon in minutes applied reversely. The result is divided by twice the *tithis*. The *valana* (deflection) in digits towards the direction of the correction (i.e., the direction in which the Sun is with reference to the Moon) is got.

169. Subtract from the *tithi* one-fifth of itself; (the measure of) the illuminated part of the Moon (phase, *sita*) is obtained. The horn of the Moon will be elongated in the direction of *valana*. The measure in digits of the elongation shall be ascertained by means of a diagram.

170-171a. *Conjunction of the planets*. The numbers 5, 6, 7, 9 and 5 (corresponding to the five planets Mars etc.) are multiplied by *Trijyā*-minus-the respective *śighrakarṇa* and (placed at two places. One set is divided, respectively by 21, 12, 6, 24 and 3 and the result is applied to other set, *i.e.*, subtracted if the hypotenuse is larger than *trijyā* and added otherwise. The results divided by 3 will be the angular diameters of the discs of the several planets beginning from Mars.

171b-172a. *Time of conjunction*. (When it is necessary to determine when two planets will meet): If the two planets are both regular or retrograde, the difference in their longitudes is divided by the difference of their rates of motion; if one is regular and the other retrograde, (the difference of their longitudes) is divided by the sum of their rates of motion. The result in days etc. would give the time to pass for their conjunction.

172b-173. *Mutual non-obscuration of planets in conjunction*. (The two planets in conjunction) should be corrected by their respective parallaxes in latitude (*nati*) according to their *śaras*, it being addition if in the same direction and subtraction otherwise. When the north-south difference of the two planets is less than half the sum of their diameters, there will be (visual) distinction between the two, (there being no obscuration). True (*sphuṭa*) results can, of course, be arrived by working with the parallax in longitude (*lambana*) etc. as in the case of the solar eclipse.

VYATIPĀTA AND VAIDHṚTA : MALIGNANT SITUATIONS OF SUN AND MOON

174. *Vaidhṛta*.[58] When the Sun and the Moon are in

the same *ayana*, *i.e.*, on the same side of either solstice, if the sum (of their longitudes) is one circle (360), and both have equal declinations, that situation is called *Vaidhṛta.*

175. *Vyatipāta.* When the Sun and the Moon are on the opposite sides of either solstice and have equal minutes of declination, that situation is called *Vyatipāta,* the sum (of their longitudes) being a half-circle.

176. *Time when declinations are equal.* When the longitudes of the Sun and the Moon corrected by the degrees of precession of the equinoxes as found by observation, is equal to 12 signs or 6 signs, respectively, compute their declinations.

177. Then, if the declination of the Moon, which is in an odd quadrant, and had been corrected for its latitude (*Vikṣepa*), is greater than the declination of the Sun, the situation of *pāta* is already past.

178. If less, it is still to come. In an even quadrant, the reverse is the case. If the Moon's declination is subtractible from its latitude, the rules as to the quadrant are to be reversed.

179. Multiply the sines of the two declinations separately by Radius (*trijyā*) and divide by the sine of the maximum declination (*parakrāntijyā, viz.*, 1397) and find the arcs (of the two results). The difference (of the arcs) or half that difference is to be added to the Moon's longitude when the *pāta* is yet to occur.

180. It is to be subtracted from the Moon's longitude when the *pāta* is past. The said (difference) when multiplied by the Sun's daily motion and divided by the Moon's daily motion, gives a correction, in minutes, to be duly applied to the longitude of the Sun, (being subtracted from the Sun if the *pāta* is past and added to it if the *pāta* is yet to occur).

181. A similar correction is to be applied, in the reverse order, to the Moon's mode. This operation is repeated until the declinations (of the Sun and the Moon) are equal.

182. *Mean time of the Pāta.* The *pāta* occurs at the moment when the declinations are equal. (To find out whether a *pāta* is past or yet to come): If the Moon's longitude at the *pāta* found by applying the correction to the Moon (vide verse 180) is less or greater than (the Moon's longitude) at

midnight (of that day), the *pāta* is past or is yet to occur, respectively.

183. *True time of Pāta.* The minutes of the interval between the Moon's longitude (at the Mean *pāta*), as ascertained, and that at midnight, when multiplied by 60 and divided by the Moon's daily motion, will give the time of the *pāta* in *nāḍikās*.

184. *Half-duration of the Pāta.* Multiply half the sum of the diameters of the Sun and the Moon by 60 and divide by the difference of their daily motions. The result will be the half-duration, (*sthityardha* (of the *pāta*), in *nāḍikā* etc.

185. *Beginning, Middle and End of the Pāta.* The true time (of the *pāta* (vide verse 183) is the middle (moment of the *pāta*). That diminished by the half-duration (vide verse 184) is the moment of its commencement and that increased by the half-duration is the moment of its end.

186. *Consequence of the Pāta.* Compared to the beginning and the end, the middle moment of the *pāta* is extremely harmful. It is like burning fire and is to be avoided in all (auspicious) rites.

187. O brāhmaṇa ! Thus has been stated, in brief, matters relating to mathematics and astronomy (*gaṇita*). I shall, now, set out horoscopy (*jātaka*) commencing with (the statement of) the nomenclature of the *rāśi-s* (signs).

CHAPTER FIFTYFOUR

NOTES

1. Hindu texts on astronomy call this section as *Tripraśna-adhyāya,* since it deals with 'problems' concerning the 'three' topics, *viz.*, time, place and direction.

2. Actually, however, this topic is not treated in the *Purāṇa.*

3. The two *vyatīpatas*, being malignant aspects of Sun and Moon, called *Lāṭa* and *Vaidhṛta,* occur at the moments when the sum of the longitudes of the Sun and the Moon is equal to 180° and 360°, respectively. These moments are considered to be highly inauspicious (*vi-ati-pāta*).

4. For the constitution and list of *Yogas,* see below, note under verse 211b. See also ch. 54, Verse 124 and footnote.

5. For the nature of *karaṇa* and the list thereof, see below, note under verse 219b. See also ch. 54, verses 126-27 and footnote.

6. The idea is that the operation could start from the unit digits *i.e.*, from the right end of the numbers, as is the general practice, or from the highest digits of the numbers at the left end.

7. For the detailed working, see *Līlāvatī* of Bhāskarācārya, (edn. Hoshiarpur, 1975). So also, for the arithmetical operations set out below.

8. Written in modern convention, this would be

$$\frac{(a+b)+(a-b)}{2} = a; \quad \frac{(a+b)-(a-b)}{2} = b$$

9. $$\frac{a^2-b^2}{a-b} = a+b$$

10. 1. Verses 32-34 give three methods to derive, on the basis of any assumed number, sets of two numbers which when squared and added together or one subtracted from the other, and reduced by 1, give perfect squares.

Method I. The numbers are : $\frac{8x^2-1}{2x}$ and $1/2\,\frac{(8x^2-1)^2}{2x}+1.$

Sum of their squares *minus* $1=64x^4-2+\frac{1}{64y}4=(8x^2-\frac{1}{8y}2)^2$

Diff. of their squares *minus* $1=64x^4+6+\frac{1}{64x}4-32x^2-\frac{1}{2x^2}=(8x^2-2+\frac{1}{8x^2})^2$

Method II. The numbers are : $(x+\frac{1}{2x})$ and 1.

Sum of their squares *minus* $1=(x+\frac{1}{2x})^2+1^2-1=(x+\frac{1}{2x})^2$

Diff. of their squares *minus* $1=(x+\frac{1}{2x})^2-1^2-1=(x+\frac{1}{2x})^2$

Method III. The numbers are : $(8x^4+1)$ and $8x^3$

Sum of their Squares *minus* $1=(8x^4+1)^2+(8x^3)^2-1=(8x^4+4x^2)^2$

Diff. of their Squares *minus* $1=(8x^4+1)^2-(8x3)^2-1=(8x^4-4x^2)^2$

Thus, all the results obtained are perfect squares.

11. Here, the first two lines give the method to calculate the last term of the series and the third line, the sum of the series. Thus, in a geometrical series, if *m* is the first member (*mukha, prāg*), *g* is the common ratio (*guṇaka*), *r* is the number of terms (*gaccha*) and *s* the sum of the series (*dhana, sarvadhana*) :

The last term $= m \times gr$

Sum of the series $= \dfrac{m(g^r - 1)}{(g-1)}$

For detailed working, see *Līlāvatī, op. cit.*, 125 (pp. 256-64).

12. Thus, in a right angled triangle, if *a* is the altitude, *b* the base, and *h* the hypotenuse, $a^2+b^2=h^2$.

13. The three sides would thus be i. $(a-b)^2+2ab = a^2+b^2$; ii. $(a+b)(a-b)=a^2-b^2$; iii. $2ab$, for $(a^2-b^2)^2(+2ab)^2 = (a^2+b^2)^2$.

14. Thus the circumference of a circle is $22/7d$.

15. Thus: $śara = 1/2\ (vyāsa - \sqrt{(vyāsa+jyā)(vyāsa-jyā)}$

$jya = 2\sqrt{(Vyāsa\text{-}śara) \times śara}$

$Vyāsa = \dfrac{(1/2 jya)^2 + śara}{śara}$

16. If *a* is the arc, *c* circumference, *d* diameter and *s* sine;

'First' $= (c-a)\ a$

Sine $= 4\ d \times \dfrac{a\ (c-a).}{5/4c^2 - a(c-\bar{a})}$

17. Arc $= \dfrac{c}{2} - \sqrt{\dfrac{c^2}{4} - \dfrac{5\ s.c^4 \div 4}{4d+s}}$

18. Different heights for different grains are suggested for the reason that when made into a conical heap, coarse grain would pile up higher while fine grain would slip down and so pile up only to a lesser height.

19. *Droṇa* is one of the bigger measures of volume used in ancient and mediaeval India.

20. The gnomon in general use in ancient India was a strong, straight, cylindrical rod, made of metal or of wood, 12 inches in height, and pointed at the tip. In use, it was fixed firmly on a hard, level surface at the centre of a graduated circle.

21. In the figure, LA=Height of the lamp

GB=Gonomon

CS=Gnomonic shadow

By the application of the rules of similar triangles, shadow,

$$CS = \frac{GC \times BC}{LA}$$

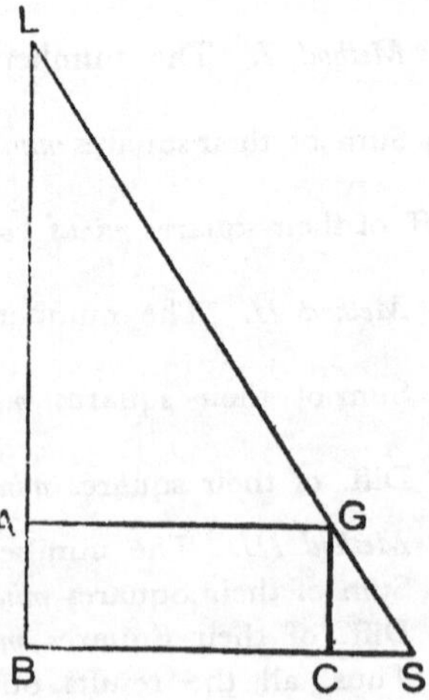

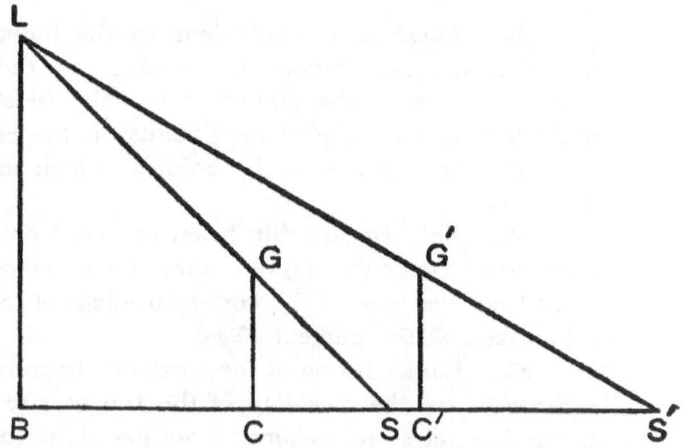

22. Height of the lamp,

$$BL = \frac{GC \times BC}{CS}$$

23. Lamp to gnomon,

$$BC = \frac{LA \times CS}{GC}$$

24. If LB, the lamp,
GC and G' C', the two gnomons,
CS and C' S', the two shadows
BS and BS', the two bases,

$$\text{Base } BS = \frac{SS' \times CS}{(C'S' - CS)}$$

$$BS' = \frac{SS' \times C'S'}{(C'S' - CS)}$$

25. $$\text{Lamp } LB = \frac{BS \times GC}{CS} = \frac{BS' \times G'C'}{C'S'}$$

26. A 'divine' year (*divya-varṣa*) is equal to 360 'mortal' years or siderial years of current astronomical parlance.

27. Manu is one of the mythical progenitors of man and the time mentioned here is called a *manvantara.* 14 *manvantaras* constitute a longer Puranic duration of time mentioned in the next verse, which is termed *Kalpa.*

28. By *Śīghrocca* is meant the farthest point from the centre of the earth in the orbit of the planet, or the higher apsis of the epicycle related to the equation of conjunction.

29. A lunar day (*tithi*) is equal to one-thirtieth of a lunar month (*cāndra-māsa*) which is the interval between two conjunctions (or oppositions) of the Moon, being the period of the moon's synodical revolution, and is reckoned either from new moon to new moon or from full moon to full moon.

30. A lunar month, extending over 29.5306, days, being shorter than a solar month of 30.4380 days, the number of lunar months in about three solar years would be one more than that of the solar months. This extra lunar month is called *adhimāsa* (additive or intercalary month).

31. A lunar day (*tithi*) being smaller than a terrestrial day (*bhūdina*), if the two begin simultaneously at a sunrise, the lunar day will end earlier. This difference will increase day by day and when it is equal to one day (24 hrs.), it constitutes one *tithikṣaya* or subtractive day.

32. The solar month (*saura-māsa*), being one-twelfth of a solar year (*saura-varṣa*) or siderial year (*nakṣatra-varṣa*), is the time required by the Sun to pass through one *rāśi* (sign or 30°) of the Zodiac and is equal to 30.4380 terrestrial days.

33. A lunar month (*cāndra-māsa*) is equal to 30 lunar days (*tithis*) and is equal to 29.5306 terrestrial days.

34. *Mandocca* is equivalent to the higher Apsis. The *mandoccas* of the Sun and the Moon are the same as their Apogees (points on the orbit farthest from the planet), while the *mandoccas* of the other planets are equivalent to their Aphelions (points on the orbit farthest from the Sun).

35. *Pāta* (node) is the point at which the orbit of a planet intersects the ecliptic.

36. The *ahargaṇa* (lit. 'total of days') or *bhūdina* at any time is the number of (terrestrial) days that have elapsed upto the previous midnight from the time of the commencement of the epoch, which latter is generally taken as the current *Yuga*.

37. Laṅkā is one of the cardinal hypothetical cities on the Earth's equator where the meridian of the Indian city of Ujjain cuts it. In Indian astronomy, days are reckoned from midnight (or sunrise, according to different systems) at the meridian of Laṅka. For a discussion on the position of Laṅkā, see *Āryabhaṭīya*, Ed. with Tr., (Delhi 1976), pp. 123-25. See also below, verses 86b-87a.

38. 1. A *Yojana*, according to this, will be about 4.95 miles or 7.56 km.

Thus, if *r* is the radius of the Earth, Circumference$=2r^2\text{x}\sqrt{10}=$ $2r\text{x}\sqrt{10}$. Here $\sqrt{10}$ is taken as π as per the formula, *cir.* $= 2\,\pi$ r. This works out of 5059.556 *yojanas*.

39. *Trijīvā*, called also *trijyā*, *tribhajyā*, *triguṇa*, *trirāśijyā*, is sine 3 *rāśis* (or 90) and is equal to the radius of the circle.

40. *Vikṣepa* (celestial latitude) is the deviation of the planets from the plane of the ecliptic.

41. Thus : The cycle=360°, *rāśi* or sign = 1/12 x 360°=30° 1/8 sign = 3°45' or 225'. This is the first of the 24 signs contained in a quarter (90° or 3 signes).

42. The second sine, being the sine for the second section (*khaṇḍa*) 225'+225'=450', would be : 225/225=1; 450-1=449'.

The third sine, being the sine for the third section (*Khaṇḍa*), 225'+225'+225=675', would be : Present quotient 449/225=2; the sum of the quotients= 2+1=3; the sum reduced from the first sine 225=225 − 3 = 222. The result added/to the second sine = 449+222=671, the third sine.

The process is repeated. The several sines calculated thus are given below :—

No.	*Khaṇḍa in minutes*	*Sine*	*No.*	*Khaṇḍa in Minutes*	*Sine*
0	0	000			
1	225	225	13	2925	2585
2	450	449	14	3150	2728
3	675	671	15	3375	2859
4	900	890	16	3600	2978
5	1125	1105	17	3825	3084
6	1350	1315	18	4050	3177
7	1575	1520	19	4275	3256
8	1800	1719	20	4500	3321
9	2025	1910	21	4725	3372
10	2250	2093	22	4950	3409
11	2475	2267	23	5175	3431
12	2700	2431	24	5400	3438

43. In Hindu astronomy, the maximum declination (obliquity of the ecliptic) is taken as 24′; and 1397 represents sine 24°.

44. While the *mandoccas* of the Sun and the Moon are the same as as their apogees, that of the other planets are equal to their aphelions. For details on the concept of and computations with *mandoccas* and *śīghroccas* in Hindu astronomy, see E. Burgess, *Translation of the Sūryasiddhānta*, ed. by P. Gangooly, Calcutta, 1935, pp. 53-56.

45. The Venkatesvara Press edn. of *Nārada Purāṇa* used for this translation, repeats, here, haplographically, two verses, thus erratically increasing serial number of the verses by two. While the repeated verses are dropped in the translation the increased serial number is retained so that there might not be any discrepancy in the number of the verses in the text edition and the present translation.

46. The Venkatesvara Press edition of *Nārada Purāṇa* used for this translation repeats here haplographically three earlier lines, increasing the serial numbering of the verses correspondingly. Here, the changed verse number is adopted according to the edition; the repeated lines are not translated.

47. *Viṣuvad-bhā* or Equinoctial shadow at a place is the shadow of the Sun cast by a gnomon of 12 digits at Midday on the day of the Vernal equipox (March 21) or Autumnal equinox (Sept.23) at that place.

48. *Kṣitijyā* (Earth-sine) is the sine of the arc of the diurnal circle intercepted between the horizon and the six o'clock line.

49. *Dina-vyāsa-dala* (day-radius), called also *dyu-jyā* ('day-sine') is the radius of the diurnal circle, in contrast to *trijyā* which is the radius of the 'great circle' or the 'tabular radius'.

50. *Prāṇa* or *Asu* ('respiration') is the period of time required for one respiration and is /equal to 4 seconds.

51. The ecliptic is divided into 27 asterisms or lunar mansions of equal extent of 13°20' or 800' each, called Aśvini, Bharaṇī etc. The *nakṣatra* forms one of the members of the five-member, almanac (*Pañcāṅga*) of the Hindus, the other four members being, *Vāra* (weekday), *tithi* (lunar day), *Yoga* and *Karaṇa*, for which see below.

52. *Yoga*, one of the members of the five-membered Hindu almanac, is used only for astrological purposes. It is a period of time of variable length during which the joint motion of the longitudes of the Sun and the Moon amounts to 13°20' or 800', being the extent of a lunar mansion. They are 27 in number, and are mentioned in Hindu almanacs for each day. They have individual names, as follows :—

1. Viṣkambha, 2. Prīti; 3. Āyuṣmān; 4. Saubhāgya; 5. Śobhana, 6. Atigaṇḍa, 7. Sukarma, 8. Dhṛti; 9. Śūla; 1p, Gaṇḍa; 11. Vṛddhi; 12. Dhruva; 13. Vyāghāta; 14. Harṣaṇa; 15. Vajra, 16. Siddhi, 17. Vyatīpāta, 18. Varīyas; 19. Parigha, 20. Śiva, 21. Siddha; 22. Sādhya; 23. Śubha; 24. Śukla, 25. Brahman, 26. Indra, and 27. Vaidhṛti.

53. The *karaṇa* is also an entity made use of only in astrology and forms a member of the five-membered (*pañcāṅga*), Hindu almanac. Each *Karaṇa* extends over half a *tithi*. The four *dhruva* ('fixed') *karaṇas viz*., *Śakuni*, *Nāga*, *Catuṣpāt* and *Kiṁstugna* occupy the four half-*tithis* as stated above, and the other seven *karaṇas* repeat eight times through the next 56 half-*tithis*, when the cycle of 60 *karaṇas* in a lunar month is completed. The cycle is then repeated.

54. *Viṣuvatkarṇa*, or equinoctial hypotenuse, is the hypotenuse of the equinoctial shadow found by calculating the square root of the sum of the squares of the equinoctial -shadow and the gnomon.

55. By 'Radius' (with capital 'R') is meant the radius of the great circle or the tabular radius. In Sanskrit it is called *trijyā*, *trijīvā*, *tribhajyā* etc., meaning the sine of three sines or 90°.

56. It might be noted that if the śara is larger and cannot be subtracted from half the (angular) diameters of the eclipsed and the eclipser, there will be no *channa* (eclipsed portion) and so no eclipse.

57. For a little time before sunrise and after sunset, the planets, near the Sun, would be invisible on account of the sun's brilliance. The times after sunset and before sunrise they would be visible are indicated here.

58. This section, called *Pātādhikāra* (Section on *pātas*) in treatises, treats of two astronomical situations called *Vyatīpāta* and *Vaidhṛta* which are highly malignant in character. They are computed and used for astrological purposes, *viz*., to avoid auspicious acts being held at these situations.

CHAPTER FIFTYFIVE

Delineation of Horoscopy

Sanandana said :

1. The twelve limbs of Kālapuruṣa, the Cosmic Being, viz. (1) head, (2) face, (3) arms, (4) heart, (5) breast, (6) entrails, (7) pelvis, (8) genital organ, (9) thighs, (10) knees, (11) shanks and (12) feet are (represented by) the twelve Signs of the Zodiac viz. *Meṣa* (Aries), *Vṛṣabha* (Taurus), *Mithuna* (Gemini), *Karkaṭaka* (Cancer), *Siṁha* (Leo), *Kanyā* (Virgo), *Tulā* (Libra), *Vṛścika* (Scorpio), *Dhanus* (Sagittarius), *Makara*, (Capricorn), *Kumbha* (Aquarius) and *Mīna* (Pisces), respectively.[1]

2. The lords of the twelve Signs (Rāśis) beginning with Meṣa (Aries) are in order (1) Mars, (2) Venus, (3) Mercury, (4) Moon, (5) Sun, (6) Mercury (7) Venus, (8) Mars, (9) Jupiter, (10) Saturn (11) Saturn, and (12) Jupiter.

3. In the odd Signs of the zodiac the first Horā i.e. 15 degree portion, is ruled by the Sun and the second by the Moon, while in the even signs the first is owned by the Moon and the next by the Sun. The lords of the three decanates i.e. 10 degree portions, in each Rāśi are those of the same Sign, the fifth one from the first and the ninth from the first respectively.[2]

4. In the odd Signs the lords of *Triṁśāṁśas* (degree portions) are Mars who owns the first 5 degrees, Saturn who owns the next 5 degrees, Jupiter who owns the next 8 degrees, Mercury who owns the next 7 degrees, and Venus who owns the last 5 degrees. This order of ownership is reversed in the case of even Signs.[3]

5. The Navāṁśas (1/9 of a Sign or 3 degrees and 20 minutes) of *Meṣa, Siṁha* and *Dhanus* begin with *Meṣa* itself; those of *Vṛṣabha, Kanyā* and *Makara*, with *Makara*; those of *Mithuna, Tulā* and *Kumbha*, with *Tulā*; and lastly those of *Karkaṭaka, Vṛścika* and *Mīna*, with *Karkaṭaka*. The lords of the *Dvādaśāṁśas* (1/12 portions of a Rāśī or 2½ degree portions) are those of the 12 Signs beginning with the same Rāśī. Thus

the six sub-divisions of a Sign are based upon the Signs of the zodiac.[4]

6. *Meṣa, Vṛṣabha, Mithuna, Karkaṭaka, Dhanus* and *Makara* are termed *Nocturnal* Signs, and these Signs rise with their hind parts first. The remaining Signs are called *Diurnal*, while Pisces rises both ways. The Signs are called *Cruel* and *Gentle* in order. They are also named *Male* and *Female* respectively.[5]

7. The three Signs beginning with Meṣa, taken at a time, represent in order *Male, Female* and *Eunuch* as well as *Movable, Fixed* and *Dual* Rāśis. The four Signs, Aries, Taurus, Gemini and Cancer, represent the four quarters, east, south, west and north respectively. The 12 Signs have their respective haunts or abode.[6]

8. The *Exaltation* Signs of the Seven planets headed by the Sun are in order *Meṣa, Vṛṣabha, Makara, Kanyā, Karkaṭaka, Mīna* and *Tulā*. Their highest exaltation points are in order the 2nd (?), 3rd, 28th, 15th, 5th, 27th and 20th degrees in their respective exaltation Signs.[7]

9. The *Debilitation* Rāśis of the seven planets beginning with the Sun are the 7th ones from their respective Exaltation Signs. The *Vargottama Navāṁśas* of the three Signs *Movable, Fixed* and *Dual*, repeated four times, are in order the first, middle i.e. 5th, and the last one. The 12 Bhāvas or houses beginning with the *Lagna* or Body constitute the whole personality of an individual.[8]

10. The *Mūlatrikoṇa* Signs of the seven planets beginning with the Sun are in order Leo, Taurus, Aries, Virgo, Sagittarius, Libra and Aquarius. *Caturasra* or Square houses are the 4th and 8th ones from a particular Sign, house (Bhāva) or a planet. The *Trikoṇa* or Triangular houses are the 5th and 9th from the house of reference or the Lagna.[9]

11. The triad of houses (that are termed inauspicious) consists of the 6th, 8th and 12th from the Lagna. The *Kendras* of *Angular* houses are the ascendant (1st), 4th, 7th and 10th. The Signs named *Human, Watery* (or Aquatic), *Reptile* and *Quadruped* are strong in the above four *Kendras* respectively.[10]

12-13. The houses immediately following the Kendras are termed *Paṇaphara*; and those following the latter, *Āpoklima*. The colours of the 12 Rāśis beginning with Aries are in order

(1) Red, (2) White, (3) Green, (4) Pink, (5) Brown, (6) Grey, (7) Variegated, (8) Black, (9) Yellow, (10) Saffron, (11) Deep Brown, and (12) Bright.

14. The seven planets beginning with the Sun represent (1) the *Soul* of Kālapuruṣa or Time, (2) His *Mind*, (3) His *Prowess*, (4) His Speech, (5) His *Wisdom* and *Happiness*, (6) His *Sexual Passion*, and (7) His *Sorrow*, in order.

15. The Sun and the Moon are the Royal planets (King and queen); Mars, the commander of the army; Mercury, the royal prince; Jupiter and Venus, the ministers; and Saturn, the messenger. This is the opinion of the leading luminaries of astrology.

16. The colours of the seven planets are in order (1) copper colour, (2) white, (3) deep red, (4) green, (5) yellow, (6) variegated, and (7) jet black. Their presiding Deities are in order (1) Rudra, (2) Goddess Durgā, (3) Śeṣa, (4) Viṣṇu, (5) Indra, (6) Indra's consort Śacī, and (7) Yama.[11]

17. The lords of the 8 quarters are in order (1) the Sun, (2) Venus, (3) Mars, (4) Rāhu, (5) Saturn, (6) The Moon, (7) Mercury and (8) Jupiter. The following are termed *Malefic* planets : The weak Moon, the Sun, Saturn, and Mercury in association with a malefic planet.

18. Mercury and Saturn are termed Eunuchs; the Moon and Venus, *Female*; and the rest, Male. The abodes of Mars, Mercury, Jupiter, Venus and Saturn are in order Fire, Earth, Ether, Water and Air.[12]

19. Venus, Jupiter, Mars and the Sun are the rulers of the *Ṛgveda*, *Yajurveda*, *Sāmaveda* and *Atharvaveda* respectively. They also preside over the four classes viz. Brāhmaṇas, Kṣatriyas, Vaiśyas and Śūdras in order. Saturn is said to be the leader of outcasts, and Rāhu, the lord of Mlecchas (barbarians).[13]

20. The Sun, Moon and Jupiter are *Sāttvika* (pure) in nature; Mercury and Venus, *Rājasa* (active or passionate); and Mars and Saturn, *Tāmasa* (dark, inert or ignorant).

21-22. Their clothes are in order (1) thick, (2) new, (3) singed by fire, (4) soft, (5) fine (strong ?) (6) silken and (7) rags. Their metals are (1) copper, (2) silver, (3) copper, (4) lead, (5) gold, (6) bell-metal, and (7) iron. These metals are to be deduced from the rulers of the decanates rising at the time. The six seasons viz. winter, spring, summer, monsoon, autumn and dewy season are ruled over by Saturn, Venus, Mars, Moon, Mercury, and Jupiter respectively.[14]

23. O Nārada, Saturn aspects fully the 3rd and 10th houses, Jupiter the 5th and 9th, Mars the 4th and 8th houses counted from the one occupied by them and all the planets cast their full aspect on the 7th house.

24. The periods allotted to the seven planets from the Sun onwards are in order. a solstice (six months), —a Muhūrta or moment, a day, two months, a month, a fortnight, and a year. Their tastes are in order pungent, bitter, salt, mixed, sweet, sour and astringent.[15]

25-26. The friends of a planet are the lords of the 2nd, 4th, 5th, 8th, 9th and 12th Rāśis counted from the *Mūlatrikoṇa* Rāśi of the planet concerned. Friends of the seven planets beginning with the Sun are : (1) Jupiter, (2) Jupiter and Mercury, (3) Venus and Mercury, (4) all planets except the Sun, (5) all except Mars, (6) all except the Sun and the Moon, and (7) all except the Sun, Moon, and Mars. Planets that are posited in the 2nd, 12th, 11th, 3rd, 4th and 10th from one are his (temporary) friends.[16]

27. O Sage (Nārada), after ascertaining the natural friends, enemies and neutrals, the temporary friends also should be determined. A natural friend who happens to be a temporary friend also, becomes an *Adhimitra* (an intimate friend). Similarly, a natural friend would become a *neutral*, if he has no temporary friendship. A natural enemy, who is a temporary friend, would become *neutral*. By the same argument a natural enemy would become a bitter enemy too.[17]

28. A planet attains *positional strength* (*Sthāna-bala*) by its occupation of its exaltation house, Mūlatrikoṇa, own house and Navāṁśa owned by itself. Murcury and Jupiter get *directional strength* (*Digbala*) when they are posited in the East; the Sun and Mars. in the South; Saturn, in the West; and the Moon and Venus, in the North.[18]

29. Planets are said to be strong in their respective seasons, and in the *uttarāyaṇa* or Winter Solstice; while others get strength by retrograde motion. Planets in conjunction being

to the north of others and possessed of brilliant rays are considered to be possessed of *Ceṣṭābala* or Motional strength.[19]

30. The *Temporal* strength (*Kālabala*) of planets is explained by scholars thus : The Moon, Mars and Saturn are strong at *night*; Mercury is strong *always*; while the rest are strong by *day*. Malefics are strong in the dark fortnight, while benefics in the bright one.[20]

31-32. Among the planets, Saturn, Mars, Mercury, Jupiter, Venus, the Moon and the Sun, each succeeding planet is stronger than its predecessor. When malefics are powerful and benefics devoid of strength; when there a eunuch planet occupies or aspects a Kendra, the birth of a sub-human being (say, animal or bird) takes place. The birth will correspond to the nature of the Aṁśa of the Sun or the Moon (whichever is stronger). When malefics are in their own Aṁśas, and benefics in those of malefics, the birth of sub-human beings is to be predicted.[21]

33-34. Where the Lagna is weak, in addition, scholars should predict the birth of an animal. In the case of quadrupeds the 12 Rāśis beginning with Meṣa represent their (1) Head, (2) Face and Neck, (3) Fore-Legs and Shoulders, (4) Back, (5) Chest, (6) Sides, (7) Stomach, (8) Anus and Hind legs, (9) Genital Organ, (10) Testicles, (11) Haunches, and (12) Tail.

35. The colour of the animal will have to be predicted from the strongest of the Rāśis represented by the Navāṁśa of the ascendant and those that are occupied by planets. The lines on the back of the animal will correspond to the number of planets in the 7th house, or the number of planets aspecting that house.[22]

36. Birds are born when the lord of the ascendant is posited in a *Bird Decanate*, and in the last Navāṁśa of a Rāśi, in conjunction with another planet. Similar is the result when the ascendant is aspected by or is conjoined with Saturn or the Moon. The nature of bird, whether belonging to water or land, is to be deduced from that of the Navāṁśa of the ascendant. [Or it may be thus :—If the decanate of the ascendant is connected with the Moon (by aspect or conjunction),

the bird must be an aquatic one, while with Saturn, it is a land bird.][23]

37. When the Lagna, the Moon, Sun and Jupiter are devoid of strength, the birth of trees should be predicted. The distinction between water and land trees is to be made on the basis of the Navāṁśa of the ascendant, as given previously.

38. The number of trees that are born on land or water corresponds to the one denoted by the number of Rāśis by which the lord of the Lagna is separated from the Lagna.

39. When the lord of the ascendant happens to be the Sun, the trees born are those that are strong internally (i.e. whose pith is strong); if it is Saturn, they would be worthless trees; if it is the Moon, they would be milky trees; if Mars, thorny ones; if Jupiter, fruit-bearing ones; and if Mercury, fruitless ones.

40. If the lord of the Lagna is Venus, the trees will be flower-bearing trees; if it is the Moon, glossy or juicy ones; if Mars, pungent ones. If the concerned planet be benefic posited in the Rāśi owned by a malefic, the result would be a good tree growing on a bad soil.

41. A retrograde planet will yield results similar to those of one posited in another's (i.e. enemy's) Aṁśa. In this world the menstrual flow of women takes place every month owing to the inter-action of the Moon and Mars.[24]

42. When the Moon in her transit comes to an *Upacaya* house (3, 6, 10 or 11 from the Lagna) in the woman's birth chart and is aspected by Jupiter, man unites with woman for impregnation. If the 7th house from the ascendant at the time of sexual union is occupied or aspected by malefics, the union takes place in a huff; if by benefics, with pleasure.[25]

43. O Foremost of Brahmins, men possessed of strong vitality (virility) would be able to beget issue, if, at the time of coitus, Venus, the Sun and Mercury be posited in their own Rāśis or Aṁśas and Jupiter in a *Trikoṇa* house from the Lagna.[26]

44. If Mars and Saturn be posited in the 7th house from the Sun and Moon at the time of sexual union, the man and woman would fall ill. The couple would meet with their end, if the luminaries (the Sun in the case of the man, and the Moon in that of the woman) should have Mars and Saturn

in the 12th and 2nd places from them, or be aspected by one of these malefics, or conjoined with them.[27]

45. For day-births Venus and the Sun are considered as *mother* and *father* respectively; and for night-births they are the Moon and Saturn respectively. When one pair acts as the parents, the other does as maternal aunt and paternal uncle respectively. If these planets occupy even and odd houses respectively, they confer auspicious results on the parents or aunt and uncle, as the case may be.[28]

46. If a weak benefic is posited in the Lagna and aspected by a malefic, or if Saturn in exaltation is posited in the Lagna, being aspected by the weak Moon, and Mars, the woman will certainly meet with death ere long.[29]

47. If the Lagna and the Moon, either together or separately, are surrounded by malefics, then the pregnant woman will die.

48. The same result will follow, if there are malefics in the 4th house counted from the Lagna and the Moon and Mars in the 8th house; or if the New Moon, and Mars and the Sun are in the 4th and 12th houses respectively.

49. If Mars and the Sun occupy the Lagna and the 7th house respectively, the woman's death takes place as a result of a surgical operation, or a weapon. Abortion is likely to take place in the particular month of pregnancy whose lord is eclipsed.[30]

50. If the Lagna at *Ādhāna* (impregnation) or the Moon are conjoined with benefics, or if the benefics are posited in the 2nd, 4th, 5th, 7th, 9th and 10th houses counted from either, and if the malefics be in the 3rd, 6th and 11th houses, without aspecting the Lagna or the Moon, as the case may be, the foetus will grow happily.[31]

51. It should be predicted that a boy will be born, if the Sun, Moon, Jupiter and the Lagna, being possessed of strength, occupy odd Rāśis and masculine Aṁśas (odd ones); or if Jupiter and the Sun at least are in odd places.[32]

52. The wise should declare the birth of a female, when the above (the Sun, Moon, Jupiter and the Lagna,) or Mars, the Moon and Venus, are posited in even Signs and even Navāṁśas.

53. If the planets (viz. Mars, Venus and the Moon) are posited in dual signs and Aṁśas, and are aspected by Mercury, twins will be born. Similarly, Saturn occupying an odd house other than the Lagna makes for a male birth.[33]

54-56. The pregnant woman gives birth to a eunuch under the following yogas :—(1) The Sun and Moon should aspect each other; (2) Mercury and Saturn should aspect each other; (3) Mars should aspect the Sun in an even Rāśi; (4) Mars aspects the Lagna and the Moon that are in odd Signs; (5) Mars aspects the Moon in an even Sign and Mercury in an odd sign; (6) Mars should aspect the odd Aṁśa (of the Lagna ?). If the Moon and Venus occupying even Rāśis are aspected by a male planet, and if the Lagna, Mercury, Mars and Jupiter occupy odd Rāśis, the result is the birth of twins. The same result will follow, if both the Lagna and Moon occupy either even Signs or dual ones. So too when Mercury situated in his own Aṁśa (or Rāśi) aspects the dual Aṁśas occupied by planets and the ascendant.[34]

57-58. Triplets will have to be predicted on the basis of Mercury's occupation of even and dual Vargas (Rāśi and Aṁśa). When the Lagna is the last Aṁśa of Dhanus, and when strong planets occupying the Aṁśa of the Lagna are aspected by strong Saturn and Mercury, there would be many children in the foetus. The lords of the 10 months of pregnancy are Venus, Mars, Jupiter, the Sun, the Moon, Saturn, Mercury, lord of Lagna, the Sun and Moon respectively.[35]

59. The welfare of the child in the womb in the different months depends on the condition of the lords of the respective months. If Mercury is posited in the 5th or 9th house, and the others weak, the child will have two faces (i.e. heads)and (four) hands and feet.[36]

60. When the malefics, the Sun, Mars and Saturn, are posited in the junctions of Rāśis viz. the last parts of Karkaṭa, Vṛścika and Mīna, the child will be dumb and without feet.[37]

61. Should Mars and Saturn occupy a Sign or Aṁśa owned by Jupiter, the child would have teeth at birth. Should the Moon occupying her own house (Karkaṭaka) which is the Lagna at birth, be aspected by Mars and Saturn, it would be

hunch-backed. If the Lagna be the last portion of Mīna and aspected by the Moon, Mars and Saturn, it would be lame.

62. If the Moon, conjoined with malefics, be posited in a Rāśi-Sandhi (i.e. the last part of Karka, Vṛścika or Mīna) without any benefic aspect, the child would be a dullard or imbecile. When the Lagna is the last part of Makara, aspected by Saturn, the Sun and Moon, the child would become a dwarf. If malefics occupy the second and third decanates, it will be born without head and feet respectively.[38]

63. When the Lagna, which is Siṁha, is occupied by the two luminaries and aspected by Mars and Saturn, the child will be blind. On the other hand, if the aspecting planets are both benefic and malefic, the child will be blear-eyed. If under the above conditions the Sun and the Moon be in the 12th house, its right and left eye respectively will be destroyed.

64. Inauspicious planetary-combinations, though aspected by benefics, do not at all give up their maleficence. If at Niṣeka (impregnation) Saturn occupies the 7th house, and the ascending Navāṁśa belongs to Saturn, child-birth will take place after three years.[39]

65. It will be after 12 years, if the planet concerned is the Moon. In this manner the time of delivery should be considered.[40]

66-67. Note the Dvādaśāṁśa Rāśi of the Moon at Ādhāna (impregnation). The delivery will take place when the Moon in transit passes though the Rāśi that is removed by the number of Dvādaśāṁśas from the Dvādaśāṁśa Rāśi. The distance in degrees travelled by the Moon in the particular Rāśi at birth, being doubled, would give the time of birth in Ghaṭīs from Sun-rise.[40a]

68. The childs' father will be away from home, if the Moon at birth does not aspect the rising Sign (Lagna) and if the Sun has fallen from the Zenith (i.e. 10th house). The father must be in a foreign country at the time, if the Sun is also in a movable Sign.[41]

69-70. The same result should be declared by expert astrologers, if Saturn be in the Lagna, and Mars in the 7th; or if the Moon be between Mercury and Venus; or if the Moon be posited in the Lagna owned by a malefic and in the decanate owned by Vṛścika, and if benefics be in the 2nd and 11th houses or if the Sun be aspected by the benefics.

71. O Great Sage, twins will be delivered from the foetus, when the Sun is posited in a quadruped Sign, and the other planets are possessed of strength.

72. If Mars and Saturn occupy Siṁha-lagna and an Aṁśa belonging to the Moon or Mercury, the child will have a cord around its limb signified by the Navāṁśa Rāśi of the Lagna. The above thing will happen if Jupiter does not aspect the Lagna, the Moon or the Lagna along with the two luminaries.[42]

73-73½. If the Sun or the Moon is conjoined with malefics (in Vṛṣabha?), the child may be illegitimate. If Mars and Saturn occupying Rāśis owned by malefics and conjoined with malefics, happen to be in the 5th or 9th from the Sun, the child's father is imprisoned in his own country or in a foreign land, according as the Rāśi occupied by the Sun is fixed or movable.[43]

74-75½. When the full Moon occupies her own Rāśi; Mercury the Lagna, and a benefic the 4th house, birth takes place in a sailing boat. Similar is the result, when the Lagna is a watery Sign and the Moon is posited in the 7th house. Undoubtedly, O Nārada, birth takes place on water, when the full Moon occupying Gemini or Virgo, aspects the Lagna, or is posited in the Lagna, 2nd or 4th house.[44]

76. Delivery takes place clandestinely, if Saturn occupying the 12th place from the Lagna or the Moon, is aspected by another malefic.[45]

77-77½. Birth takes place in a pit or dungeon, if Saturn occupies the Lagna identical with *Karka* (Cancer) or *Vṛścika* (Scorpio) or aspects the Lagna or the Moon, or is conjoined with the Moon or Lagna. If the Lagna of birth is aspected by Mercury, the Sun and Moon, the places of delivery would be a place of sport, a temple, and a barren spot respectively.[46]

77½-79. Birth takes place in a burial ground, if Mars should aspect the Lagna; in a rural place, if the Moon and Venus; in a sacrificial house, if Jupiter; in a house of ornaments and decorations, if the Sun; and in a house of fine arts; if Mercury, in all cases, the aspecting planets being strong.

80. If the lord of the Lagna is posited in his own house or Aṁśa, which is a fixed Sign, the birth takes place in the father's house; and if it is a movable Sign, in transit (during a journey), the nature of the road being determined by that of the Rāśi concerned. The child is abandoned by the mother, if the Moon occupies the 7th house which is trine (5th or 9th) to Mars and Saturn.[47]

81. However, if the ascendant is aspected by Jupiter, the child will live long and be rescued by somebody. On the other hand, if the ascendant occupied by the Moon is aspected by malefics and if Mars occupies the 7th house, the abandoned child will die.

82. If the trine (5th) from Mars and Saturn are aspected (by a benefic), the child lives happily in the protection of a stranger. If the above house be occupied by a malefic, the child will die in a month and a half, even though rescued by others.[48]

83-83½. O Sage, the birth takes place in the house of the father or mother, according as the planet owning the house is strong. If the ascendant is occupied by a debilitated benefic and the Moon and the Lagna are neither together (i.e. the Moon does not tenant the ascendant), nor aspected (by any planet), the birth takes place in a lonely place.

84-85. When the Moon is posited in the 4th house owned by Saturn or in an Aṁśa of Saturn, or aspected by Saturn, the birth takes place in darkness or in dim light and the woman lies down on the floor. Similarly, the direction of the house or the lying-in-chamber should be guessed from the nature of the Rāśi, whether it is *Śirṣodaya* (rising with its head) or *Pṛṣṭhodaya* (rising with its hind part first).

86-87. Trouble will have to be predicted for the mother, if there are malefics in the 4th and 7th houses from the Moon. When the strongest (or aspecting) planet in the chart happens to be Saturn, Mars, the Moon, the Sun, Mercury, Venus or Jupiter, the house in which the child is born should be an old house that has been renovated, a burnt one, a newly built one, a wooden house that is not very strong, one with many architectural embellishments, a new house adorned with paintings, or a strong and attractive one, as the case may be.[49]

88. The house of birth or lying-in chamber is in the *East*, if the ascendant is *Tulā*, *Meṣa*, *Karka*, *Vṛścika* or *Kumbha*; it is in the *North*, if the Lagna is owned by Mercury or Jupiter; in *West*, if it is Vṛṣabha; and in the South, if it is Siṁha or Makara.

89. The directions of the house are represented by two houses beginning with *Meṣa* for each cardinal point and a dual house for an intermediate quarter. The legs of the cot are represented by the 3rd, 6th, 9th and 12th houses respectively, as in the case of a house.

90. The number of women in attendance in the lying-in chamber corresponds to that of the planets that are situated between the Lagna and the Moon. The persons inside and outside the room are read from the planets in visible and invisible halves of the Zodiac.[50]

91. The child's body will correspond to the characteristics of the planet that occupies the Lagna, or of the one that is strongest in the chart. Its complexion will be like that of the Moon's *Navāṁśa*. The delineation of the native's limbs from head to foot, should be done on the basis of the 12 Rāśis commencing from the ascendant (as explained below).[51]

92-93. When any of the three decanates of a Rāśi rises, the native's limbs are allotted to the different houses in the following manner :—(1) When the first decanate rises, those of the 12 houses counted from the Lagna onwards represent the head, eye, ear, nostril, cheek, jaw and mouth on the right and left sides. Similarly, the second decanates of the houses represent in order the neck, shoulder, side, heart, arm, chest and navel on the two sides. The last ones likewise represent the pelvis, the genital organ, anus, thighs, knees, shanks, and feet.[52]

94-95. Whichever decanate Rāśi is occupied by malefics, will have a wound or ulcer in the corresponding limb of the native; if the planet is benefic, the particular limb will have a mole or mark. The mark will be natural or inborn, when the conjoining planet is posited in its own Sign or Aṁśa that is a fixed Rāśi; otherwise it will be an accidental one. If the planet concerned be Saturn, the wound would be one caused by wind or stone; if Mars, by poison, weapon or fire;

if Mercury, by earth (i.e. mud); and if the Sun, by wood, animals or horned animals of the class of goats.[53]

96-96½. There will undoubtedly be a wound, caused by malefics, in the limb signified by the decanate which is occupied by three planets. A decanate that is aspected (by malefics) will cause a mole in the corresponding limb, while one occupied by benefics, a good mark.[54]

97-100. The *Sun* has a square body, pink eyes, bilious constitution and sparse hair; the Moon has a round body, wind and phlegm in constitution, intelligence, measured (or slow) speech and attractive eyes; Mars is youthful, possessed of fierce eyes, fickle and bilious in constitution; Mercury has all the three humours in his constitution, practises jokes, appreciates tastes and speaks cogently (or with pun); Jupiter has pink hairs and eyes, a tall body, phlegmatic nature and great erudition and Wisdom; Venus has a charming body, attractive eyes, black and curly hair and enjoys happiness; and Saturn has tawny eyes, a bluish or black complexion, coarse hair and indolent nature.[55]

101. Muscles, bone, blood, skin, semen, marrow and fat are ruled in order by Saturn, the Sun, Moon, Mercury, Venus, Jupiter and Mars.

102. When the ascendant, the Moon and malefics are all posited in the last portion of Rāśis, 'when malifics occupy the Kendras from the Moon, when malefics and benefics occupy the first and second half respectively and when Scorpio is the rising Sign, the child will die soon.

103. If there be malefics both in the ascendant and in the 7th house and if the Moon, conjoined with malefics, be not aspected by benefics, the child would certainly meet with its end.[56]

104-104½. When the weak Moon occupies the 12th house, malefics the ascendant and the 8th house, and benefics are not in Kendras; or when the Moon, not conjoined with benefics, occupies the Lagna, the 7th, 8th or 12th house, unaspected by benefics posited in Kendra etc., the child perishes.[57]

105-105½. If the Moon be posited in the 6th or 8th house and be aspected by malefics, the child will die soon after birth. On the other hand, if the Moon in the above yoga is aspected by benefics also, it will die in 8 years. The same result i.e. death in the 8th year, will follow, if the Moon is aspected both by malefics and benefics.[58]

106-106½. When the weak Moon is in the Lagna, or is hemmed in between malefics, or when malefics occupy the 8th house or Kendras; or when the Moon is posited in the 4th, 7th or 8th house, or when the Lagna is surrounded by malefics, the child will die likewise.

107-108. The child will die along with its mother, if malefics occupy the 7th house from the Moon, provided there is no benefic aspect. The same prediction will have to be made, when the Moon occupies the end of a Rāśi without any benefic aspect, and malefics, the 5th and 9th houses; or when the Moon occupies the Lagna and malefics the 7th house.[59]

109. If the Moon is eclipsed at the time and malefics occupy the 8th house, both the mother and child will die soon. The death will be due to a surgical operation, if the Sun be in the Lagna and strong malefics in the 8th house.[60]

110. When Sign Cancer (Karka) rises along with the Moon and Jupiter in it, Mercury and Venus occupy Kendras, and the rest the 3rd, 6th and 11th house, the child will indeed be blessed with an unlimited span of life.

111. The maximum span of life is enjoyed by one, in whose birth Sign Pisces rises with its own Navāṁśa, the Moon occupies Taurus (Vṛṣa) and the 25th degree, and all the planets their exaltations.[60a]

112-114. A strong planet posited in the ascendant or a Kendra, aspected by benefics confers on the native both long life and wealth. One lives for 60 years, if the Moon is in her own or exaltation house, benefics in their own houses, and the lord of the Lagna, possessed of strength, in the Lagna itself. The longevity is of 70 years, when benefics are in the Kendras and the 8th house devoid of planets, and when Jupiter is strong (?). The native lives for 80 years, if benefics occupy their *Mūlatrikoṇa* houses, Jupiter his exaltation, and the lord of the ascendant is strong. One lives for 30 years only, when strong malefics occupy Kendras and the 8th house is free from planets.[61]

115. When the lord of the 8th occupies the 9th, and Jupiter occupying the 8th is aspected by malefics, the native

lives for 24 years. The longevity is of 27 years (or 12 years ?) if the lords of both the Lagna and the 8th house occupy the 8th.[62]

116. When the Lagna is occupied by a malefic and Jupiter, aspected by the Moon, and the 8th house is tenanted by some planet, the child will live for 20 years. The same age is to be predicted, when Saturn is in the Lagna or 9th house, Venus in a Kendra and the Moon in the 9th or 12th.

117. The span of life is 100 years, when Jupiter occupies Cancer (Karka) or when Venus and Jupiter are in Kendras. It is 40 years, when the lord of the 12th house occupies the Lagna, and the 8th house is devoid of benefics.

118. If the lords of the Lagna and the 8th house exchange their positions, the child will live for five years only. When Jupiter and Venus are combined in the Lagna, and Mercury and the Moon in the 8th house, it is 50 years.

119-119½. The above-mentioned spans of life are called those caused by Yoga or planetary dispositions. Now I shall explain the one-called *Spaṣṭa* or one based on planetary strength or longitudes. When the Sun is most powerful in the chart, the Span is called *Piṇḍaja*, whereas when the Moon is very strong, it is called *Nisargaja*; and when the ascendant is very strong, it is *Aṁśāyuḥ*. Now listen to their delineation.

120-122. The years contributed by the seven planets headed by the Sun, when they are in their highest exaltation, are in order 19, 25, 15, 12, 15, 21 and 20, in the Piṇḍāyurdāya system, while in the Nisargaja one they are 20, 1, 2, 9, 18, 20 and 50 years respectively. Subtract a planet's longitude from its highest exaltation figures. If the result is less than six Signs (Rāśis), it should be subtracted from 12 Rāśis and its Aṁśas be taken towards its contribution.[63]

123. A planet posited in an inimical house loses a part (i.e. 1/3) of its contribution except when it is retrograde. Similarly, one that is combust will lose half of its contribution. However Venus and Saturn do not lose anything on the score of eclipse.

124-124½. When there is a possibility of reduction on two counts for a planet's contribution, only the bigger one should be resorted to. When there is a malefic in the Lagna, the contribution of the Lagna should be reduced thus : Leave off the number representing the Signs in the longitude of the ascendant and reduce the degrees etc. to minutes and multiply the result by the rectified contribution of that planet. Divide the product by the number of minutes in Bhagaṇa (360°, which is 21,600). Now subtract the quotient from the rectified Āyus of that planet. The result will give the final rectified contribution of that malefic.

125-127. The contribution of a malefic (aspected by a benefic ?) is completely left out, while that of the benefic is halved. These contributions of the several planets (and the Lagna) thus rectified should be multiplied by their respective multipliers (Guṇakas) and divided by 360. The quotient will give the Āyus in years and the remainder being multiplied by 12 and divided by the above divisor will give the months. The remainder should be multiplied by 30 and divided as before by 360. The result will be days, and the remainder being multiplied by 60 and divided as before will yield Ghaṭīs etc.

127½-128½. The rectified contribution of the Lagna is got by leaving off the Rāśis in its figures and converting the degrees etc. into minutes and dividing the result by 200. The quotient gives years, and the remainder being multiplied by 12 and divided by 200, gives months etc.

129-129½. In the Aṁśāyurdāya system the longitudes of the planets and the ascendant should be converted into minutes and divided by 40. The result will give the years etc. contributed by the planets etc. I shall now explain the rectification of the contributions.

130-131. Subtract the longitude of a planet from the figures for the ascendant. If the result is less than six Signs, there should be rectification, and not otherwise. Convert the balance thus got into degrees and divide it by 30. Then reduce the quotient by 1. The result in degrees is to be divided by 30. This result again reduced by one will be the multiplier.[64]

132. The contribution of a benefic should be reduced to a half and that of a malefic to nil, without doubt. The contributions of planets when multiplied by the Guṇaka give their nett Āyus. This is what is meant by rectification.

133. The degrees etc. in the Āyus of a planet should be divided by 200. The quotient will give years, and the

remainder multiplied by 12 and divided by 200 will yield months, days etc.

134. The contribution of the Lagna multiplied by 3 and divided by 10 gives its Āyus in years. The remainder should be multiplied by 12 and divided by 10. The result will give months and days.

135-135½. When the Lagna is very strong, its nett contribution would be the above result increased by so many years as there are Rāśis in the Lagna. The degrees etc. multiplied by two and divided by 12 would give months, and the remainder being multiplied by 30 and divided as before, days etc. This is not done in the case of *Piṇḍa* and *Nisarga* systems.

136-137. The Daśā (major period) of that planet which is the strongest among the three viz. Ascendant, the Sun and Moon, will operate in the beginning. Then will come the Daśās of those that are in Kendras. In case there are many planets posited in Kendras (quadrants), then the strongest of them will have precedence over others. If two planets are equally strong, then that which contributes a greater number of years of Āyus, will operate first. In the case of planets that are associated with the Sun, the faster-moving one will come first (i.e. the one which becomes visible first).

138-140. The order of the Daśās is the following : A planet whose Ṣadvargabala is a half (of its maximum), one whose Bala is 1/3, a planet which is situated in a trine, one in the 7th (therefrom), one in the 7th itself, one in the 4th house and one in the 4th or 8th from the previous (This translation is tentative). As in the previous Āyurdāya, here too the rules regarding the precedence of Daśā with regard to the planets posited in quadrants, their order in case of a tie, are the same as noted already. The Guṇakas (multipliers) for the various types of planets are the following: for the Daśānātha (i.e. the planet whose Daśā comes first) it is 84 (or does it mean 4 or 8 according to his strength ?); for one in conjunction with another it is 4; for one posited in a line, it is 28; for one posited in the 7th house, it is 12; and for one in the 4th or 8th house, it is 21.

141. O Nārada, the Daśā period being multiplied by these Guṇakas and divided by the Guṇaikya (the combined Guṇa or product of the Guṇakas) yields the nett result in years.

When the remainder is multiplied by 12 and divided by the above divisor, months etc. are got.

142. The sub-divisions or minor periods of a Daśā are *Vidaśās* and *Upadaśās*. When the lord of the sub-period happens to be an Adhimitra (fast friend) or is posited in the former's house, exaltation or in the Lagna, the period should be increased in order by 1, 4, 1 or 7 years (?).

143. A benefic occupying a house increases its prospects, provided he is aspected by another occupying a contributory house. On the other hand, if he is posited in any other house, he will destroy it.

144. Whatever substances are allotted to a planet, all that should be mentioned as occurring in the Daśā of that planet by its occupation, aspect and conjunction, to the person concerned in his profession, life etc.

145-146. If the lord of the sub-period—Vidaśā or Upadaśā—is aspected by an inimical planet, he will cause only disasters. On the other hand, one who is aspected by a benefic, or a friend and is posited in benefic or friendly Vargas, and is strong at the time (of the sub-period) is declared to be a destroyer of all troubles. This applies also to one whose Aṣṭakavarga results are excellent.

147-148. A planet that is posited in its exaltation house identical with an auspicious house counted from the Lagna, Moon or Sun, will yield the best results, while one posited in its own house, Mūlatrikoṇa or friendly house, moderately good effects. The effect of one that is posited in an untoward house, will be undesirable. The effect, good or bad, will be intense or otherwise, according as the planet is strong or otherwise.

149. In a movable Lagna the effects of the three decanates, first, second and third, are good, middling and bad respectively; in a fixed one, they are in order bad, good and middling; and in a dual one, middling, bad and good.

150. The Lagna being aspected or joined by its own lord, Mercury or Jupiter confers excellent results on the native, while being hemmed in between malefics or being aspected or joined by malefics, it leads to his ruination.

151-152. In the Sun's Aṣṭakavarga chart he produces beneficent influences on houses, 1, 2, 4, 7, 8, 9, 10 and 11, counted from his own position; he is good in these houses counted from the positions of Mars and Saturn also; he is good in 6, 7, and 12 from Venus; he is good in 5, 6, 9 and 11 places from Jupiter; good in 3, 6, 10 and 11 from the Moon; he is good in 3, 5, 6, 9, 10, 11 and 12 places counted from Mercury; and lastly in 3, 4, 6, 10, 11 and 12 places from the Ascendant.

153-154. The Moon is beneficial in places 1, 3, 6, 7, 10 and 11 from himself; in 3, 6, 7, 8, 10 and 11 places from the Sun; in places 2, 3, 5, 6, 9, 10 and 11 from Mars; in 1, 3, 4, 5, 7, 8, 10 and 11 places from Mercury; in 1, 2, 4, 7, 8, 10 and 11 places from Jupiter; in 3, 4, 5, 7, 9, 10 and 11 places from Venus; in 3, 5, 6 and 11 places from Saturn; and in 3, 6, 10 and 11 places from the ascendant.

155-156. Mars is good in 3, 5, 6, 10 and 11 places from the Sun; in 3, 6, and 11 places from the Moon; in 1, 2, 4, 7, 8, 10 and 11 places from himself; in 3, 5, 6 and 11 places from Mercury; in 6, 10, 11 and 12 places from Jupiter; in 6, 8, 11 and 12 places from Venus; in 1, 4, 7, 8, 9, 10 and 11 places from Saturn; lastly in 1, 3, 6, 10 and 11 places from the Lagna.

157-158. Mercury is beneficial in 1, 3, 5, 6, 9, 10, 11 and 12 places from himself; in 5, 6, 9, 11 and 12 places from the Sun; in 2, 4, 6, 8, 10 and 11 places from the Moon; in 1, 2, 4, 7, 8, 9, 10 and 11 places from Mars and Saturn; in 6, 8, 11 and 12 places from Jupiter; in 1, 2, 3, 4, 5, 8, 9 and 11 places from Venus; and in 1, 2, 4, 6, 8, 10 and 11 places from the Lagna.

159-160. Jupiter is beneficial in 1, 2, 3, 4, 7, 8, 9, 10 and 11 places from the Sun; in 2, 5, 7, 9 and 11 places from the Moon; in 1, 2, 4, 7, 8, 10 and 11 places from Mars; in 1, 2, 4, 5, 6, 9, 10 and 11 places from Mercury; in 1, 2, 3, 4, 7, 8, 10 and 11 places from himself; in 3, 5, 6, and 12 places from Saturn; in 2, 5, 6, 9, 10 and 11 places from Venus; and finally in 1, 2, 4, 5, 6, 7, 9, 10 and 11 places from the Lagna.

161-162. Venus is beneficial in 8, 11 and 12 places from the Sun; in 1, 2, 3, 4, 5, 8, 9, 11 and 12 places from the Moon; in 1, 2, 3, 4, 5, 8, 9 and 11 places from the Lagna; in 1, 2, 3, 4, 5, 8, 9, 10 and 11 places from himself; in 3, 5, 6, 9, 11 and 12 places from Mars; in 3, 4, 5, 8, 9, 10 and 11 places from Saturn; in 3, 5, 6, 9 and 11 places from Mercury; and in 5, 8 , 9, 10 and 11 places from Jupiter.

163-164. Saturn is auspicious in 1, 2, 4, 7, 8, 10 and 11 places from the Sun; in 3, 6 and 11 places from the Moon; in 3, 5, 6 and 11 places from himself; in 3, 5, 6, 10, 11 and 12 places from Mars; in 5, 6, 11 and 12 places from Jupiter; in 6, 8, 9, 10, 11 and 12 places from Mercury; in 1, 3, 4, 6, 10 and 11 places from the Lagna; and in 6, 11 and 12 places from Venus.

165. In the above beneficial houses (mentioned in the Aṣṭakavarga charts of the planets) put vertical lines and in others mere dots. If these houses that contain benefic lines happen to be auspicious, when counted from one's natal sign i.e. Rāśi, and also to be owned by a benefic, friendly planet or the planet concerned or to be the planet's exaltation, the result must be wholly favourable, and in others it will be unfavourable.[64a]

166. The effects of benefic lines from 1 to 8, contained in a Rāśi, are in order (1) hardship, (2) loss of wealth, (3) trouble, (4) moderate effects, (5) acquisition of wealth and happiness, (6) influx of money, (7) happiness, and (8) accomplishment of one's ambitions.

167. The seven planets beginning with the Sun represent seven relations in order : (1) *Father*, (2) *Mother*, (3) *Enemy*, (4) *Friend*, (5) *Brother*, (6) *Wife*, and (7) *Servant*. When the Ascendant, its lord, the Moon and Sun are well-placed, the native will be blessed with wealth, fame and security.[65]

168-169. When the *Navāṁśa* (of the Lagna or 10th house) is owned by the Sun, the subject earns his living by (selling) grass, gold, horses, elephant-drivers, etc.,when it is owned by the Moon, through agriculture, marine products and women; when by Mars, through metals (or ores), weapons and adventures; when by Mercury, through poetry, fine arts (architecture etc.) and the like; when by Jupiter, through Gods (i.e. worshipping Gods), Brahmins and mines; when by Venus, through silver, cattle, gems etc.; and when by Saturn, through murderous deeds, wearisome tasks and mean activities.

170. If Saturn, Jupiter and Mars are exalted at a birth and when the ascendant is strong, the native will become a great monarch. When the Lagna is Vargottama and when the Moon is aspected by four or more planets, the same effect will follow.

171. When Mars is exalted, the Sun and Moon in Dhanus, and Saturn in the Lagna, the native becomes a landlord or king. The same effect takes place, when the exalted Sun is posited in the Lagna, Jupiter in the 10th house, and the Moon and Saturn in the 7th house.

172. When Saturn or the Moon occupies the Lagna in exaltation, the Sun and Mercury the 6th house, Venus and Mars in Tulā and Meṣa respectively; or when Jupiter is in *Karkaṭaka* Lagna along with the Moon and Mars, one becomes a King.

173. One becomes a King, if at one's birth the Moon occupies Vṛṣabha-Lagna, and the Sun, Jupiter and Saturn in the 4th, 7th, and 10th houses; or if Saturn occupies Makara-Lagna and the Moon and others the 3rd, 6th, 9th (?) and 11th (?)houses.[66]

174. When Jupiter and the Moon are together posited in Dhanus, Mars in Makara, and the exalted Sun or Venus in the Ascendant; or when the Karka-lagna is occupied by Jupiter, Meṣa by the Sun and the 11th house by Mercury, the Moon and Venus, the native becomes a King.

175. When the Lagna happens to be Vṛṣabha, occupied by the Moon, Signs *Siṁha*, *Kumbha* and *Makara* are occupied by the Sun, Saturn and Mars respectively, a king is born.[67]

176. When the Lagna is Meṣa occupied by Mars, or when it (Lagna) is Siṁha occupied by Jupiter, the native becomes a king. The same effect takes place, when Mars and the Sun occupy the 5th house, Jupiter, the Moon and Venus the 4th house, and Mercury the Lagna which is identical with Kanyā.

177. An illustrious king is ushered into the world, when the Lagna happens to be Makara occupied by Saturn, the Moon occupies Meṣa, the Sun Siṁha, and Venus and Jupiter Tulā and Mithuna respectively.[68]

178. Under the above planetary configurations even an ordinary person's son will become a king. On the other hand, O great Sage, under the following yogas only a king's son can hope to be one such.

179. One becomes a king, if three or more planets possessed of strength occupy their exaltation houses or Mūla-

trikoṇas. The same event takes place, when the Sun is posited in *Siṁha*, the Moon in the ascendant identical with Meṣa, Mars in Makara, Kumbha or Vṛścika and Jupiter in Dhanus.

180-180½. O Sage, when Venus occupies the 4th house identical with his own Rāśi, and the Moon the 9th house, either joined or aspected by benefics, and the rest the 3rd, 1st (6th ?) and 11th houses, one becomes a ruler.[69]

181-181½. A virtuous king is born, if Mercury occupies the Lagna in strength, a benefic (Jupiter) possessed of strength an auspicious house (or 9th ?) and the rest the 9th, 2nd and the Upacaya houses (3, 6, 10 and 11).

182-182½. One becomes a king with the Moon, Saturn and Jupiter occupying the 10th, 11th and the ascendant respectively, Mars and Mercury the 2nd house, and Venus and the Sun the 4th house, at one's birth.

183. When the Moon occupies the ascendant identical with Vṛṣabha, Jupiter and Saturn the 2nd and 6th respectively, and the rest the 11th house, the person concerned becomes a ruler.

184-184½. Jupiter in the 4th house, the Sun and the Moon in the 10th house, Saturn in the Lagna and the rest is in the 11th house, produce kings. Similarly, Mars and Saturn in the Lagna, the Moon, Jupiter, Venus, the Sun and Mercury in the 4th, 7,th, 9th, 10th and 11th respectively usher kings into the world.[70]

185-185½. One attains kingship or a kingdom during the major period (Daśā) of the planet posited in the ascendant or the 10th house, or of one that is very strong; whereas that of such planets as are posited in inimical houses, in debilitation etc. is productive of great troubles.

186-187. If at a birth all the planets are posited in any two contiguous quadrants (Kendras) (i.e. 1 and 4, 4 and 7, 7 and 10 or 10 and 1), the yoga named *Gadā* or *Mace* is generated. If all the planets occupy only the 1st and 7th houses, it will be called *Śakaṭa* (carriage). The *Yoga* called *Vihaga* (Bird) is caused by the planets occupying the 4th and 10th houses. *Śṛṅgāṭaka* is brought into effect by all the planets being posited in the 5th, 9th and 1st houses. The *Hala* yoga is brought about by all the planets being posited in mutual trines beginning with any house other than the ascendant.[71]

188. The yoga termed *Vajra* (*Diamond* or *Thunderbolt*) is caused by benefics being posited in the 1st and 7th houses, and by malefics in the 4th and 10th houses. *Yava yoga* (*Barley*) is the result of the benefics and malefics exchanging the positions mentioned in the previous yoga (i.e. benefics should be in 4th and 10th and malefics in the 1st and 7th houses). The *Kamala* (*Lotus*) yoga is the effect of all the planets occupying the Kendras in any manner. The *Vāpī* (*Well*) yoga is the result of the planets occupying houses other than the Kendras (i.e. in Paṇapharas or Āpoklimas).[72]

189. The *Yūpa yoga* (*Plough*) is the effect of all the planets occupying the four houses beginning with the Lagna. The *Śarayoga* (*Arrow*) is caused by their staying in the four contiguous houses from the 4th house. The *Śakti yoga* is caused, if they occupy the 7th, 8th, 9th and 10th houses. *Daṇḍa* (*Rod*) is caused by their occupying the 10th, 11th, 12th and 1st houses.[73]

190. When all the planets occupy the seven contiguous houses beginning with the Lagna, the yoga is called *Nau* (*Boat*); while the *Kūṭa* yoga (*Fraud*) is caused by the planets being in the 7 houses beginning with the 4th house. The *Chatra* (umbrella) yoga results from the planets occupying the 7 houses beginning with the 7th house. The *Cāpa* (Bow) yoga is caused by the planets occupying the 7 houses beginning with the 10th house. The *Ardhendu* (Crescent) yoga results from their occupying seven houses other than the above, i.e. beginning with any *Paṇaphara* or Āpoklima house.[74]

191-192. *Cakra* (Wheel) yoga is formed by all the planets occupying all the odd houses; and *Samudra* (Ocean), the even houses. Seven yogas called (*Viṇā* (Lute), *Dāman* (Garland), *Pāśa* (Noose), *Kedāra* (Field), *Śūla* (Spike), *Yuga* (Yoke) and *Golaka* (Sphere) are caused when all the seven planets are posited in 7 Rāśis, 6, 5, 4, 3, 2 and 1 respectively. When all the planets are in movable Rāśis, the yoga called *Rajju* (Rope) is formed.[75]

193. When the planets are only in fixed Rāśis, *Musala* (Stave) yoga is formed; in dual Rāśis, *Nala* (Reed) yoga. The *Mālā yoga* (Wreath) is formed by the benefics (Jupiter,

Mercury and Venus) occupying the Kendras; by malefics (the Sun, Mars and Saturn) therein, *Sarpa* (Serpent) yoga is formed.

194. One born under the *Rajju Yoga* becomes envious and fond of wandering; one of *Musala yoga* is blessed with wealth and honour; one born under the *Nalayoga* becomes deficient in a limb and full of prominent veins; under the *Mālā* or *Srak* yoga, commands pleasures; and under *Sarpayoga*, gets afflicted or becomes miserable.[76]

195. A person born under *Viṇāyoga* is very clever and very much interested in music and dancing; one under *Dāmayoga* becomes wealthy and munificent; and under *Pāśayoga*, possessed of wealth and character.[76a]

196. One having *Kedāra yoga* become an agriculturist; one with *Śūlayoga*, brave unharmed and poor; with *yuga yoga*, with *Gola yoga*, and slovenly.

197. In *Cakrayoga* one becomes great that his feet are worshipped even by kings; in *Samudrayoga*, one enjoys the pleasures of royalty; in *Ardhacandra*, possesses a charming body; and in *Cāmara*, becomes happy and heroic.[77]

198. Under *Chatrayoga* one helps one's friends; under *Kūṭayoga*, suffers imprisonment, and becomes a liar; under *Kamalayoga*, becomes famous and happy without doubt.[78]

199. Under *Yūpa yoga* one becomes charitable, performs sacrifices and controls his senses; under *Śara yoga*, becomes murderous and a leader of hunters; under *Śakti* low, mean, lethargic and poor; and under *Daṇḍa yoga*, suffers from separation from his beloved.

200. The yogas termed *Sunaphā*, *Anaphā* and *Duradharā* are formed when there is any planet, other than the Sun, in the 2nd, 12th and both the houses respectively. In the absence of any of these three yogas, *Kemadruma yoga* is formed.

201. A person born with the *Sunaphā yoga* at birth will enjoy the wealth earned by his own efforts, be charitable, wealthy and happy; and with *Anaphā yoga*, one becomes healthy, famous, dressed attractively and of good character.

202. Under *Durdhara-yoga* one enjoys pleasures, becomes happy, wealthy, munificent and charitable; while under

Kemadrumayoga, one becomes very dirty, miserable, mean and penniless.

203-204. O Sage, if the Sun is conjoined with the Moon, the native will become a mechanic or mason; with Mars, a wanderer; with Mercury, famours, clever, learned and wealthy; with Jupiter, engaged in helping others; with Venus, earning one's livelihood by means of weapons; and with Saturn, clever in metallurgy and pottery.[79]

205-206. O Sage, the Moon combined with Mars makes one a dealer in hammers, liquor and such other commodities, and hater of his mother; with Mercury, clever in economics, polite and famous; with Jupiter of unsteady mind, leader of his family, valiant (heroic) and rich; with Venus, seeker of pleasures (?); and with Saturn, the son of a remarried woman.[80]

207. Mars combined with Mercury makes one a single-combatant; with Jupiter, mayor of a city; with Venus, a gambler and fighter; and with Saturn, a liar and gambler.

208. O Nārada, Mercury combined with Jupiter makes one proficient in dance and music; with Venus, clever in magic; and with Saturn, greedy and cruel.

209. Jupiter combined with Venus makes one learned; and with Saturn, a cook or potter. Venus conjoined with Saturn makes one have poor eye-sight, and earn wealth through his association with a woman.[81]

210-211. Among the planets Mars, Mercury, Jupiter, the Moon, Venus, Saturn and the Sun, if any four planets should combine in the 10th or 2nd house (?), a Buddhist monk, an Ājīvaka monk, an aged mendicant, a wandering recluse, and an ascetic living on rain-water respectively are brought into existence. In case the planets owning the concerned houses are defeated in a planetary war, there will be a fall from asceticism.

212-213. Should the planets be tiny or eclipsed, one would not actually don the ochre robes; on the other hand, should they be powerful, persons would be strongly attached to their respective ascetic orders. O Nārada, one will become an ascetic, when the lord of the Lagna, being unaspected by any planet, aspects Saturn; or when Saturn aspects the lord of the ascendant that is eclipsed; or when Saturn, the Sun and the lord of Lagna occupy the Aṁśa of Mars or the Sun; or when the Moon is aspected by Saturn.[82]

214-215. One born under *Aśvinī* constellation becomes handsome, and endowed with ornaments; under *Bharaṇi*, efficient and truthful; under *Kṛttikā*, gluttonous and addicted to others' wives; under *Rohiṇi*, of stable mind and sweet-tongued; under *Mṛgaśirṣa*, wealthy and enjoyer of pleasures; under *Ārdrā*, cruel, roguish and sinful; under *Punarvasu*, Self-controlled, sickly and auspicious; and under *Puṣya*, happy and a poet.

216. One born under *Āśleṣā* will be a villain, rogue and ungrateful; under *Maghā*, sinful and eater of all and sundry (gluttonous); under *Pūrvaphalgunī*, enjoys luxuries, becomes wealthy, a devotee, donor and sweet-tongued.[83]

217. One born under *Uttaraphalgunī* becomes rich and commands luxuries; under *Hasta*, a thief, stubborn and merciless; under *Citrā*, possessed of colourful clothes, and fine eyes; under *Svāti*, without piety or kindness.

218. One born under *Viśākhā* becomes avaricious, clever and irascible; under *Anurādhā*, a wanderer and one who goes abroad; under *Jyeṣṭhā*, devoted to Dharma and content; and under *Mūla*, proud, rich and happy.[84]

219. Under *Pūrvāṣāḍhā* one becomes proud, happy and content; under *Uttarāṣāḍhā*, humble and pious; under *Śravaṇa*, wealthy, happy and famous; under *Dhaniṣṭhā*, charitable, heroic and rich.

220. One born under *Śatabhiṣak*, destroys one's enemies and gets addicted to some vice; under *Pūrva-bhādrapadā*, comes under the influence of women and becomes rich; under *Uttarā bhādrapadā*, eloquent, happy, and attractive; and under *Revatī*, heroic, wealthy and pure.

221. If a persons' natal sign (Janma-rāśi—the one occupied by the Moon) happens to be *Meṣa* (Aries), he becomes lustful, heroic and grateful; if *Vṛṣabha* (Taurus), attractive, charitable and forgiving; if *Mithuna* (Gemini), proficient in gambling, Śāstras (scriptures) and pleasing women; if *Karkaṭa* (Cancer), effeminate and short.

222. If the natal sign is *Siṁha* (Leo), one hates women, becomes short-tempered, proud, valiant, happy and of steady

mind; if *Kanyā* (Virgo), pious, tender and wise; if *Tulā* (Libra), learned, tall and rich.

223. If it is *Vṛścika* (Scorpio), one becomes sickly, respectable and receives wounds; if *Dhanus* (Sagittarius), a poet, artist and wealthy; if *Makara* (Capricorn), lazy, wanderer and possessing beautiful eyes; if *Kumbha*, stealer of others' wealth and wives.[85]

224. When the natal Sign and its lord are strong, and when the Moon also is possessed of strength, all good results will accrue to the native; otherwise they will be the opposite of what has been given above. The effects of the Sun's occupying the 12 Signs beginning with Meṣa are in order (1) fame, (2) hatred for women, (3) wealth, (4) cruelty or sharpness, (5) wisdom or learning, (6) poetic gift, (7) keeping a liquor shop, (8) riches, (9) respectability, (10) avarice, (11) penury, and (12) being without friends.

225-225½. Mars occupying *Siṁha* at birth makes one poor; *Karkaṭa*, wealthy; his own house, gluttonous; *Mithuna* or *Kanyā*, grateful; *Dhanus* or *Mīna*, famous; *Vṛṣa* or *Tulā*, having illicit connection with other women; *Makara*, blessed with many sons and affluence; and *Kumbha*, grief-stricken, wicked and a liar.

226-227½. Mercury occupying the houses of the seven planets beginning with the Sun makes one (1) hateful in the eyes of women, (2) hater of one's own kinsmen, (3) observing vows (?) (4) blessed with intelligence and wealth, (5) having honour and riches, (6) blessed with sons, and (7) getting gold from women (?) respectively. In the case of Jupiter the above results are : (1) commander of an army, (2) blessed with wife, wealth and children, (3) having efficient friends (?), (4) commanding a vast following or good clothes, (5) governor of a province, (6) having wealth and happiness. and owner of much gold (?).[86]

228-228½. The effects of Venus occupying the houses of the planets are in order (1) acquiring wealth through women, (2) riches and freedom from grief, (3) hating one's kith and kin, (4) wealth and sin, (5) wealth and intelligence, (6) uniform fame, and (7) defeat at the hands of woman.[87]

229-229½. The effects of Saturn occupying the Rāśis owned by the seven planets are in order : (1) Deficient in limbs (or with deformed limbs) and poor, (2) motherless, (3) having many friends (?) (4) afflicted by the three-fold calamities, (5) blessed with children, wife and wealth and (6) a king and (7) leader of a village or town.[88]

230-231. The Moon occupying *Meṣa*, when aspected by Mars and five other planets, produces the following effects in order : (1) kingship, (2) learning, (3) virtues, (4) mayorship of a city, (5) penury and (6) poverty; in *Vṛṣabha*, (1) poverty, (2) thievish propensities, (3) kingship, (4) learning (5) messengership and (6) sickness; in Mithuna, (1) living by working on metals, (2) kingship, (3) scholarship, (4) fearless, (5) weaver, and (6) penniless.

232. The Moon occupying her own house, produces the following effects in order, when aspected by the six planets, Mars and others : (1) a warrior, (2) poet, (3) learned man, (4) a respected teacher (or king ?), (5) metallurgist, and (6) suffering from eye-disease; and sign Siṁha, (1) astrologer, (2) wealthy, (3) respected teacher or king, (4) king, (5) barber, and (6) a great king.[89]

233. The Moon tenanting *Kanyā* and being aspected by the above planets, produces the following effects in order : (1) a pure and virtuous person, (2) a king, (3) an army-commander, (4) a skilful person, (5) a landlord and (6) a king; *Tulā*, (1) a king, (2) a goldsmith, (3) a merchant, (4) a king, (5) a goldsmith, and (6) merchant.[90]

234. The effects of the Moon's stay in *Vṛścika* under the aspects of the six planets are— (1) father of twins, (2) fond of water (?), (3) a king, (4) of defective limbs, (5) wealthy, and (6) a king; in *Dhanus*, they are : (1) protector of kinsmen, (2) a king, (3) leader of men, (4) of virtuous mind, (5) showy person, and (6) a cheat.[91]

235. In *Makara* the effects are—(1) king, (2) scholar (or ornamented ?) (3) a friendly person, (4) a sacrificer (or teacher), (5) a king, and (6) taking a boy in adoption (?); in *Kumbha* and *Mina* they are—(1) humorous, (2) learned, (3) a king, (4) learned, (5) a virtuous person, and (6) intelligent person.[92]

236. The Moon confers beneficial results, when she is joined or aspected by planets that are posited in the Rāśī or Aṁśa of the lord of the Lagna. The same result will follow, if she is combined with or aspected by those that are posited in a Rāśi that is owned by a friend of the lord of the Lagna-decanate.

237-238. The results of the Moon's being placed in the various *Dvādaśāṁśas* (1/12 of a Sign) have already been enunciated. Those of her *Navāṁśa* placements will now be explained: When the Moon is posited in the *Navāṁśa* Rāśi owned by Mars (i.e. *Meṣa* or *Vṛścika*), the native becomes a policeman (or watchman), interested in killing, single combat, and quarrels, and wealthy; when in one of Venus (*Vṛṣabha* or *Tulā*), foolish and addicted to others' spouses; when in one of Mercury (*Mithuna* or *Kanyā*), a poet, happy, dancer (actor), thief, learned and an artist (or artisan).[93]

239. When the Moon is in her own Aṁśa i.e. *Karka*, one becomes short in stature, wealthy, ascetic and greedy; when in that of the Sun, i.e. *Siṁha*, hot-tempered, owner of treasures, a minister, king, cruel and childless.[94]

240. When the Moon is in an Aṁsa of Jupiter (*Dhanus* or *Mīna*) the person concerned becomes an expert in comics, endowed with a strong physique, a minister and religious-minded (or virtuous); when she is in one of Saturn (i.e. *Makara* or *Kumbha*), he will have very few children, be wretched (distressed), indigent and associated with a wicked woman.[96]

241-242. When the Sun is aspected by the Moon and other planets, the results are the same as for the Moon being aspected by others (vide Ślokas 230-235). When a planet is posited in *Vargottamāṁśa*, own house or in another's house, the good results enumerated will be full-fledged, middling or very meagre, as the case may be : If the owner of the Aṁśa (occupied by a planet) is strong, he bestows very good results, according to the effects of the (Rāśi occupied and the aspects he receives from others.

243. If the Sun should occupy the Lagna at birth the native would become a hero, stubborn, of defective eyes

and merciless; if the Lagna is Meṣa, he will suffer from cataract in the eye and be wealthy; if it be Siṁha, night-blind.

244. If the Sun occupies the ascendant identical with *Karka* (Cancer), the native will be mean, poor and blear-eyed; if the second house, very wealthy, punished by the ruler and suffering from some facial disease.[96]

245. The Sun in the 3rd house makes one learned and full of prowess; in the 4th house, depressed (or unhappy) and afflicted; in the 5th, bereft of wealth and issue; and in the 6th house, powerful and victorious over his foes.[97]

246-246½. The Sun in the 7th house makes one under the thumb of a woman; in the 8th, have few children and poor eye-sight; in the 9th, blessed with children, wealth and happiness; in the 10th, full of heroism and learning; in the 11th, endowed with wealth and honour; and in the 12th, fallen from position, and poor.[98]

247-249. The Moon occupying the Lagna makes one dumb, deaf, blind and a servant; but if the ascendant is Cancer, Aries or Taurus, one becomes rich; in the *second* house, a religious student or rich; in the *third*, cruel; in the *fourth*, endowed with a virtuous disposition, in the *fifth*, father of girls and indolent; in the *sixth*, of poor digestion and sexual urge, and cruel, and envious; in the *seventh*, an administrator (?), and learned; in the *eighth*, afflicted with diseases; and in the *ninth*, endowed with friends and riches.[99]

250. The Moon in the *tenth* house confers virtues or piety, intelligence and riches; in the *eleventh*, fame, intelligence and wealth; and in the *twelfth*, meanness and loss of limbs. These are the results mentioned by the wise for the Moon's stay in the various houses at a person's birth.

251. Mars occupying the Lagna at birth causes wounds in the body; the *second* house, makes one eat forbidden or rotten food; the *third* house, perform virtuous deeds; the *fourth* house, sinful activities; and the remaining houses, as in the case of the Sun.

252. Mercury gives the following effects in the first eight houses beginning with the ascendant : (1) Learned; (2) Wealthy; (3) Leader of men; (4) Scholar; (5) Minister; (6) Having Enemies; (7) Appreciator of virtues; and (8) a

paragon of virtues. In the remaining four houses the effects are similar to those of the Sun.[100]

253. Jupiter produces the following effects in the 12 houses :— (1) Learned; (2) of pleasant speech; (3) Miserly; (4) Happy; (5) Wise; (6) Vanquisher of foes; (7) Intelligent; (8) Mean; (9) Ascetic; (10) Blessed and Wealthy; (11) Greedy, and (12) Wicked.[101]

254. Venus causes the following effects in the first five houses : (1) Passionate and Happy; (2) Quarrelsome; (3) Anxious for sexual pleasure; (4) Happy; and (5) Having many daughters; and in other houses he gives the same results as Jupiter.[102]

255-255½. Saturn occupying the ascendant at birth makes one penniless, sickly, voluptuous, slovenly, sickly during childhood and indolent; but if it is his exaltation, one becomes virtuously disposed, a king or administrator of a village, learned and of attractive physique. In other places he is similar to the Sun.

256-257. A planet in exaltation yields its results in *full*; in *Mūlatrikoṇa, three-fourth.*; in the house of a benefic as well as in its own house, *a half*; in the house of a friendly planet, *one-fourth*; in an enemy's house, *very little*; and in its debilitation and when it is eclipsed, the result is *nil.*

258-259. When one or more planets are posited in their own houses, Mūlatrikoṇa, exaltation or friendly houses the person becomes a worthy scion of his family, leader of the family and respected by his kinsmen; wealthy, happy, enjoyer of pleasures and a king; or enjoyer of others' wealth, protector of friends and relatives (or protected by friends and kinsmen), leader of a group:; commander or king, as the case may be.[103]

260-261. When benefic planets are posited in odd houses and in the Sun's Horā the native becomes famous, very enterprising, brilliant or valiant, intelligent, wealthy and strong; and when the benefiçs are posited in even Signs and in the Moon's Horā, he becomes lustrous, tender, attractive, enjoyer of luxuries, and wise.[104]

262. Malefics occupying even houses and the Horā of the Sun, will produce moderate results, while benefics occupy-

ing odd Rāśis and the Sun's Horā, will not yield the results expected of them (i.e. mentioned above).[105]

263. If the Moon at a birth occupies a decanate (Drekkāṇa) owned by a friendly planet, the native becomes handsome, and virtuous while in any other decanate, he gets the qualities and form appropriate to the owner of the decanate.

264-265. When the planets are posited in decanates that are designated as (1) Serpent, (2) Weapon, (3) Quadruped, and (4) Aquatic, the native becomes in order: (1) Cruel, murderous, cohabiting with revered women and wanderer; (2) thief, gluttonous, wealthy, intelligent, a king, impotent and destroyer of enemies; (3) a slave and one labouring under somebody without payment; and sinful, murderous and foolish.[105a]

266-267. The effects of *Vargottama Dvādaśāṁśas* in the Signs, *Meṣa etc.* are the same as for the Rāśis themselves. When Mars occupies his own *Triṁśāṁśa*, the native will have wife, strength, ornaments, prowess, daring spirit, and brilliance, or will be hostile to his wife and attached to other women.[106]

268-268½. When Saturn occupies his own *Triṁśāṁśa*, the person becomes miserable, untidy and endowed with followers. When Jupiter occupies his own *Triṁśāṁśa*, one gets happiness, intelligence, wealth, fame, brilliance, respect of the people, enjoyments, horses and elephants(?).[107]

269-270½. When Mercury occupies his own *Triṁśāṁśa*, one will be blessed with a highly developed intelligence, proficiency in fine arts, poetry, architecture and disputations; he will also be deceitful and well-versed in the Śāstras and be clever in adventurous deeds. When Venus occupies his own *Triṁśāṁśa*, one will have many children, happiness, health, enjoyments, an attractive personality and riches; he will have a tender body and uncontrolled senses.[108]

271-271½. When the luminaries are conjoined with Mars and other planets, the following effects are produced: (1) Heroic and obdurate; (2) Abnormal and a killer; (3) virtuous; (4) Happy and Learned; and (5) Attractive in action and body.

272-273. Planets that are posited in Kendras identical with their *own house*, *Mūlatrikoṇa* or *Exaltation*, are considered to be *Mutual Kārakas* (Significators), especially the one that is in the 10th house. A birth is highly auspicious, if the ascendant is in *Vargottamāṁśa* and if there are planets in the *Veśi* house (2nd house from the Sun).[109]

274. When *Kendras* (Quadrants) as well as the houses of the *Kārakas* (Significators) are not vacant, Jupiter and the lords of the ascendant and the lunar Sign, posited in kendras, confer beneficial results in the middle of their periods.

275. Planets posited in Rāśis that rise with their hind part foremost, in those that rise both ways—and in those that rise with their head first produce effects at the end and in the middle and in the beginning of their periods respectively. The Sun and Mars confer their results at the beginning, while Jupiter and Venus in the middle.[110]

275½. The Sun and the Moon yield their results at the end, while Mercury does it always.

276-276½. If the 5th and the 7th houses counted from the ascendant or the Moon, be aspected or joined by their own lords or by benefics, there would be all-round progress and prosperity for the two Bhāvas (i.e. issue and wife or husband); otherwise their progress would be hindered.[111]

277-278. If the Sun be posited in *Mīna*, Saturn in the 7th therefrom would destroy the wife; while Mars in the 5th from the Sun would kill the issue. Malefics in the 12th and 2nd houses or in the 4th and 8th houses from Venus would destroy the wife with fire, provided he is neither conjoined with nor aspected by benefics.[112]

279-280. [In addition to the yoga mentioned in the previous verse], if the Moon and the Sun occupy the 12th and 8th houses (or 6th ?), the man too will die along with his wife. The nature of the wife is determined from the planets occupying the 7th house. When the luminaries are situated in the 7th or 9th or 5th house, the wife would be a handicapped person. When the Sun and Venus are together in Koṇa or in the Lagna, or when Venus is in Sandhi either in the 7th or 12th house, the native's wife would be barren.[113]

281. If the 5th house is not occupied by benefics, if the ascendant, 7th and 12th houses are occupied by malefics, and if the weak Moon be in the 5th house, the native will have neither wife nor children.[114]

282. If Saturn be in the 10th house and aspects Venus posited in the 7th house, the person would be committing adultery. Should the two viz. Venus and Saturn, be combined with the Moon, the man would be adulterous along with his wife.

283. When the Moon and Venus are in the 7th house, the man, his wife or at least his son will have undeveloped organs. This defect will not arise, if they are aspected by benefics.

284. One becomes the destroyer of one's family (lineage), if the Moon, Venus and a malefic occupy the 10th, 7th and 4th house respectively. One will become an artist (artisan or architect), if the rising decanate is occupied by Mercury and aspected by Saturn occupying a kendra.[115]

285. One should be said to be born of a slave woman, if the decanate be owned by Saturn, and if Venus be in the 12th house, being debilitated. The result would follow, if both the luminaries be in the 7th house and be aspected by Saturn.[116]

286. Mars and Saturn occupying the 7th house and being aspected by another malefic, produce rheumatism; while a malefic occupying the Aṁśa of *Karka* or *Vṛścika* in a *kendra*, would cause venereal disease.

287. One is afflicted with leprosy, if the Lagna and the Moon are hemmed in between malefics, and the Sun is posited in the 7th house. One would be of defective limbs, if the Moon be in the 10th house, Mars in the 7th, and Saturn in the 2nd house from the Sun.

288-289½. If the Sun and Moon are posited in mutual Rāśis or Aṁśas, one will suffer from colic; and if the luminaries are combined, one will be lean in body. If the Sun, Moon, Mars and Saturn are posited in the 8th, 6th, 2nd and 12th house respectively, one is deprived of one's eye-sight by the affliction caused by a wandering spirit known as *Bālagraha* (which attacks children). Malefics in the 5th house, unaspected by benefics, make one deaf; while the same in the 7th house cause bad (ugly) teeth.[117]

290-291. When the ascendant is occupied by Jupiter and the 7th house by Saturn, the native will be afflicted by rheumatism. One becomes mad, if Mars occupies the 4th or 7th house and Jupiter or Saturn, the ascendant; or if Mars occupies the 5th house, Mercury the 7th and the Moon, the 12th house.[118]

292. Malefics occupying the 2nd, 5th, 9th and 12th houses cause bondage corresponding to the type of decanate occupied by them. When the decanates happen to be *Serpent*, *Fetters* and *Noose* and are aspected by strong malefics, a person suffers bondage.[119]

293-293½. When the Moon and Saturn are together and aspected by Mars, the native will be afflicted with epilepsy, be foul-mouthed and consumptive. When the Sun, Mars and Saturn occupy the 10th house, are aspected by benefics and are of bright orbs, natives become servants of the highest, moderate and low order, according to the strength of the planets.

294-295. Whatever effects have been declared for male births should be applied to female births, as far as they are applicable to them; and such effects should be declared in the case of their husbands; and in the case of death, it should be taken to apply to their husbands. Their physical features should be read from the Moon and ascendant; and paramours from the malefics occupying the 7th house.[120]

296. If both the ascendant and the Moon occupy even houses, the woman concerned will be of normal conduct; and if they are aspected by benefics, she will be of excellent character and will possess many ornaments (or will be charming).

297. If the two (Lagna and the Moon) be in Odd Signs, the woman would be masculine in physical features and mental disposition. If the two be aspected by malefics, they would be wicked (sinful) and devoid of all virtues.

298. When Mars, Saturn, Jupiter, Mercury and Venus are posited in a Sign belonging to Mars in a girl's horoscope, she will be in order (1) spoiled in girlhood, (2) a slave, (3) virtuous, (4) cunning, and (5) immoral.

299. When the Lagna and the Moon are in odd Signs, the girl will have the character and physical features corresponding to those of the planet owning the Sign, or be wicked. She will be sinful and devoid of virtues, when these two are aspected by malefics.[121]

300. When the five planets mentioned above (viz. Mars, Saturn, Jupiter, Mercury and Venus) are posited in a Rāśi owned by Venus, the respective effects would be (1) foul-tongued, (2) one remarried, (3) virtuous, (4) a scholar and (5) famous. In a house owned by Mercury the effects are : (1) deceitful, (2) impotent, (3) a devout wife, (4) virtuous, and (5) of wandering habit or fickle-minded.[122]

301. When these planets are in Gemini (*Mithuna*), she will be (1) a harlot, (2) killer of her husband, (3) virtuous, (4) artisan (artiste) and (5) ignoble. In *Siṁha* the effects are : (1) talkative, (2) a concubine, (3) passionate, (4) of masculine disposition, and (5) ugly ? (or unapproachable ?).[123]

302. In a house of Jupiter they are : (1) very virtuous, (2) having very little Sex life, (3) appreciator of merits, (4) learned, and (5) devout wife. In a house of Saturn the effects are : (1) a slave, (2) attached to a low-born person, (3) virtuous or devoted wife, (4) wicked, and (5) barren.

303-304. The above-mentioned effects for the Signs of the five planets are also applicable to the *Triṁśāṁśas* or decanate of the stronger of the two viz. Lagna and the Moon, happening to be that of one of the five planets viz. Mars, Saturn, Jupiter, Mercury and Saturn. It Venus and Saturn should occupy each other's Navāṁśa or if Venus be in *Kumbha Navāṁśa*, the woman concerned would get highly inflamed by sexual passion and have sexual congress with members of her own sex. If the 7th house be vacant and weak, the husband would be a despicable person; and if Mercury and Saturn, without receiving any benefic aspect, be posited there, he would be a eunuch. If the 7th house be a movable Sign (and its lord in a movable Sign), the husband would always be in a foreign country.

305-306. If Sun be in the 7th house, she would be deserted by her husband; if Mars, a virgin widow; if Saturn, aspected by a malefic, she remains a spinster throughout her life; if powerful malefics, a widow; and if both malefics and benefics, a widow who is remarried.[124]

307. When a weak malefic occupies the 7th house, the woman is abandoned by her husband, unless the malefic is

aspected by benefics. When Venus and Mars occupy each other's Aṁśas, the woman becomes another's mistress.[125]

308-309. When the Moon (also) is in the 7th house (in addition to Mars and Venus), she goes astray with the approval of her husband. If the Lagna be a Sign owned by Saturn or Mars and be occupied by the Moon and Venus, she would be a harlot. If in this yoga there is also malefic aspect on the Lagna, she goes astray along with her mother. If the Aṁśa of the 7th house is owned by Mars and aspected by Saturn, her genital organ will be diseased. On the other hand, if the Aṁśa belongs to a benefic, she would be loved by her husband.[126]

310-311. If the 7th house or its Aṁśa is owned by Saturn, the husband will be a foolish old fellow; if by Mars, he will be hot-tempered and libidinous; if by Mercury, learned and skilful; if by Jupiter, virtuous and self-controlled; if by the Moon, lustful and tender; if by Venus, attractive and charming; and if by the Sun, one doing very gentle deeds.[127]

312. When Venus and the Moon occupy the Lagna, she becomes happy but envious; and when Mercury and the Moon, proficient in fine arts, happy and virtuous.

313. If Venus and Mercury should occupy the ascendant, the woman would be exceedingly charming, attractive and skilled in fine arts. When there are three benefics in the Lagna, she will command immense wealth and happiness as well as virtues.

314. A woman would be widowed during the Daśā (major period) of the malefic planet occupying the 8th house or of the planet occupying the Aṁśa of the lord of the 8th house. Still she herself will predecease her husband, in case there are benefics in the second house.

315-317. A woman will have few children, if at her birth the Moon occupies *Kanyā*, *Vṛścika*, *Siṁha* or *Vṛṣabha* identical with the 5th house. A woman becomes ugly, if the Lagna is an odd Rāśi, Saturn moderately strong, the Moon, Mercury and Venus weak, and the rest strong. She becomes famous. learned in many Śāstras and a philosopher, when the Lagna is an even Sign and Jupiter, Mars, Venus and Mercury strong. She takes to asceticism of the type corresponding to the planet posited in the house, when there is a malefic in the 7th house.

318-319. All these things (mentioned above regarding a girl's horoscope) should be considered before marriage or electing a partner or at a query regarding the same. (Now about the cause of death of a person), death should be declared to be caused by the vitiation of the paticular physical constituents belonging to the strongest of the planets aspecting the 8th house. If the seven planets beginning with the Sun are posited in strength in the 8th house, the causes of death are in order : (1) Fire, (2) Water, (3) Wound caused by a weapon, (4) Fever, (5) Disease, (6) Excessive thirst and (7) Inordinate hunger.[128]

320-321. If the 8th house (as well as its lord) be in a movable, fixed or dual house, the end occurs in a far-off place from one's own house, or on the way, as the case may be. When the Sun and Mars occupy the 2nd and 4th house respectively, the death is caused by a fall from the top of a mountain, and when Saturn, the Moon and Mars are in the 4th, 7th and 10th houses in order, by a fall into a well.[129]

322. One dies at the hands of one's own kinsmen, if the two luminaries occupy Virgo (*Kanyā*) and receive malefic aspect. A person gets a watery grave, if the luminaries occupy the ascendant that is a dual Sign.[130]

323. If the Moon occupying a Sign owned by Mars is hemmed in between malefics, death is by fire or weapon; and if she be in *Makara* and Saturn in *Karka* , by dropsy.

324. If the Moon be in Kanyā under the above mentioned condition, death would be through vitiation of blood or swelling in the body; and if it be Saturn, it is due to fire, hanging or a fall. If there be malefics both in the 5th and 9th houses without receiving any benefic aspect, death would take place in captivity.[131]

325-327. If the decanate of the 8th house happens to be *Noose, Serpent* or *Fetters*, death will be in prison. If the Moon along with malefics be in *Virgo* (*Kanyā*) which is the 7th house, Venus in *Meṣa* and the Sun in the ascendant, death would take place at home as a result of womens' intrigues. If the Sun or Mars be in the 4th house, Saturn in the 10th and the weak Moon conjoined with malefics in the Lagna, 5th or 9th house, death would be through impalement (?). Death would be in the battle-field, if the Sun be in the 4th and Mars in the 10th aspected by the weak Moon. One will be beaten to death with clubs, if the 1st, 10th, 8th and 4th are occupied by the weak Moon, Mars, Saturn and the Sun respectively.[132]

328. If the above four planets viz. weak Moon, Mars, Saturn and the Sun be posited in the 10th, 9th, 1st and 5th house, death is due to suffocation by smoke, fire, imprisonment or beating[133].

329. When the 4th, 7th and 10th houses are occupied by Mars, the Sun and Saturn respectively, death is due to weapons, fire or king's displeasure. When Saturn, the Moon and Mars are in the 2nd, 4th and 10th houses respectively, it is due to wounds or worms or a fall from a tree.[134]

330. If the Sun be in the 2nd house and Mars in the 4th, death is due to a fall from a vehicle; if, in the above yoga, Mars be in the 7th house alongwith the weak Moon, it is by the destruction of a machine.[135]

331. When Mars, Saturn and the Moon are in Libra, Aries and a sign belonging to Saturn respectively, or when the weak Moon, the Sun and Mars are in the 10th, 7th and 4th house respectively, it is in the midst of filth and night-soil.

332. If the weak Moon be aspected by the powerful Mars, and Saturn be in the 8th house, the cause of death will be some disease of the privities, worms (basilli), weapons, fire or wood.

333. When Saturn is in the 7th, the Sun in the 8th, and the weak Moon conjoined with Mars in a house of Saturn; or when the Sun, Mars, Saturn, and the Moon are posited in the 1st, 5th, 11th, and 7th respectively, the native will die as a result of a fall from the top of a mountain or tree.[136]

334-335. Death will be caused by the stronger of the two planets viz. the lord of the 22nd decanate and the lord of the 8th house, through, his characteristic disease or agency. Death of a person will take place in a place corresponding to the lord of the Aṁśa occupied by the ascendant, this being influenced by the aspect and conjunction of other planets.[137]

336. The period of unconsciousness of the dying person will correspond to the Aṁśas of the Lagna that have not yet risen. If it (Lagna) is aspected by its lord, the period in to be

doubled; if by a benefic, to be trebled; and if by more benefics, it should be increased proportionately through one's intelligence.[138]

337. If the decanate of the 8th house be *Fiery*, the dead body would be burnt to ashes; if *Aquatic*, thrown to the waters; and if *Serpent*, dried by being exposed to the Sun and wind. These results are to be read from the 8th house counted from the Moon as well.[139]

338. If Jupiter be in the 8th house, the departed soul would go to the world of Gods; if the Moon or Venus, to the world of the *Manes*; if the Sun or Mars, to that of mortals (?); and if Saturn or Mercury, to the infernal regions.[140]

339. The previous world of a soul can be read from the lord of the decanate occupied by the stronger of the two viz. the Sun and the Moon. The world must have been very high or exalted, if the concerned luminary is in its exaltation; moderate, if in its own house; and low, if in debilitation.[141]

340. If the lord of the decanate of the 6th or 8th house occupies the 7th house, or if Jupiter occupies the 6th, a kendra or 8th house, or if he is in his exaltation, identical with the Lagna or the 12th house or in a benefic Aṁśa, possessed of strength, the soul attains emancipation.[142]

341. When neither the time of impregnation nor that of birth is known, the life of querists has to be predicted from the ascendant at the query. The solstices of birth has to be deduced from the two halves or Horās of the ascendant, the first standing for the winter solstice, and the second for the summer one.[143]

342. The age of the person (who asks for a *Naṣṭajātaka* as a result of his not knowing his date and time of birth) should be read from the ages of the lords of the Trines counted from the Lagna, or from the (lord of) Aṁśa (or decanate) occupied by Jupiter. The season of birth would be summer, if the Sun be in the Lagna. Similarly, the presence of other planets in it would indicate other seasons. Or it may be read from the Sign occupied by the Sun.[144]

343. The Moon, Mercury and Jupiter are to be interchanged with Venus, Mars and Saturn respectively, if necessary. If the decanate of the planet concerned that deter-

mines the season is the initial one of the Sign, the month of the season (Ṛtu) should be the first. The lunar day should be found out proportionately.[145]

344. If the Lagna of query be a *nocturnal* Sign, the ascendant at birth must be a *diurnal* one, and *vice versa*; and the time elapsed from sunrise or sunset should be read from the degrees elapsed. If the lord of the Lagna be in a *Trikoṇa* or be possessed of great strength, the Lagna of birth would correspond to the star ruling at the time of query (?).[146]

345-347. Subtract the longitude of the Moon from the position of the ascendant at query. The natal ascendant would be so far removed from the Moon at query as is represented by the balance. Multiply *Vṛṣabha* and *Siṁha* by 10; *Mithuna* and *Vṛścika* by 8; *Meṣa* and *Tulā* by 7; *Makara* and *Kanyā* by 5; and the remaining Rāśis viz. *Karka*, *Dhanus*, *Kumbha* and *Mīna* by their respective numbers. Jupiter, Mars, Venus and Mercury are to be increased (?) by 3, 1, 11 and 11 respectively. The calculation of the lunar mansion (*Nitya-nakṣatra*) as well as of the *Ahargaṇa* (the total number of days elapsed), is done by multiplying it by 7 and dividing by 27. The remainder will give the *Nakṣatra* in question.[147]

348. By adding to or subtracting from the above shown result, 9, double the figure. You get the year, season and month. The fortnight and lunar day are got by multiplying it by 8. The same being multiplied by 7 will yield the day, night and asterism; and being multiplied by 5, the degree of the ascendant as well as the time of birth in *Ghaṭis*.[148]

349. The following are the characteristics of the first, second and third decanates of *Meṣa* (Aries): (1) It is a man holding an axe, dark in complexion, with red eyes, and capable of protecting others. (2) It is a woman wearing red garments, pot-like in shape, with canine face, ugly feet and sore (?) eyes. (3) It is a man, of brown complexion, blind, cruel, wearing red cloths, and who has broken his vow or promise.[149]

350-351. Those of the decanates of Taurus (*Vṛṣabha*) are : (1) A man oppressed by hunger and thirst, wearing singed clothes, and with his trimmed hair hanging. (2) Man, hungry, dirty, with a goat-like face, but clever in agriculture etc. (3) Man with an elephantine body, impatient (hurrying), pink in complexion, and with a perplexed mind.[150]

352-352½. Those of the decanates of Gemini (*Mithuna*), are : (1) A woman engaged in needle-work, beautiful, chaste, issueless and with raised hands. (2) A man in a garden wearing armour, holding a bow, intent on sport, and with an aquiline face. (3) A man well-versed in dance and other fine arts, holding a bow, and possessing a vast treasure of gems like *Varuṇa*.

353-354. The characteristics of the decanates of Cancer (*Karka*) are : (1) A man with an elephantine face and neck, or with hog's face, standing in a forest and shooting arrows (or hunting Śarabhas and snakes). (2) A woman, who is very coarse from head downwards (or who is coarse and has a snake on her head), and who shrieks holding the branch of a Palāśa tree. (3) A man with a flat face, having a serpent coiling round his body, and sailing in a boat for the sake of a woman.[151]

355. The characteristics of the decanates of Leo (*Siṁha*) are : (1) A monkey (or a man with a dog) who has caught an eagle and jackal, cries aloud on (or near) a silk-cotton tree. (2) A man, holding a bow, wearing the skin of an antelope, roars aloud like a lion, and is sickly. (3) A man with a beard, with a bear's face, acting like a monkey, and destroying (for) fruits and meat.[152]

356-357. Those of the decanates of Virgo (*Kanyā*) are : (1) A girl in unclean clothes, wearing lots of flowers on her locks, (2) A bowman, harming and causing loss to others, dark, a writer, and hairy. (3) A very tall woman of golden complexion, wearing clean, washed clothes, holding a pot in her hand, in a tempie.[153]

358. The characteristics of the decanates of Libra (Tulā) are : (1) A man engaged in weighing with a balance and measuring commodities in a shop, thinking of the prices of articles (or costly things); (2) A man oppressed by hunger and thirst, holding a pot, with an aquiline face, and accompanied by wife and children. (3) An archer, wearing a golden armour, behaving like a Kinnara (a semidivine being with a horse's face), and pursuing an animal (or deer).

359-360. The decanates of Scorpio (*Vṛścika*) are represented by (1) a woman seated on a lion (?) going to a well, with many snakes curling round her legs; (2) a woman, having husband and wealth (or for the sake of her husband), with the form of a tortoise, with her body covered with serpents, and yearning for happiness; and (3) a man having the face of a tortoise and hunting lions, dogs, hogs and deer.[154]

361-361. Those of Sagittarius (*Dhanus*) are represented by (1) a boy with the body of a dog (or a man with a tail and horse's body), holding a bow, and protecting ascetics and sacrificial performances; (2) a middle-aged woman seated on a seat bedecked with Campaka-flowers, and opening a lion's mouth (or, looking after elephants); and (3) a man with the complexion of Campaka, seated on a straw seat, holding a rod in a forest of Kuśa grass (or, having a piece of silk over his face).[155]

362-363. The decanates of Capricorn (*Makara*) are the following:—(1) A man with an aquiline face, holding an axe (?), and eager for oils, wine and food. (2) A woman who has been burnt (?), holding iron, and having ornaments, valuable things or pots and dirty things. (3) A man full of treasures or pots, with hairy ears, dark in complexion, wearing a crown, and holding fruits and machines in his hands.[156]

364-365. The decanates of Aquarius (*Kumbha*) are the following:—(1) A man seated in boat, with his hands adorned with all kinds of gems, who is anxious for collecting ornaments and decorative articles; (2) a woman sailing in a boat towards the shore, whose face is like the Campaka flower (in colour), and who is followed by her retinue; and (3) a naked man coiled by a serpent sitting in a cavern and weeping, as he is troubled by robbers and fire. These are the 36 decanates that have been delineated in proper sequence.[157]

366. O great Sage, in this manner horoscopy has been expounded to you succinctly. Now you will know the branch of astrology known as *Saṁhitā-Skandha* (a compilation of all useful thinking which is highly beneficial for worldly activities.

CHAPTER FIFTYFIVE

1. In Sanskrit the word *Kāla* is used in many senses. It means time, the God of Death, the Cosmic Being, the Supreme Lord etc. It is derived thus: संकलयति कालयति इति कालः', 'स सूक्ष्मामपि कलां न लीयते इति कालः' कालशब्दात्ककाराकारौ लीधातोश्च लकारमादाय कालशब्दनिष्पत्तिः ।' 'कलनात्सवधातूनां स कालः परिकीर्तितः । सुख-दुःखाभ्यां भूतानि योजयतीति कालः । कालयति संक्षिपतीति वा कालः । मृत्युसमीपं नयतीति वा कालः ।' The Bhāgavata has the following to say : 'कालो बलीयान् बलिनां भगवानीश्वरोऽव्ययः । प्रजाः कालयते क्रीडन् पशुपालो यथा पशून् ।' "Time is called Kāla, because it controls the life and death of all beings; it does not leave even the minutest part of time, Kalā; it seizes or gathers together all beings; it drives beings; it invests all beings with weal and woe; it contracts their span of life; or it leads them to abode of Death.

Varāhamihira too says : "कालाङ्गानि वराङ्गमाननम्....." "The use of Greek words such as Kriya and Āsphujit, indicates that the chapters bearing on astrology are not very ancient. They may even be post-Varāhamihira. The printed text reads 'कोडान्त बस्तिव्यञ्जसोनखः," which is palpably wrong. It should be 'क्रोडान्त्रवस्तिव्यञ्जनोरवः'.

2. There was a dispute about the origin of the word Horā. Burgess first thought that it was borrowed from the Greeks, but later he changed his view. However, the word *Drekkāṇa* or *Dreṣkāṇa* is evidently a Greek word. In each Sign there are two Horās and three decanates. In Meṣa, Mithuna, Siṁha and other odd Rāśis the first half or 15 degree portion is presided over by the Sun, while the next half by the Moon. In the even Signs i.e. Vṛṣabha, Karkaṭaka, Kanyā etc. they are ruled by the Moon and the Sun respectively. There are three decanates in each Sign, the dimension of each being 10 degrees. In each Rāśi the first part or decanate is owned by the same Rāśi and its lord; the second by the Rāśi that is 5th from it; and the third by the Rāśi that is 9th from the original. For example, take Sign Cancer. Its three decanates are called respectively Cancer, Scorpio and Pisces. Their lords too are in order the Moon, Mars and Jupiter.

3. *Triṁśāṁśa* is 1/30 of a Rāśi which consists of 30 degrees. So one *Triṁśāṁśa* means one degree. But in Hindu astrology each degree is not given a ruler. On the other hand these 30 degrees are distributed among the non-luminaries. In the odd Signs, Meṣa, Mithuna etc., Mars, Saturn, Jupiter, Mercury and Venus own in order 5°, 5°, 8°, 7° and 5°. In the even Signs, Taurus, Cancer etc. This order is reversed. In other words, the first 5° are ruled by Venus, the next 7° by Mercury, the next 8° by Jupiter 'the next 5° by Saturn and the last 5° by Mars.

4. There are two printing mistakes in the text viz. क्रियण for क्रियैण, and षडर्ग for षड्वर्ग. The *Navāṁśas,* (3°-20' portions of a Rāśi) of each Sign bear the names of nine Signs and are owned by their lords.

The first Navāṁśa of Aries is owned by Aries itself and its lord is that of Aries viz. Mars; the second by Taurus whose lord is Venus; the third by Gemini ruled by Mercury; the fourth by Cancer and the Moon; the 5th by Leo and the Sun; the sixth by Virgo and Mercury; the 7th by Libra and Venus; the 8th by Scorpio and Mars; and lastly the 9th by Sagittarius and Jupiter. This method should be followed in the case of Leo and Sagittarius also. So it will be seen that for *Meṣa, Siṁha* and *Dhanus* the first *Navāṁśa* is Meṣa and the last one *Dhanus*. Similarly in the case of *Vṛṣabha, Kanyā* and *Makara* the first Navāṁśa is *Makara* itself and the last one Kanyā. In the case of *Mithuna, Tulā* and *Kumbha* the first and last ones are *Tulā* and *Mithuna* respectively. In respect of the last group of *Karkaṭaka, Vṛścika* and *Mīna,* They are *Karkaṭaka* and *Mīna* respectively. Here it can be seen that every Rāśi participates in the *Navāṁśa* scheme in one way or other. In every triad of Signs the first owns the first Navāṁśa, the second the middle one, and the third the last Navāṁśa. Thus Taurus, Leo, Scorpio and Aquarius own their middle or fifth Navāṁśas; and Gemini, Virgo, Sagittarius and Pisces own their last Navāṁśas. If a planet is posited in one and the same Rāśi and *Navāṁśa* it is said to be in *Vargottamāṁśa*.

5. The first quarter of the verse is wrongly printed and should read 'गोजाश्वकर्कयुग्मैणाः'. The statement made here to the effect that Sign *Mithuna* is *Pṛṣṭhodaya* (rising with its back first) is not corroborated by ancient authorities. On the other hand it rises bothways, because the male and female face each other. (See 'Fundamentals of Astrology', Page 9). *Śīrṣodaya* or those that rise with their heads foremost are *Siṁha, Kanyā, Tulā, Vṛścika* and *Kumbha*.

6. In this verse the 12 Rāśis are distinguished on the basis of their sex, nature, quarters they own and their habitats. For the first two 3 Rāśis are taken at a time and the process repeated. Thus we get four signs under each : *Meṣa, Karkaṭaka, Tulā,* and *Makara* are *Male* and *Movable*; *Vṛṣabha, Siṁha, Vṛścika* and *Kumbha, Female* and *Fixed*; and lastly *Mithuna, Kanyā, Dhanus* and *Mīna, Eunuch* and *Dual*. Next four Signs are taken together at a time to represent the four cardinal points. For showing eight quarters we have to consider *Meṣa* and *Vṛṣabha*—as forming the *East* and *Mithuna* the *South-East* and so on. For knowing the habitats of the Signs one has to understand, their forms. For example, Aries is represented by a *Ram,* Taurus by a *Bull,* Gemini by a human couple, and so on. So the habitats of the 12 Signs are in order (1) Forest or Plateau, (2) Field or Meadow, (3) Bed chamber or village, (4) Pond, (5) Mountain cave, (6) Land with water and vegetation, (7) Market-place, (8) Hole, (9)Battle-field, (10) Forest with plenty of water, (11) Place of potters, and (2) Water.

7. The extant reading उच्चानि द्विति... gives the 2nd degree as the Sun's highest exaltation point in Aries, which is definitely wrong. It is well known that that point is the 10th degree. It is possible that the manuscript was illegible here.

8. The Vargottama Aṁśas have already been explained under verse 5 *supra*. The Debilitation Signs of the planets are Libra, Scorpio,

Cancer, Pisces, Capricorn, Virgo and Aries. Here the readings चराद्येषु, भावा द्वादश and मूर्तिमान् require emendation as चराद्येषु, भावा द्वादश and मूर्तित: Here Mūrti should connote the ascendant (Lagna).

9. The reading 'सिंहोक्षाविस्त्रश्च...' should be corrected as 'सिंहोक्षाविस्तयश्व...' The words *Mūlatrikoṇa* and *Trikoṇa* are to be distinguished. The former are certain Signs where the planets find special kinship and strength, while the latter are those reckoned from a particular Rāśi or Lagna.

10. The word त्रिक here stands for the three untoward houses: 'षष्ठं द्वादशमष्टमं च मुनयो भावाननिष्टान्विदु:' । It is to be remembered that many of the words such as Kendra, Paṇaphara, Āpoklima, Rippha etc., are of foreign origin. Kendra means right angle i.e. the four kendras at a distance of 90° from one another. *Mithuna, Kanyā, Tulā,* the first half of *Dhanus,* and *Kumbha* are termed *human* Signs; Signs *Karkaṭaka, Vṛścika, Makara* and *Mīna, Watery*; *Karkaṭaka, Vṛścika* and *Mīna, Reptile*; and *Meṣa, Vṛṣabha, Siṁha,* the letter half of *Dhanus* and the first half of *Makara Quadruped. Human* signs are strong when they occupy the ascendant (Lagna); *Watery* ones, the 4th house; *Reptile* ones, the 7th house; and the *Quadruped* ones, the 10th house.

The reading 'नृपाद: कीट....' should be corrected as 'नृपाथ: कीट....'

11. The readings of the text in the second line are hopelessly corrupt. Hence the meanings given above regarding the presiding Deities of the Sun, Moon, Mars and Saturn are only tentative. For another list of deities please refer to fundamentals of Astrology, page 14.

12. The reading in the text, 'शिखिभूमिपयोवारिवाज्ञिनो भूसुतादय:' is wrong. It may be read as : शिखिभूखपयोवायुवासिनो etc.

13. According to Varāhamihira and others both Jupiter and Venus rule over the Brāhmaṇa class; the Sun and Mars over the Kṣatriyas. The reading वेदोज्ञो should be read as वेदेशा.

14. The reading 'मद्यद तथा makes no sense. It must be मृदु (soft) दृढं (strong) तथा'. There is no word for the raiments of Venus in this verse. स्थलं is a misprint for स्थूलं. Similarly 'ताम्रपुनिस्तथा' is wrong. It should be 'ताम्रं तथा त्रपु'

15. Here *bitter* and *salt* tastes are assigned to the *Moon* and *Mars* respectively. It should have been *salt* and bitter respectively.

16. According to the rule enunciated here the Sun must have Jupiter, who owns the 5th and 8th houses from his Mūlatrikoṇa, Mars owning 4th and 9th; and the Moon owning the 12th house, as his friends. However, the author gives only Jupiter. Similarly, for the Moon, the Sun and Mercury become friends. For Mars they are the Sun, Moon and Jupiter; for Mercury, the Sun and Venus; for Jupiter, the Sun, Moon and Mars; for Venus, Mercury and Saturn; and for Saturn, Mercury and Venus. The reading 'सुखखोद्यप:' should be emended as 'सुखस्वाधिप:' and सान्त्यधा as सान्त्यधी.

17. The reading in the first half is woefully corrupt and hence it is impossible to correct. The author's intention has been explained in the

translation. In the second line मत्काल should be read as तत्काल Just as natural friends are determined by the rule given in the previous verse, even so the following rule will help us to find out the natural enemies of the planets. Here too the calculation is to be done from the planet's Mūlatrikoṇa Rāśi. The lords of the 3rd, 6th, 7th, 10th and 11th houses counted from the Mūlatrikoṇa of the planet concerned, are his natural enemies, provided they come twice in this reckoning (in the case of those owning 2 houses). There is an exception to this rule : A planet, though a *natural enemy* of another, according to this rule, becomes only a *neutral*, if his exaltation house is owned by that planet. For example, for Mars, Saturn becomes a *natural enemy*, since the latter owns 2 houses viz. 10th and 11th from his Mūlatrikoṇa, Meṣa. Still he is only a *neutral*, as the exaltation sign of Mars, Makara, is owned by Saturn.

18. The reading गेहा प्र should be corrected as गहस्व. The directional strength is otherwise stated thus : Jupiter and Mercury are strong in the Lagna; the Sun and Mars in the 10th house; Saturn in the 7th house; and Venus and the Moon in the 4th house.

19. Planets' strength is measured in respect of six things viz. *Kāla, Ceṣṭā, ucca, Dik, Ayana* and *Sthāna* (i.e. time, motion, exaltation, direction, declination and position). Here the word conjunction is used by the author in the sense of *War.* The Summer Solstice or *Dakṣiṇāyana* gives strength to Mercury, Saturn and the Moon, while the rest get strength in the winter Solstice. The non-luminaries get strength when they are retrograde. The reading in the text, खादृतूदगनेन्ये is corrupt. It may be read as : स्वतूंदगयने-ऽप्यन्ये.

20. In astrological works Venus is said to be strong at night.

21. The reading विवक्षा must be changed to विवर्शा and तदूशनाद to तदीक्षणाद्.

22. 'इष्टं रेखां should be read as 'पृष्ठरेखाः'.

23. The reading बलाग्नगे should be read as विलग्नेशे; वांशे may have to be changed to अंशैः; सौरेर्द्वीक्षा is to be read as सौरेन्द्वीक्षा. The last decanate of Taurus is called Vihaga or Bird. The *first* of *Siṁha* and *Kumbha* and the *middle* of Tulā are called *Gṛdhrāsya* or *Vulture-faced.*

24. The part of this verse relating to menses reminds us of a similar verse by Varāhamihira : कुजेन्दुहेतु प्रतिमासमार्तवं गते तु पीडर्क्षमनुष्णदीधितौ ।

25. The first half of this verse is rather unintelligible. It is felt that it is nothing but a paraphrase of the second half of the verse quoted above.

26. ईज्य चाङ्ग should be read as ईज्ये चाङ्ग *Trikoṇa* or trines are the Lagna, 5th and 9th houses.

27. अस्त्रे ऽर्केन्दो should be read as अस्तेऽर्गेन्द्वोः and व्ययखगो as व्ययस्वगो.

28. The reading वा पद्मोजि is utterly corrupt. It may be corrected as वा तावोजे.

29. The reading, मृत्युमेत्य गता should be corrected as मृत्युमेत्यङ्गना

30. Pregnancy lasts for 10 months based on the sidereal calendar. Each of the months is ruled by a planet. The condition of the foetus will depend on the strength etc. of the planet ruling the month. The following are the rulers of the 10 months in order : Venus, Mars, Jupiter, the Sun, Moon, Saturn, Mercury, the planet that owns the Lagna at impregnation, the Moon, and lastly the Sun.

31. In the text we find the reading सुखी गर्भो रवीक्षितः which cannot be accepted as genuine. The original reading must have been सुखी गर्भो न वीक्षितः, which means that the foetus would be happy, if the malefics do not aspect the Lagna or the Moon.

32. In astrology the strength of Navāṁśas and their lords plays an important role. In this verse two criteria are mentioned for determining the sex of the child. These rules can be applied to a nativity, query or impregnation chart.

33. The second half looks like a copy of *Varāhamihira's* line : "विहाय लग्नं विषमर्क्षसंस्थः सौरोऽपि पुञ्जन्मकरो विलग्नात् Here the counting is done not from Meṣa, but from the Lagna which is first house. It is not clear as to what is meant by the word स्वपक्षे. It may also mean, in their respective Aṁśas.

34. In verse 54 'समगं रविः' is wrong for समगं रविम्. Similarly, the reading ओजे जज्ञौ should be rectified as ओजेऽब्जज्ञौ. In verse 56 'द्व्यङ्गांशान् stands for द्व्यङ्कांशान्.

35. The reading बहवोगिनः should be read as बहवोऽङ्गिनः. There is a difference between this work and others on astrology regarding the lordship of the last two months.

36. The word 'weak' here includes the condition of eclipse. The reading अह्निकपान्वितः should be corrected as अङ्घ्रिकरान्वितः।

37. The reading अवागावाटावशुभैः should be corrected as अवागपादो ह्यशुभैः। The second half is utterly unintelligible owing to its gumbled words.

38. The last line being corrupt does not make construction easy. The reading is धीनयोदयगैस्त्यंशैः पापास्ते रसिरोह्रदाः। It may be read as : धीनवोदयगैस्त्र्यंशैः पापैस्तैरशिरोऽपदः. The meaning given above for this portion is tentative. Elsewhere the conditions are given thus: When the rising decanate is occupied by Mars (the other conditions being the same for dwarfness), it will be headless, armless or devoid of feet, according as the decanate is the first, second or third (See "Fundamentals of Astrology" page 118).

39. There appears to be some mistake in the reading नेष्टा योगा, whose sense is against astrological conventions. Hence we may have to change the reading as इष्टयोगाः

40. 'सुतावपि' should be changed to 'सूतावपि'.

40a. In verse 66 the word पापाः makes no sense. It must be याताः according to the context. Let us say that the Moon at conception occupies Vṛṣabha and her longitude is 15-25°-46'. The Dvādaśāṁśa of the

Moon is the 11th counted from Vṛṣabha. So the Moon's Dvādaśāṁśa Rāśi happens to be Mīna. Now counting will have to be made from this Rāśi i.e. Mīna. 11 Rāśis should be counted from Mīna, which comes to Makara. So we must say that delivery is likely to occur when the Moon passes through Makara Rāśi.

41. From verse 65 to 68 only single lines i.e. 2 quarters, are taken as full verses without any rhyme or reason. There is a metrical flaw too in the second line. The reading नारिजन्म वै makes no sense. It may be corrected as चारिजन्मगे. Similarly जनने should be read as जनके.

42. The reading साक्यरिसिंहोज्ञाजांसे is wrong. It should be आक्यारौ सिंहे ज्ञाब्जांशे.

43. The reading 'सपापगोऽर्को जायो' should be read as 'सपापगोऽर्कोऽब्जातो' It is suspected that the word गो in this reading may mean *Vṛṣabha*. In the second line the substantive of the dual, पापभस्थौ, is missing. The author must have the two malefics, Mars and Saturn, in mind. The reading, सूर्याधीनत्रिकोणगौ is wrong. It must be read as सूर्यस्थानत्रिकोणगौ. 'पितावृद्धः' should be read as पिता बद्धः.

44. 'यातेंगना नारी प्रसूयते' should be as 'यानेऽङ्गना नीरे प्रसूयते'. The reading, अब्धांगमन्भगः पूर्णे ज्यो वा' may have to be corrected as युग्माङ्कनाभगः पूर्णोऽब्जो वा.

45. The reading गुह्यां should be corrected as गुप्त्यां and अज as अब्ज.

46. 'कर्काति' should be read as कर्कालि. It is strange that the author gives 'barren ground' as the effect of the Moon's aspect. It ought to be a good place of decoration or recreation.

47. The reading भासमाने सरे is unintelligible. It should be read as भसमाने चरे. Here too the word अब्ज in for गेऽब्ज is wrongly spelt as गेज

48. The meaning given here is tentative. The word भवे may mean, at birth, in the Lagna, in the 11th house or the 5th. So we can translate it thus as well: 'When Mars and Saturn occupy the 11th and when the ascendant is (or these two planets are) aspected by a benefic....' The reading यतायुः.....मासः सार्यैः should be emended as गतायु.....मासैः सार्धैः. The plural usage here is archaic.

49. The reading न वा should be emended as नवं; and दृढे रम्ये as दृढं रम्यं.

50. In the Zodiac one half is above the horizon and the other below it. So they are called *Dṛśyārdha* (visible half) and *Adṛśyārdha* (invisible half). The 8th, 9th, 10th, 11th, 12th. and the portion of the Lagna that has risen come under the *Visible Half.* The 7th is called the *Astarāśi* or Setting Sign. Even in this Sign there are two parts as in the Lagna.

51. According to Varāhamihira the colour or complexion corresponds to, चन्द्रसमेतनवांशपवर्णः, that of the lord of the Moon's Navāṁśa Rāśi. It is possible that this author too means the same thing.

52. Suppose the first decanate of Meṣa rises. Then the first ones of the 12 houses will represent in order the head, the right eye, right ear, right nostril, right cheek, right jaw, mouth, left jaw, left cheek, left nostril, left ear and the left eye.

53. The reading तद्युते should be rectified as सद्युते. Similarly भुज needs to be changed to भूजो and जेतु: into जन्तो:.

54. The reading तिलकृन्मसकृदष्ट should be corrected into तिलकृन्म शकृददृष्ट:. Here मश means मशक a mole-like thing. Cf. बृहत्संहिता LII.10.

55. The reading पिंगके श्लक्षणो should be emended as पिङ्गकेशेक्षणो.

56. The reading चन्द्र: कूरयुतै: शुभै: should be read as चन्द्र: क्रूरयुत: शुभै:.

57. The reading केन्द्राद्याहस्तसन्खेटै: is corrupt and may be corrected as केन्द्राद्यारूढसत्खेटै: Here केन्द्रादि should be taken to mean केन्द्र, own house or exaltation.

58. The reading षष्ठेमेब्जे should be emended as षष्ठेऽष्टमेऽब्जे.

59. The reading त्रिकोणोपस्तै: should be corrected as त्रिकोणोपगतै:.

60. The reading सृज्यवात्मजयो: makes no sense. It should be emended as जनन्यात्मजयो:

60a. The reader should bear in mind the fact that all the 7 planets cannot be exalted at the same time. For, when the Sun is exalted in Meṣa, Mercury cannot be so. A planet is said to be in Vargottama when it occupies the same Sign both in the Rāśi chart and the Aṁśaka Chart.

61. सवीर्ये सत्सु is grammatically wrong. The author intends probably to convey the idea : सवीर्येषु असत्सु.

62. The printed text gives 'जिता:' which can mean only 'defeated'. It may be some other word standing for some number. It must be जिना: which would give the number 24. The word भाब्द may yield the number 27 which is the number of stars, or 12 which is the number of Rāśis.

63. After subtracting the planet's longitude from its highest exaltation, see if the result is less than 6 Rāśis. If so, subtract it from 12 Rāśis and reduce the result to minutes and multiply it by the planet's years. Then divide the product by 21,600. The quotient represents years etc. contributed by that planet. The reading नो ग्रह: should be read /as यो ग्रह:.

64. The reading षड्रात्यं is a mistake for षड् भाल्पं.

64a. According to the plan given in/the previous verses for putting benefic lines in the Aṣṭakavarga chart for each planet, we have to view the different houses containing benefic dots from the point of the planet concerned. For example, the Sun is good in transit in the 3rd, 6th, 10th, and 11th from one's natal Moon (Rāśi). If these also happen to contain more than 4 benefic lines, the effect of the Sun's transit through these houses will be excellent.

65. The translation of the second half is tentative.

66. The text invariably gives अज (Moon) for अब्ज The reading अर्यकांश is corrupt and has been corrected as अर्यङ्काय.

67. The reading एषे षांग्रेंर्कपपासृज: is utterly corrupt. It should be read somewhat as वृषेऽङ्गेऽर्कयमासृज:

68. The reading लग्नगै: सौरेजाब्जर्क्षहरय: सया:। कविक्षौ is corrupt. It may be corrected as लग्नगे सौरेऽजेऽब्जेऽर्को हरिसंस्थित:। कवीज्यौ...।

69. The reading त्रिलग्नभवगै: would mean the 3rd, ascendant and the 11th house.

70. 'भवे करै' should be read as भवे परे; 'सुखास्तु' as सुखास्त.

71. As usual the readings are corrupt : Instead of putting गदाख्य: the editor of the Purāṇa has given us the reading वर्गदाख्य:. Similarly धिगौगस्थै: should be read as धीगोऽङ्गस्थै:.

72. वर्जोङ्गेस्थे should be read as वज्र ऽङ्गेऽस्ते; and वाया as वापी.

73. शक्ति दंड should be read as शक्तिदण्ड.

74. नुर्यत: should be read as तुर्यत:; and स्वभाद्यायो as खभाञ्चापो.

75. षह्यु is unintelligible. राजयोग: should be read as रज्जुयोग:

76. The reading व्यंगा स्थिरा लो... may have to be read as व्यङ्ग: शिरालो.

76a. According to other authorities *Pāśayoga* does not lead to good character.

77. अर्द्धचंपात् should be read as अर्द्धचन्द्रोत्थ:.

78. The reading तौज: सकीर्ति: possibly stands अब्जे सकीर्ति: Here अब्ज means *Lotus*.

79. Here too the readings are very bad : The expression शाजोको must be corrected as साञ्जोऽर्को; 'भौमपुष्करुर्तेब्वग:' should be read as 'भौमग्रहयुतोऽब्वगम्'. सुज्ञ stands for सज्ञ:. सेन्यो is to be read as सेज्यो.

80. The सज्योऽस्थिरवयं is to be changed to सेज्योऽस्थिरहृदं; ससितोसुकवेत्तारं to ससित: सुखवेत्तारं; and सार्किपोनभवं to सार्कि: पौनर्भवं.

81. 'स मन्दमन्दाक्षा व वनिश्रय:...' should be read as 'समन्दे मन्दाक्षो वनिताश्रय...'

82. The expression मंदकागणे may have to be read as मन्दार्काङ्कपे. In the last condition we can also add the condition viz. when the Moon, *being posited in the Aṁśa of Mars or the Sun*, is aspected

83. पत्रे should be read as पित्र्ये.

84. मढचो आठनो should be read as मैत्रे चाटनो.

85. It is strange that the author has omitted Sign Mina (Pisces) while giving the effects of the various natal Signs.

86. नियरत्य: is to be changed to नियमस्थ:, सपुत्रस्त्रीसर्ण: to सपुत्र: स्त्रीस्वर्ण: and द्रक्षमैश्य: is दक्षमित्र:

87. The reading धनाघवान् may stand for धनौघवान्. In that case under 4 we have to take the meaning as "lot of wealth."

88. The reading, व्यंगजार्थो खप्रसूको विधिमित्रो सुखत्रय: makes no sense. So it has to be read as व्यङ्गजोऽर्थी ह्यप्रसूको बहुमित्रोऽसुखत्रय:. The असुखत्रय or

triad of troubles consists of आधिभौतिक, आध्यात्मिक and आधिदैविक. The reading ग्रामे शोकादिभेर्कजे should be read as ग्रामेशोऽर्कादिभेऽर्कजे.

89. 'नु खलु' should be taken as नखलु and नृपेज्याज्ञादि as नृपेशादि.

90. The reading नैपुण्यवतिताशया: should be changed to नैपुण्यवनिपेश्वरा:.

91. जनयाश्चाये should be read as जनपाश्चापे, सद्भिर्दर्मी to सद्धीर्दम्भी.

92. The meanings given under *Kumbha* and *Mīna* are tentative. मण्डित should be read as पण्डित; भूयान्यदारिकौ as भूपान्यदारकौ; and सद्भिः as सद्धीः.

93. आरक्षेको....क्षितिजांशस्थे should be read as आरक्षिको.....क्षितिजांशस्थे.

94. सख should be emended as सस्वः.

95. विद्योधा should be read as विद्यो वा, and दुःखितो खो as दुःखितोऽस्वो.

96. नीचोधोस्वः should be read as नीचोऽयास्वः, and उद्बुदाक्षः as बुद्बुदाक्षः.

97. अपत्योक्तितो is to be read as अपत्योज्झितो. The expression शत्रुजितः would mean, vanquished by enemies, but the author means the opposite of that and had to resort to this expression for the sake of metre.

98. सुखभा is to be read as सुखभाग् and पतितो खोऽव्यये as पतितोऽस्वो व्यये.

99. These verses contain many unintelligible readings : प्रेष्यो जेगे should be read as प्रेष्योऽब्जेऽङ्गे; खाच्चाजगे as स्वे चाजगे (tentatively), तन्त्रिमदोज्ञखे is a hard nut to crack; it may be read as तन्त्री मदे ज्ञपः (tentative) or सुस्त्रीमदो हये for हय stands for 7, the meaning of सुस्त्रीमदः being—'one enjoying sexual pleasures with an excellent damsel'; भानुर्द्धनगे is metrically an impossibility and should be read as भाग्ये.

100. Read गाधो as बुधो and ज्ञेयस्तो as ज्ञेयस्ततो.

101. स वाच्यः should be read as सुवाक्यः; सुखाक्षो as सुखी ज्ञो; रिपुगृद्धिमान्. as रिपुहृद् धीमान् (though the metre becomes faulty); and चष्णवनी possibly as धन्य धनी.

102. मुखी should be read as सुखी; and तनपस्ये च as तनयापत्यः or स्त्रैणापत्यश्च.

103. The reading 'खभराकादिके' is highly corrupt. It might be taken as स्वभमूलादिके. 'खेटे घ्रें का' is to be read as 'खेटेष्वेका.'

104. 'संस्थिते शुभभेषु च' should be read as संस्थितेषु शुभेषु च.

105. गतः पापः should read as गताः पापाः and भास्कर्या as भास्कर्यां.

105a. The first line should be read as—व्यालायुधचतुष्पादाब्जेषु च त्र्यंशकेषु च.

106. खाये should read as स्वीये; and त्रिशांसे सृजि as त्रिशांशेऽसृजि.

107. कीर्त्यालः should read as कीर्त्याढ्यः. The reading नीरगुह्यभवान् is unintelligible. It may be taken as तुरगेभ... The meaning given above is tentative. Read ख as स्व.

108. रोग should read as भोग.

109. There are three yogas viz. *Vesi*, Vāsi and *Ubhayacarī*, when there

are planets (except the Moon) in the 2nd, 12th and both respectively. (Vide "Fundamentals of Astrology" p. 149).

110. The reading पृष्ठोभवकोदयर्क्ष should be emended as पृष्ठोभयकोदयर्क्ष. Here क means, head.

111. Read अन्यथाथांगतोदय: as अन्यथास्तङ्गतोदय:।

112. सिमातुर्या should read as सितात्तुर्या.

113. The translation given above of verse 279 is tentative. Another meaning of verse 280 is :— The wife would have defective limbs, if the Sun and Venus together occupy the 5th or 9th house. If Saturn is posited in the Lagna and Venus in Sandhi.., *Koṇa* being one of the synonyms of Saturn.

114. पापे should read as पापै: and क्षीणजन्मा as क्षीणे जन्मा–.

115. व्योशे should be read as व्यंशे.

116. अर्केन्दो: should read as अर्केन्द्वो:.

117. 'सौम्या दृष्टा न' should be read as सौम्यदृष्टा न.

118. संज्ञे should read as सज्ञे. The expression सोन्मद: is used सोन्माद: for metrical necessity.

119. याशाठ्यै: should read as पाशाढ्यै:.

120. 'फलं पण्यस्त्रीणां' must be wrong. It should be read as फलं यद्यत्स्त्रीणां; and 'यादयूपपीतद्युने' as 'पापादुपपतिं द्युने'.

121. This verse appears so be a repetition of verse 297. Here the word दृष्टा या makes no sense. It may be दुष्टा. The translation is only tentative.

122. दुष्णवाक् should read as दुर्वाक्.

123. The word अगम्यता may stand for अगम्यता or अरम्यता.

124. 'आग्नेयैर्विधवा' reminds us of the Bṛhajjātaka expression.

125. मिथोंऽशगै: should read as मिथोंऽशगौ.

126. अनुसया should read as अनुज्ञया.

127. वृद्धौ should read as वृद्धो.

128. The reading हितं युक्तं भगात्तोस्थोपथभूरिभि: ....बहुजो is highly corrupt; अग्न्यक्षत should read as अग्न्यम्बुक्षत. The corrupt portion might mean the following :—When the lord of the 8th house occupies it and is aspected by benefics, the native's death takes place in a peaceful and ideal manner.

129. The ready मन्दभूजै: is wrong both metrically and grammatically. So it should be corrected as मन्दचन्द्रभूजै:.

130. 'पापदृक्तयो:' should be emended as पापदृष्टयो:, and 'तोयमृतो रवीदृतुस्यातां या द्युभयोदये' as 'तोये मृसी रवीन्दू तु स्यातां यद्युभयोदये'.

131. वाज्वग्नि should be read as रज्ज्वग्नि.

132. 'सयासशयं' should read सपाशसर्पं; and स्त्रीकृते as स्त्रीकृतं. The expression 'सकृत्' is hard to understand. It must be something शुभेऽसित: or असित: In that case it may be read as क्षीणचन्द्रेऽशुभेऽसित:, असित: meaning, from the sword.

133. 'धूमानि' should be read as धूमाग्नि, and कुदनैः as कुट्टनैः.

134. क्षतक्रेभ्यंगया ततः should be read as क्षतक्रम्यगपाततः.

135. यंत्रोसीदुनतः should be read as यन्त्रोत्सादनतः.

136. मृतो should be read as मृतौ; भुव्य-संयुते. as भूजसंयुते If भुव्यसंयुते be correct, we may have to construe it thus : The weak Moon in the 4th house without any other planet in it. लग्नध्यायुस्तपः स्वर्क० should be read as लग्नध्यायास्तगैरर्के०; and चन्द्रनिशाकरैः as मन्दनिशाकरैः; शैलशृंगस्वरुग्रपातौ as शैलभृङ्गात् तरोरग्रात्पातैः.

137. दृक्कोंत्तरे should read as दृक्के खरे.

138. मोदो should read as मोहो.

139. बिन्दुतः should read as इन्दुतः

140. The reading पित्रतिरक्तोथ is unintelligible. It may have to be read as पित्रतिरिक्तोप०.

141. "बलवश्रंश" is to be read as बलवत्व्यंश. 'सांदनूके' must be स्यादनूके.

142. बलान्यतः should be read as बलाश्रितः.

143. आधाने जन्माज्ञाने should read as आधानजन्मा ज्ञाने; वृक्षतां as पृच्छतां; and वाच्यपने as वाच्यायने.

144. ग्रीष्मोगे should read as ग्रीष्मोऽङ्गे. 'रम्यापनतांपृतुरकंभात्' is highly corrupt. It may be something like 'रन्यायनतामृतुरर्कभात्'.

145. वृत्यस्याः is to be read as व्यत्यास्याः.

146. The second half which reads thus : 'त्रिकोणोत्तमवार्यं हि लग्नं वा लभनाभने' is woefully corrupt and obscure. It may be corrected as "त्रिकोणोत्तमवीर्यं वा लग्नं कालभनामतः" or so. Another interpretation of this line proposed is : "If the Lagna at query is very strong, then the natal ascendant may be a sign which is a trine (Trikoṇa) to this Lagna; or it may correspond to...."

147. In verse 346 'खसंख्यया' may be स्वसङ्ख्यया. The reading 'राघवाधायरेज्ञवत्' is difficult to decipher. Some tentative meaning has been proposed above. खेटवशावद्धर्गणाः probably stands for खेटवशादहर्गणाः.

148. सप्तघ्न होनिशा should read as सप्तघ्नेऽह्नोनिशा. In the following verses, from 349 to 365, the characteristics of the 36 decanates are described.

149. हृष्टतिकपदा may be दृष्ट्यातिकपदा or हृष्टातिकपटा which would mean : Jolly and very cunning; the latter may be preferred.

150. दुग्धपटो should be read as दग्धपटो; and सरभयात् as सरभसः.

151. शरमाहिकः may be read as शरमाश्रितः or शरभाहिकः; आतव्य as आलम्ब्य; and पालाशी as पालाशीं.

152. श्वा नरो may be वानरो or as it is; सिंहवाश्वोन्नतमातुरः as सिंहवाशी चोन्नतमातुरः.

153. विद्येल्ला is unintelligible; व्ययापकृत् may also be read as व्यवायकृत्; and अंशुकात्सुच्चा should be read as अंशुकात्युच्चा.

154. सिंधे should read as सिंहे; कूजं as कपं; सर्पसितांहिका as सर्पावताङ्घ्रिका; and सिंह:श्व as सिंहश्व.

155. वास्य: श्वकाय: may be बाल: श्वकाय: or वाल्यश्वकाय:; सिन्धुरत्नविवर्द्धिनी may be सिंहवक्त्रविवर्द्धिनी or सिन्धुरव्रजवर्द्धिनी; and कौशेयकानिनी may be कौशेयकानने or कौशेयकानन:.

156. दग्धानस्था may be दग्धावस्था or दग्धवस्त्रा (with burnt clothes) or दग्धासनस्था (seated on a burnt seat).

157. ध्वौसं may be ध्यायन्; एतादृशां क्रियां शा: स्तु should be read as एतादृशा: क्रियाद्यास्तु (or क्रियादीनां); षड्विंशत् is wrong for षट्त्रिंशत्. In the text there are no lines to describe the three decanates of Mina. The omission must have been due to the scribe's inadvertence.

CHAPTER FIFTYSIX

Natural Astrology

Sanandana said:

1-2a. *Lord of the year etc.* (In one year), the Sun transits into (the twelve) *rāśis* (or signs of the Zodiac) Aries (*Meṣa*) etc.[1] during the (twelve) months beginning with *Caitra* etc.[2] The King of the year is (the lord of) the week-day of the first day of the bright fortnight of the month of *Caitra*. The Commander of the year is (the lord of the week-day on which) the Sun transits into the sign of Aries and the Lord of Vegetation is (the lord of the week-day) on which the Sun transits into the sign Cancer, *Kaṭaka*.

2b-3. As the Lord of the year, the Sun is of middling benefit while the Moon would be extremely beneficial. Mars is not beneficial but Mercury, Jupiter and Venus are highly beneficial. Saturn is least beneficial of all. In due consideration of the strength or otherwise of these (planets) should be indicated the general benefice of the year.

SUN: RAVICĀRA

4. *Significance of snn-spots*. Spots on the Sun of the shapes of a rod, corpse, crow and pillar, respectively, portend, (to the king), disease, turbulance, (trouble from) thieves and loss of wealth.

5. (Sun-spots of the shape of) the umbrella, chaurie, banner, rain-cloud, smoke and sparks, portend the destruction of the land.

6. O sage: If these spots are, respectively, white, red, yellow or black in colour they will afflict the four castes *Brahmins*, *Kṣatriyas*, *Vaiśyas* and *Śūdras*. If they appear in two or three of these colours, they will afflict the royalty.

7. *Significance of the Sun's beams*. If the (upward) beams emanating from the top of the Sun's disc are reddish, the commander of the army will die, if the beams be yellow, the prince, if white, the chief priest, and if variegated the people.

8a. If the downward beams are dark, they foretell disaster to the king and if reddish yellow, to the clouds (indicating rainlessness).

8b-9. *The Sun's hue.* The Sun is auspicious in *śiśira*, the cool season, if copper-red, in spring if saffron-hued, in summer if greyish, in the rainy season if variegated, in autumn if lotus-red, and in winter if crimson-coloured.

10. If the Sun be yellowish, bright-white and crimson, respectively, in winter, rainy season and summer, it portends, O sage: diseases, drought and calamities.

11. A sun appearing in a rainbow causes a fight between kings. And, if the Sun appears with hue of the hare's blood, there will ensue shortly a world war.

12. If the Sun appears with the hue of the peacock's feather, there will be no rains for twelve years. A moon-like Sun will cause the replacement of the king of the land.

13. If the Sun is darkish, there would be fear from locusts and, if greyish like ash, there would be contrywide distress. When a hole is seen in the Sun's disc an emperor will die.

14. *Orb of the Sun.* (The Sun's orb) appearing like a pot will cause famine (in the country); if like an arch it will cause the destruction of the capital; and, if like an umbrella, the destruction of the country. A split Sun will cause the death of the monarch.

15. If at sunrise or at sunset, there occur (against the sun's disc) lightning, meteor and thunder, then, one can fortell the death of the king or fight between kings.

16. If for a fortnight or half a fortnight, the Sun and the Moon appear with a halo around (*pariveṣa*), both day and night, it will cause the replacement of the king, which will happen, also if they appear crimson at rising and setting (during the said period).

17. If the Sun is obscured at sunrise and at sunset by clouds having the shape of weapons, there will be war; and, (if those clouds have the shape of) sinful animals like the camel, the war would be terrible.

THE MOON: CANDRACĀRA

18. In the signs Pisces and Aries, the crescent Moon with

the southern horn higher (than the northern horn) is beneficent, while in the signs Gemini and Capricorn, the Moon with the northern horn higher is auspicious.

19-20a. In the signs Aquarius and Taurus, the Moon is auspicious if the horns are equal, and in Cancer and Sagittarius, if they look like arrows. In the signs Scorpio and Leo (the Moon) is auspicious, if it has the shape of a bow, and in the signs Libra and Virgo, if it has the shape of a javelin. In the reverse positions, the Moon causes famine and war.

20b-21a. When the Moon courses south of the asterisms[3] Pūrvāṣāḍha, Uttarāṣāḍha, Mūla and Jyeṣṭha there will occur fires, drought and the destruction of forests and (the appearance of) snakes.

21b-22a. (The time when) Moon courses south of the asterisms Viśākhā and Anurādhā is inauspicious; and its coursing north of the asterisms Maghā (*pitṛdaivatya*) and Viśākhā (*dvidaiva*), is medially beneficial.

22b-23a. With reference to auspicious Moon, the six asterisms from Revatī (*Pauṣṇya*) are (called) 'Conjunction to be' (*aprāpya-yoga*), the twelve asterisms from Ārdrā (*Rudra*) as 'In conjunction' (*Madhya-yoga*) and the nine asterisms Jyeṣṭhā (*Vāsava*) are called 'Past conjunction' (*Atīta-yoga*).

23b-24a. The 'half-asterisms' (*Ardha-tārakas*) are Bharaṇī (*Yama*)Jyeṣṭhā (*Indra*), Āśleṣā (*Ahiśa*), Śatabhiṣak (*Toyeśa*) and Svātī (*Marut*); the 'more-than-half asterisms' (*Adhyardha-tārakas*) are: Dhruva, Punarvasu (*Aditi*) and Viśākhā (*Dvideva*); the remaining asterisms are 'full' (*Sama*).

24b-25a. The Moon with its south horn higher (than the north horn) is extremely beneficial and that with the north horn higher is generally auspicious. The illuminated portion decreases and increases alternatively.[4]

25b-26a. The Moon with a broad orb is a harbinger of plenitude, while that with a narrow orb would cause loss of wealth. If it appears to hang with face down, there will be a threat from weapons and if (elongated) like a rod, there would be disputes.

26b-27a. If its horns or orb are crossed by Mars and other planets, effects such as destruction of welfare, wealth, rains, kings and people, will follow.

MARS : KUJACĀRA

27b-28a. When, (after retrogression), Mars has risen in an asterism, which thus forms its 'rising asterism', (*udaya-nakṣatra*) if it again goes into retrogression in the 7th, 8th or 9th asterism counted from its 'rising asterism', such a retrogression is called *Uṣṇa*, then will occur distress to people and damage by fire.

28b-29a. The retrogression at the 10th, 11th and 12th asterism is called *Aśrumukha*. It keeps off rains and destroys crops.

29b-30a. When the retrogression of Mars is in the 13th or 14th asterism, it is called *Vyālavakra*. Therein will occur the destruction of vegetation and of the rains.

30b-31a. The retrogression on the 15th or 10th asterism is *Rudhirānana*. Mars will then cause famine, starvation and diseases.

31b-32a. In the 17th and the 18th, the retrogression is called *Musala*. It will be attended with famine and will be terrible on account of heavy loss of wealth and grains.

32b-33a. If Mars rises in the asterisms of Pūrva or Uttara Phalgunī and retrogrades in Uttarāṣāḍha (*Vaiśvadeva*) and sets in Rohiṇī (*Caturāsyārkṣa*), it destroys three worlds.

33b-34a. Mars which rises in Śravaṇa and retrogrades in Puṣya is inauspicious to kings in general and will threaten (especially) the kings of that direction in which Mars rises.

34b-35a. If Mars courses through the (four) stars of the Maghā constellation and retrogrades in the same constellation, it will cause fear from drought and weapons and destroy the Pāṇḍya king.

35b-36a. If Mars crosses the asterisms Mahā (*pitṛ*), Viśākhā (*Dvidaiva*) and Rohiṇī (*Dhātṛ*), it will then cause famine, death and disease.

36b-37a. If Mars courses through the three *Uttaras*, (viz., *Uttaraphalgunī*, *Uttara-āṣāḍha* and *Uttara-bhādrapada*), Rohiṇī, Mūla (*Nairṛta*), Śravaṇa and Jyeṣṭhā (*Indrabhā*) or courses south of Rohiṇī, it will cause drought.

37b-38a. Mars coursing north of any constellation will be auspicious; while coursing south thereof, it will be inauspicious and cause dissentions amongst the people.

MERCURY : BUDHACĀRA

38b-39a. If Mercury rises, being afflicted by a portent (*utpāta*), it will cause drought, fear from fires, calamities and war between kings.

39b-40a. If Mercury courses across the asterisms Dhaniṣṭhā (*Vasu*), Śravaṇa (*Vaiṣṇava*), Uttarāṣāḍha (*Vaiśva*), Mṛgaśīrṣa (*Indu*) and Rohiṇī (*Dhātṛ*) it will threaten with distress and drought.

40b-41a. If Mercury is seen among (*five*) constellations from Ārdrā to Maghā, it will then threaten with famine, war, disease and drought.

41b-42a. Mercury traversing across the six constellations beginning with Hasta will cause welfare, prosperity, health and destruction of diseases.

42b-43a. Mercury coursing across the constellations Uttara-bhādrapada (*Ahirbudhnya*), Uttara-phalguni (*Aryama*), Kṛttikā (*Āgnaya*) and Bharaṇī (*Yama*) will bring distress to physicians and sea trade.

43b-44a. If Mercury crosses the three constellations beginning with Pūrva-, (*viz.*, Pūrva-phalgunī, Pūrva-āṣāḍha and Pūrva-bhādrapada, it will then threaten people with starvation, weapons, fire and robbers.

44b. The motion of Mercury in the constellations Bharaṇī (*Yāmya*), Kṛttikā (*Agni*), Rohiṇī (*Dhātṛ*) and Svāti (*Vāyavya*) is said to be *Prākṛta* (natural).

45. In the constellations Ārdrā (*Raudra*), Mṛgaśiras (*Indu*), Āśleṣā (*Sarpa*) and Maghā (*Pitrya*), its motion is called *Miśra* (mixed) and in the constellations Pūrva-phalgunī (*Bhāgya*) Uttara-phalgunī (*Aryamā*), Puṣya (*Ijya*) and Punarvasu (*Aditi*), its motion is termed *Saṅkṣipta* (concise).

46. The motion amongst the constellations Pūrva-bhādrapada (*Aja-caraṇa*), Uttara-bhādrapada (*Ahirbudhnya*) is called *Tikṣṇa* (Sharp). *Yogānta* is the term for the motion of Mercury in the constellations Uttarāṣāḍha (*Viśva*), Pūrvāṣāḍha (*Ambu*) and Mūla.

47. Its motion is called *Ghora* (Cruel) in the constellations Śravaṇa (Hari), Citrā (*Tvāṣṭra*), Śraviṣṭhā (*Vasu*) an Śatabhiṣak (Varuṇa). Pāpa (sinful) is the name of its motion

through the constellations Viśākhā (*Indrāgni*), Anurādhā(*Mitra*) and Hasta (*Mārtaṇḍa*).

48. Mercury which has risen with one or the other of the motions *Prākṛta* etc. will be visible for as many days as it will be invisible (later).

49. Mercury (completes the motions *Prākṛta* etc.), in order, in the following number of days : (*Prākṛta*) 45 (*Miśra*) 30, (*Saṅkṣipta*) 22, (*Tīkṣṇa*) 20, (*Yogānta*) 9, (*Ghora*) 15 and (*Pāpa*) 11.

50. Mercury, in its *Prākṛta* motion, brings welfare, health and prosperity. During the motions *Miśra* and *Saṅkṣipta*, it is of mixed benefit, and, during the other (motions), it produces rain.

51. If Mercury remains visible during the months Vaiśākha, Śrāvaṇa, Pauṣa and Āṣāḍha it will bring distress to the world; during the other (months) it is beneficial.

52. However, if it is visible during the months of Āśvina (*Iṣa*) and Kārttikā (*Ūrja*), there will be fear from weapons, famine and fire. If Mercury rises with the brilliance of silver and crystal, it will be most auspicious.

JUPITER : GURUCĀRA

53. (In the case of Jupiter), two constellations make up the months Kārttika (*Ūrja*) etc.; however, three constellations make up the fifth, twelfth and eleventh months. The year should be named by the constellation in which Jupiter rises.[5]

54. The years Kārttika and Mārgaśīrṣa (*i.e.*, the Jovian years in which Jupiter rises in the constellations Kṛttikā and Mṛgaśira, respectively) are inauspicious to people, the years Pauṣa and Māgha are auspicious, and, the years Phālguna and Madhu (Caitra) would be of medium benefit.

55-56a. The year Mādhava (*Vaiśākha*) is auspicious while Jyeṣṭha is of medium benefit. The year Śuci (*Āṣāḍha*) is, again, of medium benefit but Nabhas (*Śrāvaṇa*) is extremely beneficial, while Bhādrapada is so at some places and for some people. The year Iṣa (*Āśvina*) is most auspicious. Thus has been stated the effect of the different months.

56b-57a. Jupiter traversing to the north of the asterisms is productive of welfare, health and prosperity. If otherwise (*i.e.*, traversing south) it will have the opposite effect. If it traverses through (the asterisms), it will have mixed effect.

57b-58a. Jupiter having the hues—yellow, fire-bright, dark, green and red, will threaten creatures respectively with disease, arson, loot, weapons and missiles.

58b-59a. Jupiter, if smoke-hued, will cause drought. If it is sighted during day, it will cause the death of the king or the destruction of the country.

59b-60a. The constellations Rohiṇī and Kṛttikā are said to be the 'body' of the year. The two Āṣāḍhās, (*viz.*, Pūrva and Uttara) form its 'nipple'. Ārdrā is its 'heart' and Maghā, its 'flower'.

60b-61. If the 'body' (of the year) comes into conjunction with a 'cruel' planet, there will be fear from famine, fire and wind; if the 'nipple' (is attacked), there will be fear from starvation; if the 'flower', roots and fruits will be destroyed; and if the 'heart', destruction of crops will follow. On the other hand, if the conjunction is with auspicious (planets), the results also will be auspicious.

62-64. (The following are the effects, in order, when) Jupiter traverses the 27 asterisms commencing with Maghā: Increase in crops; Health of the people; War; Food; Drought; Calamities; Distress to brahmins; Great happiness to cows, to kings; and to women. Quiet rain; Rain of snakes; Welfare; Rejoicing; Great Wealth; Prosperity; Destruction of the country; Torrential rains; Friendliness; Disease; Freedom from fear; Threatened disease; Vegetation, Rain; Disease; Grain; and Invisibility of the skies.

VENUS : ŚUKRACĀRA

65. Three lanes (*vithi*) each of Venus have to be conceived, situated, respectively, north, middle and south (of the Sun's path). The lanes have to be reckoned from the asterism Aśvinī (*dasrabhā*), at the rate of three asterisms each.

66. Thus will be formed nine lanes (*vīthis*) which are termed, respectively, (1) *Nāga*, (ii) *Ibha*, (iii) *Airāvata*, (iv) *Vṛṣabha*, (v) *Go*, (vi) *Jaradgava*, (vii) *Mṛga*, (viii) *Aja*, (ix) *Dahana*.

67. Venus, traversing the three northern lanes produces the plenitude of grains, wealth, rains and vegetation.

68a. In the three middle lanes, (it causes medium effects in these (matters) and in the three southern lanes)[6] the effects in all cases are completely adverse.

68b-69. Jupiter traversing across the five asterisms beginning with Maghā (*Pitṛ*) produces rain, and so does it in the western direction while traversing the three asterisms beginning with Svāti. Conversely, drought results. However, if it is in conjunction with Mercury, there will be rain.

70. If Venus rises or sets on the eighth or fourteenth day of the dark fortnight, or on the full moon day the land will be flooded.

71. If both Jupiter and Venus be in the seventh sign (Libra) and later pass on to the eastern lane, they will cause drought, famine and war.

72. If Mars, Mercury, Jupiter and Saturn, precede Venus, they will cause, respectively, war, whirlwind, famine and drought.

73. Venus is productive of plenty while traversing the asterisms Pūrvāṣāḍha (*Jala*), Anurādhā (*Mitra*), Uttaraphālguni (*Aryamā*), Āśleṣā (*Ahi*) and Jyeṣṭha (*Indra*). In Mūla, it threatens with hunger, weapons and drought, and in Uttarabhādrapada (*Ahirbudhnya*) and Revatī it produces fear.

SATURN : ŚANICĀRA

74. Saturn coursing amongst the asterisms Śravaṇa, Svāti (*Anila*) Hasta, Ārdrā, Bharaṇī and Pūrvaphalguni (*Bhāgya*) produces for people plenitude, health and vegetation.

75-77. (In the asterismal conception) reckoned from the asterism in which Saturn rises: One in the head: (the next) three in the face; two in the vital parts,[7] two in the eyes, five stars in the heart; four in the left hand; three in the left leg and three stars in the right leg, and four stars in the right arm, the occurrence of Saturn (in the said nine limbs) will produce, respectively: Disease, profits, misfortune, profits, peace, imprisonment, difficulties, exalted pilgrimage, and acquirement of wealth, in order.

78. When Saturn is retrograde, the effects are also retrograde. That is, the effects are in order for the right motion

(of the planet) and when it is fast (in retrograde motion), the effects are in the reverse order.

SHADOW OR DRAGON'S HEAD : RĀHUCCHĀYĀ

79. The slow-moving (Rāhu), is the demon's head which had been cut off by Viṣṇu's discus, but which attained immortality on account of its having tasted ambrosia and so was raised to planethood.

80. Through the power of a boon conferred on him by the Creator, Rāhu eclipses, at the syzygies, the Sun and the Moon, on account of latitude (*vikṣepa*) and declination (*avanati*).

81-82a. Once in six months the possibility of eclipses should be checked. There are seven Lords of the syzygies, who have been functioning from the commencement of the aeon (*kalpa*). They are Brahmā, Indu, Indra, Kubera, Varuṇa, Agni and Yama.

82b-83. (If an eclipse occurs) in the syzygy, of which Brahmā is the lord, there will be prosperity for cattle, vegetation and the twiceborn. Similar is the effect besides trouble to brahmins, when Indu (Soma) is the overlord of the syzygy. When Indra is the lord, there will be enmity between kings, calamity and destruction of vegetation.

84. During the lordship of Kubera, there will be loss of wealth to the wealthy; there will also be increase in grains. During Varuṇa's lordship, there will be distress for the kings, but peace for others.

85. During Agni's lordship of the syzygies, there will be plenty of rains, increase in vegetation and peace. During the lordship of Yama over the syzygies, there will be drought, loss of crops and adversity.

86. If an eclipse occurs before the computed time, there will be destruction to crops and fierce battles amongst kings, (if it occurs) after (the computed time) there will be destruction of flowers, fear and loss of crops.

87. If eclipses of both the Sun and the Moon occur during the same month, there will be enmity amongst the rulers of the land, loss of wealth and absence of rains.

88. If the rising or setting Sun or Moon is eclipsed, the destruction of kings and grains will result; if (in such cases),

the Sun and the Moon are eclipsed completely, they will cause starvation, disease and arson.

89. An eclipse during the northward course of the Sun (*saumyāyana*) is destructive of royalty and brahmins and that in the southern course is destructive of the other (castes). Rāhu observed in the four directions, reckoned from the north will destroy (the four castes), brahmin etc., in that order.

90. There are ten types of immersion, and, in the same manner, ten types of emergence as well. These cannot be properly identified even by Gods; then, what of ordinary men?

91-92a. Having derived the true positions of planets by calculations, one should cogitate about their respective rates of motion (*cāra*). Rate of planetary motion (*grahacāra*) is the means of ascertaining auspicious and inauspicious times. Hence, the wise should strive to ascertain those times.

TAIL OF THE DRAGON : KETUCĀRA

92b-93a. The rising and setting of comets (*Ketu-s*) are in the form of forebodings to men. They are of three types, *Divya* ('Divine'), *Antarikṣa* 'Atmospherical', and *Bhauma* ('Earthly') and yield auspicious and inauspicious fruits.

93b-95a. The *Antarikṣa* ones are said to occur in the shape of sacrificial flags, missiles, houses, chariots, trees and elephants, and, also, of the shape of posts, javelins and hooks. The *Divya* types occur in the asterisms and the *Bhauma* ones on the earth. A comet (*Ketu*), though really one, appears in different shapes, to destroy creatures on the earth.

95b-96. As many days as a comet continues to be visible in one or the other of its different shapes, its effect will extend over so many months; and, as many months (as it is visible, its effect will extend over so many) years. The 'Divine' comets continue to be effective for a life-time.

97. A comet which is short, resplendent, fair or white causes rain. A tall comet sets in a short time and causes drought.

98. A comet of the shape of a rainbow brings ill luck, and one like a spear with two, three or four points is said to destroy the land.

99. Resplendent comets of the from of a gem, garland, or gold, rising in the east or west, are injurious to kings.

100. Comets having the hue of the (red) *bandhūka* flower, blood (*kṣataja*), parrot's beak etc., are born of Fire and are (as destructive as fire).

101. The comets born of the Earth have the glaze of water or oil, and are circular; they cause starvation and fear. White comets, born of the Moon, bring about prosperity and peace.

102. *Brahmadaṇḍa*, the comet, born of Brahmā, is three-hued and three-horned and is known to raze down the entire population (of a country).

103. The white comets that show up in the north-east are born of Bhārgava (Venus) and are harbingers of ill luck. The two-horned comets, which are born of the 'Slow-moving' (Saturn) and are called Kanaka, also bring ill luck.

104. The comets called *Vikaca-s*, born of Jupiter, are inauspicious even if they occur in the south. The tiny white comets, born of Mercury, threaten with robbers and disease.

105. The Mars-born comets, called *Kuṅkuma-s*, red-hued and javelin-like, are harbingers of ill luck. However, the Fire-born comets called *Viśvarūpa-s* and of the hue of fire, are producers of happiness.

106. The darkish comets, called *Aruṇa-s*, born of the Sun, are inauspicious. However, the star-shaped comets born of Venus bring auspiciousness.

107. A comet which occurs in the constellation of Kṛttikā, causes the destruction of the people, while one seen over a palace, tree or hill causes the destruction of the king.

108. The comet called *Kaumuda*, resembling a lily, brings prosperity but the comet called *Āvartaketu*, with three horns (*triśiraḥ*), is inauspicious if it rises at dusk.

THE YEAR : SAṀVATSARA

109. *Measures of time and their use.* Measures of time are nine, being, *Brahma*, *Deva*, *Manu*, *Pitrya*, *Saura*, *Sāvana*, *Cāndra*, *Ārkṣa* and *Guru*.

110. From among these nine measures, practical reckoning is done only through five. The practical use of each is set out here.

111. The motion of the planets is reckoned through the

solar measure (*saura-māna*). The reckoning of the rainy season and pregnancy of women are reckoned through the civil measure (*sāvana-māna*).

112a. (Times for) rains and the pregnancy, of clouds are reckoned through the siderial measure (nākṣatra-māna).

112b-113a. Times for setting out on a pilgrimage (*yātrā*) marriage, religious fasts and tonsure, lords of the *tithi* (lunar day) and the year, the day of the syzygies, setting up a house, observance of religious fasts etc., are all fixed through the lunar measure (*cāndra-māna*).

113b-114. *The year*. The years *Prabhava* etc. are reckoned on the basis of the Jovian measure (*Guru-māna*). A year by each measure is made up of 12 months of that measure. The years *Prabhava* etc. are measured off by the mean motion of Jupiter.

115-120. (The sixty Jovian years are) : (1) Prabhava, (2) Vibhava, (3) Śukla, (4) Pramoda, (5) Prajāpati, (6) Aṅgiras, (7) Śrīmukha, (8) Bhava, (9) Yuvā, (10) Dhātā, (11) Īśvara, (12) Bahudhānya, (13) Pramāthi, (14) Vikrama, (15) Vṛṣa, (16) Citrabhānu, (17) Subhānu, (18) Tāraṇa, (19) Pārthiva, (20) Vyaya, (21) Sarvajit, (22) Sarvadhāri, (23) Virodhi, (24) Vikṛta, (25) Khara, (26) Nandana, (27) Vijaya, (28) Jaya, (29) Manmatha, (30) Durmukha, (31) Hemalamba, (32) Vilamba, (33) Vikārī, (34) Śārvarī, (35) Lava, (36) Śubhakṛt, (37) Śobhana, (38) Krodhi, (39) Viśvāvasu, (40) Parābhava, (41) Plavaṅga, (42) Kīlaka, (43) Saumya, (44) Sādhāraṇa, (45) Virodhakṛt, (46) Paribhāvī, (47) Pramādī, (48) Ānanda, (49) Rākṣasa, (50) Anala, (51) Piṅgala, (52) Kālayukta, (53) Siddhārtha, (54) Raudra, (55) Durmati, (56) Dundubhi, (57) Rudhirodgārī, (58) Raktākṣa, (59) Krodhana, and (60) Kṣaya.

121a. These sixty years have, all, effects according to their nomenclature.

121b-123a. Five years make up a *Yuga*; thus, there are 12 *yugas* (in a Jovian cycle). Their lords are, in order: (1) Viṣṇu, (2) Bṛhaspati (Devapurohita), (3) Purandara, (4) Lohita, (5) Tvaṣṭṛ, (6) Ahirbudhnya, (7) Pitṛs, (8) Viśve-devas, (9) Śaśī, (10) Indrāgni, (11) Aśvins and (12) Bhaga.

123b. The lords of the different years of the *yuga* are:

(1) Agni, (2) Ina or Sūrya, (3) Indu or Candra, (4) Vidhi or Brahmā, and (5) Īśvara or Śiva.

124. One should announce the effects (of a year) only after fully ascertaining (and balancing) the strength and weakness of the lords of the year, commander-in-chief and the lord of vegetation and also the motion of the planets at the time.

125. *Uttarāyaṇa and Dakṣiṇāyana.* Reckoning from the commencement of Capricorn, six months, in the solar measure constitute *Uttarāyaṇa* (the northward course of the Sun) ; this is also the day time of the gods. (The six months) beginning from cancer is *Dakṣiṇāyana* (southward course of the Sun) and that forms the night (of the gods).

126-127a. During *Uttarāyaṇa* should be performed all such auspicious rites as the first entry into the house, marriage, consecration of idols, ritual tying of the girdle made of *muñja* grass, sacrifices etc. (*yajñādi*). During *Dakṣiṇāyana* is to be done all inauspicious acts.

127b-128. *The seasons.* Two months each, as reckoned from Māgha constitute the (six) seasons Śiśira etc. Thus, during *uttarāyaṇa* occur (the three seasons) *Śiśira* (cool), *Vasanta* (Spring) and *Grīṣma* (hot), commencing from capricorn. And, during *dakṣiṇāyana* occur (the three seasons) *Varṣā* (rainy), *Śarad* (autumn) and *Hemanta* (winter).

129. *The months.* Lunar months are reckoned up to the end of the new moon and solar months from *Saṅkrānti i.e.*, entry of the Sun into the relevant signs of the Zodiac). In 30 days would one revolution of the Moon be completed, as also one siderial (*nākṣatra*) month.

130-131a. The names of the 12 months from Caitra are, in order : (1) Madhu, (2) Mādhava, (3) Śukra, (4) Śuci, (5) Nabha, (6) Nabhasya, (7) Iṣa, (8) Ūrja, (9) Saha, (10) Sahasyaka, (11) Tapa and (12) Tapasyaka.

131b-132a. That constellation in which the full moon occurs in any month , that month is named after that constellation. That full moon is also named with (the name of the constellation tacked to it).

132b-133a. *The fortnights.* The two fortnights, *viz.*, *śukla* (bright) and *kṛṣṇa* (dark) of the month are termed *daiva* (pertaining to the gods') and *pitrya* (pertaining to the manes). he two are specified for the performance of auspicious and inauspicious rites, respectively.

TITHIS : LUNAR DAYS

133b-135. *Lords of the days.* The lords of the lunar days are in order: Brahmā, Agni, Viriñci, Viṣṇu, Sailajā, Vināyaka, Yama, Nāga, Candra, Skanda, Arka, Vāsava, Mahendra, Vāsava, Nāga, Durga, Daṇḍadhara, Śiva, Viṣṇu, Hari, Ravi, Kāma, Sarpa, Kali, Candra, Viśvedevāḥ, and Darśa. So also are the manes.

136-137a. The names of the (fifteen) lunar days are, Nandā, Bhadrā, Jayā, Riktā and Pūrṇā, these being repeated thrice.[8] During the bright fortnight, their effect should be counted as non-beneficial, medium and beneficial. In the dark fortnight, however, the reckoning should be beneficial, medium and non-beneficial, in order.

137b-138a. *Auspicious and inauspicious days.* (In a fortnight, five days, being) the eighth, twelfth, sixth, fourth and fourteenth are called *pakṣa-randhra* ('holes in the fortnight') and are declared to be highly dreary.

138b-139a. If it is desired to perform any auspicious act in the said five nonauspicious days, one should reject 7, 14, 9, 9 and 24 *nāḍikās*, respectively, (as reckoned from the commencement of the day).

139b-140a. Except for *amāvāsyā* (the new moon) and *navamī* (the 9th), the odd days are commendable (for auspicious rites). The *pratipad* (first day) is always of medium (benefit).

140b-141a. One should abstain from an oilbath on *ṣaṣṭhī* (the 6th), meat on *aṣṭamī* (the eighth), haircut on the day of Kali (*i.e.*, the first), and recourse to women on full moon and new moon.

141b-142a. One should never clean the teeth on new moon, *pratipad* (1st), *dvādaśī* (12th), the *pratiparva* (*i.e.*, full moon) and *Navamī* (9th).

142b-143a. One should not take an oilbath on days of *Vyatipāta*,[9] *saṅkrānti*, *ekādaśī* (11th), full and new moon days, *ṣaṣṭhī* (6th) and on Sundays and Tuesday; so also on days of *Vaidhṛta*.[9a]

143b-45a. If one takes a bath in *āmalaka* water[10] on *daśamī*

(10th), he will lose his son; if on *trayodaśī* (13th), he will suffer from loss of wealth; if on *dvitīyā* (2nd), without doubt, he will lose his wealth and his son; and if on the new moon, *navamī* (9th) and *saptamī* (7th), his clan will be ruined.

145b-46. *Anumati, Rākā, Sinīvālī and Kuhū.* On a full moon day, (if due to astronomical circumstances) the moon is seen (even) during day-time, that full moon day is called *Anumati*; it is called *Rākā* when there is Moon (only) during the night, In the same manner, the new moon is also of two types; when moon is visible (at some part of the day), it is called *Sinīvālī* and when Moon is never visible, it is called *Kuhū*.

147-48. *Days of the commencement of the Yugas.* The first day of *Kṛtayuga* fell on the 9th day of the bright half in the month of Kārttika. The auspicious first day of *Tretāyuga* was on the 3rd day of the bright fortnight in the month of Mādhava. The first day of *Dvāparayuga* was the 15th day of the dark fortnight in the month of Māgha. And, the first day of *Kaliyuga* was the 13th day of the dark fortnight in the month of Nabhasya.

149-152a. *Days of commencement of the* 14 *Manus that make up a Kalpa.* (1) 12th day in the bright fortnight of the month of *Ūrja* (Kārttika) (2) 9th day, bright fortnight of *Āśvayuj* (Āśvina); (3) 3rd day, bright fortnight of Caitra, (4) 3rd day, bright fortnight of Bhādrapada; (5) 11th day, bright fortnight of Pauṣa; (6) 10th day, bright fortnight of Āṣāḍha; (7) 7th day, bright fortnight in Māgha. (8) 8th day, dark fortnight in *Nabhasya* (Śrāvaṇa); (9) New moon in Śrāvaṇa; (10) Full moon in Phālguna; (11) Full moon in Āṣāḍha, (12) Full moon of Kārttika; (13) Full moon in Jyeṣṭha; and (14) Full moon in Caitra; the abovesaid days, which are the days of commencement of the *manvantaras*, are, for men, extremely meritorious in the matter of worshipping the manes (*śrāddha*).

152b-153a. *Gajacchāyā.* On the 13th day of the dark fortnight in the month of Bhādrapada, if the Moon occurs in the constellation Maghā or the Sun in the constellation Hasta, the situation is called *Gajacchāyā*, which is infinitely productive if a *śrāddha* (is performed then).

153b-54a. *Intercalary tithis etc.* If three lunar days occur on a civil day, there will be a *tithikṣaya* (expunged lunar day).

On the other hand, if a *tithi* extends over three civil days, there will be an *adhika* (intercalary) *tithi*.[11] Both are nonauspicious.

154b-55a. A *tithi* that extends upto (or beyond) sunset in a civil day is said to be *Akhaṇḍa* ('full') ; if the *tithi* is short (of sunset) it is called *Khaṇḍa* ('broken').[12]

155b-56a. The fifteen parts of a *tithi* are called, in order, *Pratipad* etc. Halves thereof are called *Kṣaṇa-ṣ* in their (*i. e.*, of *Pratipad* etc.) half-measures.

THE DAY OF THE WEEK : VĀRA

156b-57a. *Nature of the week-days.* Sunday is 'firm', Monday 'moving', Tuesday 'cruel', Wednesday 'whole', Thursday 'light', Friday 'soft' and Saturday 'sharp'.

157b-58. *Effects of the week-days.* A man who takes an oilbath on Sunday will be in distress, on Monday handsome, on Tuesday diseased, on Wednesday fortunate, on Thursday poor, on Friday depleted and on Saturday prosperous.

159. The beginning of the week-day is reckoned from its occurrence in Laṅkā.[13] Beyond or before it (*i.e.*, east or west), the day will vary depending on terrestrial longitude (of the place) and the time of half ascensional difference in *nāḍikās* (at the time of the year).

160. Any act (performed on the day) of a strong planet will be effective, while the same act performed on the day) of a weak planet will be hardly productive.

161. The day of Moon, Mercury, Jupiter and Venus (*i.e.*, Monday, Wednesday, Thursday and Friday) are effective for all acts; the other days yield result in the case only of cruel acts.

162-163a. The Sun is dark-red, the Moon white, Mars pale-red, Mercury (dark-green) like the *dūrvā* grass, Jupiter yellowish, Venus white, and Saturn dark. Each is beneficial to actions of those who are of the respective complexion.

163b-65. (Inauspicions periods due to) the *Upagrahas* (secondary planets) *Kulika*, (called also Gulika), Upakulika, and Vāravelā ('time when no work should be undertaken'), occur on each day of the weak, as specified below). The reckoning is in terms of *praharas*, ($3\frac{1}{2}$ nāḍikās each) commencing from Sunday. Kulika : Sunday, at the 7th *prahara*; Monday,

5th; Tuesday, 4th; Wednesday, 6th; Thursday, 4th; Friday, 7th; and Saturday, 5th; Upakulika: Sunday 3rd; Monday, 2nd; Tuesday, 4th; Wednesday, 2nd; Thursday, 5th; Friday, 3rd; and, Saturday, 1st Vāravelā, Sunday, 8th; Monday, 2nd; Tuesday, 7th; Wednesday, 3rd; Thursday, 1st; Friday, 6th; and Saturday, 6th. The duration of each is half a *prahara* (*i.e.*, one and three fourths *nāḍikās*).

166-67a. *Lords of the hour*. If the lord of the hour 'kāla-horeśa', for any particular time, *kṣaṇa-vāra*, (within a day) is required, take the lord of that day as the lord of the first hour (of 2½ *nāḍikās*), the sixth as the lord of the second hour and the sixth from that as the lord of the third hour. Counting repeatedly the sixth of the previous, the lords of the *kāla-horās* for each hour of 2½ *nāḍikāṣ*, for whole day and night are got, in that order.[14]

THE ASTERISMS : NAKṢATRAS

168b-70. *The lords af the nakṣatras*. The lords of the asterisms are, in order : (1) Aśvinī—Dasrau (Aśvins); (2) Bharaṇī—Yama; (3) Kṛttikā—Vahni, (Agni); (4) Rohiṇī—Brahmā; (5) Mṛgaśiras—Candra; (6) Ārdrā—Īśa (Rudra); (7) Punarvasu—Aditi; (8) Puṣya—Jīva, (Bṛhaspati); (9) Āśleṣā—Ahi (Sarpa); (10) Maghā Pitṛs; (11) Pūrvaphalgunī—Bhaga (12) Uttaraphalgunī—Aryamā; (13) Hasta—Arka (Sūrya); (14) Citrā—Tvaṣṭṛ; (15) Svāti—Marut (Vāyu); (16) Viśākhā—Śakrāgnī (Indrāgnī, Dvideva), (17) Anurādhā—Mitra; (18) Jyeṣṭhā—Vāsava (Indra); (19) Mūla—Nirṛti; (20) Pūrva-āṣāḍha—Udaka (Āpaḥ); (21) Uttara-āṣāḍha—Viśvedevāḥ; (22) Śravaṇa—Govinda (Viṣṇu); (23) Dhaniṣṭhā (Śraviṣṭhā) Vasu; (24) Śatabhiṣak—Toyapa (Varuṇa); (25) Pūrva-Bhādra-pada—Aja Ekapād; (26) Uttara-bhādrapada—Ahirbudhnya; and (27) Revatī—Pūṣā.

171. *Downlooking asterisms*. The nine asterisms Pūrva-phalgunī, Pūrva-āṣāḍha, Pūrva-bhādrapada, Maghā, Āśleṣā (Ahi), Kṛttikā (Agni), Viśākhā, Bharaṇī (Yama) and Mūla are downward-looking asterisms.

171b-172. (During their currency, the under-mentioned acts are) ordained : Entering a cave, diagrammatic and other matters based on mathematics, architectural work, digging of wells, retrieval of treasures etc.

173. *Sideways-looking asterisms.* The nine asterisms Anurādhā (Mitra), Mṛgaśiras (Indu), Citra (Tvaṣṭṛ), Hasta, Jyeṣṭhā (Indra), Punarvasu (Aditi), Revatī (Bhāntya), Aśvinī and Svāti are sideways-looking.

173b-174 During their currency, the undermentioned acts are ordained: Driving the plough, travel, riding the bullock cart (*gantri*) driving machines, elephants and camels, and directing chariots drawn by asses and oxen, floating naval vessels, and work with buffaloes and horses.

175a. *Upward-looking asterisms.* The nine asterisms Rohiṇī (Prajāpati), Śravaṇa (Viṣṇu), Ārdrā (Maheśa), Puṣya (Arya) Śatabhiṣak, Dhaniṣṭhā (Vasu), Uttaraphalgunī, Uttara-āṣāḍha and Uttara-bhādrapada, are upward-looking.

175b-76. (During their currency, the undermentioned acts are ordained: Royal consecration, marriage, hoisting the flag on the rampart, and erection of palaces, arches, gardens and forts.

177. *Classification of asterisms.* The (four) asterisms Rohiṇī, Uttara-phalgunī, Uttara-āṣāḍha and Uttara-bhādrapada are 'fixed' (*sthira*). The (three) asterisms Hasta (*Sūrya*), Aśvinī and Puṣya are 'light' (*Kṣipra*). Viśākhā (*Dvidaivatya*) and Kṛttikā (*Vahnibhā*) are 'medium'.

178. The (five) asterisms Dhaniṣṭhā (Vasu), Punarvasu (*Āditya*), Śatabhiṣak (*Ambu*), Svāti and Śravaṇa (*Viṣṇu*) are 'moving' (*Cara*). The (four) asterisms Mṛgaśīrṣa (*Indu*), Anurādhā (*Mitra*), Citrā and Revatī (*Antya*) are 'soft' (*mṛdu*). And, the (five) asterisms Pūrva-phālgunī, Pūrva-āṣāḍha, Pūrva bhādrapada, Maghā and Bharaṇī (Antaka, *Yama*) are 'violent' (*ugra*).

179a. The (four) Asterisms Mūla, Ārdrā Āśleṣā (Indra) and Jyeṣṭhā (Indra) are 'sharp' (*tikṣṇa*). All have effects in consonance with their nomenclatures.

179b-80a. *Karṇavedha.* It is auspicious to perforate the ears of boys in Citrā, Punarvasu (*Āditya*), Aśvinī, Śravaṇa (Viṣṇu), Revatī (Antya, Hasta (Ravi), Anurādhā (Mitra), Śraviṣṭhā (Vasu), Mṛgaśiras and Puṣya (*Ijya*).

180b-81. *Dealings with elephants and horses.* All matters

relating to elephants (like their taming, sale, purchase etc.) should be done in the asterisms Aśvinī (*Dasra*), Mṛgaśiras (*Indu*), Punarvasu (*Aditi*), Puṣya (*Tiṣya*), Hasta, Citrā and Svāti. All matters relating to horses should be done in (the duration of) the 'fixed' stars (*viz.* Rohiṇī, Uttaraphālgunī, Uttarāṣāḍhā and Uttarabhādrapada), and especially on Sundays.

182. *Cattle. Trade etc. in cattle* is recommended in Citrā, Śatabhiṣak (*Varuṇa*), Rohiṇī (*Vairiñci*), Uttaraphālgunī, Uttara-āṣāḍha and Uttara-bhādrapada. This should, however, be never done on *aṣṭamī*, *caturdaśī* and the new moon day.

183. *Agriculture.* The first driving of the plough (in a season) shall be done with oxen, in the (20 asterisms) consisting of the *mṛdu*, *dhruva* (*sthira*), *kṣipra* and *cara* groups,[14a] Viśākhā, Maghā (*Pitṛ*) and Mūla.

184-85. In the *Lāṅgala-cakra* ('diagram of the plough' with the asterisms represented on it), three asterisms reckoned from the one in which the Sun is at the time of consideration, tend to destroy the oxen; the next three, which from the tip, tend to the production of plenty; the next five, which form the sides, tend to happiness; the next nine forming the three spikes, lead to death; the next five lead to prosperity and the last three, towards the tail end are extremely beneficial.[15]

186. *Sowing.* Sowing (crops) would be highly fruitful if done under the *mṛdu*, *dhruva* (*sthira*) and *Kṣipra* groups of asterisms as also under Maghā (*Pitṛ*), Svāti (*Vāyu*), Dhaniṣṭhā (*Vasu*) and Mūla.

187-88. (In the *Phaṇicakra*, the 'diagram of the serpent Rāhu', with the asterisms represented on its body) the three asterisms reckoned from the asterisms in which Rāhu occurs at the time under consideration will form its hood; (if sowing is done under those asterisms), the crops will be destroyed. The next three asterisms which form the neck will conduce the growth of weed (*kajjala* or *śyāmikā*). The next twelve asterisms forming the body will conduce to plenitude. The next four asterisms forming the tail will conduce to the dearth of grains. The (remaining) five asterisms, which are outside (the serpent diagram), portend destruction to the crop.[16]

189. *Bath after recovery from illness.* One should not give a

bath to a person recovered from illness; under the asterisms of the *sthira* group, Punarvasu (*Aditi*), Āśleṣā (*Sarpa*), Revatī (*Antya*), Maghā (*Pitṛ*) and Svāti (*Maruts*), and, so also, on Monday and Friday.

190. *Dance.* Commencement of dance is recommended in the asterisms Uttara-phalgunī, Uttara-āṣāḍha, Uttara-bhādrapada, Anurādhā (Maitra), Jyeṣṭhā (Indra), Dhaniṣṭhā (Vasu), Śatabhiṣak (Varuṇa), Puṣya, Hasta (Arka), and Revatī (Pauṣṇya).

191-92a. *Conjugal felicity.* Six asterisms beginning with Revatī (Pauṣṇa) form the first group, twelve asterisms beginning from Ārdrā (*Rudra*) form the middle group and nine asterisms from Jyeṣṭhā (*Indra*) form the final group, in order, in the consideration of the conjugal felicity of couples.

192b-93. *Size of the asterisms.* The smaller asterisms (*Jaghanya*) are Śatabhiṣak (*Toyapa*), Ārdrā, Āśleṣā (*Ahi*), *Svāti* (*Pavana*), Bharaṇī (*Yama*) and Jyeṣṭhā (*Nākapa*).

The bigger Stars. Dhruva, Punarvasu (*Aditi*) and Viśākhā (*Dvidaivatya*) are the bigger stars (*bṛhat*); their measures in *nāḍī's* are 30, 90 and 82. The remaining asterisms are medium (*Sama*) in size.

194. Prices are reduced to half during the asterisms Aśvinī, Kṛttikā (*Agni*), Puṣya (*Ijya*), Mūla (*Nairṛtya*), Citrā *Tvāṣṭra*), Uttaraphalgunī, Uttarāṣāḍha and Uttarabhādrapada.

195-96a. *Kula-asterisms and victory in battle* : The *Kula*-asterisms are Maghā (*pitṛ*), Viśākhā (*Dvidaivatya*) and Dhaniṣṭhā (*Vasu*). The *Akula*-asterisms are: Rohiṇī (*Dhātṛ*), Jyeṣṭhā, Punarvasu (*Aditi*), Svāti, Revatī (*Pauṣṇa*), Hasta (*Arka*), Śravaṇa (*Hari*), Pūrvabhādrapada (*Aja*), Bharaṇī (*Antaka*) and Āśleṣā (*Bhaujaṅga*). The remaining stars are *Kulākula*.

166b-98a. From among these, if kings set out for battle during the *Kula*-asterisms, they will suffer defeat, while in *Akula*-asterisms, assuredly, they will win. During the *Kulākula*-asterisms there would be equality (of results) and peace will follow.

198b-199a. *Puṣkara, the inauspicious combination.* If an odd quarter of the (Pūrva)-bhādrapada falls on a Sunday, Saturday or Tuesday, (the inauspicious *yoga* of) *Tripuṣkara* occurs and will have the (destructive) effect of three *Puṣkaras*. If the combination is with an even quarter of the asterism (it will be *Dvipuṣkara*) having double the (destructive) effect.

199b-200a. In order to destroy the evil effect of the former, gift away three cows or their value in money; in the case of the *Dvipuṣkara*, gift away two (cows). The inauspicious effect of the asterism would then be obviated.

200b-201a. *Effect of Puṣya.* The asterism Puṣya aspected by a cruel (planet) or in combination with it, is always beneficial in all auspicious rites except in marriage.

201b-103. *Number of prominent stars in the asterisms.* The number of bright stars called *Yogatārās*, in the asterism-groups beginning with Aśvanī (*Dasra*) are in order: (Aśvinī)3, (Bharaṇī) 3, (Kṛttikā) 6, (Rohiṇī) 5, (Mṛga-Śiras) 3, (Ārdrā) 1, (Punarvasu) 4, (Puṣya) 3, (Āśleṣā) 5, (Maghā) 5, (Pūrvaphālgunī) 2, Uttaraphālgunī) 2, (Hasta) 5, (Citrā) 1, (Svāti) 1, (Viśākhā) 2, (Anurādhā) 4, (Jyeṣṭhā) 3, (Mūla) 11, (Pūrvāṣāḍha) 4, (Uttarāṣāḍha) 2, (Śravaṇa) 4, (Dhaniṣṭhā) 3, (Śatabhiṣak) 100, (Pūrvabhādrapada) 2, (Uttarabhādrapada) 2, (Revatī) 32.

204-10. *Favourite trees of the asterisms.* The trees favourite to the different asterisms are : Aśvinī: *Vṛṣa-vṛkṣa*; Bharaṇī : *Yamakara*; Kṛttikā: *Udumbara*; Rohiṇī: *Jambuka*; Mṛgaśiras: *Khadira*; Ārdrā: *Kṛṣṇaplakṣa*; Punarvasu: *Vaṁśa* (bamboo); Puṣya: *Pippala* (Peepul); Āśleṣā: *Nāga*; Maghā: *Vaṭa* (banyan); Pūrvaphalgunī: *Palāśa*; Uttaraphalgunī: *Akṣa*: Hasta: *Ariṣṭā*; Citrā: *Śrīvṛkṣa* (*Vilva*); Svāti: *Arjuna*; Viśākhā: *Vikaṅkaṭa*; Anurādhā: *Bakula*; Jyeṣṭhā: *Viṣṭi*: Mūla: *Sarja*; Pūrvāṣāḍhā: *Vañjula*; Uttarāṣāḍhā: *Panasa* (Jack tree); Śravaṇa: *Arka*; Dhaniṣṭhā: *Śamī*; Śatabhiṣak: Kadamba; Pūrvabhādrapada: *Cūta* (mango); Uttarabhādrapada: *Picumandaka*; and Revatī: *Madhu*.

211a. One (born in a particular asterism) should endeavour to worship the relevant tree when Saturn is in the particular asterism.

YOGA

211b-12a. *Lords of the Yogas.* The presiding deities of the 24 *Yogas*[17] are: (1. *Viṣkambha*): Yama; (2. *Priti*): Viśvedevāḥ; (3. *Āyuṣmān*): Moon; (4. *Saubhāgya*): Dhātā; (5. *Śobhana*): Jīva (Bṛhaspati); (6. *Atigaṇḍa*) : Moon; (7. *Sukarmā*): Indra;

(8. *Dhṛti*) : Varuṇa (Toya) ; (9. *Śūla*) : Ahi ; (10, *Gaṇḍa*) : Agni ; (11. *Vṛddhi*) : Sūrya ; (12. *Dhruva*) : Bhūmi ; (13. *Vyāghāta*) : Rudra ; (14. *Harṣaṇa*) : Brahmā (Ka) ; (15. *Vajra*) : Varuṇa (Toyapa) ; (16. *Siddhi*) : Gaṇeśa ; (17. *Vyatīpāṭa*) : Rudra ; (18. *Variyas*) : Kubera (Dhanada) ; (19. *Parigha*) : Tvaṣṭā, (20. *Śiva*) : Mitra ; (21. *Siddha*) : Ṣaḍānana, (22. *Sādhya*) Sāvitrī, (23. *Śubha*) : Kamalā ; (24. *Śukla*) : Gaurī, (25. *Brahman*) : Nāsatyas (26. *Indra*) : Pitṛs : and (27. *Vaidhṛti*) : Aditi.

212b. *Effects of the yogas*. The *yogas*, *vaidhṛti* and *vyatīpāta* are always highly catastrophic.

213-15a. The first half of *Parigha* is abhorred for all rites. In *Viṣkambha* and *Vajra*, the first three *nāḍikās*, in *Gaṇḍa* and *Atigaṇḍa* six, in *Vyāghāta* nine, and in *Śūla* five *nāḍikās* are to be rejected.

215b-16a. *Kharjūrikā diagram.* The asterisms Punarvasu (*Aditi*), Mṛgaśiras (*Indu*), Maghā, Āśleṣā (*Ahi*), Aśvinī, Mūla, Hasta (*Maitreya*) Puṣya (*Ijya*), with their diagrams have to be understood as the Head-asterisms (*mūrdha-bhā*), in order.

216b-18a. Draw a vertical line and 13 lines across it. In that diagram called *Kharjūrikā-cakra*, place the Head-asterism. Between the Sun and the Moon marked on the vertical line, mark the (26) asterisms, leaving out Abhijit (the 28th *nakṣatra*). (The pair of asterisms) on each cross line (*Ekārgala*) aspect each other.

218b-19a. *Duration of a yoga.* A *yoga* extends to two *nāḍikās* and 12 *vināḍikās*, and the *yogas* are 27 in number, in order (in a lunar day).

KARAṆA

219b-220a. *Lords of the Karaṇas.* The lords of the 11 half-*tithis* (*Karaṇas*) are : (1. *Bava*) : Indra ; (2. *Bālava*) : Prajāpati ; (3. *Kaulava*) : Mitra ; (4. *Taitila*), Aryamā ; (5. *Gara*) : Bhuḥ (Earth) ; (6. *Vaṇij*) : Lakṣmī (Haripriyā) : (7. Viṣṭi) : Kīnāśa ; (8. *Śakuni*) : Kali ; (9. *Nāga*) ; Rudra : (10. *Catuṣpada*) : Ahi, (11. *Kiṁstughna*) : Marut.

220b-21a. The six *karaṇas* from *Bava* to *Vaṇij* are auspicious. However, *Viṣṭi*, either in the beginning or in the end, is not desirable for any auspicious rite.

221b-22a. *Karaṇa diagram.* (In the diagrammatic representation of the *Karaṇas*), five would be in the face, one in the neck, eleven in the chest, four in the navel, six at the waist and three in the tail, in terms of *nāḍikās*.

222b-13a. Those in the face indicate obstruction to one's acts; in the neck, death; in the chest, penury; in the waist, madness; in the navel, loss; but in the tail sure success.

223b. Of the (24 *karaṇas*), the *sthira-karaṇas*, (*viz.*, Śakuni, Nāga, Catuṣpāda and Kiṁstughna) are of medium effect; and, of them too, the middle ones, Nāga and Catuṣpāda.

MUHŪRTA

224b-25a. *Lords of the muhūrtas.* The *muhūrtas* of daytime are lorded over by fifteen (deities, as under): Rudra, Ahi, Mitra, Pitṛs, Vasu, Varuṇa (Udaka), Viśvedevas, Vidhātā, Brahmā, Indra, Indrāgnī, Vasu, Varuṇa, (Toyapa), Aryamā and Bhaga.

225b-26a. (The lords of the *muhūrtas* of the night are): Īśa, Aja-Ekapād, Ahirbudhnya, Pūṣā, Aśvins, Yama, Agni, Dhātṛ, Indra, Aditi, Ijya (Bṛhaspati), Viṣṇu, Arka, Tvaṣṭṛ and Vāyu.

226b-27a. The measure of a *muhūrta* is one fifteenth part of the day-time and so also night-time (*i.e.*, 2 nāḍikā) with their lords as stated above.

227b-228. *Muhūrtas to be avoided.* On the (seven) weekdays beginning with Sunday, (the undermentioned seven sets of *Muhūrtas*) should be rejected for all auspicious rites: (1. Sunday): Uttaraphalgunī (Aryamā); (2. Monday): Mūla (Rākṣasa) and Rohiṇī (Brahmā); (3. Tuesday): Maghā (Pitṛ) and Kṛttikā (Āgneya); (4. Wednesday): Abhijit; (5. Thursday): Mūla (Rākṣasa); (6. Friday): Rohiṇī (Brahmā) and Maghā (Pitṛ); and (7. Saturday): Āśleṣā (Bhujaṅga).

229. *Muhūrtas and Nakṣatras.* Whatever rite has been ordained to be performed in specific *nakṣatras*, all those acts, including pilgrimages, shall be done during the *muhūrtas* lorded over by the respective deities.

UPAGRAHA (SECONDARY ATMOSPHERIC PHENOMENA)

230-33a. *Portentuous natural phenomena.* Earthquake in the seventh asterism from Hasta (Sūryabham), lightning in the fifth; *Śūla* in the eighth, thunder in the tenth, comet in the eighteenth, Daṇḍa in the fifteenth, meter in the nineteenth, thunder-strike in the fourteenth, fall of thunderbolt in the fourteenth, and atmospheric haze (*moha*), thunder, earthquake, thunderbolt and halo (round the moon) respectively in the twentyfirst and further asterisms (are inauspicious) and no auspicious rite should be performed in the asterisms in which the above occur along with the Moon.

233b-35a. *Other inauspicious combinations* (*Yogas*). The Moon occurring in the asterisms Āśleṣā (Sarpa), Maghā (Pitrya), Citrā (Tvāṣṭra) Anurādhā (Mitra) and Revatī (Antya), causes an inauspicious *yoga* to occur in the asterism as much removed from Aśvinī as each of these are removed from Hasta (Sūryabha), So also in Śravaṇa (Viṣṇubha).

235b. The said two *yogas* are called respectively *Caṇḍiśa* and *Caṇḍāyudha.* No auspicious rite should be performed then.

236a. *Krakaca-yoga.* A *krakaca-yoga* 'cutting saw combination' will occur when the sum of lunar day and week-day is 13. This is to be rejected for any auspicious rite.

236b-37a. *Saṁvartayoga.* When Sunday falls on the seventh lunar day or Monday on the first lunar day, a *saṁvarta-yoga* ('dissolution combination') will occur. This is all-destructive.

237b-40a. *The twenty-eight asterismal yogas.*[18] The following eight *yogas* produce effect, as per their meanings; *Ānanda* (pleasure), *Kāladaṇḍa* (Death's rod), *Dhūmra* (Smoky), *Dhātṛ* (protectivc), *Sudhākara* (ambrosial), *Dhvāṅkṣa* (crow) *Dhvaja* (flag), *Śrīvatsa* (Viṣṇu's gem), *Vajra* (thunderbolt), *Mudgara* (spade), *Chatraka* (umbrella), *Mitra* (friend), *Mānasa* (heart), *Padma* (lotus), *Lumbaka* (cutting), *Utpāta* (calamitous), *Mṛtyu* (death), *Kāṇa* (blind), *Siddhi* (achievement), *Śubha* (auspicious), *Amṛtyu* (deathlessness), *Musala* (pestle), *Antaka* (death), *Kuñjara* (elephant), *Rākṣasa* (demoniac), *Cara* (moving), *Sthairya* (firm) and *Vardhamāna* (increasing).

240b-41. These *yogas* are to be reckoned, in order, from Aśvinī (Dasrabha) on Sundays; from Mṛgaśiras (Indubha) on Mondays; from Āśleṣā (Sarpa) on Tuesdays; from Hasta on Wednesdays; from Anurādhā (Maitrabha) on Thursdays; from Uttarāṣāḍha (Vaiśvadeva) on Fridays and from Śatabhiṣak (Varuṇa) on Saturdays.[19]

242-43a. *Siddhiyogas for the week-days*. Hasta on Sunday, Mṛgaśiras (candrabha) on Monday, Aśvinī (Dasrabha) on Tuesday, Anurādhā (Mitrabha) on Wednesday, Revatī on Thursday, Puṣya (Tiṣya) on Friday and Rohiṇī on Saturday; these are called as *Siddhi-yogas* (combinations for achievement).

243b-44a. *Effect of tithis classified as Nandā, Bhadrā etc.*[20] It is not auspicious to have *Nandā* on Sunday and Tuesday, *Bhadrā* on Friday and Monday, *Jayā* on Wednesday, *Riktā* on Thursday and *Pūrṇā* on Saturday.

244b-45a. (On the other hand), *Nandā* on Friday, *Bhadrā* on Wednesday, *Jayā* on Tuesday, *Riktā* on Saturday and *Pūrṇā* on Thursday are termed *siddha*, (indicating achievement).

245b-46. *Dagdhayoga*. Monday on the eleventh lunar day, Sunday on the twelfth, Thursday on the sixth, Wednesday on the third, Friday on the eighth, Saturday on the ninth and Tuesday on the fifth are declared as *dagdhayogas* (destructive combinations).

247-48a. *Some destructive Yogas*. Bharaṇī on Sunday, Citrā on Monday, Uttarāṣāḍhā (Viśvabha) on Tuesday, Śraviṣṭhā on Wednesday, Uttaraphalgunī (Aryamābha) on Thursday, Jyeṣṭhā on Friday and Revatī on Saturday are destructive to one born in the respective asterisms.

248b-49a. Viśākha, Āśleṣā (Ahi) and *Caturvarga* are declared as the three *asiddhi-yogas*, *Utpāta*, *Mṛtyu* and *Kāṇa*, in order, for the days beginning from Sunday.

249b-50a. In other lands like Hūṇa, Vaṅga aud Khasa, the *Yogas* calculated on the basis of the lunar day cum week-day are not to be applied, but those calculated on the basis of week-day cum asterisms are auspicious.

SAṄKRĀNTI (SUN'S TRANSIT INTO A SIGN)

250b-51a. *Week-days and Saṅkrānti*. The Sun's transits (*Saṅkrāntis*) on the several week-days commencing from Sunday are called, respectively, *Ghorā*, *Dhvāṅkṣī*, *Mahodarī*, *Mandā*, *Mandākinī*, *Miśrā* and *Rākṣasikā*.

251b-52a. These transits will bring happiness, respectively, to the Śūdra, thief, vaiśya, brāhmaṇa, king, cow and all the beings not included above.

252b-54a. *Time of the transits*. The Sun's transit occurring during the forenoon is harmful to the kings, to the brāhmaṇas at noon, to the vaiśyas in the afternoon, to the śūdras at sunset, to the ghosts, at dusk, the demons in the night, the actors after midnight, the cowherds at sunrise and the religious students at dawn.

254b-55a. *Effects of the Sun's transit into Aries*. *Meṣasaṅkrānti* (Sun's tratsit into Aries, and, so, the beginning of the year), occurring during day-time is productive of calamity and quarrel; if it occurs during night, there would be sumptuous plenitude; and if it occurs during the twilights, rains will be ruined.

255b-58a. *Personification of the Saṅkrāntis*. The personification of the *Saṅkrāntis* when they fall in one or the other of the eleven *karaṇas*, from *Bava*, are endowed with the following mounts: Lion, tiger, bear, ass, elephant, buffalo, horse, dog, goat, ox and cock. Weapons carried in their hands are Bhuśuṇḍi, mace, sword, rod, bow, javelin, pike, rope, hook, missile and arrow, respectively. The food offerings prescribed for them are, respectively, rice, rice cooked in milk, rice obtained by begging, cake, milk, curd, sweet rice, molasses, wine, ghee and sugar.

258b-60a. *State of the personifications while in the Karaṇas*. The Sun's personification is deemed to be 'sitting' if the transit occurs in Vaṇij, Bālava, and Gara; it is said to be 'erect' (*i.e.*, standing) in Kaulava, Śākuna and Kiṁstughna; the Sun is supposed to make the transit 'sleeping' if it occurs during Catuṣpada, Taitila and Nāga. (The effect of the said three states) in the matter of the performance of ordained duties, longevity and rains would be medium, excellent and depletion, respectively.

260b-61a. The above-said weapons, mounts and food if adopted by the people will also be beneficial to them, as also their condition as sleeping, sitting or standing (at the time of *saṅkrānti*).

261b-62a. *Classification of the asterisms*. The asterisms are also classified into four types, designated, respectively, as *Andhaka Manda*, *Madhya* and *Sulocana*, as counted from Rohiṇī.

262b. *Viṣṇupada.* The transit of the Sun into the 'firm' asterisms, (*viz.*, Uttaraphalgunī, Uttarāṣāḍhā and Uttarabhādrapada and Rohiṇī, is called *Viṣṇupada.*

263. *Ṣaḍaśītimukha and Viṣuvat.* The transit of the Sun into the double-natured signs,[21] (*viz.*, *Mithuna*, *Kanyā*, *Dhanu* and *Mīna*) is called *Ṣaḍaśītimukha*, while the transit into the signs *Tulā* and *Meṣa* is called *Viṣuvai* (Equinox).

264a. During the southward course of the Sun (*Yāmyāyana*) the former, (*viz.*, the double natured signs) are firm (*sthira* in relation to the Moon and the asterisms, and *Cara* ('moving') in the northward course of the Sun (*saumye*).

264b-265. *Holy time at equinox* (*Puṇyakāla*). At the Equinoxes, sixteen *nāḍikās* (before it and 16 after it, making a total of 32 *nāḍikās* are said to be holy *nāḍikās*, suitable for meritorious rites. Dusk (*sandhyā*) extends through three *nāḍikās* before the rising of the centre of the Sun's orb (in the morning) and after the setting thereof, in the evening. If (the *Saṅkrānti*, *i.e.* Sun's transit, occurs) before or after midnight, the holy time, (one half of which is of 15 *nāḍikās*), extends through (the afternoon of)the previous day and (the forenoon of) the next day.

266. (By performing meritorious rites at the time of *saṅkrānti*) one reaps results corresponding to the nature of the Sun and the Moon in the relevant sign, according as the Sun or the Moon is benevolent or otherwise.

267. *Expiation for Unholy time at Saṅkrama.* Take the degrees that the Sun, after making a transit (into *Meṣa* or *Tulā*), has to go to reach the transit into the *ayana*; if at one's birth asterism occurs within that period on either side of the transit into the sign, the two are not auspicious for fasts and marriages. In order to counteract the evil, spread out sesame and draw on it a circle, trident and a triangle, place a bit of gold on it and gift it away.

268-70. *Power of Saṅkrama.* The Moon is strong on account of the strength of the asterisms and the Sun at transit is strong on account of the Moon. In the same manner, the planets are also strong (at the time of the Sun's transit).

GOCARA (CURRENT MOTION OF THE PLANETS)

271. *Effect of the planets occupying the different signs.*[2] O

sage ! the Sun is benefic when it occupies the 3rd, 11th, 10th or 6th sign counted from the birth-sign (of the person under consideration), if it is not affected[23] by planets other than Saturn[24] occupying the 9th 5th, 4th, (*ambu*) 12th (*rippha*).

272. The Moon is benefic if it occupies the 7th (*dyūna*) 1st, 11th, 6th (ari) 10th or 3rd sign from the birth-sign, if it is not affected by planets other than Mercury in the 5th, 8th, 12th, 4th and 9th (*dharma*) signs.

273. Mars is benefic if it occupies the 3rd, 11th or 6th sign from the birth-sign if it is not affected by Saturn, Mercury or Sun occupying, respectively, the 12th (*vyaya*), 5th and 9th signs.

274. Mercury is benefic if it occupies the 4th, 6th, 8th 10th or 11th sign from the birth-sign if it is not affected by planets other than the Moon in the 5th (*dhi*), 3rd, 9th, 1st, 8th and 12th signs.

275. O great sage ! Jupiter is benefic in the 11th, 9th 4th or 7th sign from the birth-sign, if it is not affected by the planets in the 12th, 8th, 10th, 4th and 3rd signs.

276. Venus is benefic in the 1st to 5th (*āsuta*), 8th, 9th 12th or 11th signs from the birth-sign, if it is not affected by planets in the 8th, 7th, 1st, 10th, 5th, 11th, 6th and 3rd signs.

277. No planet will be benefic if its current position is affected (by another planet). Hence good and bad results shall be predicted only after duly considering planetary affectation.

278. A planet which has turned malefic on account of being adversely affected (by a planet) can still be benefic if aspected by a beneficent planet, while even a beneficent planet might be productive of evil effects if aspected by an evil planet.

279a. Two (inimical) planets will not produce their individual effects if they aspect one another.

279b-80a. A planet occupying the sign of an evil planet or the house of an enemy planet, or if it has already set will not produce its good or bad effects.

280b-81a. When planets occupy malefic places, one should take steps to perform propitiatory rites, for one's progress and regress are dependent upon the planets, for which reason they are worthy of worship.

281b-82. *Precious Stones.* Towards the propitiation of the planets Sun etc., one should wear, in order, the precious stones: (Sun) pearl, (Moon) coral, (Mars) emereld, (Mercury) Topaz (Jupiter) diamond, (Venus) Sapphire and (Saturn) Opal.

(CANDRA-TĀRĀBALA: STRENGTH OF THE MOON AND PLANETS)

283. *Nature of the Moou.* One to whom the moon is benefic on the first day of the bright fortnight, to him it will be beneficent throughout that fortnight; on the contrary, in the dark fortnight it would be malefic.

284. In the bright fortnight, the Moon is benefic on the second, ninth and fifth days. It would be benefic also on the 12th, 9th and 4th days if it is not affected by other planets.

285. *Birth asterisms.* Birth, wealth, danger, welfare enemy, benefactor, death, friend and intimate companion have always to be ascertained from the birth asterism.

286-87a. The birth-asterism and the 3rd, 5th and 7th therefrom do not yield benefits. In order to ward off the evil effects (of these four), one should gift to brahmins (the four objects) vegetables, molasses, salt, and gold with sesame, in that order.

287b. The asterisms are particularly potent during the dark fortnight and the Moon is similarly potent during the bright fortnight.

287c-88a. *States of the Moon.* The Moon has twelve states (*avasthās*) in the (twelve) signs. And, these states will have effects in accordance with their nomenclatures, (given below, in verse 289), with regard to pilgrimage, marriage etc. undertaken at those times.

288b-c. (In order to calculate the state of the Moon at any time), multiply the number of the current asterism (reckoned from Aśvinī) by 60, add the number of *nāḍikās* elapsed at the desired time (in the current asterism), multiply the result by 4 and divide by 45 (*iṣu-veda*). Divide the quotient by 12 (*bhānu*). (The result would be the current state of the Moon).

289. The (twelve *avasthās* are *Pravāsa* (exile), *Naṣṭa* (loss), *Mṛta* (death), *Jaya* (victory), *Hāsya* (laughter), *Rati* (pleasure), *Muda* (joy), *Supti* (sleep), *Bhukti* (feast), *Jvara* (fever), *Kampa*

(tremour) and *Susthiti* (firm establishment). Their effect is in consonace with their nomenclatures.

(SARVALAGNA : RISING OF THE SIGNS)

290. *Rise of Aries* (*Meṣa-lagna*). When the sign of Aries is rising (the undermentioned acts) will be successful: Royal coronation, marching of the army, peace, war, making of ornaments, extraction of minerals from mines and wars.

291. *Rise of Taurus* (*Vṛṣabha-lagna*). When the signTaurus is rising, will be successful: Auspicious rites, firm actions, digging of wells for water, construction of houses agriculture, trade, raising of cattle, etc.

292. *Rise of Gemini* (*Mithuna-lagna*), When the sign Gemini is rising should be done: Engagement in art and architecture, acceptance of ornaments, invitation, for sacrifice, dealings relating to elephants, marriage and consecration.

293. *Rise of Cancer* (*Karkaṭa-lagna*). When the sign Cancer is rising, should be performed: Work relating to the collection and release of water in tanks, wells and lakes, physical nourishment and writing and literary activities.

294. *Rise of Leo* (*Siṁha-lagna*). When the sign Leo is rising will be successful the following: work relating to the cultivation of sugarcane and grains, trade and adventurous onslaughts by kings, etc.

295. *Rise of Virgo* (*Kanyā-lagna*). When the sign Virgo is rising, should be performed acts relating to: Study, architecture, medicine, ornaments, middling matters which are both firm and otherwise, physical nourishment and all auspicious acts.

296. *Rise of Libra* (*Tulā-lagna*). When the sign Libra is rising, should be done acts pertaining to agriculture, trade, travel, cattle, marriage, fasts and *tulābhāra* (religious weighing of oneself in a balance).

297. *Rise of Scorpio* (*Vṛścika-lagna*). When the sign Scorpio is rising, should be taken action on all matters which are of a firm, permanent (*sthira*) nature as also service to the royalty, consecration and burglary.

298. *Rise of Sagittarius* (*Dhanu-lagna*). When the sine sagittarious is rising, should be performed the following: Religious fasts, marriage, travel, matters relating to horses and elephants,

arts, and actions relating to matters which are of a miscellaneous and quasi-permanent nature.

299. *Rise of Capricorn* (*Makara-lagna*). When the sign Capricorn is rising should be performed: Stringing of bows and shooting of arrows, cultivation, matters relating to cattle and horses, setting out on a journey, tending of cows, servitude etc.

300. *Rising of Aquarius* (*Kumbha-lagna*). When the sign Aquarius is rising should one engage himself in agriculture, trade rearing of cattle, digging for water, architecture, the fine arts, voyage, practice of missiles and weapons, etc.

301. *Rising of Pisces* (*Mīna-lagna*). When the sign Pisces is rising, are auspicious acts relating to religious fasts, marriages, consecration, inauguration of water reservoirs and housing colonies, wearing of ornaments and using of water vessels.

302. *Potency of the rising signs.* Success in actions, as stated above, would accrue in respect of the rising of the signs which are clear i.e., vacant (or occupied by beneficent planets). However, if the signs are aspected by malefic planets or occupied by terrible planets, the results will also be terrible.

303. The Seven signs, *viz.*, Aries, Taurus, Cancer, Virgo, Pisces, Libra and Sagittarius are beneficent (by nature) since they are occupied by beneficent asterisms; the other signs are evil-natured.

304. (Over and above this), the signs attain their (ultimate) strength from the combination of planets occupying them and by the aspecting of other planets on them. If neither of the above is applicable, the signs will exhibit only their primary nature.

305. Towards the beginning (of their rise) all the signs will have their full strength, in the midd'e medium strength and towards the end little strength.

306. First determine the rising sign (at the desired time) and then the strength of the Moon. If the Moon is strong, the planets in the seventh sign will also be strong.

307. The strength of the Moon is the base, (as the sustainer, and supporter), and that of the other planets is only secondary (contained, supported). It is obvious that the supported is held by the snpporter.

308. If Moon is benefic, all the other planets will also be

benefic and if Moon is malefic, (all the others) would also be rendered malefic, except the Sun.

309. The planet occupying those degrees of a sign which have risen, gets the strength of the first part of the sign and the one coming after, that of the second part.

310. The strengths of the planets in the other sections are also to be reckoned in this same manner. By this procedure one can select a rising sign endowed with all qualities.

311.12a. All men always wish for the minimum of bad effects and the maximum of good effects. Bad effects are inherent in time and even the creator is incapable of eradicating them completely. Hence it is necessary to look for the minimum of bad effects and the maximum of good effects.

PRATHAMA-ĀRTAVA (FIRST MENSTRUATION)

312b-13a. *Inauspicious days of prathamārtava—Prathamārtava* is inauspicious on new moon, the *rikta*[25] lunar days (*viz.*, 4th, 9th aud 14th), 8th, 6th, 12th, 1st, the first half of (the *yoga* called) *Parigha,*[26] *Vyatipāta*, *Vaidhṛta*, the (three) *sandhyās* (of dawn, noon and dusk), invasion by an enemy and (the *Karaṇa* called) *Viṣṭi.*[27]

314. *Prathamārtava on the week-days.* The result of *Prathamārtava* occurring on the week-days from Sunday are: (Sunday:) Ill-health; (Monday:) Dear to the spouse; (Tuesday:) Unhappiness, (Wednesday:) Much-daughtered; (Thursday:). Sensuous: (Friday:) Chaste, and (Saturday) Having Heavy tresses.

315. *Inauspicious asterisms and months*—The following asterism are inauspicious (in *prathamārtava*): Bharaṇī. Kṛttikā, Ārdrā, Pūrvaphalguni, Āśleṣa, Viśākhā, Jyeṣṭhā Maghā and Pūrvāṣāḍhā. The following months, too, are not auspicious: Caitra (Madhu), Kārttika (Ūrja), Aṣāḍha (Śuci) and Pauṣa.

316a. One having *prathamārtava* on the *bhadrā* lunar days, (*viz.*, 2nd, 7th and 12th), the transit of the Sun into a sign, sleep, and the lunar and solar eclipses would be unchaste.

316b-17. To ward off all evil the effects of *prathamārtava* on malignant occupation and undesirable asterisms and week-days, the wise should offer oblations of sesame, ghee and *dūrvā* grass, repeat the *gāyatri mantra* a hundred times and gift away gold, cows and sesame.

ĀDHĀNA (CONCEPTION)

318a. For conception, the first four nights (of menstruation) are to be avoided; the further days are permissible.

318b-19. One who had been endowed with the sacred thread, if he desires for a male issue should resort to a woman when the Moon occupies an odd sign, the then rising sign aspecting a male planet[28], the lunar day being even, the asterisms being not one of Revatī (*Pauṣṇa*), Mūla, Viśākhā (*Ahi*) and Maghā (*Pitrya*); and the sacrificial fire having not been fed by him (that day).

PUṀSAVANA: RITE FOR THE BIRTH OF A MALE CHILD

320a. *Puṁsavana.*[29] When conception has been confirmed, in the first third or second month, the *Puṁsavana* ceremony has to be performed.

320b-21. *Simantonnayana* (*Parting of the hair*). The *Simanta* ceremony should be performed in the fourth, sixth or eighth month (of pregnancy) when the lord (of the month is strong,[30] (the other conditions being that) the Moon and the asterisms relating to the couple are strong;

322. The lunar day not being *riktā* (*viz.*, 4th, 9th, 14th), new moon or full moon; the week-day being Tuesday, Thursday and Sunday, (being the 'male' *days*); the asterism being male, but omitting the *tikṣṇa* (sharp) one's (viz. Mūla, Ārdrā, Jyeṣṭhā, and Āśleṣā), the *miśra* (mixed) ones, (*viz.*, Kṛttikā and Viśākhā) and the *ugra* (violent) ones, (*viz.*, Pūrvaphalgunī, Pūrvāṣāḍha and Pūrvabhādrapada, Bharaṇī and Maghā); the Moon being in a male asterism;[31]

323. The 8th house (indicating death) from the birthhouse being clear, the rising signs of the couples being not the eighth being aspected by beneficent planets and not aspected by malefic planets;

324. Beneficent planets occupying the 3rd (*dhi*), 9th *dharma*), and *Kendra* and malefic planets occupying the three evil houses, the Moon being not in the 12th (*antya*, loss) or 6th (*ari*).

325. If any of the cruel planets which is strong, occupies the 12th, 5th (*ātmaja*) or the 8th place, assuredly it will kill the pregnant lady, whose *sīmanta* is being performed or the child in the womb.

JĀTAKARMA AND NĀMAKARAṆA (BIRTH RITE AND NAMING CEREMONY)

326. The birth rite (*jātakarma*) of the child should be performed on the *muhūrta* of birth or at the end of the birth-pollution and should be preceded by the worship of the manes.

327. When the birth-pollution has ended, the naming ceremony should be performed according to family practices. The name given shall be ancient, renowned and composed in auspicious syllables.

328-30a. If due to the exigencies of place, time, invasion etc., there had been delay, the father of the child should perform the above two ceremonies when the planets Jupiter and Venus have not set, in the asterism Puṣya, during the northward course of the Sun, in an asterism belonging to the groups *cara, sthira, mṛdu* or *kṣipra*,[32] in an auspicious week-day, the day being endowed with potency in consideration both of the Moon and the asterisms, during the rising of an auspicious sign and in an auspicious division thereof, and when the 8th house (indicating death) is clear.

ANNAPRĀŚANA (THE FIRST FEEDING)

330b-31a. It is auspicious to perform the First feeding ceremony of male children in the sixth or eighth month, and of female children in the fifth or the seventh month (after birth).

331b-32a. It is ordained to be performed on an auspicious week-day, on any lunar day except *riktā* (4th, 9th and 14th), the omitted lunar day,[33] *nandā* (1st, 6th and 11th) and 12th and 8th.

332b-34. The first feeding ceremony would be auspicious in the asterisms of the *cara, sthira, mṛdu* and *kṣipra* classes, the eighth house (indicating death) being vacant, the 10th house also being vacant, during the rise of an auspicious sign and in an auspicious division thereof, in the forenoon, when (the rising sign is) occupied or aspected by beneficent planets, when the

3rd, 6th and 11th (*lābha*) houses are occupied by evil planets while the *kendra*, 3rd (*dhi*) and 9th (*dharma*) are occupied by beneficent planets, and the Moon is in the 12th (*vyaya*), 6th (*ari*), or the 8th (*nidhana*).

CAULA (TONSURE)

335. The tonsure of boys should be performed in the third or the fifth year, in accordance with the family practice and as ordained by the *Gṛhya-sūtra* which one follows.[34]

336. The tonsure ceremony should be performed in the northward transit of the Sun, when the Jupiter and Venus have not set, on a lunar day other than the full moon and new moon days and the *riktā* days (*viz.*, 4th, 9th and 14th), on a Friday, Thursday, Wednesday or Monday.

337. For the tonsure ceremony, the asterisms Aśvinī, Punarvasu, Puṣya, Mṛgaśiras, Jyeṣṭhā, Revatī, three from Hasta, (*viz.*, Hasta, Citrā and Svātī), three from Śravaṇa, (*viz.*, Śravaṇa, Śraviṣṭhā and Śatabhiṣak) are auspicious.

338. One's birth asterism is auspicious for coronation, tonsure, first feeding and educational initiation into (Vedic) study and wearing the sacred thread), but not in other ceremonies.

339. (Tonsure should be performed) when the 8th house is clear, during the rise of an auspicious sign and in an auspicious division thereof; when the Moon does not occupy the 8th house from the birth-house, and avoiding the sixth, eighth and twelfth houses.

340. When the second (*dhana*), *trikoṇa*-s and (1st, 5th and 9th houses) and *kendras* (1st, 4th, 7th, and 10th houses) and occupied by beneficent planets and the 3rd, 11th and 6th houses by the other planets.

340b-41a. (Tonsure should not be performed) after an oilbath, at dawn or dusk, on Tuesdays and Saturdays (*āra*), at night, after meals, in battle, when one is angry, wearing ornaments, riding in a vehicle or on the ninth lunar day.

341b-42a. Trimming of the moustaches is recommended for kings regularly every fifth day; it o be done on the asterisms recommended for tonsure (but if the fifth day does not tally with the asterisms it may be done) at the time of rise of such an asterism (inconsiderate of other factors).

342b-43a. Tonsure is productive of beneficial results if done on the direction of kings and brahmins, on the occasion of sacrifice, death, release from bond, marriage and on (the ordained) week-days, asterisms and lunar days.

AṄKURĀRPAṆA : AUSPICIOUS SOWING

343b. At the beginning of all auspicious rites, *aṅkurārpaṇa*, 'sowing of the seed', should be done with a view to gain auspiciousness (for the rite).

344-45. On the ninth, seventh, fifth, or third lunar day, on an asterism recommended for sowing,[35] on an auspicious weekday, when an auspicious sign is rising, the houses should be well decorated by awnings, banners and arches, and auspicious words of blessing should be caused to be uttered by auspicious ladies (*i.e.*, those who are not widows).

346-47. Then (the master of the rite), preceded by the playing of musical instruments, dancing etc., should proceed in the north-easterly direction and collect from there sand and soft mud. Returning to the house, he should fill earthen or bamboo vessels (with the sand and mud brought) and pour over it water into which different seeds and flowers have been put.

MAUÑJĪBANDHANA AND UPANAYANA : TYING THE MAUÑJĪ BELT AND COMMENCING STUDIES

348. *Mauñjībandhana* (*lit.* 'tying the belt made of *mauñji* grass)[36] is recommended on the eighth year after conception for *brahmins*, on the eleventh year for *kṣatriyas* and on the twelfth year for *vaiśyas*.

349. *Upanayana* could be performed even, at the fifth year, since the boy endowed with the sacred thread done could become well versed in the Vedas and *Śāstras* and be endowed with prosperity.

350. To the boy, even a week Venus or Jupiter would be beneficent. *Upanayana* should be performed only at the years ordained therefore and not at other times.

351. (*Upanayana* should be performed) when Jupiter, Venus and the lord of the (relevant) Veda are visible. The lords of the (four) Vedas are, in order: (*Ṛgveda*) Jupiter; (*Yajurveda*), Venus; (*Sāmaveda*:) Mars and (*Atharvaveda*:) Mercury.

352. The appropriate seasons for the *Upanayana* of the three classes of twice-borns are, Autumn (*Śarat*), Hot season (*Grīṣma*) and Spring (*Vasanta*), taken in the reverse order. In general, the time ordained for them are the five months beginning with Māgha (*Tapas*).

353. (One who wears the sacred thread) in the months of Māgha and Phālguna will become well versed in the hereditory practices of his family; if in the month of Caitra he would become a knower of ordained duties, wealthy and an expert in the Vedas and Vedāṅgas.[37]

354. One who wears the sacred thread in the month of Vaiśākha would become wealthy, an expert in the Vedas, Śāstras and the sciences, and physically strong; if in the month of Jyeṣṭha, he would be a knower of ordained rules.

355. For *Upanayana*, the most auspicious days are : In the bright fortnight, the 13th, 10th, 7th, 11th, 6th and the 12th, the other days are of middling benefit. In the dark fortnight, the 2nd, 3rd and 5th days are of middling effect and the rest are extremely bad.

356-57. The asterisms favourable for *upanayana* are : Hasta, Citrā and Svātī (*arka-traya*), Revatī, Puṣya (*Ijya*), Ārdrā (Rudra), Punarvasu (Aditi), Uttaraphālgunī, Uttarāṣāḍha and Uttarabhādrapada, Śravaṇa Dhaniṣṭhā, Śatabhiṣak (*Viṣṇutraya*), Aśvinī, Anurādhā (*Mitra*) and Rohiṇī (*Abjayoni*).

358-59a. The tenth asterism from the birth-asterism is called *Karma*, the sixteenth *Saṅghāta*, the eighteenth *Sāmudāya*, the twenty-third *Vināśana*, and the twenty-fifth *Mānasa*. No auspicious rite should be performed in these asterisms.

359b-60a. The week-days pertaining to Ācārya, Saumya and Kāvya, (*viz.*, Thursday, Friday and Wednesday) are auspicious, the days pertaining to the Moon and the Sun are middling and the remaining two are detestable for commencing religious studentship (*vrata*).

360b-61a. Divide daytime into three. During the first

part one should perform acts relating to the gods, during the second part, acts relating to men, and during the third part acts relating to the manes. (*Upanayana*, which comes under the first category, should therefore be performed only in the first part of the day.)

361b-62a. If Jupiter, Venus or the lord of one's Veda or their divisions are in debilitation (*nīca*), or are situated in enemy asterisms or divisions the student will lose his family status and his character.

362b-363a, Again, Jupiter, Venus or the lord of one's Veda[38] occupies an inimical house or its division, the student will be the perpetrator of great sins.

363b-64. If, however, Jupiter, Venus or the lord of one's Veda or their divisions are in exultation (*ucca*) or occupy their own houses or their *rāśigaṇas*, or the quadrant (*kendra*) or trine (*trikoṇa*), the boy will be extremely wealthy and well versed in the Vedas and the Vedāṅgas.

365. If Jupiter, Venus or the lord of one's Veda is in high exaltation and the eighth house is clear, the boy will be well versed in the Vedas and Śāstras.

366. If Jupiter, Venus or the lord of one's Vedas or their divisions are in friendly houses or in their divisions or are in exaltation he will be endowed with knowledge and wealth.

367. It is rare that in the case of boy all the three, *viz.*, the week-day of the lord of one's Veda, the strength of the lord of one's Veda and the rising sign of the lord of one's Veda occur simultaneously.

368. Thus, when the Moon is in the division of the lord of the Veda, the student would become learned, but if in the division of an evil sign or in a division of his own sign, he would be poor and constantly distressed.

369. When the asterisms Śravaṇa or Punarvasu (Aditi) (prevail and the Moon is in a division of Cancer, the student would be endowed with the knowledge of the Vedas and the sciences and with wealth and foodgrains.

370-72. All the signs are commendable (if the time for the studentship ceremony is fixed) in an auspicious *lagna*, in an auspicious division thereof, when the eighth house is clear, the *lagna*, which is not in the eighth house is occupied or aspected by beneficent planets or by the five planets Jupiter, Sun, Moon, etc., when they are friendly and strong or by four auspicious planets fully endowed with strength of position etc. or aspected by them, and devoid of the twentyone great blemishes (possible in a day)[39].

373. However, only the auspicious divisions of the nine-fold division (*navāṁśa*) of the said signs are to be selected. But the division of Cancer should never be selected even if it is aspected by a beneficent planet.

374. The divisions of Vṛṣabha and Mithuna, and Libra and Virgo are also auspicious. Studentship ceremony is to be performed only in a *navāṁśa* selected in the above manner.

375-76. If evil planets occupy the 3rd, 6th and 11th (*āya*) houses, beneficent planets are not to be found in the 6th, 8th and 12th houses, and if the Moon does not occupy the 6th, 8th or the 12th house from the *lagna*, the boy who takes the vow of studentship will be pennyless and always consumptive even if the Moon is in exaltation in its own house.

377. If the Sun is exalted in the quadrants, the student's parents will die. A *lagna* which does not have any of the above five faults is productive of auspicious results in *upanayana*.

378. The studentship ceremony should not be performed other than in spring, nor in the *galagraha* days, the days of non-study,[40] the 6th nor in (the *karaṇa* called) *Viṣṭi*[41].

379. The eight *galagraha* (lit. 'gripping the throat') days. *viz*., the four days from the 13th, the three days from the 7th and the 4th (of the dark fortnight) are declared to be inauspicious.

KṢURIKĀBANDHANA—(GIRDING THE SWORD)

380a. Now, shall I set out *kṣurikābandhana* 'the girding of the sword', a ceremony (ordained) for kṣatriyas, before their marriage.

380b-83. The *Kṣurikābandhana* ceremony should be performed after worshipping the gods and the manes, in the month recommended for marriage, in the bright fortnight, when Jupiter, Venus and Mars have not set, on days prescribed for *Mauñjibandhana* ('tying the belt of mauñji grass'),[42] on a week-day other than Tuesday, a day endowed with the strength of the

Moon and the asterisms, in a *navāṁśaka* except the 8th, of the performer, the 8th house being clear, the Moon being in the *lagna* leaving out the 6th, 8th and 12th houses, and with beneficent planets occupying the 2nd (*dhana*) house, the trines (*trikoṇa*) and the quadrants (*kendra*), while the others occupy the 3rd, 11th (*āya*) and 6th (*ari*) houses.

384. First the sword should be duly worshipped, placing it in front of the deities. Later, in an auspicious *lagna*, the sword endowed with proper form and proportions should be tied to the performer's waist.

385-386. *Prognostication by Āya.* Divide half the length of the sword by the breadth of the blade. The remainders are called *āya*.[43] (Remainder 1, called) *Dhvaja-āya*, foretells destruction of foes; (Rem. 2) *Dhanur-āya* foretells death; (Rem. 3) *Siṁha*, Victory; (Rem. 4) *Śvāna*, ill health; (Rem. 5) *Vṛṣa*, gain of wealth; (Rem. 6), *Gardabha*, sorrow;

387a. (If the Rem. is 7, it is) *Gaja-āya* when there would be great happiness, and (if the Rem. is 8) it is *Dhvāṅkṣa* (Kāka) when there would be loss of wealth.

387b-89. *Prognostication through scars.* Multiply the length of the sword, measured in one's own *aṅgulis* (two-finger breadths) by the length of the dagger (*khaḍgaputrikā*) and divide by 11. (If a scar or flaw occurs in the sword at distances from the handles indicated by) the several remainders, the effect would be, in order : (1) birth of a son, (2) death of the enemy, (3) acquisition of a wife, (4) travel, (5) auspiciousness, (6) loss of wealth, (7) gain of wealth, (8) satisfaction, (9) attainment (of desires), (10) victory and (11) praise.

390-91a. A scar in the first part (of the *aṅgula* is inauspicious in the *Dhvaja* and *Vṛṣa āyas*. It is inauspicious if it occurs in the middle of the *Siṁha* and *Gaja-āyas* prevail. It is so towards the end, if the *Śvāna* and *Kāka āyas* prevail. In the *Dhūmra* and *Gardabha āyas*, a scar will not bring prosperity if it is at the very end (of the *aṅgula*).

SAMĀVARTANA-(RETURN FROM STUDIES)

391b-94a. The 'tonsure after return' (*Samāvartana-muṇḍana*)[44] should be performed on the twice-borns when they return from their teachers' homes after exerting themselves (in their studies).

(The ceremony is to be conducted) during the north-ward course of the Sun; when Jupiter and Venus are visible; in the asterisms Citrā, Uttaraphalgunī, Uttarāṣādhā, Uttarabhādrapada, Puṣya (Ijya), Revatī (Antya), Śravaṇa (Hari), Anurādhā (Mitra) and Rohiṇī (*Vidhātā*); on the week-days of Sun, Moon, Mercury, Jupiter and Venus, and in their (auspicious) *lagnas* and divisions thereof and leaving out the 1st (*pratipat*), 4th, 9th and 14th (*riktā*)[45], new moon 8th and the 'omitted day' (*dinakṣaya*)[46]

VIVĀHAPRAŚNA : (SOLICITATION FOR MARRIAGE)

394b-95a. *Ascertainment of auspicious time* : O great brahmin ! Of all the stages of life, that of the householder is the most exalted. There, too, happiness depends on the wife being of good character.

395b-96a. Her acquiring commendable character depends upon the beneficent *lagna* (at the time of wedlock). Hence I shall set out below the ascertainment of the purity of the *lagna*, taking into cognizance what has been stated on the subject by Brahmā.

396b-97. On an auspicious day, (the enquirer) taking with him betel leaves, fruits, flowers etc., should approach, with folded hands, a well-qualified astrologer, who is comfortably seated and is having a clear mind (at the moment), and consult him, with attention, as if to a deity. (He should then convey to the astrologer the birth-sign, birth-asterism etc. of the proposed couple.)[47]

398. If (at the time of the enquiry), the planet in the *lagna* is cruel and there is Mars in the seventh (house therefrom), the death of the couple should be predicted within eight years.

399. If the Moon occupies the *lagna* and Mars is in the seventh house, the wise should anticipate the death of the husband within eight years.

400. If there be a malefic planet in the fifth house from the *lagna*, who is aspected by an enemy planet and is in debilitation, the girl will, without doubt, have her son still-born or will turn unchaste.

401. The Moon, occupying the 3rd, 5th, 7th, 11th (*āya*)

or 10th (*karma*) house from the *lagna*, if aspected by Jupiter, will bring about the union of the (proposed) couple.

402. If the sections in the *lagna* relating to Libra, Taurus and Cancer are occupied or aspected by Venus or Moon, then the people who solicit for the bride will get her.

403. If the *drekkāṇa* or *navāṁśa* is female[48] and the *lagna* even and aspected by the Moon or Venus, then also the bride who is solicited for will be obtained.

404. In the same manner, the bride will secure the solicited bridegroom if the *lagna* or *navāṁśaka* of the solicitor (*i.e.*, at the time of the enquiry) is male or is aspected by male planets.[49]

405. If the query is made in the dark fortnight, when the Moon occupies an even sign from the *lagna* or is aspected by an evil planet or is in the 8th house (*randhra*), the marriage (solicited) will not take place.

406. If, at the time of enquiry, auspicious indications and omens are seen, they tend to the welfare of the couple, and if these be inauspicious, they tend to undesirable consequences.

407-409a. *Kanyāvaraṇa, solicitation for the bride.* On a day which is pure in respect of the five constituents (of the almanac)[50], endowed with the strength of the Moon and the asterisms, at the rise of the marital asterism, the solicitation for the bride (*Kanyā-varaṇa*) should be made with the utterance of the *praṇava* (syllable *Om*) by the bridegroom, through his elders, at the bride's house, to which place he should go with flowers, betel leaves, fruits, fragrant unguents and sanctified grain (*akṣata*) and white garments, (the procession being) accompanied by music, musical instruments and words of benediction, warding off obstacles.

409b. The bride's father should, then, offer him the bride with pleasure.

410. To the bridegroom endowed with family status, character, youth, handsomeness, wealth and learning, should be offered the bride, beautiful and young.

411-13. The bride should then worship Goddess Śacī, who is the source of all good qualities, the most beautiful in the three worlds, is adorned with divinely fragrant unguents, garlands and garments, is endowed with all auspicious marks, wears all ornaments and illuminates all the directions by means of her superior gemset chains, is attended day and night, by thousands of beauteous maids, and pray to the Goddess thus:

414. "O Goddess Indrāṇi, the dear consort of God Indra! bestow on me, at my marriage, fortune, health and male offspring."

MARRIAGE

415. It is desirable to conduct the marriage of girls in the even years of their birth, and that of boys in the odd years (of their birth). Otherwise, it would be destructive of both.

416. The months of Māgha, Phālguna, Vaiśākha and Jyeṣṭha are auspicious; Kārttika and Mārgaśīrṣa are middling; the rest are censurable.

417. Never should marriage, installation of deities and *upanayana* be performed in ten asterisms from the time that the Sun enters the asterism Ārdrā.

418. Marriage should not be performed when Jupiter or Venus have set or when they are in the stages of childhood and old age (*i.e.*, just after they have risen or when they are about to set). Neither when Jupiter is in the sign Leo or in a Leo-part (in any other sign).

419. For thirteen days after its rise in the west or in the east[51] Venus would be in the 'child's stage' and for five days before setting, in the stage of 'old age'. In the case of Jupiter both stages would be of 15 days duration.

420. So long as God Viṣṇu (Hṛṣīkeśa) is asleep, it is not auspicious. There is nothing more auspicious than the festival day of Viṣṇu (Vāsudeva).

421. The marriage of the firstborn, whether boy or girl, should not be conducted in the month of their birth, nor in the asterisms of their birth, nor in the week-day of their birth.

422. In the month of Jyeṣṭha the marriage of both the Jyeṣṭhaputrī and Jyeṣṭhaputra (eldest daughter and the eldest son) should not be performed. It is best to have one 'Jyeṣṭha' at a time, not otherwise.[52]

423. A marriage should not be performed for a week after a natural visitation (*utpāta*) (like the appearance of a

comet, earthquake etc.) nor a complete eclipse. If the eclipse is partial (the prohibition is) for three days. (Similarly, prohibited are the intercalary lunar day) which touches three civil days (*tridyusprk*) and the expunged lunar day.[53]

424. (In the case of planetary obscuration), three days after their setting and three days before their rise should be eschewed. So far as their dusks are concerned, three days before setting and seven days before rising should be eschewed. (?)

425. Five days towards the close of the (lunar) month should be eschewed. So also the 8th and the *riktā* days, (*viz.*, 4th, 9th and 14th). The *yogas Vyatīpāta* and *Vaidhṛti*, in their entirety, and half of *Parigha* are also to be eschewed.[54]

426. Marriage is recommended in the following asterisms: Revatī (*Pauṣṇa*), Uttaraphalgunī, Uttarāṣāḍha and Uttarbhādrapada (*tryuttara*), Anurādhā (*Maitra*), Svātī (*Marut*). Mṛgaśīrṣa (*Candra*) Hasta (*Arka*), Maghā (*Pitrya*) and Mūla, when these are not in *vedha*, *i.e.*, not mutually afflicted.[54a]

427. If, in a marriage, the potencies of Jupiter and the Sun[55] are required for the couple, effort should be made to worship those two weak planets.

428. The strengths of *gocara*[56], *vedha*[57] and *aṣṭavarga*[58] reckoned in *rūpa*[59] are higher in the ascending order. The strength *gocara* is of a general nature (compared to the others).

429-30a. The potencies of the Moon and the asterisms should be considered and then the strength of the five constituents of the *pañcāṅga*. (Of the latter, if) the strength of the *tithi* is one, that of the weekday is two-fold, that of the asterism is three-fold, that of *yoga* is fourfold and that of *karaṇa* (*tithyardha*) is fivefold.

430b-31. The (prognostication as reckoned in the) *muhūrta* is more strong and *lagna* is still stronger. *Horā*[60] is stronger and *Drekkāṇa*[61] is still more so. *Navāṁśa*[62] is more strong and *Dvādaśāṁśa*[63] stronger than that.

432. *Triṁśāṁśa*[64] is stronger than the previous, The combined strength of the above has to be duly considered. All the signs which are beneficently aspected are commended in fixing a marriage.

433-34a. The signs occupied by the five planets Moon, Sun, Jupiter, (Mercury and Venus) are acceptable. That is an auspicious *lagna* where all the four (Moon, Mercury, Jupiter and Venus) are in strength and which is devoid of the blemish of *Jāmitra*[65] or the twentyone great faults (mentioned below).

434b-35a. *Twentyone Major blemishes* (*Ekaviṁśatimahādoṣa*). O Nārada ! Listen now, to the names and effects of the twenty-one 'Major blemishes', being set out below.

435b-36. (i). *Pañcāṅgaśuddhi-rāhitya* is declared as the first blemish. (ii) The second is *Udayāstaśuddhi-hīna-Sūryasaṅkrama*, (iii) The third is *Pāpaṣaḍvarga*. (Then follow) : (iv) *Bhṛgu-ṣaṣṭha* (v) *Kujāṣṭama*;

437-39a. (vi) *Gaṇḍānta*; (vii) *Kartarī*, (viii-ix) *Rippha-ṣaḍaṣṭendu*, (x) *Sagraha*, (xi-xii) *Aṣṭama-lagna* and *Aṣṭamarāśi* of the couple, (xiii) *Viṣaghaṭī*, (xiv) *Muhūrtadoṣa* (*Durmuhūrta*), (xv) *Vāradoṣa*, (xvi) *Ekārgala* (*Kharjūrikā-samāṅghribha*), (xvii) *Grahaṇotpātabha*, (xviii) *Krūraviddharkṣa*, (xix) *Krūrasaṁyutarkṣa* (xx) *Kuṇavāṁśa*, and (xxi) *Mahāpāta-Vaidhṛti*.[66]

439b-440 (i). *Nonpurity of Pañcāṅga. Pañcāṅga* is constituted by *Tithi*, *Vāra*, *Nakṣatra*, *Yoga* and *Karaṇa*. The purity (of the five items) constitutes the *purity of pañcāṅga*. When there is a blemish in the *pañcāṅga*, mere merit in *lagna* would not bring the desired result.

441a. *Discard Pañceṣika* ('Five arrows', *iṣikā-bāṇa*)[67] as if it is milk mixed with poison.

441b-42. If (at the selected moment, *muhūrta*) the *lagna* and *lagnāṁśaka* are not aspected by or are together with their respective lords or by their mutual lords or auspicious friends, (such a *muhūrta* should be rejected). If the *lagna* be the 7th or the 7th section, the bridegroom will meet with death.

443a. If they (the *lagna* and the *lagnāṁśaka*) are not aspected or are together, as indicated above, the death of the bride will result at the time of the marriage.

443b-44a. (ii). *Saṅkrama*. In marriage etc. sixteen *nāḍikās* each have to be eschewed before and after the transit of the Sun into a sign.

444b. (iii). *Pāpa-Ṣaḍvarga*.[68] In fixing a marriage etc. the auspicious (findings as read off from) *Ṣaḍvarga* are greatly commended (and, so, the inauspicious times as reckoned by the *ṣaḍvarga* reckonings should be avoided.

445. (iv). *Venus in the sixth house*. The blemish of *Bhṛgu*.

ṣaṣṭha occurs when Venus occupies the sixth house. Even if Venus is in exaltation and occupies the *lagna* with an auspicious planet, such a *lagna* should always be rejected.

446. (v). *Mars in the eighth house.* The great blemish *Kujāṣṭama* will occur when Mars occupies the eighth house from the *lagna.* Reject the *lagna* even if it is occupied by three benefic planets if there is alongside Mars in exaltation.

447. (vi). *Gaṇḍānta. Gaṇḍānta* (relating to *tithi* or lunar days) occurs for two *nāḍikās* each at the junctures of the (three) *Pūrṇā tithis* with the (three) *Nandā tithis*, (*i.e.*, between the 5th and the 6th, 10th and 11th, and 15th and 1st).[69] This time is deadly in the matter of birth, travel, marriage etc.

448. *Gaṇḍānta* (relating to *lagna*) occurs for half a *nāḍikā* each at the junctures of Cancer and Leo, Scorpio and Sagittarius and Pisces and Aries; this time is deadly.

449. *Gaṇḍānta* relating to asterisms occurs at the junctures of the ending sixteen *nāḍikās* of the three asterisms Āśleṣā (*Sarpa*), Indra (*Jyeṣṭha*) and Revatī (*Pauṣṇa*) with the first quarters of the respective succeeding asterisms (*viz.*, Maghā, Mūla and Aśvinī).

450a. The said three tapes of junctures form three different types of *Gaṇḍāntas*, which are all highly harmful.

450b-51a. (vii). *Kartarī.* The crossing, (in their motion), of two evil planets, one in regular motion and the other in retrograde motion, while facing the *lagna*, is known as *Kartarī*; it will cut the throats of couple (like a pair of scissors).

451b-52a. Discard the *lagna* which is tainted by the blemish of *Kartarī* even if it be occupied by auspicious planets endowed with all good qualities.

452b. (viii-ix). *Ripphaṣaḍaṣṭendu.* When Moon occupies the 6th, 8th and 12th (*Rippha*) houses, the blemish of that name is caused.

453-54a. Discard, even with effort, the abovesaid *lagna*, even if it be occupied by Jupiter and Venus. For a *lagna* within an enemy house even if occupied by friendly planets, either in exaltation or debilitation, and even if invested with all qualities, is deathly to couples.

454b-55a. (x) *Sagraha.* When the Moon is in conjunction with some other planets, the 'blemish' by name *Sagraha* occurs. Do not perform marriages (at a *muhūrta*) when the said blemish prevails.

455b-57. When Sun is in conjunction with the Moon, to be sure, poverty will result; with Mars, disease; with Mercury, childlessness; with Jupiter, misfortune; with Venus, having a co-wife; with Saturn, turning a recluse; with Rāhu, destruction of family base; and if the Moon is in conjunction with Ketu continued suffering and poverty will result.

458-59a. If the Moon is in conjunction with evil planets the death of the couple will result. However, if the Moon, in exaltation, is in conjunction with beneficent planets in friendly signs, the *lagna* does not turn evil but always tends to their welfare.

459b-60a. On the other hand, Moon, in exaltation or in its asterism or in a friendly house, if it is in conjunction with an evil planet will cause their death.

460b-61a. (xi-xii). *Aṣṭama-lagna and Aṣṭama rāśi.* The eighth *lagna* or the eighth sign (of birth) of the couple, if it occupies the *lagna* (of the time of the marriage) that too would cause the death of the couple.

461b-62a. Even if the said sign or the *lagna* is occupied by a benevolent planet, discard that *lagna*, and its divisions and also other houses governed by the lords (of the eighth houses of the couple).

462b-63a. The twelfth *lagna* or sign (of birth of the couple, occupying the *lagna* (of the marriage) will result in their loss of wealth. Hence discard the lord of that division of the *lagna*.

463b-64a. The rise of the birth sign and the rise of the birth *lagna* are auspicious. If the *lagna* (of the *muhūrta*) is in the *upacaya-s*[70] of the above two, it is extremely auspicious.

464b-68. (xiii). *Viṣaghaṭī*. Four *ghaṭikās* each in continuation of the undermentioned *ghaṭikās*, respectively, in the twentyseven asterisms are called *Viṣaghaṭikās*. They should be eschewed in fixing times of marriages etc., even if endowed with other qualities. They are, in order from the asterism Aśvinī: (1. Aśvinī) : 50, (2. Bharaṇī) : 24; (3. Kṛttikā) : 30; (4. Rohiṇī) : 40; (5. Mṛgaśiras) : 13; (6. Ārdrā) : 21; (7. Punarvasu): 30; (8. Puṣya); 20; 9. Āśleṣā); 32; (10. Maghā) : 30; (11. Purvaphalgunī): 20; (12 Uttaraphālgunī): 18; (13. Hasta): 20; (14. Citrā 20; (15. Svātī); 14; (16. Viśākhā): 14; (17. Anurādhā): 10; (18. Jyeṣṭhā): 14; (19. Mūla): 56; (20. Pūrvāṣāḍha); 24; (21. Uttarāṣāḍha): 20; (22. Śravaṇa): 10; (23. Śraviṣṭhā): 10; (24. Śatabhiṣak): 18; (25. Pūrvabhādrapadā); 16; (26. Uttarabhādrapadā): 24; (27. Revatī): 30.

469 (xiv). *Muhūrtadoṣa.* Such *muhūrtas* in the week-day from Sunday, as are censured (for other auspicious rites) are to be censured also for marriage etc., even if invested with good qualities.[71]

470 (xv). *Vāradoṣa.* Such days of the week for which blemishes have been indicated, in order, beginning with Sunday, are to be eschewed also for (marriage, which is) the most auspicious rite, even if the days are endowed with all qualifications.[72]

471. (xvi). *Ekārgala.* Discard a *lagna* which encompasses even a fourth part of (an asterism having) the blemish of *Ekārgala,* as if it is milk mixed with poison, even if (the *lagna* is) occupied by Venus and Bṛhaspati.[73]

472. (xvii). *Grahaṇotpātabha.* (In an auspicious rite, like marriage), the asterism in which an eclipse or an *Utpāta* (like the fall of a meteor or occurrence of an earthquake) occurs should be discarded for three succeeding seasons (*i.e.* six months), thereafter as charred firewood, except when they are occupied by the moon and left (*bhuktvā muktam bham*).

473. (xviii-xix). *Krūraviddharkṣa and Krūrasaṁyuta.* In auspicious rites (like marriage) discard all asterisms which are afflicted (*viddha*)[74] or in conjunction with violent planets, as *pañcagavya*[75] to which a drop of wine has been added.

474. If the asterism in question had been afflicted only by its fourth part and that, too, by benefic planets, the whole asterism is not rendered inauspicious. However, if the affliction or being in conjunction is by cruel planets, the whole asterism has to be discarded.

475-77a. (xx). *Kunavāṁśaka.* The *navāṁśas* Libra, Gemini and Virgo and the Second half of Sagittarius are auspicious except the ending in each. The ending will also be auspicious if they are of the *vargottama* category.[76] The other *navāṁśakas* are not to be selected since they are *Kunavāṁśakas* ('Evil *navāṁśakas*'). A *lagna* in which there is a *Kunavāṁśaka* is to be rejected even if endowed with all other qualifications.

477b-78a. (xxi). *Mahāpāta Vaidhṛti.*[77] The day on which the *mahāpāta Vaidhṛti* occurs should be eschewed in auspicious rites (like marriage), even if endowed with all qualities, for it would cause the death of the couple.

478b-79. *Minor blemishes* (*Svalpadoṣa*). Minor blemishes, not mentioned (above) also exist, like for instance, lightning and hailstorm; mock-sun, halo round the Sun and the Moon, rainbow, and thunder of clouds: *Lattā*; minor tremours etc., lunar days called 'burnt month' (*dagdhamāsa*).

479. *Dagdha-lagna* (burnt *lagna*), and the *lagnas* with the appellation 'blind', 'deaf' and 'lame'. Now, the explanation of these is given below.

480. *Lightning and hailstorm.* Lightning and hailstorm, which occur at unexpected times, will indeed, be injurious to auspicious rites, though, in course of time, they will become noninjurious.

481. There is, however, no doubt that anyone of Jupiter, Venus or Mercury will obviate the effect of these groups of blemishes if it is in a quadrant (*kendra*)[78].

482-84a. *Vedha* (*Piercing Affliction*). (Draw a diagram with) five vertical lines, five across, and two each diagonally. Mark the asterism Kṛttikā (*Agnidhiṣṇya*) at the end of the second diagonal in the north-east and the other asterisms, including Abhijit (in order, in a clockwise direction). The mutually 'pierced' asterisms are those at the ends of the lines.[79]

484b-85a. *Lattā.* The Sun and other planets affect, for a day, an asterism, ahead of or behind it, (alternately). Thus, the Sun affects the 12th asterism (ahead of it); Moon, the 22nd (behind it); Mars, the 3rd (ahead of it); Mercury, the 7th (behind it); Jupiter, the 6th (ahead of it); Venus, the 5th (behind it); Saturn the 8th (ahead of it); and Rāhu, the 9th behind it. (These days are to be scrupulously avoided in fixing *muhūrtas.*)

485b-86a. *Pātabha* (*Malignant asterism*). Count from Hasta (*Sūryabha*) the asterism Āśleṣā (*Sarpa*), Maghā (*Pitrya*), Revatī (*Antyā*), Citra (*Tvāṣṭra*), Anurādhā (*Mitra*) and Śravaṇa

(*Viṣṇubha*) and count off those numbers from Aśvinī. The asterisms got would be malignant asterisms (*pātabha*) (?)

486b. In Saurāṣṭra and the Sālva country the blemish of *Lattā* is not taken note of.

487. *Pātita* (*Minor tremour*) is not considered auspicious in Kaliṅga (Orissa) and Vaṅga (Bengal) countries. In Bālhīka, Kuru country and certain other regions, however, it is not a blemish at all.

488. *Dagdha-tithi* and *Dagdha-lagna*. The 'burnt' lunar days and the 'burnt' *lagnas* are eschewed in Madhyadeśa (Madhya Pradesh) but not considered inauspicious in other areas.

489. The 'lame', 'blind' and 'deaf' *lagnas*[80] and the signs which do not contain the ending of a lunar month are rejected in the Gauḍa and Mālava regions, but not censured in other areas.

490. Every moment is infested with some blemish or other, and it would be impossible even for the creator to wipe off the blemishes completely. Hence one should opt for the maximum of auspiciousness and the minimum of blemishes.

491a. *Marriage altar*. In an auspicious *lagna*, (decided upon) in consideration of the above, should be arranged the mutual viewing of one another by the couple.

491b-95. The couple should then be made to ascend an auspicious altar on which holy fire is kept—an altar which is one cubit high, a square of four cubits on all sides; supported by four polished pillars; slightly slanting to the left; with a pavilion around, beautified by steps on the four sides; elongated on the east and the north; beautified by the planting of plantain trunks; ornamented by (replicas of) swans and parrots, painted pots, and shoots placed on the arches; decked with heaps of love-inciting flowers and colours; sanctified by the benedictions of brāhmaṇas and pleasing with auspicious and divinely beautiful ladies; and making the heart merry with musical instruments, dance and songs.

496. *Mutual horoscopical agreement of the couple*[81]. Eight are the mutual compatabilities which conduce to sons and grandsons: (i) *Rāśi*, (ii) *Strīdūra*, (iii) *Gaṇa*, (iv) *Rāśīśa*, (v) *Yoni* (vi) *Varṇa*, (vii) *Rajju* and (viii) *Vaśya*.

497-98a. *Agreement of Rāśi.* Different asterism for the couple in the same *rāśi* is excellent. Middling is to have different *rāśis*, but the same asterism. The marriage of a couple born in the same asterism in the same *rāśi* results in death.

498b-99a. *Strīdūra.* A distance within the first nine asterisms for the male horoscope from the asterism of the female is highly inauspicious, the second nine is middling and the third nine is excellent.

499b-500a. *Agreement in Gaṇa*[82]. The asterisms in the human group (*martya-gaṇa*) are : The three *pūrvas* and *uttaras*, (*viz.*, Pūrvaphalgunī, Pūrvāṣāḍha, Purvabhādrapada, Uttaraphalgunī, Uttarāṣāḍha and Uttarabhādrapada), Rohiṇī (*Dhātṛ*), Bharaṇī (*Yāmya*), Ārdrā (*Maheśa*).

500. Those of the divine group are : Śravaṇa (*Hari*), Vasu (*Āditya*), Hasta (*Arka*), Svātī (*Vāyu*), Revatī (*Antya*), Anurādhā (Mitra), Aśvinī, Puṣya (Ijya) and Mṛgaśīrṣa (Indu).

501. Asterisms of the demonic *gaṇa* (*Rakṣo-gaṇa*) are : Maghā (*Pitṛ*), Citrā (*Tvāṣṭra*), Viśākhā (*Dvidaivatya*), Kṛttikā (*Agni*), Jyeṣṭhā (*Indra*), Dhaniṣṭhā (*Vasu*) Śatabhiṣak (*Vārīśa*), Mūla, and Āśleṣā (*Ahi*).

502. If the birth-asterism of the couple is the same, it would be pleasing in many ways. It is middling if one is human and the other divine. Death will result (if the human and the divine are united) with the demonic.

503. *Agreement between the lords of the rāśi* : If the lords of the *rāśis* of the couple are one in the 6th house and the other in the 8th, death will result. If it be fifth and ninth, there would be childlessness. Second and twelfth houses, too, are not desirable. In the others, there will be excellent mutual attraction between the couple.

504. If the said lords are identical or friendly, the marriage will be happy. It might be so even in the case of two and twelve and the trines (*trikoṇā*), but never in the case of six and eight.

505-6. *Agreement of Yoni.*[83] The animals relating to the asterisms Aśvinī etc. are in order: (1. Aśvinī) : Horse; (2. Bharaṇī): Elephant; (3. Kṛttikā): Goat; (4. Rohiṇī): Serpent; (5. Mṛgaśiras) : Snake; (6. Ārdrā): Dog; (7. Punarvasu): Cat; (8. Puṣya): Goat; (9. Āśleṣā): Cat; (10. Maghā): Rat; (11. Pūrvaphalgunī): Mouse; (12. Uttaraphalgunī): Cow; (13. Hasta): Buffalo; (14. Citrā): Tiger; (15. Svātī): Buffalo; (16. Viśākhā): Tiger; (17. Anurādhā): Deer; (18. Jyeṣṭhā): Deer; (19. Mūla): Dog; (20. Pūrvāṣāḍha): Monkey; (21. Uttarāṣāḍha): Ox; (22. Śravaṇa): Monkey; (23. Śraviṣṭhā); Lion; (24. Śatabhiṣak): Horse; (25. Pūrvabhādrapadā): Lion; (26. Uttarabhādrapadā): Cow; (27. Revatī): Elephant.

507. The pairs Dog and deer, Mongoose and serpent, Goat and monkey, Lion and elephant, Cow and tiger, Rat and cat, and Buffalo and horse are inimical.

508. *Varṇa* (*caste*)[84]. Pisces, Scorpio and Cancer are brāhmaṇas; the further ones belong to the other castes.[85] If the male's *rāśi* is lower than that of the female in caste, it is inauspicious[86].

509-10a. *Rajju* or *Nāḍi*. (The 27 asterisms are in the form of a zigzag rope, each loop carrying 3 asterisms, thus forming three columns (*nāḍis*) of 9 asterisms each, (If the asterisms of the boy and the girl fall) in the same column, it indicates death and not so in adjacent columns.)[87]

510b-11a. *Different types of marriages*. (The three types of marriages) *Prājāpatya*, *Brāhma* and *Daiva* are approved by the sage, and if performed at the said (auspicious) times, would be extremely beneficial.

511b. (The *Āsura* marriage is achieved through the payment of money and *Paiśāca* by kidnapping the bride. The *Rākṣasa* marriage is done by winning over the bride in battle and *Gāndharva* is made by mutual understanding.)[88]

512-13a. *Abhijit and Godhūlikā*.[89] The fourth *lagna* from the *lagna* at sunrise is called *Abhijit* and the seventh is called *Godhūlikā*. Both these are auspicious for marriage and (will bless the couple) with sons and grandsons. For the Easterners (belonging to Bengal, Assam etc.) and the people of Kaliṅga (Orissa), *Godhūlikā* is important.

513b-14. *Abhijit* is considered as important in all regions as a destroyer of blemishes. The *muhūrta* (of two *nāḍikās*) when the Sun is at the zenith is called *Abhijit*. It wipes off all blemishes as the Pināka-bowed (Śiva) wiped out the Tripuras.[90]

515. *Prohibitions in marriages*. A daughter's marriage should

not be conducted for three seasons after a son's marriage, neither should be performed the sacrament (for the change to married life, *vrata*). When there has been an auspicious event, there shall not be another auspicious event closely following.

516. If the marriages of two sisters are conducted within six months of each other, one of them will surely become a widow within three years.

517. Mutual marriages should not be performed nor should two daughters be married to the same groom, nor two daughters born of the same parents to two brothers born of the same parents.

518a. Nor should two marriages be conducted at the same time, nor two tonsures.

518b-19a. If a marriage is performed during *Gaṇḍa*[91], the child if born during day-time will kill his father, if during night, his mother, and if during the (morning and evening) twilights, himself. There is no exception to *Gaṇḍa*.

519b. A son and a daughter born in the asterism Mūla will positively kill the father-in-law, but not one born in the ending quarter of that asterism.

520a-20b. A boy, but not the girl, born in the first quarter of Āśleṣā and the latter two quarters of Jyeṣṭhā will also (kill the father-in-law).

521. A girl born in Mūla or Pūrvāṣāḍha will not harm the father or the mother, but the one born in Jyeṣṭhā will kill the elder brother of the husband, and one born in Viśākhā (*Dvidaiva*) the younger brother.

521-23. *Vadhūpraveśa*. For the auspicious entry of the bride into her husband's household, the sixth, eighth, tenth or seventh day counted from the day of marriage is recommended. (If it is delayed), the marriage journey should be made leaving out the second (and other even) years and eschewing the bride's birth asterism, birth-lagna, and birth-day, and also avoiding position to Venus.[92]

INSTALLATION OF DEITIES

524a. The installation of any deity during the northward course of the Sun will conduce to prosperity.

524b-25. The installation would be auspicious if made at a time when both Mercury and Venus are visible, in the five months from Māgha, but omitting Citrā; in the bright fortnight and, if in the dark fortnight, in the first eight days, the lunar day being selected in accordance with the day patronised by the particular deity;

526-527a. On the two lunar days beginning with the second, the three days beginning with the fifth, the four days beginning with the 10th, especially on full moon day;

527b-28a. On the asterisms, the three *Uttarās* (*viz.*, Uttara-phālgunī, Uttarāṣāḍhā and Uttarabhādrapadā), Mṛgaśiras, Revatī, Hasta, Citrā, Svātī and Puṣya; and also on Aśvinī, Rohiṇī, Pūrvāṣāḍhā, Śravaṇa, Anurādhā, and Dhaniṣṭhā;

528b-29. On week-days excepting Tuesday, when the Sun is strong with regards to the master (of the installation), when the potencies of the Moon and the asterisms are forthcoming; in the forenoon of that auspicious day, when the *lagna* and the division thereof are auspicious, and when no (asterism) deadly to the master is rising.

530. *Nature of the signs and houses.* All the signs are auspicious if occupied or aspected by benefic planets, the *Pañcaka* (Five sources of energy)[93] being auspicious and the 8th house, indicating death, is vacant.

531. The Moon, Mars, Sun, Node, Tail and Saturn would be harmful to the master if they occupy the *lagna*, while the other planets would bestow wealth, grain and happiness.

532a. In the second house, the evil planets will not bestow any desired fruit, while the benefics and the Moon will bestow wealth.

532b. In the third house, all the planets bestow sons, grandsons and happiness.

533a. In the fourth house, the benefic planets bestow happiness, while the violent planets bestow unhappiness.

533b. In the fifth house, the violent planets produce distress, while the benefic planets bestow sons and happiness.

534a. In the sixth house the benefic planets become enemies, while the evil planets would destroy one's enemies.

534b. In the seventh house, the evil planets cause disease, while the benefic planets bestow auspicious fruits.

535a. In the eighth house, all planets occupying it cause the death of the master.

535b. In the ninth house which indicates *dharma*, the evil planets cause distress, but the benefic planets are auspicious and bestow happiness.

536a. In the tenth house which indicates *Karma*, the evil planets give trouble but the benefic planets and the Moon bring glory.

536b. In the eleventh house, indicative of profit, all planets tend to bestow the maximum income (profit) (to the master).

537a. All the planets occupying the twelfth house indicating expenditure will make (the master) spend incessantly.

537b-38a. The images of deities, installed, if not endowed with wealth, will harm the master, and harm the priest if not properly invoked with sacred chants. If not sculptured according to specifications, they will injure the master's wife. Indeed, there is no act so inimical (as an installation (which has not been properly performed).

538b-39a. If the installation is done during a *lagna* highly endowed with auspicious qualities, and if the blemishes are very little, the installation of deities would bestow upon the master all his desires.

(VĀSTULAKṢAṆA: CONSTRUCTION OF HOUSES)

539b-400a. *Testing of the ground.* Towards the construction of a town, village, house etc, first examine the ground for its qualities of smell, colour and taste.

540b-41. For brāhmaṇas, (kṣatriyas, vaiśyas and śūdras), it is auspicious if the earth has, respectively, the smell of honey, flower, sour fruit and flesh; has, respectively, the colours white, red, green and dark; and has, respectively, the tastes sweet, hot, bitter and astringent.

542. It is beneficial for all people if the ground slopes towards north-east, east or north. Slopes towards the other directions would always be highly harmful to them.

543. Dig a (cubical) pit of the depth of one cubit and fill it (with the excavated earth). It would be extremely beneficial if there is earth to spare, if less, it is inauspicious and if just enough (to fill the pit), it is middling.

544. Dig a similar pit at duskand fill it with water. When examined in the morning, if there is water still, the place would be prosperous, if there is just slush, it would be middling, and if it is dry, it is inferior.

545. *Orientation* (*East-west determination*). When a ground with good characteristics as above has been selected, prepare a level surface in its middle and draw a circle thereon, for determining the east-west line.

546a. Fix a 12-inch gnomon at its centre and with its help, determine the directions.[94]

546b-47a. *Construction of the building.* In the ground measured out as a rectangle and tested through the sixfold divisions (Ṣaḍvarga),[95] a beautiful edifice should be erected, along the lines drawn.

547b-48. *Windows in the outer walls of the residential enclosure.* Along the directions on the four sides, reckoned from the east, eight gates each should be put up. In the clockwise order they will have the undermentioned effects:

549. *East*: (i) Misfortune, (ii) Loss of wealth, (iii) gain of wealth, (iv) propitiation of the king, (v) great wealth, (vi) big theft, (vii) rage and (viii) fear.

550. *South*: (i) Death, (ii) imprisonment, (iii) fear, (iv) attainment of riches, (v) increase in wealth, (vi) freedom from doubts (vii) fear from diseases, and (viii) destruction of creatures.

551. *West*: (i) Loss of a son, (ii) prosperity to the enemy, (iii) attainment of riches, (iv) receipt of wealth, (v) happiness, (vi) extreme misfortune, (vii) unhappiness, and (viii) distress.

552. *North*: (i) Loss of one's wife: (ii) destruction of creatures, (iii) Misfortune, (iv) attainment of grains and wealth, (v) wealth, (vi) prosperity, (vii) intense fear, and (viii) hunger.

553. *Doorways.* The main doorway to the house is to be in the west or the south, its height being twice its breadth.

554. 81-*division concept.*[96] Divide the ground inside the boundary walls into 81 squares (by dividing the sides into nine equal divisions). Nine squares in the centre form the *Brahmasthāna* ('place of Brahmā'), which is highly inauspicious (for residential quarters).

555-56a. The thirytwo squares close to the outer wall, (*i.e.*, the border squares, all round) pertain to the ghosts. Residential construction in the ghost region will result in unhappiness, distress and fear.

The other squares (are auspicious and) tend to bless one with sons, grandsons and wealth for one's constructing the house.

556b-58a. The east-west and north-south lines in the construction form its bloodvessels. The *Brahmā* squares, the ghost squares and the intersecting points of the bloodvessels are to be understood as the vital junctures of the construction. The vital junctures are not commended for residential use.[97]

558b-59a. *Time for building construction.* The months Mārgaśiras (*Saumya*), Phālguna, Vaiśākha, Māgha, Śrāvaṇa and Kārttika conduce to sons, health and wealth (to one who builds a house during these months).

559b-60. *Digvargayoni.* The (eight) groups (*vargas*) beginning with *a* (*viz.*, (1) the vowels *a* etc., (2) *ka-varga*, (3) *ca-varga*, (4) *ṭa-varga*, (5) *ta-varga*, (6) *pa-varga*, (7) *ya-ra-la-va* and (8) *śa-ṣa-sa-ha*) are placed, in order, against the (eight) directions beginning with the east. (The eight animals and birds, *viz.*) (1) eagle, (2) cat, (3) lion, (4) dog, (5) serpent, (6) rat, (7) elephant and (8) deer are the *yoni-s* (animal-births) of the (eight) said direction-groups. Of these the fifth counted from its group is its enemy.[98]

561. *Auspiciousness based on Varga-cakra.* (In order to determine whether the selected spot would be beneficial for the owner's residence), the *varga* of the *sādhya* (here, the village) and that of the *sādhaka* (owner) are separately (calculated) and each divided by 8. If the remainder got from the *Varga* of the sādhaka is greater, the land is good for him, otherwise, it will destroy him.[99]

562. Or, count the asterisms from the asterisms of the *sādhaka* (owner) to that of the *sādhya* (village), multiply that number by 4 and divide by 7. The greater the remainder, the owner will fare better in that land.[100]

563. *Auspiciousness based on area.* The product of length and breadth forms the area of a house. From it is calculated, in order, the numbers indicating (the nature of) its positiveness, negativeness, income, asterism, week-day and *navāṁśa.*[101]

564. Positiveness conduces to prosperity, while negative-

ness is inauspicious. An odd number indicating income points to auspiciousness while an even number indicates penury.

565. *Auspiciousness based on asterisms.* The third asterism (of the house) from that of the master of the house indicates depletion of wealth, the fifth asterism indicates depletion of prestige, and the seventh asterism foretells death.

566. *Auspiciousness based on the signs.* The second and twelfth sign conduces to poverty and triangular sign conduces to sonlessness. The sixth and eighth signs indicate death. The other signs are auspicious.

567. *Auspiciousness on the basis of week-days.* Sundays and Tuesdays conduce to fear of fire. The days pertaining to the other planets conduce to the fulfilment of all desires.

568-69a. *Deity of the dwelling and entrance to the house.* The Deity of the dwelling (*Vāstu-pumān*) would be lying prostrate on the house-site with his head towards the east during the three months beginning with Nabhasya (*i.e.*, Bhādrapada, Āśvina and Kārttika). This pot-bellied deity, called also *Cara* 'the moving' shifts its position anticlockwise every three months, (thus remaining with his head towards north during Mārgaśīrṣa, Pauṣa and Māgha, west during Phālguna, Caitra and Vaiśākha, and south during Jyeṣṭha, Āṣāḍha and Śrāvaṇa).

569b-70. The main entrance to the house should be in the direction in which the head of the Deity of the dwelling is (at the time when construction is started). A house with its entrance turned opposite to the said direction will bring disease and distress (to the master of the house). This drawback will not affect a house which has entrances on all sides.

571. *Commencement of construction.* A mud pot, with gold, gems, grain and lotus seeds should be placed in a pit of the depth of a cubit in the centre of the house (-site) as a deposit).

572a. The middle point of the longer side of the house-site is termed (*nābhi*) (navel) and an area of three digits around it is its belly.

572b-74. At the navel a gnomon adorned with gold, clothes, etc., and conducive of sons and grandsons, has to be fixed. The measure of the gnomon for (the houses of) Brāhmaṇas, (Kṣatriyas, Vaiśyas and Śūdras) are, respectively, 24, 23, 16 and 12 digits. The gnomon should be constructed from the wood of *khadira*, *arjuna*, *sāla* and *pūga* or from red sandal, *palāśa*, *raktasāla* or *visāla*.

575. Divide the gnomon into three, construct a square around it, then an octogon and then an unbroken circle (?) (*anasram ṛjum āvaraṇam*).

576-78. Fix the gnomon prepared as above at the appropriate place duly marked with a string used to mark off the quadrants, signs etc. (*ṣaḍvargaśuddhisūtreṇa*),[102] on an auspicious day, the prevailing asterism being one of the *mṛdu*, *dhruva* or *kṣipra* classes[103] the lunar day being not newmoon or one of the *riktā* 'empty' days (*viz.*, the 4th, 9th and 14th *tithis*), the day being not Sunday nor Tuesday, the *lagna* and the eighth house being not occupied by evil planets, the eighth house being vacant, the *lagna* being auspicious, and so also the *navāṁśaka* division thereof, and the *lagna* being occupied or aspected by beneficent planets.

579-80a. The fixing of the gnomon should be accompanied by the utterance of sacred hymns and the sounds of musical instruments played by the most auspicious ladies. The *kendra* and *trikoṇa* houses (quadrants and trines) should be occupied by beneficent planets, the third and the eleventh (*āya*) and sixth houses being occupied by the other planets, and the Moon occupying the sixth house from *lagna*.

580b-82. *Classification of dwellings.* There are six types of dwellings having, respectively, one, two, three, four, seven and ten halls; each of these are of sixteen types, which carry the appellations: *Dhruva*, *Dhanya*, *Jaya*, *Nanda*, *Svara*, *Kānta*, *Manorama*, *Sumukha*, *Durmukha*, *Krūra*, *Śatru*, *Svarṇaprada*, *Kṣaya*, *Ākranda*, *Vipula* and *Vijaya*.

583-84a. The possible types of dwellings can be calculated by the method of permutation and combination (as is done in metrics, where, in order to find the number of possible forms of a metre, the following procedure is adopted): Place the short syllable below the long syllable; and further, too, place the syllables, progressively. Thus fill the set entirely with long syllables and then add one with all short.[104]

584b-85a. *Verandah.* Construct narrow verandahs (*alinda*) round the building, starting from the entrance. Considering the verandahs from the east, there can be sixteen types of houses.

585b-87a. *Location of the rooms.* The bathroom shall be to the east and the kitchen to the south-east. The room for sleeping shall be to the south and the armoury to the southwest. To the west shall be the dining room and the granary to the northwest. The room for worship is to be in the north and the room for the storing of milk, curds etc. to the north-east.

587b-89a. Rooms for (1) bed, (2) urine, blood and faeces; (3) food, (4) auspicious things, (5) grain, (6) enjoyment with women, (7) wealth, and (8) ornaments, are to be located (in between the eight rooms mentioned above) beginning with the north east-east. Construction of residences in this manner is auspicious.[105]

589b-90a. *Birds, beasts etc. of the direction.* Flag, smoke, lion, dog, cow, ass, elephant, and crow—these eight are ascribed, in order, to the directions beginning with the east.[106]

590b-91. *Inauspicious trees around the house. Plakṣa, udumbara, cūta, snuhi, nimba, vibhītaka,* thorny trees, milktrees, *vaṭa, aśvattha, kapitthaka, agasti, sindhuvāla* and *tintiḍīka* are not recommended (for being planted around a residence).

592a. An elder brother's house to the south or west (of one's own) (is recommended) as that of one's own father. (?)

592b. The foundations of a house are to be commended if they are level and the pillars equal (in height), not otherwise.

593. The walls should not be too high nor too low, the height being fixed as one likes it. So also, the storeys, one over the other. In all such cases, the above shall be the consideration.

594-95. *Drains and gagoyles.* Drains in houses are of eight types (as obtaining in different regions). They are, in order: Pāñcāla, Vaideha, Kaurava, Kaujanyaka, Māgadha, Śūrasena, Gāndhāra and Āvantika. In all these the breadth is one fourth of the height.

596. The Pāñcāla type is the smallest and the others, Vaideha etc., are larger, in that order.

597-98. The Pāñcāla measure is applicable to all. However, for the residences, in two or three storeys, of brāhmaṇas etc., drains of special suitability are those of the Avanti measure to Brāhmaṇas, Gāndhāra measure to Kṣatriyas and Kaujaneya measure to Vaiśyas.

599-600a. *Stables.* Stables for camels and elephants should have their heights with accord with the *dhvaja or gaja* measures. However, for cattle and horses, the height of the tables shall accord with the *dhvaja* or *vṛṣa* measures. The entrance, place for penning and place for feeding should accord respectively, with the *dhvaja*, *siṁha* and *vṛṣa* measures.[107]

600b. *Vāstupūjā.* I shall now set out the procedure for the worship of the building before it is occupied.

601. On husked rice spread in the centre of the house, draw ten lines, (west to) east, a cubit in the length, and ten lines (across south to) north, thus forming 81 squares.

602. Mark the 45 deities mentioned below (in the appropriate squares), 32 of them in the border squares and 13 inside.

603. Now, shall I state their names and places, in order. Here are the 32 deities (to be marked) from the northeast.

604-5a. (1) Śiva, (2) Parjanya, (3) Jayanta, (4) Indra, (5) Sūrya, (6) Candra, (7) Bhṛśa, (8) Ākāśa (Antarikṣaka), (9) Vāyu, (10) Pūṣā, (11) Nirṛti, (12) Gṛhākṣata, (13) Yama (Daṇḍadhara), (14) Gandharva, (15) Bhṛṅgarāja (Bhṛgurāja), (16) Mṛga, (17) Pitṛgaṇādhīśa (18) Dauvārika, (19) Sugrīva, (20) Puṣpadanta, (21) Varuṇa (Jalādhīśa), (22) Asura, (23) Śeṣa (? Śoṣa), (24) Pāpa (Rājayakṣmā), (25) Roga, (26) Nāga (Bhogi), (27) Mukhya, (28) Niśākara (? Bhallāṭa), (29) Soma, (30) Śūnya (? Sarpa), (31) Aditi, and (32) Diti. These are the 32 deities.

605b-7a. (As has already been noted, Brahmā occupies the nine squares at the centre). Outside (this *Brahmapada*), are the four deities, Āpaḥ, Sāvitra, Jaya and Rudra in the corners, beginning from northeast.

607b-9a. Again, in the alternate squares around *Brahmapada*, beginning from the east, are the eight deities Aryamā, Savitā, Vivasvān, Indra (vibudhādhipaḥ), Mitra, Rājayakṣmā, Pṛthvīdhara and Āpavatsa. These are the 55 deities (to be marked in the squares)[108].

609b-11. *Classification of the deities.* Āpas, Āpavatsa, Parjanya, Agni and Diti—these deities, form in order, (five) square-groups in all the corners. From among the deites, twenty are always two-square deities. Aryamā, Vivasvān, Mitra, Pṛthvīdhara who are on the four sides of Brahmā are three-square deities.

612. *Worship of the deities.* The knower of house construction should worship Brahmā and the two-square and three-square deities with the hymn of house-building and with *dūrvā*-grass, curds and rice grains.

613. With the chanting of the Brahmā-hymn shall be offered two white pieces of cloth. In due order shall be performed the invocation of the deity and the bestowing of honours.

614. Offering of three types of cooked rice shall be made, as musical instruments are played, (after which) betel shall be offered. Then shall the master of the house pray (as follows):

615. "O lord ! Deity of the dwelling ! Obeisance to you, who are intent on lying on the ground ! May you make my dwelling always rich in cash and grains."

616. Having prayed thus, he should pay the priest *dakṣiṇā* according to his mite and later feed the brāhmaṇas in consonance with his capability.

617. One who performs properly the worship of the dwelling in this manner, will attain health, birth of a son, wealth and grains.

618. On the contrary, one who enters (and dwells) in the residence without performing the worship of the dwelling, will have to endure disease, all kinds of difficulties and every calamity.

619. Enter not a house which is either doorless or roofless, or for which neither sacrifice has been made nor people fed, for such a house is a source of danger.

TRAVEL : YĀTRĀ

620. I shall now set down the dictums for travel for kings and all others whose time of birth is correctly known.

621. In the case of those whose time of birth is not known the attainment of the predicted result would be by chance, like letters carved out by a worm.[109] However, in their case also correct results can be predicted through (such methods of astrology as) *Praśna* and *Nimitta*.[110]

622. *Inauspicious days for travel.* Travel on sixth, eighth and twelfth (lunar days), 'empty' days (*viz.*, fourth, ninth and fourteenth), full moon and first of the bright fortnight will tend to penury and distress.

623. *Auspicious asterisms for travel.* Travel during the asterisms Anurādhā (Maitra), Punarvasu, (Aditi), Mṛgaśiras (Indu), Hasta (Arka), Revatī (Antya), Śravaṇa (Hari), Tiṣya (Puṣya) and Dhaniṣṭhā (Vasu) and also those other than the seventh, fifth, third and first, will yield one's desires.

624. *Śūla (Spear) on Week-days.* Travel not towards the east on Saturday and Monday, not southwards on Thursday, not westwards on Friday and Sunday, and not northwards on Wednesday and Tuesday.

625a. *Śūla on asterisms.* (Travel is inauspicious on account of) Śūla towards the four directions, from east, in order, on the asterisms: (east): Jyeṣṭhā; (south): Pūrva-Bhādrapadā; (West): Rohiṇī; and (north): Uttara-phālgunī.

625b. *Auspicious asterisms for all directions.* The (four) asterisms, Anurādhā (Mitra), Hasta (Arka), Puṣya (Ijya) and Aśvinī are prescribed for (travel) in all directions (*sarvadvāra*).

626-27a. *Blemish of Parigha-daṇḍa.* Seven asterisms each, counted from Kṛttikā (*Agnidhiṣṇya*) are prescribed for free (travel) in (the four) specific directions (*dig-dvāra*) (reckoned from east). The (diagonal) line from south-east to north-west is called *Parigha-daṇḍa*, ('cross-bar') which should not be crossed (in travel as above).[111] However on night travel south-east in the asterisms specified for the east, the same rule is applicable in the case of the other directions also (i.e., southern asterisms for southwest etc.).

627b. The *rāśis* of the directions (*dig-rāśi*) are Meṣa etc. counted in continuation 'in order' (from the east).[112] (One can cut the *parigha-daṇḍa* in travel if the *dig-rāśi* is favourable).

628a. *Lalāṭikā-yoga.*[113] (The lords of the directions are, in order: East: Sun; SE: Venus; South: Mars; SW: Rāhu; West: Saturn; NW: Moon; North: Mercury, and NE: Jupiter.)[114] When the lord of the direction (towards which one travels) is in the *lalāṭa yoga*, the traveller will not return home.

628b. The Sun in the *lagna* would be *lalāṭaga* (*i.e.*, in the *lalāṭa yoga*) for one travelling east.

629. Venus in the 12th and 11th houses would be *lalāṭaga* in the south-east. Mars in the 10th house would be *lalāṭaga* in the south.

630. Rāhu in the 9th and 8th houses would be *lalāṭaga* in the southwest. Saturn in the 7th house from *lagna* would be *lalāṭaga* in the west.

631. The Moon in the 6th and the 5th houses would be *lalāṭaga* in the north-west. Mercury in the 4th house would be *lalāṭaga* in the north.

632. Jupiter in the 2nd and 3rd houses would be *lalāṭaga* in the north-east. One who loves his life would keep away from *lalāṭa-yoga*.

633. *Effect of retrograde planets.* If the planet in the *lagna* at the commencement of the journey is retrograde, that will cause the defeat of the king; so also the *vargas* of those planets, if in retrograde motion.

634. *Effect of Ayana.* Travel in the direction of the (northward or southward) course of the Sun and the Moon is beneficial (if both move in the same direction). If otherwise (*i.e.*, if the Sun and the Moon move in opposite directions), the journey should be begun during the day (if the journey is in the direction of the Sun's motion) and during night (if the journey is in the direction of the Moon's motion).[115]

635. *Effect of Venus.* (Journey undertaken) when Venus has set will not be successful, while that against the course of Venus would end in failure. The adverse effect of going against Venus cannot be counteracted by other planets (even if they be in favourable positions).

636. However, persons belonging to the five gotras, Vasiṣṭha, Kāśyapa, Ātreya, Bhāradvāja and Gautama, will not be affected by travelling against (the course) of Venus.

637. Neither travel against Venus will affect their journeys within the same village, in famine, during wars between kings, and agitation against brahmins or kings.

638. Venus will defeat the purpose of the traveller if it is in debilitation (*nīca*), is in enemy planets' house, in retrogression or in defeat. On the other hand, if it is in exaltation, it will bring success.

639. *Prognostication based on one's janma-lagna.* (If travel is commenced) in the 8th house as reckoned from one's *janma-lagna*, or in the 8th *rāśi*, or in the 8th *lagna* or *rāśi* of one's enemy

or in the *rāśi* of the lords of the above, no doubt, the traveller will meet with his death.

640. However, if the lord of one's *janmalagna* and that of the 8th *lagna* are friendly, the blemishes resulting from the *janmarāśi* and 8th house will be counteracted.

641. Houses aspected or occupied by violent planets (*viz.*, Sun, Saturn and Mars) and those of a double nature (*viz.*, Gemini, Virgo, Sagittarius and Pisces) will bring about failure. Travel is not recommended during the rising of the 'firm' (*sthira*) asterisms (*viz.*, Uttaraphalgunī, Uttarāṣāḍha, Uttarabhādrapadā and Rohiṇī). On the other hand, houses aspected or occupied by benefic planets are good for travel.

642. During the five asterisms (actually four and a half) from Dhaniṣṭhā (Vasu) to the middle of Revatī (*antyārdha*), should not be done the following five things; (Dhaniṣṭhā): cutting grass, (Śatabhiṣak): collecting firewood; (Pūrvabhādrapadā): travel south; (Uttarabhādrapadā): constructing cots; and (Revatī): repairing houses.

643. (Of a king) who starts (for war) when the then *lagna* is his *janma-lagna* on *janma-rāśi*, or the lords of these two are in the then *lagna*, or the then *lagna* is the 3rd, 11th (*āya*), 6th (*ari*) or 10th house as reckoned from the above two, *viz.*, *janmalagna* and *janmarāśi*, the enemy will perish.

644. If a *śirṣodaya-rāśi* (sign rising with head)[116] is rising, the *dig-lagna* is in the *lagna*, or a beneficent *varga* is in the *lagna*, (at the start of the journey) then, too, the enemy will perish.

645. (If the journey is commenced by the king) at the enemy's *janmalagna*, *janmarāśi* or *death-lagna* (*i.e.*, 8th house), or in the *signs* occupied by the lords of the above, then, also, the enemy will perish.

646. (If a king starts) when Pisces is rising (*Mina-lagna*) or in the Pisces-division of another sign, his journey will be tortuous (and unsuccessful). Similarly, the sign Aquarius or its section (in any other sign) is not recommended for any type of journey.

647a. For (starting) a naval expedition or travel over the waters, the rising of 'watery' signs(*jala-rāśi*)[117] or the sections thereof in other signs, is auspicious.

647b-48. *The twelve Bhāvas (Houses)*. The twelve houses

(relating to any time) are designated as follows, commencing from the then rising sign (*udaya-lagna*: (1) *Mūrti* (Body), (2) *Kośa* (Treasury), (3) *Dhanvin* (Archer), (4) *Vāhana* (Vehicle), (5) *Mantra* (Counsel), (6) *Śatru* (Enemy), (7) *Mārga* (Way), (8) *Āyus* (Age), (9) *Manas* (Mind), (10) *Vyāpāra* (Occupation), (11) *Prāpti*(Attainment) and (12) *Aprāpti* (Non-attainment).[118]

649. The violent planets (*viz.*, Sun, Mars and Saturn), are destructive in all the houses except the 3rd and the 11th (*āpti*). Sun and Jupiter do not harm the 10th house (*Vyāpāra*). The benefic planets (*viz.*, Jupiter, Venus, Moon and Mercury) make all houses except the 6th (*Ari*) flourish.

650a. Venus, when set, does not benefit any house and the Moon does not benefit the 1st (*Mūrti*) and the 8th (*Mṛtyu*) houses.

650b-51. *Effect of Abhijit.* To travellers in all directions except to the south, the asterism Abhijit will fulfil all desires. This asterism is effectively beneficial even on a day which is not pure in relation to its five aspects (*Pañcāṅgaśuddhi*).[119]

652a. *Combination benefic for travel.* Multifarious are the combinations for travel (*yātrā-yoga*). I shall, therefore, set forth those combinations.

652b-53a. A combination would be effective, in the case of a brahmin, in view of the *lagna*; in the case of a kṣatriya in view of the asterisms and in view of the auspicious moment (*muhūrta*) in the case of others. So far as a thief is concerned, the omens count most.

653b-654a. In the *kendras* (quadrants, *viz.*, 1st, 4th, 7th and 10th houses) and *trikoṇas* (trines, *viz.*, 1st, 5th and 9th houses) a (benefic) *yoga* would be constituted by any one of Venus, Mercury and Sun. A double *yoga* (*adhi-yoga*) would be constituted by two of them, and by three a super *yoga* (*yogādhi-yoga*).

654b-55a. A *yoga* would afford protection (*kṣema*) and in an *adhiyoga* one would be successful. And, in *Yogādhiyoga*, protection, success and prosperity would result.

655b-56a. The Moon, Saturn and Sun occupying, respectively, the 10th (*Vyāpāra*), 6th (*Śatru*) and 1st (*Mūrti*), houses, will ensure the victory of the king who is setting out for war.

656b-57a. The enemy's forces will melt like lac in fire before a king who has marched when the planets Venus, Sun, Mercury, Saturn and Mars were occupying, respectively, the 1st (*lagna*), 7th (*Mārga*), 11th (*Āya*), 3rd and 6th (*Śatru*) houses.

657b-58a. The enemy's army will be transported to the abode of Death by a king who had set out when Venus occupied the 1st house (*lagna*) and the other planets, the 2nd (*Dhana*) and the 11th (*Āya*) houses.

658b-59a. A king who sets out when Venus is in the *lagna*, the Sun in the 11th (*Lābha*), and the Moon in the 2nd (*Bandhu*), will destroy the horde of enemies just as a lion would destroy a herd of elephants.

659b-60a. One who sets out when Venus is in exaltation, (the lord) of the *lagna* is also in exaltation and the Moon is in the 11th house would have all miseries destroyed as Keśava destroyed Pūtanā.[120]

660b-61a. If the *kendra* and *trikoṇa* houses are occupied by the benefic planets and the cruel planets occupy the 3rd, 11th and 6th houses, misfortune will seek out the traveller as a wanton woman (*abhisārikā*) (would go out in search of her lover).

661b-62a. In front of a king who sets out when Venus, Sun and Moon occupy, respectively, 1st, 6th and 12th (*randhra*) houses, the enemy would not stand firm, as (the instable) friendship between evil persons.

662b-63a. The enemy's land would be within the grasp of a king who sets out for battle when Saturn and Mars are strong in the 3rd (*trikhaḍa*) and 11th (*Āya*) houses.

663b-64a. If a king sets out when Venus, which is in exaltation, occupies the *lagna* and the Moon is in the 11th house (*lābhagata*), he will destroy his enemies, as Lord Śiva, with his bow Pināka, destroyed the Tripura demons.[121]

664b-65a. A king who sets out (for war) when Venus, which is in exaltation, occupies the *lagna*, and Jupiter occupies the 11th house (*lābhaga*) will kill his enemies just as God Kumāra killed the demon Tāraka.[122]

665b-66a. A king who marches (for battle) when Jupiter

occupies the *lagna*, *kendra* or *trikoṇa*, will consume his enemies just as fire burns out the forest.

666b-67a. Kings (who go for battle) when Mercury occupies the *lagna*, a benefic planet in the *kendra* and Venus (*Dhiṣṇya*) is in a (favourable) division (*upakula*), will dry up the enemies just as the rays of the Sun dry up the lake during summer.

667b-68a. A king going out when a benefic planet occupies a *trikoṇa* or *kendra* and the Sun or the Moon the 11th house (*Lābha*) will drive away the enemies just like the Sun drives out darkness.

668b-69a. A king will destroy his enemies just as fire burns cotton if benefic planets occupy their own houses, the *kendra*, *trikoṇas* and the 11th house (*Āya*) when he sets out.

669b-70a. A king who goes out (for war) when Moon occupies its own house, Jupiter is in a *kendra* and Śukra (*Mantrī*) is in the 7th house, will destroy all his enemies like the sacred *Pañcākṣara* destroys all sin.[123]

670b-71a. A king who sets out when Venus, which is in the *lagna*, occupies also the *vargottama* division in it,[124] will destroy the horde of enemies just as the remembrance of Hari (*Harismṛti*) would destroy all accumulated sin.[125]

671b-72a. (A king starting on an expedition) when the *kendra* is occupied by a benefic planet and the Moon in the *trikoṇa* is also in the *vargottama* section, will crush his enemies along with their clan just as Indra crushed the (flying) mountains.[126]

672b-73a. A king will kill his enemies just as the kite kills serpents, (if he starts for battle) when Jupiter occupies a friendly house and Venus occupies the *kendra* or *trikoṇa*.

673b-74a. (If a king) sets out when a benefic planet occupying the *kendra* or the *trikoṇa* is also in the *vargottama* division (of the *navāṁśa*), he will wash away his enemies just as (the sacred river) Ganges (Bhāgīrathī) washes off sins.[127]

674b-75a. Those kings who set out to conquer their enemies in the above yogas called 'Royal yogas' (*nṛpāhvaya*) (will be victorious and) their fire of anger would be put out by the tears of the enemy queens (who would be weeping on their fresh widowhood).

675b-76a. The tenth day of the bright fortnight of the month of Āśvina is called Vijaya. For those who go out to fight that day there might be truce, but never defeat.

676b-77a. For omens and portents the mental attitude is most important. Hence it is up to all serious-minded people to cultivate the mental attitude.

677b-78. One who desires to continue alive should not undertake a journey when a festival, the ceremonies of bestowing the sacred thread, marriage and installation of a deity, and pollution due to death or child birth (which is in force) has not been duly completed.

678b-79a. A king should not set out when there is going on a buffalo fight or a goat fight, a quarrel between his queens or they are in their monthly course, clothes have been soiled, and when angry words have been uttered.

679b-80a. *Food before setting out.* A king will conquer his enemies if he starts towards the (four) directions beginning with east after a repast, in order, of rice with ghee, cooked sesame balls, dish of fish, and rice cooked in milk with ghee added.

680b-81a. On the week-days beginning from Sunday, (he should set out) after taking a food of (1) *majjaka,* (2) rice cooked in rice, (3) *kañjika,* (4) water, (5) curd, (6) milk and (7) cooked sesame.

681b-84. A king will conquer his enemies if he sets out on the 27 asterisms beginning with Aśvinī, accompanied by his army consisting of elephants, chariots, horses and infantry, after having his repast on : (1) *Kulmāṣa,* (2) cooked sesame, (3) curd, (4) milk, (5) wine, (6) ghee, (7) water, (8) venison, (9) blood from the preceding, (10) rice cooked in milk, (11) bird's flesh, (12) Venison, (13) hare's flesh, (14) rice, (15) *priyaṅgu* (mustard), (16) rice cakes cooked in oil, (17) variegated egg, (18) fruits, (19) flesh of tortoise, (20) of *śvāvid* (21) of *godhā,* (22) of *śalyaka,* (23) sanctified food (*haviṣya*), (24) cooked rice-sesame mixture (*kṛśarānna*), (25) cooked gram, (26) balls of cooked *yava* flour, (27) dish of fish, (28) variegated cooked rice, and (29) curd rice.[128]

685-86a. *Procedure for the march.* The king should first offer oblations of sesame in the (sacred) fire and then worship the lord of direction (in which he is to proceed). He should then pay obeisance to the deities and brāhmaṇas and start after receiving their blessings. (The worship of the respective deities) should be according to the prescribed specifications of complexion, dress, unguents etc. and with the chanting of their *mantras*.

686b-87a. Indra should be worshipped as mounted on (his white elephant) Airāvata, resplendent with (his consort) Śacī, as holding the thunderbolt in his hand, as of golden complexion and as adorned with divine ornaments.

687b-88a. Agni should be worshipped (in an idol having seven hands, seven tongues, six faces, seated on a goat, with his consort Svāhā, red-complexioned, and holding the *palāśa* twig and sacrificial ladle as weapons.

688b-89a. Yama should be worshipped as holding the rod as a weapon, with red eyes, mounted on a buffalo, seated with his consort Śyāmalā, red-complexioned, looking up and beneficent.

689b-90a. Nirṛti should be worshipped as holding the sword and shield, blue-complexioned, mounted on a man as his vehicle, with raised hair, odd-eyed, with a high neck and lordly.

690b-91a. Varuṇa should be worshipped as holding the serpent-rope, yellow-complexioned, seated on a whale, with his consort Kālikā and adorned with gem-set ornaments.

691b-92a. Vāyu should be worshipped as the life of living beings, two-armed, holding a rod and riding a black antelope with his consort Añjanī.

692b-93a. Kubera should be worshipped as riding a horse, holding a pitcher in his hand, two-armed, golden-head, accompanied by his consort Citralekhā and lording over the (semidivine) Yakṣas and Gandharvas.

693b-94a. (Īśāna) should be worshipped as holding the bow Pināka in his hand, seated on the bull, with his consort Gaurī, as the best of all, fair-complexioned with the crescent moon on his crest and with his sacred thread formed by a serpent.

694b-95a. *Procedure when march is delayed.* In case a king cannot move off immediately for some reason or other, he should (still) make a start along with his flag, weapons, missiles and vehicles (exactly at the auspicious time determined as above).

695b-96a. The place up to which he should march (before stopping) shall be two hundred *daṇḍa*-measures, or forty or even twelve, (as convenient).

696b-97a. The king should not stay for more than seven days at one place and the others five days. In case of a longer delay (the ceremony of) starting should be made at another (auspicious) *lagna* (to be determined as before).

697b-98a. If there is untimely rain accompanied by lightning and thunder, or the three types of (major) natural calamities, the king should not move forward for three days.

698b-99. *Omens at the time of march.* The sounds of *ratnakuḍya*, she-jackal, crow and pigeon and of *ruru*, parrot etc. (if heard from) the left and of *potaki* and the bird *bharadvāja* from the right (are auspicious).

700. The forest-crow is inauspicious, while four-legged animals on the right are auspicious. And, so is being stared at by a chameleon, but not by one of black colour.

701. Hearing the boar, hare, *godhā*, cat and serpent being spoken about is auspicious but the sound made by them or seeing them is not auspicious. It is the contrary in the case of the monkey and the bear (which can be seen and heard but not spoken about).

702. The peacock, deer, mongoose, wild, crow and pigeon are auspicious at being seen at the commencement of a journey; the reverse is the case when one returns (home).

703. A corpse, without any mourning, if seen (at the commencement of a journey), will fulfil the objective of the journey. On the other hand, a corpse, accompanied by mourning, seen on the return, will turn one into a corpse.

704-6a. The following, if seen at the time of setting out, will destroy the aim (of the journey) : An outcaste, eunuch, bearded, drunk, vomit, medicine, one bathed in oil, fat, bone, skin, charcoal, diseased, molasses, cotton, salt, threat from an enemy, thirst, serpent, sterile woman, dwarf, saffron-clothed, clean shaven, hungry and the naked.

706b-9. On the other hand, the following seen/heard (at the start of a journey) will fulfil its aim : Blazing fire, horse, throne, brāhmaṇas, unguents, flowers, sanctified rice grain, umbrella, chowrie, swing, king, foodstuff, sugercane, fruits, bengal gram, cooked rice, honey, ghee, curd, cow, bull, fish, flesh, wine, white cloth, sound of conch, flags, courtesans, filled pitchers of water, gem, gold vessel, mirror, the sound of cattle drums, *mṛdaṅgas*, *paṭahas*, bells and lutes, and the auspicious chant of the Vedas.

710. If one sees an adverse omen for once, he might remember his personal deity (and proceed); if he sees it for a second time he might worship the brahmins (and proceed); if he sees it for the third) he must return home.

711. Sneezing heard from any side is inauspicious and the sneezing of cows is deadly. However, it is harmless if done by children, old men, diseased persons and persons suffering from cold.

712. *Binding on the conqueror.* The conqueror who has taken the enemy's capital should not touch another's woman, nor the wealth of brahmins and gods, nor the elephants, and horses, nor the distressed and the disarmed.[129]

RETURN TO THE CAPITAL

713. *Occupation of a new residence.* The first occupation of a newly built house should be done during the northward course of the Sun and after worshipping and offering oblations to the Building, the previous day.

714. (Occupying the house) during the months of Māgha, Phālguna, Vaiśākha and Jyeṣṭha is auspicious, while it is middling in the months of Mārgaśīrṣa (*Saumya*) and Kārttika.

715. Occupation (of the house) is auspicious in the asterisms of Mṛgaśiras (*Śaśi*), Puṣya (*Ijya*), Revatī, Śatabhiṣak (*Varuṇa*), Citra (*Tvāṣṭra*), Anurādhā (*Mitra*) and the fixed asterisms, (*viz.*, Uttaraphalguni, Uttarāṣāḍhā, Uttarabhādrapada and Rohiṇī), (care being taken to see that) Jupiter and Venus are visible (*i.e.*, not set).

716. Occupation is auspicious both during day and night, on week-days other than Sundays and Tuesdays, and *tithis* other than the empty lunar days (*riktā*, *viz.*, the 4th, 9th and 14th) and new moon.

717. Thus, at an auspicious time, on an auspicious day, in the forenoon, when both the Moon and the asterisms are strong,[130] in a fixed *lagna* (*i.e.*, when the 'fixed' signs, Taurus, Leo, Scorpio and Aquarius, are rising), and in a 'fixed' division of that *lagna*, not affected by deadly indications, characterised by blemishlessness.

718. When the benefic planets occupy the *trikoṇas* and the *kendras*, while the others occupy the 3rd, 11th and 6th houses, when the Moon occupies a house other than the 6th and the 8th from *lagna*.

719. In the birth asterism or birth-sign of the master or when they are in exaltation, the occupation will result in prosperity, otherwise misery and penury will result.

720. The wise man shall enter the charming and attractive house, accompanied by variegated and auspicious sounds (of music and instrumentation), with the Sun on the left and with a pot of water carried in front.

PROGNOSTICATION OF RAIN

721-22a. If (when the possibility of rains is considered) it is the advent of the rainy season, the Moon being in a 'watery sign' (*Jala-rāśi*)[131], in the *kendra* if it is the bright fortnight and is aspected by benefic planets, there would be heavy rains. On the other hand, if the aspection (of the Moon) is by malefic planets and if it is summer, there would only be a little rain.

722b. The same will occur also when Venus is characterised by the different things mentioned for the Moon.

723. If in the rainy season, the Moon occupies the seventh house from Venus and is aspected by benefic planets, or in the *trikoṇa* or 7th house from Saturn, there would be (immediate) rain.

724. Venus will produce immediate rain if it is near Mercury. If, however, the Sun occurs between the two, there would be no rain.

725. Venus in the five asterisms beginning with Maghā (*i.e.*, Maghā, Pūrvaphalgunī, Uttaraphalgunī, Hasta and Citrā) will cause rain, if the three asterisms Svāti, Viśākhā and Anurādhā follow (*i.e.*, in the regular motion of the planet). If

otherwise (*i.e.*, in the retrograde motion of the planet), there would be no rains.

726. Planets near the Sun cause rains when they are just before or behind the Sun (in their regular motion), but not in their retrograde motion.

727. Venus coursing on the left will bring about rains if it is moving south. There would be rains in the morning and in the evening as the Sun enters the asterism Ārdrā.

728. There would be increase in vegetation during the twilights (due to rains falling at these times) and there would be prosperity on all counts for people during nights. Light rains will then reduce prices and no rains will increase crops.

729. If there is a division in the rising of Ārdrā, there will, no doubt, be a calamity. If, however, the Moon, Jupiter or Venus is in a *kendra*, the calamity will not occur.

730. The Sun occupying the asterism Pūrvāṣāḍhā and surrounded by clouds, will cause noticeable rains on all days from Ārdrā to Mūla.

731-32a. If there had been rains on Revatī (*Pauṣṇabha*), there would be no rains for ten days. If Siṁha is divided, how can there be rains and if Karkaṭa is divided, how can there be no rains. If the rise of Kanyā is divided there would always be plenty of rains.

732b-33a. (Rains in) Uttarabhādrapada are indicative of vegetation in the beginning and Revatī of vegetation in the end. Rains in Bharaṇī are indicative of vegetation throughout, while Aśvinī is indicative of destruction of all vegetation.

733b-34a. When Venus is in the 7th sign ahead of Jupiter, there would be heavy rains, especially if the rainy season is at its height.

734b-35a. If a halo (*pariveṣa*) occurs around the Moon, extending to seven asterisms (from it), there would be rains, heavily interspersed with lightning and accompanied by the croaking of frogs.

735b-36a. If the clouds in the centre of the sky are inclined towards the west or towards the south, there would be rains shortly.

736b-37a. Cats pawing the ground, encrustations occurring on metal and children building bunds on the pathways are indicative of rains.

737b-38a. Moving rows of ants, profusion of glow-worms, serpents climbing up trees are indicative of (immediate rains).

738b-39a. The Sun and the Moon, at rising or setting, appearing dull or coloured like honey and if there be severe wind at that time, heavy showers would follow, immediately.

(KŪRMAVIBHĀGA : DIVISION OF THE GLOBE)

739b-40a. This land (of India) has been laid out as if divided into nine sections (*maṇḍala*) and set in a clockwise direction on nine parts (of the body)of a tortoise facing east.

740b-41. The (central) navel region consists of Antarveda and Pāñcāla. The face-region, in the east, is formed by the region forming Magadha and Lāṭa. The (right) fore-leg is formed by Strī-(rājya), Kaliṅga and Kirāta.

742. The (right) flank region consists of Avanti, Drāviḍa and Bhilla. The (right) hind leg region is constituted of by the countries of Gauḍa, Koṅkaṇa, Sālva, Āndhra, and Pauṇḍra.

743. The tail-region is formed by Sindhu, Kāśī, Mahārāṣṭra and Saurāṣṭra. The (left) foot-region consists of Pulinda, Cīna, Yavana and Gūrjara.

744. The (left) flank region is made up of Kuru, Kaśmīra, Mādreya and Matsya. The (left) foreleg region is constituted of by Khasa, Aṅga, Vaṅga, Vālhīka and Kāmboja.[132]

745. In the nine parts commencing with the navel place three asterisms each, beginning with *Kṛttikā.* When any of these stars is aspected by malefic planets, there would be misery (for the region represented by it), and when aspected by benefic planets, (there would be happiness for the region).

(UTPĀTA : PORTENTUOUS PHENOMENA)

746. (Portentuous phenomena are said to present themselves) when (idols of) deities (in temples) frequently dance, fall and burn; weep, sing, sweat and laugh;

747. Vomit fire, fumes, oil, blood and water; stand upside down and move from place to place.

748. Such freak occurrences seen in the idols of deities

(constitute portentuous phenomena). So also are mansions in the air (*gandharva-nagara*), asterisms becoming visible during day;

749. The fall of a mighty meteor and the raining of twigs, grass and blood, atmospheric smoke in mansions in the air, and earthquake during day or night;

750. Sparks without fire and flames without fuel, rainbow during night, *maṇḍūkaśikhara*, and white crow;

751. Sparks of fire emanating from cows, elephants, horses and camels, two-headed and three-headed animals being born from unnatural wombs.

752-53a. Mock-suns in the four directions along with the (real) Sun; jackals inhabiting villages; and the appearance of comets; and agitated flock of crows, in the night and pigeons during the day.

753b-54a. So also trees flowering out of time and seen bearing fruits likewise; they should first be cut down by the wise and then rites for averting the evil foretold should be performed.

754b-55a. Many are such portentuous phenomena which are destructive in the different regions. Some bring about death and some others fear from enemies.

755b-56a. An anthill covered with honey (at the nine places, *viz.*,) the top (and the eight directions from the east) is indicative, respectively, of fear, fame, death, depletion, reputation, happiness, misery, prosperity and loss of wealth.

756b-57a. O great brahmin! at the occurrence of all such portentuous phenomena, (if of an inauspicious nature), rites for averting evil should be performed with care as specified by the ritual texts.

757b-58. O brahmin! Thus has been narrated to you the discipline of *Jyotiṣa* in all its aspects. I shall now set out the exquisite science of metrics.

CHAPTER FIFTYSIX

1. he twelve *rāśis* or signs, of 30° each, which make up the zodiac (360°) are: (1) *Meṣa* (Aries); (2) *Vṛṣabha* (Taurus); (3) *Mithuna* (Gemini); (4) *Karkaṭaka* (Cancer); (5) *Siṁha* (Leo); (6) *Kanyā* (Virgo); (7) *Tulā* (Libra); (8) *Vṛścika* (Scorpis); (9) *Dhanus* (Sagittarius); (10) *Makara* (Capricorn); (11) *Kumbha* (Aquarius) and (12) *Mīna* (Pisces).

2. The twelve months are : (1) *Caitra*, (2) *Vaiśākha*, (3) *Jyeṣṭha*, (4) *Āṣāḍha*, (5) *Śrāvaṇa*, (6) *Bhādrapada*, (7) *Āśvina*, (8) *Kārttika*, (9) *Mārgaśīrṣa*, (10) *Pauṣa*, (11) *Māgha and* (12) *Phālguna*.

3. Very often the asterisms are referred to in the *Purāṇa* not by their proper names, but by names of the presiding deities of the relevant asterisms. The following table gives the asterisms with the presiding deities noted against each.

Asterisms and their deities

1. *Aśvinī*—Aśvins	2. *Bharaṇī*—Yama
3. *Kṛttikā*—Agni	4. *Rohiṇī*—Prajāpati
5. *Mṛgaśiras*—Soma	6. *Ārdrā*—Rudra
7. *Punarvasu*—Aditi	8. *Puṣya*—Bṛhaspati, Ijya or Tiṣya.
9. *Āśleṣā*—Sarpa, Ahi	10. *Maghā*—Pitṛs.
11. *Pūrva-phalgunī*—Bhaga	12. *Uttara-phalguni*—Aryamā
13. *Hasta*—Savitā	14. *Citrā*—Tvaṣṭā
15. *Svāti*—Vāyu	16. *Viśākhā*—Indrāgnī, Dvideva
17. *Anurādhā*—Mitra	18. *Jyeṣṭhā*—Indra
19. *Mūla*—Nirṛti	20. *Pūrva-āṣāḍha*—Āpaḥ.
21. *Uttara-āṣāḍha*—Viśvedevāḥ	22. *Śravaṇa*—Viṣṇu
23. *Dhaniṣṭhā* or *Śraviṣṭhā*—Vasus.	24. *Śatabhiṣak*—Varuṇa
25. *Pūrva-bhādrapada*—Aja Ekapād	26. *Uttara-bhādrapada*—Ahirbudhnya
	27. *Revati*—Pūṣā.

4. The lines which are corrupt in the *Purāṇa* are translated according to the parallel texts in the *Nāradīya-Saṁhitā*, 2. 27-8 (edn. Varanasi, 1905).

5. The conception here is as follows: In the 60-year cycle of Jupiter, let the several years be given the names of the 12 lunar months reckoned from Kārttika. Then, the first four months, Kārttika, Mārgaśīrṣa, Pauṣa and Māgha, will have two constellations each, the fifth month, Phālguna, will have three constellations, the next five months two constellations each and the eleventh and the twelfth months, Śrāvaṇa, Bhādrapada, Āśvina, will have three constellations each, thus completing the circle of 27 constellations. The names of the years mentioned in the following verses refer to the above special connotation.

6. Some portion omitted here by haplography, in the Venkatesvara Press edn. of the Purāṇa is rendered and inserted here from the parallel passage occurring in the *Nāradīya Saṁhitā*, (edn. Banares, 1905), 2.7.4.

7. The Venk. Press edn. has: "One in the face, two in the anus, three on the head". The emendation is from the parallal passage in the *Nāradīya-Saṁhitā* (edn. Banares, 1905), 2.8.3.

8. Thus, Nanda days are : I, 6, 11; Bhadrā : 2, 7, 12; Jayā : 3, 8, 13, Riktā : 4, 9, 14 and Pūrṇā : 5, 10, 15.

9-9a. On *Vyatīpāta* and *Vaidhṛta* see above, ch. 54, verses 174ff.

10. That is, water in which *āmalaka* (myrobalan) fruit has been boiled, in view of its medical properties.

11. This occurs for the reason that civil days and lunar days are of variable lengths and do not coincide. Thus, when a civil day is 24½ hrs. and the relevant lunar day is 24 hrs. and commences 15 minutes after the civil day, that civil day will contain, in it, three lunar days, the first for the first 15 minutes, the second for 24 hrs. and the third for the last 15 minutes. And, to correlate the lunar days with the civil days, one *tithi* will have to be expunged. The converse is the case when the lunar day happens to be longer than the civil day, which latter commences a little after the lunar day has commenced.

12. This happens because the lunar day and civil day can commence at different times. A lunar day which has commenced much later than the previous sunset will, naturally, extend to beyond sunset of the relevant civil day and a lunar day which has commenced earlier than the previous sunset will fall short of the next sunset.

13. Laṅkā (not modern Ceylon) is a hypothetical city conceived to be situated on the equator at the zero meridian of Indian astronomy. The time of sunrise at Laṅkā is taken as mean and local time calculated therefrom. On Laṅkā see above ch. 54, Verses 85-87.

14. For a detailed elucidation of the calculation of the lords of the hour and the rationale of the calculation thereof, see *Muhūrtacintāmaṇi* of Rāma-Daivajña, 1. 55-56, and the com. *Pīyūṣadhārā* by Govinda Jyotirvid (edn. N. S. Press, Bombay, 1945, pp. 49-50).

14a. For the asterisms comprising these groups, see above, under verses 177-79.

15. On the *Lāṅgala-cakra* or *Halacakra* and the citation of authorities in the matter, including the verses of Nārada translated here, see Com. *Pīyūṣadhārā* by Govinda Jyotirvid on the *Muhūrtacintāmaṇi* of Rāmadaivajña, (edn. N. S. Press, Bombay, 1945, pp. 73-74). *Lāṅgalacakras*, with 28 asterisms, including Abhijit, have also been conceived. For the description of such a *Cakra*, see *Narapatijayacaryā*, (*Kashi Skt. Ser.* 205, Varanasi, 1971), pp. 201-02.

16. For details about this serpent diagram and for further authorities in the matter, see the com. *Pīyūṣadhārā* by Govinda on the *Muhūrtacintāmaṇi* of Rāmadaivajña, 2. 29 (edn., N. I. Press, Bombay, 1945, pp. 72-73) and *Narapatijayacaryā*, *op. cit.*, pp. 202-03.

17. The *Yoga* as noted earlier (see fn. to Ch. 65, verse 124), is a period of variable length, during which the joint motion in longitude of the Sun

and the Moon amounts to the span of an asterism in the zodiac, *viz.*, 13° 20'. The 27 *yogas* contained in 360° are wholly of astrological significance, not astronomical. Being one of the five items (*pañcāṅga*) the *yoga* for each day would be specified in the Hindu almanacs.

18. Since 28 *yogas* are mentioned here, the asterism Abhijit has also to be reckoned along with the accepted 27 asterisms.

19. The reckoning is made thus: Consider the asterism prevailing on the relevant day. Count its number from Aśvinī on Sunday. Mṛgaśiras on Monday, etc. The *yoga* of that number (counted from Ānanda) will be prevailing on that day.

20. The fifteen lunar days are divided into five classes : 1. *Nandā* : 1, 6, 11; *Bhadrā* 2, 7,, 12; *Jayā* 3, 8, 13; *Riktā* : 4, 9, 14, *Pūrṇā*: 5, 10, 15. They have effects according to the meanings of the different terms. See above, vv, 136-37.

21. The twelve signs of the zodiac are classified into three: *Cara* or 'moving', being Meṣa, Karka, Tulā and Makara, *sthira* or 'fixed', being Vṛṣa, Siṁha, Vṛścika and Kumbha, and *dvisvabhāva* or double-natured', being Mithuna, Kanyā, Dhanu and Mīna.

22. The sign of the Zodiac (which corresponds also to the 'house' and 'mansion' in a horoscopic diagram) which the Moon occupies at the time of one's brith is termed the 'Birth-sign' (*janma-rāśi*) of the individual concerned. Other signs are counted taking the 'birth-sign', as the first.

23. If a planet is 'affected' (*Viddha*, 'pierced', *i.e.*, under *Vedha*) it might turn into a malignant sign even if it had been primarily benefic.

24. The presence of Saturn in the prohibited signs 9, 5, 4 and 12 is tolerated because, being the son of Sun, it would not turn malefic against its own father. The rule is that neither will a son be malignant towards his father nor a father towards his son. The rule is applicable in the cases also of Moon and Mercury, below.

25. The fifteen lunar days (*tithis*) are classified into five, being *Nandā*: 1, 6, 11; *Bhadrā*: 2, 7, 12, *Jayā*: 3, 8, 13; *Riktā*: 4, 9, 14; and *Pūrṇā*: 5, 10, 15 each possessing effects according to their nomenclature. See above, vv. 136-37.

26. *Parigha* is the 19th of the 27 *yogas* enumerated and described earlier (see ch. 54, verse 124).

27. *Viṣṭi* is one of the *Karaṇa* divisions of time, each of the duration of half a lunar day, enumerated and described above(ch. 56, verses 219b-220a.)

28. The planets are classified as Male: Sun, Mars, and Jupiter; Female: Moon and Venus; and Neuter: Mercury and Saturn.

29. *Puṁ-savana* ('Male production rite') and *Sīmantonnayana* (parting of the hair) are two Vedic rites performed so that the child born is male and the delivery be safe.

30. The lords of the months of pregnancy are : 1st month: Venus; 2nd, Mars; 3rd Jupiter; 4th, Sun; 5th Moon; 6th Saturn; 7th Mercury; 8th, the lord of the rising sign at the time of conception; 9th Moon; and 10th Sun. *Cf.*, *Muhūrtacintāmaṇi* of Rāma, 5.9.

31. The male asterisms are: Aśvinī, Bharaṇī, Puṣya, Āśleṣā, Maghā,

Uttaraphalgunī, Svāti, Viśākhā, Jyeṣṭhā, Mūla, Pūrvāṣāḍha, Uttarāṣāḍha, Śravaṇa and Pūrvabhādrapada.

32. That is, excluding the three further groups, *viz.*, *tīkṣṇa* ('sharp') *ugra* ('violent') and *miśra* ('mixed'). On the classification of the asterisms into seven groups having qualities indicated by their nomenclature, see above, under verses 177-79.

33. *Dinakṣaya* (*Tithikṣaya*, 'omitted lunar day', lit. loss of a lunar day) refers to the lunar day which is completely contained within a civil day (the lunar day being shorter than the civil day) and, so, is left out of count. On this, see above, ch. 54, verse 71 and ch. 56 verses 153b-54a and the notes thereon.

34. The *Gṛhyasūtras* are auxiliary texts appertaining to the different Vedas, prescribing the *gṛhya* 'household' rituals of an orthodox Hindu, like the five daily sacrifices (*mahāyajñas*), the sixteen sacraments (*ṣoḍaśasaṁskāras*) like conception, birth rites, tonsure, *upanayana*, marriage etc. Each Veda has its own *Gṛhyasūtra*, which the followers of the different Vedas adopt in performing their rituals.

35. For the asterisms recommended for sowing, see above Verse 186. The asterisms recommended are those of the *mṛdu*, *sthira* and *kṣipra* groups and Maghā, Svātī, Dhaniṣṭhā and Mūla.

36. For this a triple cord is plaited out of the *mauñjī* or *darbha* grass and is ceremonially used in three loops round the waist of the boy who is invested with the sacred thread (*yajñopavīta*) and initiated into Vedic study (*upanayana*).

37. The *Vedāṅgas* are auxiliary texts which instruct in the correct recitation and right understanding of the Vedas and prescribe the exact performance and punctual observation of Vedic ritual. Each Veda has its own auxiliary texts which fall into six categories (*ṣaḍvedāṅgas* dealing respectively with : (1) *Śikṣā* (Phonetics), (2) *Vyākaraṇa* (Grammar), (3) *Nirukta* (Etymology), (4) *Chandas* (Metrics), (5) *Jyotiṣa* (Astronomy) and (6) *Kalpa* (Ritual), divided into three—*Gṛhya* 'household ritual', *Śrauta*, sacrificial ritual' and *Śulba* 'construction of altars'.

38. The lords of the Vedas are: *Ṛgveda.* : Jupiter, *Yajurveda*: Venus; *Sāmaveda* : Mars, and *Atharvaveda*: Mercury: See above, verse 351.

39. These blemishes are listed in the following verse :

Ulko-rvīcalan-oparāga-gulikāḥ ṣaṣṭhā-ṣṭam-āntyendv-asad-
dṛṣṭārūḍhavimuktarāśi-sitadṛk-sāyāhnasandhyādayaḥ |
gaṇḍānt-oṣṇa-viṣaṁ sthiraṁ ca karaṇaṁ riktā-ṣṭamī-viṣṭayo
lāṭaikārgala-vaidhṛtāhiśirasaḥ sarvatra varjyā amī ||

Muhūrtapadavī of Māthūr Nampūtiri (Ed. Panchangam Press, Kunnamakulam (Kerala), 1955), Verse 1.

The days on which these 'blemishes of day' (*nityadoṣa*) occur should be rejected in fixing the date for any auspicious rite and if they cannot be avoided, due expiation prescribed for obviating the evil effect of each of these blemishes has to be duly performed before commencing the auspicious rite.

These 'blemishes of the day' are: The four blemishes on account of portentuous natural phenomena (*utpāta*), being : (1) *Ulkā* (meteor), (2) *Urvīcalana* (earthquake), (3) *Uparāga* (eclipse), (4) Gulika; the five blemishes due to the positions of the planets, being (5) Moon in the 6th house, (6) in the 8th house and (7) in the 12th house, (8) *Asad-dṛṣṭārūḍhavi-mukta-rāśi* (the house which has been aspected, occupied or left by the evil planets *viz*., Sun, Mars, Saturn and Rāhu, (9) Aspecting by Venus (*Sitadṛk*); one blemish due to the time of the day, being (10) *Sāyāhnasandhyā* (dusk); three blemishes due to asterisms, being (11) *Gaṇḍānta*, (12) *Uṣṇa-(śikhā)*, (13) *Viṣa*; four blemishes of lunar days (*tithi*), being (14) *Sthira-karaṇa*, (15) *Riktā*, (16) *Aṣṭamī* and (17) *Viṣṭi-(karaṇa)*; and four blemishes due to the positions of the Sun and the Moon, being (18) *Lāṭa*, (19) *Ekārgala*, and (20) *Vaidhṛta*, and (21) *Ahiśiras*.

40. The *anadhyāya* or non-study days are: 1st, 8th, 14th and 15th days of the dark and bright fortnights; 2nd day of Jyeṣṭha, 10th of Āṣāḍha, 4th and 12th of Māgha, all in the bright fortnight; and the days of *saṅkrānti*, when the Sun transits from one sign to another.

41. *Viṣṭi* is one of the half-*tithi* durations of astrological importance into which the lunar month is divided, on which see above, ch. 54, vv. 126-27 and the notes thereon.

42. On *Mauñjī-bandhana*, an auxiliary ceremony of *Upanayana*, see above, vv. 348 ff.

43. Prognostication by *āya* is more commonly made in the case of buildings where the length of the bulding is multiplied by its breadth and the product divided by 8, and the remainders are called *āya*, on the basis of which future is foretold. Thus, Remainder 1. called *Dhvaja* foretells, for the master of the house, fame; 2. called *Dhūma*, sorrow; 3. *Siṁha*, victory, 4. *Śvā*, enmity, 5. *Vṛṣa*, wealth; 6. *Gardabha*, penury; 7. *Gaja*, happiness, and 8. *Dhvāṅkṣa*, illness.

44. *Samāvartana* means literally 'return', here, 'return of the Vedic student to his own house from his teacher's house after successfully complet-ing his studies. At the ceremony conducted on the occasion, the grass-belt (mauñji) that he would be wearing throughout his studentship is removed and he is given a ritual tonsure (*muṇḍana*), called generally, *go-dāna* (*go*—hair, *dāna*—cutting), and, thus, prepared for his entering the next stage of life, namely, that of the householder.

45. For the *riktā* days, see above under verses 126—37a and the notes thereon.

46. On *dinakṣaya* ('omitted day'), see above vv. 153b—54a and ch. 64, verse 71, and the notes thereon.

47. This half verse which is needed in the context, but which is not to be found in the Venkateswara Press edn. of the Purāṇa, has been restored from the corresponding section of the *Nāradīya-Saṁhitā*, 27. 4.

48. The odd numbers are considered males and the even numbers female.

49. Of the seven planets, Sun, Mars and Jupiter are males, Moon and Venus are females, and Mercury and Saturn eunuchs.

50. The 'five constituents' (*pañca-aṅga*) of a day, on the basis of which the nature of the day is determined in Indian astrology, are *nakṣatra* (asterism), *tithi* (lunar day in the bright or dark fortnight) *vāra* (week-day), *yoga* and *karaṇa*. Since Indian almanacs mention these five constituents for every day of the year, these almanacs are, by extension, called *Pañcāṅgas*.

51. It may be noted that Venus rises in the west after its invisibility in its right motion (*krama-mauḍhya*) and in the east after its invisibility in its retrograde motion (*vakra-mauḍhya*). It may also be noted that since Jupiter moves outside the orbit of the Earth, it becomes invisible only in its right motion, and not in its retrograde motion.

52. The idea is this : The grouping of the *Jyeṣṭha* month, *Jyeṣṭha* daughter and *Jyeṣṭha* son (*jyeṣṭha-trayam*), is not auspicious in marriage. To marry off a jyeṣṭha daughter or a *jyeṣṭha* son in the *jyeṣṭha* month, in which case a group of two jyeṣṭhas is formed, is middling. What is auspicious is to have only one *jyeṣṭha* at a time. In other words, it would be auspicious to marry off the eldest daughter and an eldest son separately and in months other than *Jyeṣṭha*.

53. On these days, see above verses 153b-54a and the notes thereon.

54. On *Vyatīpāta* and *Vaidhṛti* and *Parigha*, being the 17th, 19th and 23rd of the 27 yogas, see above, ch. 54 verse 124.

54a. *Vedha* (lit. 'piercing', *viddha* 'pierced') refers to the mutual affliction between pairs of asterisms that happen to be at the ends of the lines in the *Pañca-śalākā-cakra* (five-spike-diagram) and *Sapta-śalākā-cakra* ('seven-spike-diagram') which might be represented as follows:—

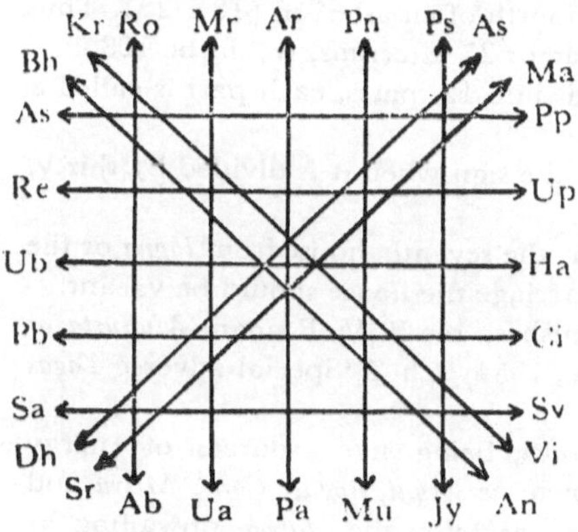

Pañca-Śalākā-Vedha-Cakra

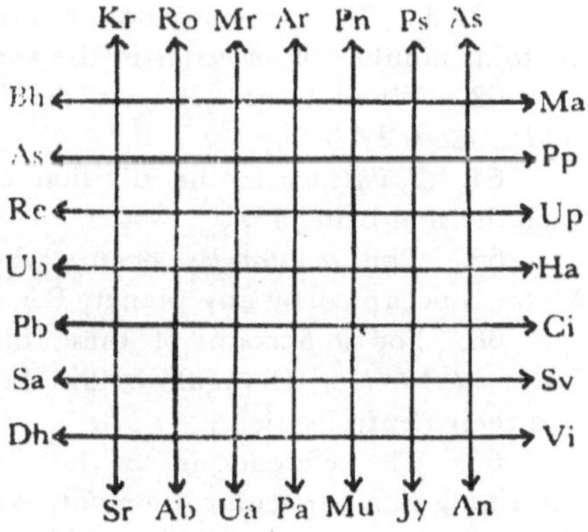

Sapta-Śalākā-Vedha-Cakra

In the first diagram, asterisms such as *Aśvini* and *Pūrvāṣāḍhā* and *Bharaṇī* and *Anurādhā*, and in the second diagram *Bharaṇī* and *Maghā*, and *Kṛttikā*, and *Śravaṇa* are mutually afflicted. The former 'affliction' is to be considered for the entrance of the bride into the groom's house, offer and acceptance of the bride and marriage, and the latter for other allied rituals.

55. The planets, on account of certain positions in the heavens, and the 'houses' (*bhāvas*) on account of their being occupied or aspected by certain planets aequire certain sources of strength and weakness, called *graha-bala* 'planetary potency' and *bhāva-bala*, 'potency of the house'.

56. *Gocara* See above, under vv. 271-82. for prediction based on *Gocara* see Ch. 34, '*Gocara* or Results of transits' in B. V. Raman, *Hindu Predictive Astrology*, Bangalore, 7th edn., 1054.

57. *Vedha*, see above, verse 426.

58. *Aṣṭavarga* or *Aṣṭakavarga* refers to the eight sources of energy which each of the seven planets and the ascendent (*lagna*) as the eighth attain as a result of its own transit from *rāśi* to *rāśi* and its being aspected by the other seven. For details see Ch. 18. The *Aṣṭakavarga* system: Strength for transiting planets, in B. V. Raman, *Hindu Predictive Astrology*, (Bangalore, 7th edn., 1959).

59. *Rūpa* forms the unit of measuring the potency of planets and houses.

60. By *Horā* is meant the strength of the 'planetary hour'. Each hour of a week-day is governed by a different planet in a certain order, the first hour being governed by the lord of the day. On 'Planetary hours' and a table thereof, see B. V. Raman, *Muhūrta or Electional Astrology*, Bangalore, 2nd edn., 1954, pp. 215-16.

61. *Drekkāṇa* (decanate)). The zodiac of 360° is divided into 36 *drekkāṇas*, each extending the 10°. Thus, each sign will contain three *drekkāṇas*. On this see Ch. 36. 'Drekkāṇas and stellar influences', in B. V. Raman, *Hindu Predictive Astrology*, Bangalore, 7th edn. 1959.

62. *Navāṁśa* is the division of the sign (30°) into 9 parts, each extending to 31/3°. This corresponds to one-fourth of an asterism (13 1/2°). Thus the total number of *navāṁśas* in the zodiac or 27 asterisms, would be 108.

63. When a sign (30°) is divided into 12 parts, each part is called a *dvādaśāṁśa* ś(2 1/2°).

64. *Triṁśāṁśa* is the division of the sign when it is divided by thirty, each division being 1°.

56. The *Jāmitra-doṣa* occurs when the seventh house from *lagna* or the Moon is occupied by any planet. For marriage the house should be vacant.

66. For an account of these blemishes, see B. V. Raman, *Muhūrta or Electional Astrology*, (Bangalore, 2nd Edn., 1954) Ch. 5 'Special adverse *Yogas* and their neutralisation'.

67. The reference is to the *Pañcaka*, being five sources of energy pertaining to a particular moment, known as *Agni*, *Roga*, *Cora*, *Mṛtyu* and *Rāja*. The numbers of the *tithi*, *vāra*, *nakṣatra* and *lagna* prevailing at the moment under consideration are added up and divided by 9. If the remainder is 1, it is *Mṛtyu-Pañcaka*, indicative of danger; if 2. *Agni*, indicative of risk of fire; if 4. *Rāja*, bad results; if 6. *Cora*, evil happenings; and if 8. disease. Remainders 0, 3, 5 and 7 are *niṣpañcakas*, free from the blemish of *Pañcaka*, and so such moments are auspicious.

68. The *Ṣaḍvarga* is a group of six independent divisions of the zodiac

and the day, each being used differently to read the future. The six vargas are : *Rāśi, Horā, Drekkāṇa, Navāṁśa, Dvādaśāṁśa* and *Triṁśāṁśa*, the second being a division of the day and the others of the Zodiac, prognostications being made in a different way for each. (For details, see B. V. Raman, *Hindu Predictive Astrology*, op. cit., pp. 92-97).

69. On the classification of the lunar days into *Nandā, Bhadrā, Jayā, Riktā* and *Pūrṇā*, see above, under verse 136.

70. *Upacaya* is a term for the 3rd, 6th, 10th and 11th signs from the *lagna*.

71. The *muhūrta* referred to here is the time-measure of 2 *nāḍikās* (48 minutes.). The *muhūrtas* to be rejected in the seven week-days are: On Sunday, the 14th; Monday 8th and 12th; Tuesday, 4th and 11th; Wednesday (the *muhūrta* called *Abhijit*); Thursday, 12th and 13th; Friday, 4th and 8th and Saturday, 1st and 2nd, as reckoned from sunrise on the several days.

72. Tuesdays and Saturdays are to be invariably avoided for marriages.

73. On *Ekārgala* see above, under verses 214b-218a.

74. On *Vedha* 'Affliction' add *viddha* 'afflicted', in relation to asterism, see above, note under verse 426.

75. *Pañcagavya* (a mixture of five products of the cow, being milk, curd, ghee, urine and dung), is used as a holy liquid for the religious bathing of idols during worship.

76. *Vargottama-navāṁśakas.* Of the *navāṁśakas*, the first *navāṁśaka* in a *sthira-rāśi* , the fifth in a *cara-rāśi* and the ninth in a *dvisvabhāva-rāśi* are especially benefic and so are called *vargottama-navāṁśakas.* On *navāṁśaka*, see above note under verse 430 and on the division of the *rāśis* as *sthira* etc., see above under verse 430b.

77. On *Vaidhṛti*, see above, under ch. 64, verses 174 ff.

78. The *kendra* (quadrant) positions in a 12-member chart are the 1st, 4th, 7th and 10th.

79. For the diagram, see above, under verse 426.

80. 'Lame' : Kumbha (Aquarius) during day time and Mīna (Pisces) during night.

'Blind' : Siṁha (Leo), Aja (Aries) and Vṛṣa (Taurus) during day-time and Kanyā (Virgo), *Mithuna* (Gemini) and *Karkaṭa* (Cancer) during night. 'Deaf' : *Tulā* (Libra) and *Vṛścika* (Scorpio) during day and *Makara* (Capricorn) and *Dhanus* (Sagittarius) during night.

81. These are called *kūṭa-s*.

82. The 27 asterisms are divided into three *gaṇas* (groups), called respectively, *Daiva* (divine), *Mānuṣa* (human) and *Rākṣasa* (demoniac), the persons born on the different asterisms possessing the innate qualities expressed by these terms. The agreement in *gaṇa* indicates compatability in temperament between the couple.

83. *Yoni-kūṭa* indicates sexual compatibility.

84. *Varṇa* (caste) is indicative of the spiritual and egoistic development in a person.

85. This would mean that, Aries, Leo and Sagittarius are Kṣatriyas, Taurus, Virgo and Capricorn are Vaiśyas, and Gemini, Libra and Aquarius are Śūdras.

86. Conversely if the caste of male's *rāśi* is the same or higher than that of the female's *rāśi*, it is auspicious.

87. The translation here does not follow the textual verses. *Rajju* or *Nāḍī Kūṭa* is extremely important in matching horoscopes, for it indicates the compatibility in physiological and hereditory temperaments. the three columns, shown below, represent the three humours (*nāḍī-s*), *Vāta, Pitta* and *Kapha* :

Vāta	*Pitta*	*Kapha*
Aśvinī	Bharaṇī	Kṛttikā
Ardrā	Mṛgaśiras	Rohiṇī
Punarvasu	Puṣya	Āśleṣā
Uttaraphal.	Pūrva-phal.	Maghā
Hasta	Citrā	Svāti
Jyeṣṭhā	Anurādhā	Viśākhā
Mūla	Pūrva-āṣā.	Uttara-āṣā.
Satabhiṣak.	Dhaniṣṭhā	Śravaṇa
Pūrvabhādra	Uttarabhādra:	Revatī

Persons of the same humour (*nāḍī*) would not be mutually compatible, especially those under the *Pitta* humour.

88. Threc lines are left out in the Venk. Press edn. of the *NP*. Their rendering is added here from the corresponding verses in the *Nārada-Saṁhitā*, 27. 141-42.

89. This *muhūrta* is called *Godhūlikā* because it occurs at dusk when cows return home from pasture, happy and expectant, running and raising a cloud of dust.

90. The reference is to the complete uprooting by Śiva of the three demoniac cities (*Tripura*) with a single shot of His arrow. For the story and references, see *Puranic Encyclopaedia*, pp. 793-94.

91. *Gaṇḍa*, Lit. 'neck' which is the junction of the head and the body, is of different kinds, *e.g.*, the junction of the asterisms, *tithis*, *lagna*, *yogas*, *karaṇas*, *years*, *ayanas*, seasons, months, fortnights, days and nights. Some of these, specified in astrological texts, are extremely inauspicious and it is these that are referred to here. On *Gaṇḍa* see also above, verses 448-50a.

92. *Atiśukra* (*Pratiśukra*) or 'journey opposed to Venus' will occur if Venus appears in the sky opposite or to the south of the direction in which the bridal party has to travel.

93. On *Pañcaka*, see above under verse 441.

94. For the method to determine the directions, see above ch. 64, vv. 128-31.

95. The *ṣaḍvarga* is primarily the divisions of the circle, *viz.*, *Rāśi*, *Horā*,

Drekkāṇa, Navāṁśa, Dvādaśāṁśa and *Trīṁśāṁśa.* See note under verse 430b, above.

96. On this see *Bṛhatsaṁhitā*, of Varāhamihira, 53. 42 ff.

97. On the bloodvessels (*śirā*) and vital points (*marmasandhī*). see *Bṛhatsaṁhitā, op. cit.*, 53. 63-65.

98. Thus, (1, 5) eagle and serpent, (2, 6) cat and rat, (3, 7) lion and elephant, (4, 8) dog and deer are enemies by nature.

It is stated elsewhere that these *vargas* have the values, called *śaras* ('arrows') respectively, as (1) 8, (2) 5, (3) 6, (4) 4, (5) 7, (6) 1, (7) 3 and (8) 2 (*Narapati-jayacaryā - Svarodaya* by Narapati (*Kashi Skt. Ser.*, No. 205, Varanasi, 1971, p. 271). These numbers are used as the basis for different types of computations for the prognostication of different matters. These numbers have been used for the calculations in the next two verses of the *Purāṇa*.

pa-varga 1 Rat	ya-varga 3 Elephant	śa-varga 4 Deer
ta-varja 7 Serpent		a-varga 8 Eagle
ṭa-varja 4 Dog	ca-varga 6 Lion	ka-varga 5 Cat

N ↑

99. The *Varga* of the village and that of the owner are found by adding up the values of the individual consonants and the vowels in their names. Thus, if Gokula is the name of the village, its *varga* would be 5+8—5—8—3—8=37. For an owner by name Rāma, the *varga* would be 3—8—1 +8=20. The respective remainders, on dividing the *vargas* are 5 and 4. Since 5 is greater than 4, Gokula will not be suitable for Rāma to construct his residence.

100. For a further reading on the basis of these *varga*-numbers, see below, verses 589b-60a, and the notes thereon.

101. Different calculations the adopted in this behalf. For some of these, see *Muhūrtacintāmaṇi, op. cit*, 12. 3-4 (pp. 415-17) 12. 11-12 (pp. 422-24).

102. On *ṣaḍvarga*, see above, under verse 430b.

103. On the classification of the asterisms, see above, verses 177-79.

104. This method, called *Chandaḥ-prastāra* or *Chandaś-citi*, has been set out both in mathematical texts like Bhāskara's *Līlāvatī, Gaṇitapāśavyavahāra*, 261-66, Edn. K. V. Sarma, *op. cit.*, pp. 459-64 and Kedārabhaṭṭa's *Vṛttaratnākara* (6. 1-8). Thus, the *prastāra* for the 6-lettered foot of the *Gāyatrī* metre would be given by the arrangement of the syllables as 6/1, 5/2, 4/3, 3/4, 2/5, 1/6, giving the results 6, 15, 20, 15, 6, 1, respectively, when one long syllable, two long syllables etc. occur, making a total of 63. When the single case with all short syllables is added, the total possible number of arrangements of the letters would be 64.

105. The allocation of the rooms in the sixteen directions differs, to

some extent, in the different texts. For the different authorities on the subject, see *Muhūrtacintāmaṇi, op cit.*, 12. 21, pp. 432-33.

106. This verse which does not have any significance here, should actually come after verse 562, being a continuation of the subject of *Digvarga-yoni*, making use of the *Varga*-numbers. For this continuity, see *Narapati-jayacaryāsvarodaya, op. cit.*, pp. 271-73, where readings are made on the basis of these birds, beasts, etc. in the *Āyacakra*.

107. *Dhvaja, gaja, vṛṣa*, etc. are comparative measures derived by dividing the area of a building by eight. The divisions are used for various other purposes. On this see *Muhūrtacintāmaṇi, op, cit*, 12. 4-5, pp. 417-18.

108. The distribution of the deities in the 81-square diagram (*Vāstu-cakra*) might be represented thus :

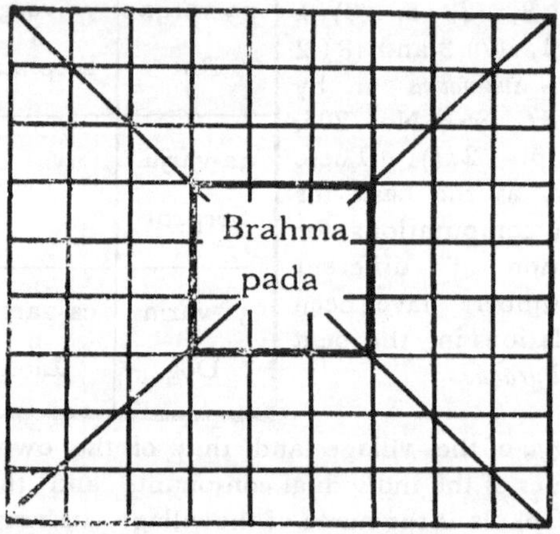

109. The reference is to the *ghuṇākṣara-nyāya*, the instance of the mark of gnawing of a worm on a piece of wood resembling a letter, by chance.

110. These are branches of astrology for the prediction of future events on the basis of *Praśna* or questions articulated by an enquirer, and the time, manner and circumstances under which they are put. *Nimitta* or omenology relates to prognostication based on natural and other phenomena at the time under consideration.

111. This travel diagram (*Yātrā-cakra*) could be represented as follows:

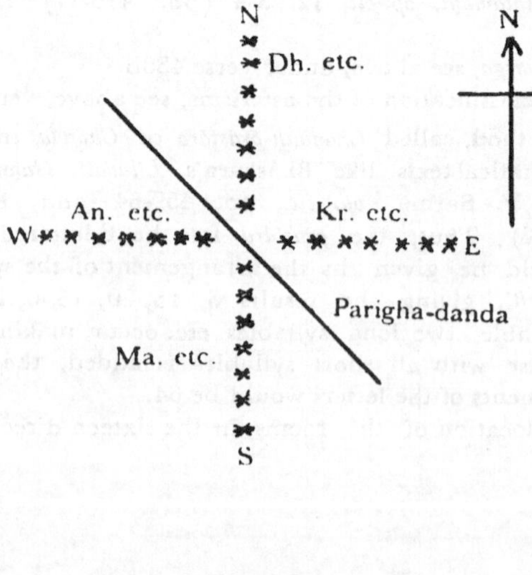

112. The *dig-rāśis* reckoned in this manner would be : East: Meṣa, Siṁha and Dhanu; South : Vṛṣabha, Kanyā and Makara; West : Mithuna, Tulā and Kumbha; and North : Karka, Vṛścika and Mīna.

113. A *lalāṭikā-yoga* would occur if the lord of the direction which a traveller takes, occupies certain specified house in relation to the *lagna* at the time at which the journey is commenced.

114. This information which is necessary here, but is omitted in the *Nārada Purāṇa* is taken from elsewhere.

115. Since the motions(*ayana*)of the Sun and the Moon are only towards the north and the South of the Zodiac, while the cardinal directions include also east and west, it is explained in astrological texts that 'north' takes in also east, and 'south' takes in also west.

116. The twelve signs (*rāśis*)are classified into three types in consideration of the posture presented by the figures of the animals etc. in which they appear, as upright, inverted etc. Thus, the *Sīrṣoday-rāśis* (signs rising with the head up, *i.e.* upright) are : Leo, Virgo, Libra, Scorpio and Aquarius. The *Pṛṣṭhodaya-rāśis*(signs rising with their hind parts, *i.e.*, inverted) are : Aries, Taurus, Cancer, sagittarius and Capricorn. The *Ubhayodaya-rāśis* (signs of a combined nature)are Pisces and Gemini.

117. In the classification of the signs on diverse bases, the 'watery' signs are Cancer, the latter half of Capricorn and Pisces.

118. The twelve 'houses' are given below under their better-known designations, with those aspects of man's life to which they are related:

1. *Tanu-bhāva* (Body, build, appearance).
2. *Dhana-bhāva* (Wealth, property, family, vision, relatives).
3. *Bhrāṭṛ-bhāva* (Brothers, intelligence, strength, help, army).
4. *Sukha-Bhāva* (Happiness, vehicles, education, friends, residence).
5. *Putra-bhāva* (Children, fame, pregnancy).
6. *Śatru-bhāva* (Enemy, debts, disease, misery).
7. *Kalatra-bhāva* (Wife or husband, death, gambling).
8. *Āyur-bhāva* (Longevity, gifts, intrigues, war, victory and defeat).
9. *Dharma-bhāva* (Piety, god, teacher, father, travels, fortune).
10. *Karma-bhāva* (Occupation, Philosophical bent, activity).
11. *Āya-Bhāva* (Income, profits, gains).
12. *Vyaya-Bhāva* (Expenditure, loss, salvation).

119. These five aspects of a day are its *tithi* (lunar day), *vāra* (week day), *nakṣatra* (asterism), *yoga* and *karaṇa* (see above notes on cha. 54, vv 124-27). A day is declared as *pañcāṅga-śuddha* (pure in relation to its five aspects). When these, individually, are in combination, are blemishless.

120. The reference is to the episode in the *Bhāgavata Purāṇa* (*Skandha* 10) describing how Lord Kṛṣṇa (Keśava) residing in Gokula during his childhood, destroyed the demoness Pūtanā who had been sent out by king Kaṁsa to kill him.

121. The episode of god Śiva destroying three demonic cities, *Tripuras*, and the three demons occupying them, with the shooting of a single arrow

from his bow, forms the basis of a lengthy episode described in the *Padma-Purāṇa*, chs. 13-14, and 33-34,*Bhāgavata*, *Sk.* 7, chs. 31-34.

122. For a detailed account of the devastation of the world by the demon Tāraka and the destruction of that demon by Kumāra (God Skanda) born of the union of God Śiva and goddess Pārvatī, daughter of Himavān, see *Skanda Purāṇa*, *Sambhava-Khaṇḍa*, *Mahābhārata*, *Vanaparva*, ch. 223 *Anuśāsana-parva*, ch. 85, *Vālmīki-Rām*, Bāla. ch. 36. The episode forms the basis of *Kumārasambhava*, a long poem in Sanskrit by Kālidāsa.

123. On the efficacy of this five-syllabled *mantra*, *na-maś-śi-vā-ya*, 'obeisance to Lord Śiva', see the section on *Pañcākṣaramāhātmya*, in the *Śivapurāṇa*, *Vāyavīya-saṁhitā*, Chs. 82-84.

124. The *Vargottamāṁśa-s*, being the most effective section in the *navāṁśa*-division of the rāśis are the following : (1) The first *navāṁśa* in the case of the 'Moveable signs' (*cara-rāśis*), *viz.*, Aries, Cancer, Libra and Capricorn; (2) the fifth *navāṁśa* in the case of the 'Fixed signs' (*sthira-rāśis*), *viz.*, Taurus, Leo, Scorpio and Aquarius, and (3) the ninth *navāṁśa* in the case of the 'Double-natured signs' *Dvisvabhāva rāśis*), *viz.*, Gemini, Virgo, Sagittarius and Pisces.

125. There are several episodes in the Purāṇas to vindicate the efficacy of uttering the name of Hari (Viṣṇu). For example, see the story of Ajāmila, the depraved brāhmaṇa who gained salvation at the utterance of the name of Viṣṇu (*Bhāgavata* P. *Sk.* 8, Ch. 1).

226. On Indra's cutting of the wings of the destructive flying mountains *cf.*, the episode narrated by Mt. Maināka to Hanumān, *Vālmīki-Rāmāyaṇa*, *Sundarakāṇḍa*, ch. 1.

127. On the episode of Bhagīratha, king of the solar dynasty, bringing the divine Ganges down to the earth to resurrect his ancestors and the river getting the appellation *Bhāgīrathī* on that account, see *Mahābhārata*, *Vanaparva*, ch. 108; *Vālmīki-Rāmāyaṇa*, *Bāla*. Canto 42; *Brahmāṇḍa P.* ch. 91; *Padma P.* Pt. 4, Ch. 21.

128. It may be noted that the prescription is for the 28-cycle of asterisms, including Abhijit, it being number 22 in the list.

129. It is worth while to note the ideals of chivalry and non-injury advocated by the Purāṇa in this verse which restricts a conquerer from indulging in pillage, plunder and insult. More explicit is the injunction of the *Varāha-Purāṇa* which says: "The distressed, the frightened, the disarmed, the fleeing and those who have surrendered with grass in their mouths, those with broken arms and those who have got down from their horses and elephants—these should not be killed nor tortured. The lone heir to the family,those who have surrendered, with folded hands, saying. "I am yours', should not be attacked and those (like sages), children, and those protected by women should not be killed nor tortured."

130. On *Candrabala* and *Tārābala*, the astrological strengths of the Moon and the asterism relating to a person, see B. V. Raman *Muhūrta* (Bangalore, 2nd edn., 1954), Ch, III. 'The birth-star and the birth-moon'.

131. The 'Watery signs' are Cancer, the latter half of Capricorn and Pisces.

132. The division of the country, made as above could be represented thus:

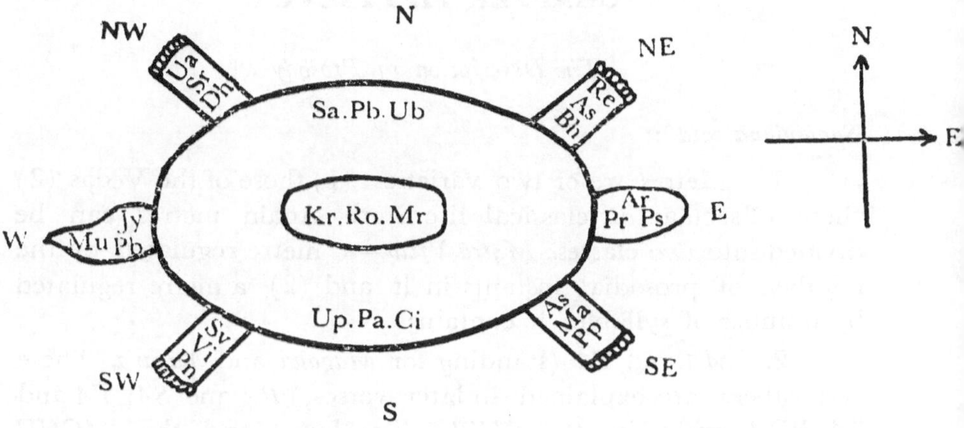

CHAPTER FIFTYSEVEN

The Description of Prosody

Sanandana said :

1. Metres are of two varieties: (1) those of the Vedas (2) those of secular or classical literature. Again metres can be divided into two classes: *Mātrā-Vṛtta*—a metre regulated by the number of prosodial instants in it and (2) a metre regulated by number of syllables it contains.

2. *MA* and *YA* (standing for *Magaṇa* and *Yagaṇa.* These and others are explained in later verses,) *RA* and *SA*, *TA* and *JA*, *BHA* and *NA*, the *GURU* (i.e. long) and the *LAGHU* (short), O Brāhmaṇa, these are said to be the basis in prosody as explained by experts in the science of Prosody.

3. *Magaṇa* is that set of three syllables where all are long ones (— — — Mollosus). *Yagaṇa* is that set of three syllables where the first syllable is short (v — — Bacchius). The *Ragaṇa* is that set of three syllables), in which the middle one is short (— v — Amphimacer), and the *Sagaṇa* is that set of three syllables in which the last one is long (vv—Anapestus).

4. The *Tagaṇa* is that set in which the last one is short (— — v Antibacchius). The *Jagaṇa* is that set of three syllables in which the middle one is long (v—v Amphibrachys) and the *Bhagaṇa* is that set of three syllables in which the first one is long (—v v Dactylus.) The *Nagaṇa* is said to consist of three short syllables (v v v Tribrachys). O sage, the *Gaṇas* or sets of syllables contain three in each.

5-6. Five *Gaṇas* are mentioned with four short syllables. They are admitted in the *Āryā* and other metres. If a conjunct consonant, the aspirate *Visarga* or the *Anusvāra* comes after a short syllable that short syllable is considered to be prosodially long. The abbreviated term for a long syllable is *GU* and that for a short syllable is *LA*. A fourth of a verse is called a *Pāda* (foot). A break in the middle is called a *Yati* (Caesura).

7. O Nārada. a *Vṛtta* (metre) is classified into three : *Sama*, *Ardhasama* and *Viṣama*. If all the four feet have the same characteristics, the metre is called *Sama*.

8. If the first and the third feet have one set of characteristics (i.e. combination and arrangement of the Gaṇas) and the second and the fourth feet have another set of characteristics, the metre is called *Ardhasama*. If all the four feet have different characteristics it is called *Viṣama*.

9. There are verses with one syllable in each foot. This number is increased one by one upto twentysix syllables. Each one thus constitutes a separate metre.

10. Beyond that the metres evolved are called *Daṇḍakas* the first of which is *Caṇḍavṛṣṭi Prapāta*. If each verse consists of three feet or six feet it is called a *Gāthā*. Now listen to the names of the metres in order.

11-13. *Name of the metre*	*No. of syllables in each foot*
Uktā	One
Atyuktā	Two
Madhyā	Three
Pratiṣṭhā	Four
Supratiṣṭhā	Five
Gāyatrī	Six
Uṣṇik	Seven
Anuṣṭubh	Eight
Bṛhatī	Nine
Paṅkti	Ten
Triṣṭubh	Eleven
Jagatī	Twelve
Atijagatī	Thirteen
Śakvarī	Fourteen
Atiśakvarī	Fifteen
Aṣṭi	Sixteen
Atyaṣṭi	Seventeen
Dhṛti	Eighteen
Vidhṛti (? *Atidhṛti*)	Nineteen
Kṛti	Twenty
Prakṛti	Twentyone
Ākṛti	Twentytwo
Vikṛti	Twentythree

Saṁkṛti (? *Saṁskṛti*)	Twentyfour
Atikṛti	Twentyfive
Utkṛti	Twentysix

14-15. These are the names of the different metres. By means of *Prastāra*[1] they may have many combinations. In the *Prastāra* for each metre, first take one foot with all long syllables. Beneath the first long syllable put a short syllable. All the remaining syllables must be as they are above. In the next line do like-wise until all of them become short.

16-20. (These verses form a group requiring arithmetical calculations. An explanatory translation with illustrations is necessary in stead of a literal one. Here *Prastāra, Naṣṭa, Uddiṣṭa, Ekadvyādi-la-ga-kriyā, Saṅkhyāna* and *Adhva-yoga* are the technical terms in Sk. Prosody.[2] These are retained as the explanation of these terms will be more useful than their word-to-word rendering.)

Prastāra means "A representation or enumeration of all the possible combinations of certain given numbers or of short or long syllables in a metre". If a *Prastāra* is *Naṣṭa* (lost) and needs ascertainment of the 'lost' *Vṛtta*, the procedure is called *Naṣṭa-pṛtayaya*. The variety (*Bheda*) of *Prastāra* is determined in the following way:

If the *Naṣṭa* number be even, one should record a *Laghu* (v) for it. The number is to be halved and if it be still even, one is to record another *Laghu* (v) for it. If the *Naṣṭa* number is odd (not divisible by 2), record a *Guru* (—) for it. Add one to that odd number and divide it half. If that number be uneven, record a *Guru* (—) for it. This should be continued till the number of syllables in that foot is completed.[3]

If the type or *Bheda* of a *Prastāra* is known but not the number of its variety *Uddiṣṭāṅka*), it is ascertained as follows:

In the *Uddiṣṭa*, there are signs of *Laghu* and *Guru* (in a certain arrangement). One should write the number 1 over the head of the first syllable and go on doubling the numbers over the heads of the subsequent syllables. One should add number 1 to the number above the *Laghu* (v) syllable and that is the number of the *Uddiṣṭa* or variety of that *Prastāra*.

(For example: We want to know the number of a variety

of a four-syllabled metre with the following distribution of *Laghu-Guru* syllables in its metrical foot:

1	2	4	8
Guru	Guru	Guru	Laghu/

As the number 8 is above the head of *Laghu,* we should add 1 to it. And 8 + 1 = 9 is the *Uddiṣṭāṅka* of the variety of the metre.)

The next two processes are a bit complicated. But briefly they are as follows:)

Eka-dvyādi-la-ga-kriyā is the method of ascertaining the complete number of Prastāras of a particular Chanda. It is called calculation or *Saṅkhyāna.* We hereby know the number of *Laghus* and *Gurus* in a *Prastāra.* Thus in a *Prastāra* of a metre with four-syllabled foot, there will be the following varieties:

	No.
(1) All the four syllables *Laghu* . . .	1
(2) One *Guru* + three *Laghu* syllables . . .	4
(3) Two *Gurus* + Two *Laghus* . . .	6
(4) Three *Gurus* + One *Laghu* . . .	4
(5) All four *Guru* Syllables . . .	1
	Total : 16 Vṛttas

Thus 16 is the total number of Prastāras according to the *Saṅkhyāna.*

This total can be arrived at by adding one to the Uddiṣṭāṅka. As noted above the numbers of Uddiṣṭas are: 1+2+4+8 = 15 + 1 = 16

By deducting one from doubling the number of *Prastāra* is also called *Adhva* by the wise people.[4]

21. O sage ! I have lightly indicated to you the characteristics of *Chandas Śāstra* (the Science of Prosody). The details of subtle varieties of *Prastāras* are infinite.

CHAPTER FIFTYSEVEN

1. *Prastāra*—A tabular representation of the long (*Dīrgha*) and short (*Laghu*) syllables of a metre with all possible varieties.

2. *Prastāro naṣṭam uddīṣṭam eka-dvyādi-la-ga-kriyāḥ /*
Saṅkhyānam adhva-yogaś ca ṣaḍ ete pratyayāḥ smṛtāḥ //
—Vṛtta-Ratnākara VI-I.

3. For example : The 6th type of a four-syllabled (footed) metre will give us the arrangement of the syllables in its foot as follows:

Now the number 6 is even, so it is to be marked as *Laghu* (v). Its half: 6/2=3, an odd number and hence is to be marked as *Guru* (–). No. 3 being an odd number 1 is to be added and the total is to be divided by 2. It is $\frac{3\times1}{2}$= 2. This being an even number is to be noted as a *Laghu* (v). Further this 2/2=1 which is an odd number and should be marked as a *Guru* (–).

Thus this 6th variety of a four-syllabled metrical foot will be : Laghu-Guru-Laghu-Guru as the arrangement of syllables per foot.

4. These last 5 verses of this Chapter of the NP. are the same as those in Kedāra Bhaṭṭa's *Vṛtta Ratnākara.* It appears that both N P. and Kedāra Bhaṭṭa used a common source. For the interpretation of above verses, I have used the Comm. *Vṛtta-ratnākara-pañcikā* on Vṛtta Ratnākara by the Simhali scholar Śilaskandha Mahā Sthavira (Nirnaya Sagar Edt., 1908).

CHAPTER FIFTYEIGHT

*Śuka's Temptation**

Nārada submitted:

1. When there was a reference to the term *Anūcāna* (well-versedness in Vedas) all the *Vedāṅgas* (ancillaries to the Vedas) were heard (by me) from your lotus-like mouth (as they were being explained) partially in brief and partially in details.

2a. Narrate to me in details the (story of) the birth of Śuka, O highly intelligent sage.

Sanandana narrated:

2b-3. It is reported that formerly, on one occasion, on the peak of mount Meru, in an extensive forest of Karṇikāra trees, Lord Mahādeva accompanied by multitudes of terrible goblins sported himself. The daughter of the Lord of mountains, goddess Pārvatī, was also there with them.

4-5a. The holy sage Vyāsa (Kṛṣṇa Dvaipāyana) performed a divine penance there. He was devoted to the practice of Yoga. By dint of his yogic power, he entered (withdrew) in the soul and performed *Dhāraṇā*. That excellent-most sage performed those austerities for the sake of a son.

5b-7a. "May my son have the virility of Fire, Earth, Wind and Ether all round†". With this solemn vow of performance of penance, he practised severe austerities and sought after the Lord of gods who is impossible to be attained by persons who are not self-possessed.

7b-8a. It is reported that the powerful sage stood for one hundred years, subsisting on the air only, and pro-

---

* This chapter incorporates chapters 323 (from v. 11 onwards), 324, 325 of the *Śānti Parva* of the *Mbh.* In the notes on these, Mbh=*Mbh. Śānti* Parva, the next reference is to chapter No. and Verse Nos.

† For *abhitaḥ* of the NP. *aṁbhasaḥ* would be a better reading as the puissance of five *Mahābhūtas* is desired. The Mbh. also includes 'water' in the list of *Mahābhūtas* whose strength is requested.

pitiated the multi-formed great god (Mahādeva), the consort of Umā.

8b-12a. There were (in attendance) all Brāhmanical sages, heavenly sages, guardians of the worlds, demigods like Sādhyas, along with eight (twelve) Ādityas, Rudras, the Sun god and the Moon god, Gandharva (king) Viśvāvasu, Siddhas, bevis of divine damsels. There the great god Rudra, wearing an auspicious garland of Karṇikāra flowers, shone like the Moon in the autumn.

12b-13a. It was surprisingly mysterious to all the three worlds that his (Vyāsa's) complexion did not fade nor exhaustion overcame him.

13b-14a. As he, of immeasurable splendour, was absorbed in Yoga, the locks of his matted hair due to his splendour appeared to glisten like the blazing flames of fire.

14b-15. O Nārada ! Pleased at heart with this type of penance and such devotion of the sage, the great god Mahādeva made up his mind (to bestow favour on him) and the three-eyed Lord spoke to him smilingly.

16. "Your son shall be as pure as the Fire, as the Wind, as the Earth, as the Water and as the Sky.

17. He will be the partaker of consciousness of himself being the Brahman; his intelligence and mind shall be concentrated on the Brahman; he shall be permanently established in the Brahman. By dint of his (Brahmanic) splendour, he will be renowned all over the three worlds."

18. After having obtained that excellent boon from the Lord, Vyāsa, the son of Satyavatī, was one day engaged in churning the sacrificial sticks, with the desire of making a fire (for sacrificial purpose).

19. At that time, the illustrious sage happened to see a heavenly damsel called Ghṛtācī who, in consequence of her brilliant splendour, possessed excellent beauty.

20. Seeing that celestial damsel, in that forest, the great sage Vyāsa became instantly passionately enamoured of her.

21. After making Vyāsa deeply agitated with passion, the most beautiful Ghṛtācī, transforming herself into a she-parrot, approached him.

22. Even after seeing the celestial lady disguised in

another form, he was overcome with cupid (passionate love) who spread in every part of his body.

23. With great (moral) courage, the sage tried to restrain his passion. But his mind being extremely agitated, Vyāsa was unable to control it.

24-25. Due to the inevitability of Destiny (lit. what was to happen) the heart of the sage was fascinated by the (beautiful) form (of Ghṛtācī). With the desire to do this (viz. the kindling of fire) while he was suppressing his passion with special efforts, all of a sudden his semen fell on the churning sticks. It was thus that the great ascetic Śuka was born, while Vyāsa continued the churning of sacrificial sticks.

26-27. The foremost of sages, the great Yogī, was (thus) born of (lit. from the womb of) two (sacrificial) churning sticks. Just as a blazing sacrificial fire after being fed with oblations of ghee, sheds his effulgence all around, in the same way Śuka was born as if blazing with his brilliance, assuming a wonderfully beautiful form and excellent, unsurpassable complexion, O, foremost of Brāhmaṇas.

28.* The Gaṅgā, the greatest of all rivers, assumed her (godly) form and coming to the top of the Meru bathed Śuka (with her own waters after his birth), O Nārada.

29. There fell from the sky to the ground a deer-skin garment for Śuka (to wear it). The Gandharvas constantly performed their musical concerts and the various groups of celestial nymphs indulged in dances.

30-31a. High sounding heavenly kettle-drums began to beat lustily. Gandharva Viśvāvasu, Nārada and Tumburu, and the pair of Gandharvas Hāhā and Hūhū eulogised the nativity of Śuka.

31b-33a. There arrived the regents of different worlds of whom Indra was the leader, and gods, heavenly sages and Brahmanical sages as well. And the wind-god showered all varieties of heavenly flowers. (In this manner) all the world, the mobile and immobile, became highly delighted.

33b-34a. The highly resplendent, noble-souled god Mahādeva along with the goddess Umā performed with due

* Grammatically the verse is loose and defective.

formalities the ceremony of investiture of thread of the sage's son (i.e. Śuka) as soon as he was born.

34b-36a. To him gifted Indra, the Lord of gods, a wonderful-looking heavenly water-pot (*Kamaṇḍalu*) out of love and gods gave him clothes. Thousands of swans, peacocks, cranes, parrots and blue jays hovered around him clockwise, O Nārada.

36b-37a. The highly intelligent great sage, having obtained his divine nativity from the two sacrificial sticks, stayed there, observing his holy vows with great attention.

37b-38a. As soon as he was born, the Vedas with all their esoteric secrets and all their abstracts, approached him for dwelling in him even as they approached his father.

38b-39a. Although he was conversant with Vedas, Vedāṅgas (accessories of the Vedas) together with their commentaries he remembering that it was his duty (to have a guru, as per ancient religious practice), selected Bṛhaspati as his preceptor, O prominent Brāhmaṇa.

39b-40. Having studied all the Vedas along with their mysteries and abstracts as well as *Itihāsa* (History, like the *Mahābhārata*) and all the sciences and scriptural texts based on the Vedas, the great sage paid his tuition-fees to his preceptor and performed the rite of *Samāvartana* (the formal conclusion of the life as a religious student).

41-42a. Observing the vow of celibacy, he, with great concentration, began to perform severe austerities. Even though he was a child, the great ascetic became worthy of being honoured and consulted due to his knowledge and penance.

42b-43. The mind (intelligence) of Śuka who was the observer of the path leading to Emancipation (from the cycle of *Saṁsāra* did not take interest in the three *Āśramas* (stages of life) depending on the house-holder's stage of life.*

44-45a. Desirous as he was of the highest beatitude and endowed with humility as he was, he bowed down to him and requested him: 'You are an expert in the religious path that leads to Emancipation from Saṁsāra. May you be pleased to elucidate that to me, so that I may be blessed with Supreme tranquility of mind."

---

* Here ends chapter 324 of the *Mbh. Śānti.*

45b-46a. Hearing the words of his son, the great sage advised him, "Do you learn the scripture pertaining to Mokṣa as well as all other different religious duties."

46b-47a. At the behest of his father, Śuka, the excellent-most among the knowers of the Brahman (or Vedas) learnt the entire *Yoga-Śāstra* and the (*Sāṅkhya*) philosophy of Kapila completely.

47b-49a. Seeing his son resplendent with the splendour of the Vedas* and endowed with the glory of Brahman and thoroughly conversant with *Mokṣa-Śāstra,* he directed him then "Go to Janaka, the king of Mithilā. That king will explain to you everything about the meaning of the *Mokṣa-Śāstra.*

49b-50a. At the behest of his father, Śuka went (was about to go) to Janaka, the king of Mithilā, in order to enquire about the definite knowledge (*niṣṭhā*) about duties leading to *Mokṣa* and the nature of that ultimate goal.

50b-54. (As he was about to depart) he was instructed (by his father). "You go by the way traversed by ordinary mortals." Śuka was not surprised (at this instruction). He was further advised : "You should not go through the sky by your Yogic power. You should proceed there with simplicity and straightforwardness and not for seeking pleasure. Specialities (friendship etc.) should not be seen (formed) by you, as those specialities (or contacts) become binding. Even though the king is adopted by us as one on whose behalf sacrifices are to be performed by us, you should not entertain any pride about it. You should stay in his premises. He will dispel all your doubts as the king is proficient in *Dharma* (religious duties) as well as scriptures regarding (the path to) *Mokṣa.* You should abide unhesitatingly by whatever he asks you to do."

Being thus instructed, the righteous-souled sage Śuka proceeded to Mithilā.

55. Though he had the capability of traversing through the sky the whole of the earth alongwith the oceans, he crossed on foot the mountains and reached the sub-continent called Bhārata.

---

* NP. reads : *Śataṁ brāhyā Śriyā yuktam.* But *Śataṁ brāhyā* is meaningless and an obvious miscopying of *Sa taṁ brāhmyā* of the *Mbh. Śānti.* 325.5a.

56. The great sage passed through different prosperous and rich countries. At last reaching the country (known as) Videha, he approached Janaka.

57. When he arrived at the gate of (Janaka's) palace, he was stopped by the door-keepers. The great Yogin stood there unaffected by hunger or thirst.

58-60a. O Nārada, even in the heat of the sun, he was not distressed by exhaustion or dejection and was absorbed in meditation. One of the porters who was posted there saw Śuka standing, blazing like the mid-day sun. He worshipped Śuka with due formalities and paying obeisance to him with his palms joined, led him to the second apartment of the king's palace.

60b-61. Near the harem, there was a beautiful garden like Caitraratha park (of Kubera). It abounded in trees in full blossom and had separate swimming pools and playgrounds. Showing him that garden, the porter made him sit and humbly reported (his arrival) to the king.

62. Having heard that Śuka had arrived, the king appointed courtesans for his service as well as to gauge the disposition and the inclinations of his mind.

63. All those damsels were young, beautful-looking with fine tresses of hair, possessing excellent hips, clad in red clothes of fine texture and decked with ornaments of burnished gold.

64-65a. All of them were experts in agreeable conversation, competent to read the minds of man and skilled in all (amorous) acts. They were more than fifty. They arranged for his reception with water for washing feet etc. They gratified him with such articles of food as were agreeable in the season.

65b-66a. When he had eaten his food, they showed him beautiful parks in the town one by one, O Nārada.

66b-67a. Sporting, giggling and singing, those ladies, conversant with male psychology, entertained that noble-souled sage.

67b-68. The pure-souled ascetic, born of sacrificial firesticks, had conquered his anger and had subdued his sense-organs. He was always absorbed in meditation. He was neither delighted nor angry at these.

68b-69a. Śuka washed his feet and after completing his

Sandhyā prayer, seated himself on a holy seat meditating on that object for which he had come there.

69b-70a. In the earlier part of the night, he became absorbed in meditating upon Nārāyaṇa. In the middle part of the night he duly went to sleep.

70b-71a. Getting up early in the morning and after performing the necessary rites of bodily purification and ablution, the highly intelligent sage, though he was surrounded by women, was once again absorbed in meditation.

71b-72. It is in this manner that he spent the remaining part of the day and that night in the palace of the king, O Nārada.*

* Here ends ch. 325 in the Mbh. *Śānti*.

CHAPTER FIFTYNINE

*The dialogue between Śuka and Janaka**

Sanandana continued:

1-3a. The next morning, O excellent Brāhmaṇa, with the family priest at the head (of the procession), the king accompanied by his ministers and all the members of his harem, approached the preceptor's son (Śuka). He carried the articles of worship (*arghya*) on his head and took with him a highly valuable seat bedecked with all (kinds) of precious stones. He offered that extremely suitable seat to Śuka, the son of his preceptor.

3b-4a. When Śuka, the son of Kṛṣṇa-(Dvaipāyana Vyāsa) occupied the seat, the king worshipped him according to the prescribed rites. At first he offered him water to wash his feet. He then presented him a cow alongwith articles of worship.

4b-5a. The excellent Brāhmaṇa accepted the worship offered in accompaniment of the prescribed *Mantras*. The highly resplendent ascetic enquired after king's unfailing welfare and prosperity.

5b-6a. The noble-minded monarch with his entourage of noble men and officers duly reported about his welfare to the son of his preceptor. With his permission, he sat on the ground.

6b-7a. Conversant with etiquettes and proper procedure as he was, the king enquired of Śuka, the son of Vyāsa after his welfare and asked him the object of his visit.

Śuka replied:

7b-8. Prosperity be unto you ! My father has informed me that "the King of Videhas known all over the world as Janaka, is my first[1] (disciple ?), is well-versed in the virtuous path leading to *Mokṣa*, you therefore go to him quickly. If you have any doubt

---

* This chapter consists of ch. 326 and of a few more verses from ch. 327 of the *Mbh. Śānti.*

in your heart regarding the religion of *Pravṛtti* (sacrifices and such other ritualistic matter) or about the religious path of renunciation (*Nivṛtti*), he will definitely dispel them all."

9. At the command of my father, I have therefore, come here to you to discuss with you (these matters). Hence, it behoves you, O foremost among the upholders of *dharma* to instruct me precisely.

10. What should be done by a Brāhmaṇa here? What is the essence of those religious duties which are conducive to Liberation ? How is the Liberation (from Saṁsāra) to be achieved ? Is it obtainable by (spiritual) knowledge or by penance.

Janaka replied:

11. Listen to me, dear child, what are the duties of a Brāhmaṇa since his birth. After the investiture of the sacred thread, he should devote himself to the study of the Vedas.

12. By performing penance, services to his preceptor and observance of celibacy and by remaining devoid of greed and jealousy, he should do his duties to Devas and *Pitṛs*.

13. Having studied the Vedas regularly and controlled his senses, and after paying off the tuition-fee of his preceptor, and after taking the permission of his teacher he should formally conclude his stage of religious studentship (by performance of *Samāvartana* ceremony).

14. After completion of the *Samāvartana*, he should betake himself to the householder's stage of life. (After marriage) he should live in the company of his spouse, devoid of malice and jealousy, and he should duly and continuously maintain domestic (sacrificial) fire.[2]

15. After procreating sons and grandsons, he should retire as a hermit to a forest and continue to worship the same (domestic) sacrificial fires and receive lovingly guests with due hospitality.

16. Thereafter, the knower of Dharma should establish all (sacrificial) fires within his soul and rising above the pair of opposites, and banishing all passionate attachment from his soul, he should pass his life in the stage of life called *Brahmāśrama* (or Sannyāsa).

Śuka enquired:

17. (It may be true that) when perfect spiritual knowledge dawns and the eternal entity (the Brahman) is realised directly, (*Mokṣa*) is automatically attained). But they say that attainment of (true spiritual) knowledge is not possible without direct association with and personal stay with the spiritual preceptor.

18. Is it necessary for a person to go through the three stages of life (studenthood, the life of a householder and that of a forest-hermit)? This is what I ask you. It behoves you to explain this.

Janaka explained:

19. Attainment of Liberation from Saṁsāra is not possible till one accomplishes knowledge (understanding the nature of Brahman etc. theoretically from the scriptural studies) and the true conception of Reality. But the knowledge (or the nature of Brahman) is not possible without association with the (spiritual) preceptor.[3]

20. The preceptor is the pilot or helmsman, while spiritual knowledge is the boat. After attaining knowledge and crossing the ocean of Saṁsāra, one may abandon both.

21. In order to prevent the annihilation of worlds and for forestalling the destruction of acts (on which the existence of the world depends), a person performs both auspicious and inauspicious deeds. It is only after that, that the Liberation is achieved.

22. When (through performance of penanee) one becomes perfectly purified in one's soul, by means of purificatory causes[4] in the course of many births in the world, he attains Liberation from Saṁsāra even in the first (*Brahmacarya*) stage of life.

23. What paramount desirable object is to be achieved by going through the three stages of life by a person who has attained Liberation from Saṁsāra, or by a learned person who has seen the Reality.

24. One should always cast off defects or faults caused by the attributes *Rajas* and *Tamas*. Adhering to the path charact-

erised by *Sattva,* he should behold the Supreme soul, by means of (or within) his own individual soul.

25. Realizing his own soul in all created beings and beholding all creatures within his soul, he should behave (without being attached to anything in the *Saṁsāra*) like an aquatic animal which does not become wet though moving through waters.

26. Transcending the pairs of opposite attributes and associated with auspiciousness, he becomes completely liberated (from *Saṁsāra*) after casting off the physical body and attains Infinity in the next world like a bird, soaring up high in the sky above (the currents of) the wind.

27. In this context, listen to the *Gāthās* sung in ancient times by King Yayāti. They are remembered in their hearts by all twice-borns who are experts in the philosophy of Liberation.

28. The resplendent lustre (i.e. the Supreme soul) is in one's soul. It is a jewel[5] there itself. It is possible to be observed by oneself, but only with concentrated mind.

29. He who behaves in such a way that others are not afraid of him and when a person is not inspired with fear at the sight of another person, he who neither covets nor hates anything, attains to the Brahman.

30-31. When a person does not entertain evil thoughts about any of the living beings, when one abides by the path of virtue (or religious duty) called *Caturāśrama Dharma* (A Dharma constituted of four stages of life) which has been practised by one's ancestors, when according to the serial order of these *Āśramas* (stages of life) he performs (for many births) good actions physically, mentally and verbally, he attains (realizes) the Brahman.

32. If a person, eschewing malice that deludes people and having cast off passion and greed (from the mind), unites his soul with penance, he attains the state of (being one with) *Brahman.*

33. When one is equally disposed to all beings whether visible or audible, and supersedes the (reactions at) naturally opposite pairs (like pleasure and pain), one gets to the Brahman.

34-35. When one looks upon with an equal eye (without feeling attraction of repulsion), to naturally opposite pairs

(*Dvandvas*) like praise and blame, a piece of gold and iron, pleasure and pain, cold and heat, attainment of worldly prosperity and adversity, pleasing and displeasing, life and death—then one attains to the Brahman.

36. Just as a tortoise spreads out its limbs and withdraws again (within itself), in the same way, the sense-organs are to be restrained by the recluse through his mind.

37. Just as one's place of residence plunged in darkness is seen with (the light emanating from) a lamp, in the same manner it is possible to visualize the *Ātman* with the brilliant light of intelligence.

38. I, however, can clearly see that you are endowed with all these (within you), O prominent one among the intelligents. If there be anything else to be known, your worship will know it fundamentally (and correctly).

39. O Brahmanical sage, you are already famous as one who have transcended (lit. gone to the other end of) worldly objects of sense through the grace of your spiritual preceptor as well as through your personal discipline (i.e. disciplined way of life).

40. It is through the grace of that great sage that the refulgent divine knowledge has revealed itself to you. You are known to me on account of that (spiritual knowledge).

41. Your knowledge about *Mokṣa* is more profound; your understanding is deeper, your spiritual glory is so immense that you don't realize it yourself.

42. Maybe due to immaturity or due to doubts or fears caused by delusion, some people do not attain that spiritual goal (*Mokṣa*) even though knowledge leading to *Mokṣa* is dawned in them.

43. When all the doubts have been dispelled by persons like me, they, by dint of their pure determined efforts, cut the knots (of doubt) in their heart and do not fall a victim to distress (i.e. are not distressed).

44. Your honour is a person in whom perfect knowledge has been generated and is steady in intellect and are free from covetousness. One, however, cannot attain that goal (of *Mokṣa*) without determined efforts.

45. You entertain no differentiation between pleasure

and pain and attach no importance to objects of senses. You have no curiosity and attraction for dancing and music. Nor does any passion overpower you.

46. You feel no bonds to your kinsmen. You are not inspired with fear at fearful objects. I find that to you censure and praise are all equal.

47. I see that you are a person among other wise persons who have taken to the highest imperishable path devoid of ailments.

48. O Brāhmaṇa you are already existing in that state (called *Mokṣa*) which is the fruit attained by a Brāhmaṇa and it is not a particular region. What else do you (want to) ask me about ?"

Sanandana said:

49.* Having heard this exhortation (of Janaka), Śuka who was self-controlled and had determined (to see the *Ātman*), began to abide in his soul mentally (by withdrawing himself from worldly objects) and he realized the (Universal) soul within his individual *Ātman*.

50-51a. Having accomplished his object, he was filled with bliss and (mental) tranquillity. He silently proceeded to the north. On reaching the *Śaiśira* (the Himālaya) mountain, he espied Vyāsa, the son of Parāśara who was teaching his disciples like Paila and others, the compilations of the Vedas.

51b-52. Śuka (the sage born of Araṇī) of extremely pure mind (soul) and brilliant like the sun-god, respectfully clasped his father's feet and felt delighted at heart. The noble-minded Śuka reported everything to his father.

53-54. Having heard the dialogue between Śuka and king Janaka on the means of getting *Moksa* (liberation from *Saṁsāra*), Vyāsa, the author (arranger) of the Vedas, embraced his son with a heart full of ecstatic delight and seated him by his side.

55. Thereafter, the Brāhmaṇas like Paila and others completed their course of Vedic study under Vyāsa. They came down to the earth from the mountain-summit and engaged themselves in teaching the Vedas and performing sacrifices.

**vide* Mbh. *Śānti* 327.1 and 2.

CHAPTER FIFTYNINE

1. NP reads *ādyaḥ* 'first' but the substantive qualified by it being absent I proposed "disciple". But Mbh. *ibid* 10b reads *yājyaḥ* i.e. 'for whom we perform sacrifices' 'our *Yajamāna.*'

2. For *āhitāgnir anādṛte* of the NP. Mbh. (*ibid*) v. 17 reads *āhitāgnis tathaiva ca.*

3. vide. 'naiṣā tarkeṇa matirāpaneyā' etc.—Kaṭha. 12. 9. tadvijñānārthaṁ sa gurum evābhigacchet—Muṇḍaka I. 2. 12.

4. Mbh. (*ibid*) v. 26a reads *bhāvitaiḥ karaṇaiḥ* in stead of *Kāraṇaiḥ* of the NP. The Mbh. verse means "through penance performed in many births, a man is able to have pure, cleansed sense-organs (of which mind is the eleventh one) and the soul" etc.

5. NP reads *ratnaṁ tattraiva caiva tat* but Mbh. (*ibid*) v. 32 reads *sarva-jantuṣu tat samam* / 'It (the soul) exists in all beings.'

CHAPTER SIXTY

The Dialogue between Śuka and Sanatkumāra

Sanandana continued[1] :—

1. When the Brāhmaṇas (disciples of Vyāsa) descended (from the height of Vyāsa's hermitage) or departed, the intelligent Vyāsa with only his son (Śuka) as the companion, remained silently absorbed in meditation in the hermitage.

2. An incorporeal voice[2] addressed Vyāsa along with his son : "O great sage : O descendant of Vasiṣṭha : (How is it that) there is no chanting sound of the Vedas (in your hermitage) ?

3. Why are you sitting thus silent and absorbed in meditation, as if you are (anxiously) brooding over something? This mountain devoid of the vibrant echoes (of Vedas) does not appear splendid.

4. O venerable Sir, with a delighted heart, recite the Vedas along with your intelligent son who is well-versed in the Vedas."

5. On hearing that speech addressed to him by the ethereal voice, Vyāsa began to chant the Vedas along with his son Śuka.

6. While both of them were chanting the Vedas for a pretty long time, there arose, O excellent Brāhmaṇa, a violent wind which was as if driven by the gales that break out on the seas.

7-8. Then Vyāsa prohibited his son from continuing the Vedic study, as it was not the time suitable for studies (and hence a holiday). As soon as he was so bidden (to suspend Vedic recitation), Śuka, out of curiosity asked his father : "whence is the wind blowing ? It behoves you to explain to me all the activities of the wind."

9. Vyāsa was extremely surprised to hear these words of Śuka. He replied to Śuka that it was an ill omen which indicated the suspension of the recitation of the Vedas.

10. "You are blest with the spiritual vision. Your steady

mind has been at ease; you are free from the attributes of *Rajas* and *Tamas*. You are well established in the Truth.

11. Hence realising the Vedas in your own self do you reflect and meditate : the path pertaining to the Supreme soul is known as the path of gods (*Deva-yāna*). The path that is made of *Tamas* is called the path of *Pitṛs* (*Pitṛ-yāna*).

12a. Both of these have come to be realized[3]—one as leading to the heaven and the other to the world below since the winds blow over the world and high up in the atmosphere.

12b-13a. The winds go on blowing both on the surface of earth as well as in the sky. They blow in seven courses. Listen and understand as I recount them one after another.

13b-14a. The (physical) body is endowed with senses which are domineered over by the (semi-divine beings called) Sādhyas and many (other) great powerful beings. They brought forth an unconquerable son called *Samāna*.[4]

14b-15a. From *Samāna* was born a son called *Udāna*; from *Udāna* sprang *Vyāna*; from whom was created *Apāna*. From *Apāna* arose lastly the vital air called *Prāṇa*.

15b-16a. The invincible tormentor of enemies, the *Prāṇa* was issueless (as had no further function of such production) I shall now recount to you the different functions of these vital winds (as they are factually observed).

16b-17a. The vital wind causes all the various functions of all living beings and because living creatures are made to be pleased[5] (NP) (are enabled to live—Mbh—*ibid* v. 35).

17b-18. The wind mentioned first (in the above list) and which is known by the epithet *Pravaha* (or Samāna) impels the masses of clouds born of smoke and heat, to go by the first track. Moving through the sky and coming in contact with the water contained in the clouds, the wind manifests itself in its brilliance among the flashes of lightning.

19-20a. The second wind known as *Āvaha* goes on blowing with a loud noise. It is due to (the power of) this wind that Soma and other luminaries rise and appear (our body is a replica in miniature of the cosmos). Within the body this wind is known as *Udāna* by the learned and the wise.

20b-21a. The wind holds (within itself) the waters from

the four oceans and having taken up the water gives it to the clouds for the sake of Protection.[6]

21b-22a. The winds having equipped (filled) the clouds with waters, presents it to the presiding deity of rains. It is the mighty wind, third in the above enumeration and is famous as *Udvaha.*

22b-23a. The wind carries the blue big clouds and divides them into various portions, which it makes them shower rain and the clouds become solidified.

23b-24a. It is that wind which carries the celestial cars of gods. It is that fourth wind (in the list) called *Saṁvaha* which is capable of subduing mountains.

The fifth wind called *Vivaha* is full of great might and speed. By that hard blowing wind, the internal juices of trees are made sick or dry.

24b-25a. It holds up (supports from below) all the heavenly waters in the sky and prevents them from falling down. Supporting up the sacred waters of the celestial Gaṅgā, the wind blows to prevent them from flowing downwards. And the holy river water stays on (high up in the sky).

25b-26a. The Sun is the source of thousands of rays and it throws (a flood of) light on the earth. But it is through the obstruction of this.

26b-28a.* Through the action of that wind, the Moon, after waning, waxes again till he shows his full disc. That wind is known as *Parivaha* and it is the excellent among the living beings[7] and from it Soma, the divine store of nectar, is obtained.

28b-29a. That wind takes away the life of all living creatures at the time of death. His Law is abided by Death and god Yama, the son of the sun-god.

29b-30a. That Law becomes the source of immortality which is attained by Yogins of quiescent mind (intellect) who are ever engaged in Yogic meditation.

30b-31a. By resorting to this wind, thousands of Dakṣa's grandsons through his (Dakṣa's) ten sons quickly and with

*NP reads *yāti vasundharām*—'goes to the earth.' Mbh. (ibid) v. 47 reads *bhāti vasundharām* 'enlightens or sheds light on the earth'. I prefer the Mbh. reading.

speed attained the limits of the universe (broke through them to reach *Mokṣa*).

31b-32a. It is the wind called *Parivaha* which is irresistible by anybody[8] overwhelmed with whose showers he does not revert (?)

32b-33a. In this way all these wind-gods, the sons of Aditi, are extremely miraculous. They blow about (without being attached to anybody) everywhere. They have access everywhere and are the end of everything.[9]

33b-34a. It was indeed a great miracle that this excellent mountain was suddenly shaken by the blowing of that wind.

34b-35. This wind is the exhalation from (the nose of) Viṣṇu. When it blows forcibly, O child, the whole world gets agitated. Hence when a stormy wind blows violently persons well-versed in the Veda do not recite it.

36-37a. The Vedas are a form of the wind. If uttered with force and loudly (at this time) the external wind gets pained." (Hence one should not recite the Vedas when stormy winds blow).[10]

After addressing these words to his son, the spiritually powerful son of Parāśara asked his son to resume the recitation of the Vedas (when the storm subsides). He then left to take his ablutions in the heavenly Gaṅgā.

37b-38a. Thereafter when Vyāsa departed to take his bath, Śuka, the foremost among the knowers of the Vedas and the master of the Vedas and accessories to Vedas (like *Śikṣā*, *Kalpa* etc.) resumed his self-study (and recitation) of the Vedas.

38b-39. Then Venerable Sanatkumāra[11] approached Śuka, the son of Vyāsa who was engaged in the recitation of the Vedas in solitude, O sage. Śuka, the son of Kṛṣṇa Dvaipāyana got up and the son of god Brahmā (Sanatkumāra) was received by him.

40. O excellent Brāhmaṇa ! Then Sanatkumāra who was prominent among the knowers of the Veda enquired, "O highly fortunate son of Vyāsa, O highly brilliant sage ! What are you doing (now)?"

Śuka said :

41. O son of Brahmā, I am now engaged in the self

study of the Vedas. It is a (great) holy merit of mine whereby I have been able to see you.

42. I wish to ask you something about the principle that is conducive to the attainment of salvation. Please recount it, O highly blessed one, so that I may attain that perfect knowledge.

Sanatkumāra said :

43. There is no (other) vision on a par with learning, there is no (other penance on a par with learning. There is no (other misery on a par with sensuous attachment. There is no other happiness on a par with renunciation.

44. Refraining from sinful activities, being continuously engaged in meritorious activities, good behaviour and adherence to conventional duties—these are the most excellent things contributing to welfare.

45. Having obtained the birth as a human being (the life in) which is fraught with sorrow he who becomes attached to it becomes stupefied; such a man is incapable of being emancipated from sorrow. Attachment (to worldly objects) is an indication of misery.

46. The intellect of one attached to the worldly affairs heightens one's vicious snare of delusion. One ensnared by delusion attains misery here and hereafter.

47. Restraint of lust and fury by all means must be pursued by one who seeks welfare. These two are conducive to the destruction of (spiritual) welfare (the moment) they crop up.

48. One must continuously guard one's penance against fury; one must save one's splendour and glory from (indecent) rivalry; one must save one's learning from being over-honoured and disrespected; one must save oneself from blunders.

49. Absence of cruelty is the greatest *Dharma*, forbearance is the greatest strength; knowledge of the *Ātman* is the greatest knowledge and truthfulness is the greatest of benefits.

50. He is an erudite scholar who renounces everything. He moves about the objects of the sense-organs by means of those sense-organs that are fully submissive to himself.

51-52a. He who is not getting entangled; he whose soul is quiescent; he who is without aberration; he who has concentration; he who does not identify himself with those beings that do not become one with the Ātman, that is, he who is with them and without them, becomes liberated and ere long attains the greatest welfare.

52b-53a. One who never sees others, never touches others, never talks with others, soon accomplishes his *summum bonum*. O sage.

53b-55. No one shall injure any living being; one shall move on friendly terms with all the living beings. After attaining this birth no one shall be inimical to anyone. Voluntary indigence, perfect contentment, indifference and absence of fickle-mindedness—these, they say are conducive to the welfare of one who is the knower of the *Ātman*, of one who has conquered the *Ātman*.

56-57a. Disengaging oneself from all attachment, O child, you subjugate all your senses and by that means attain the state of sorrowlessness, both here and hereafter. Those who have no desire do not feel aggrieved. One shall avoid and eschew all types of desire within the Ātman.

O gentle one, by abandoning all desires you will be released from hosts of miseries.

57b-58a. You must be permanently engaged in austerities and silent self-control. You must restrain yourself. You must be desirous of conquering what is not conquered, viz. the *Brahman*. You must not be entangled in any close attachment.

58b-59a. A Brāhmaṇa (one who is engrossed in the meditation of (Brahman) uninvolved in the close intimacies due to the *Guṇas* and always engaged in the only activity (of meditation), ere long attains the excellent happiness.

59b-60a. It is the unfortunate and wretched sage who takes delight in the pairs of *Dvandvas* (mutually clashing opposites). He is satisfied with a little knowledge. But he who is satisfied with perfect knowledge does not feel aggrieved.*

---

*This verse in the NP is a bit obscure; the corresponding verse No. 24 in the *Mbh. Śānti* ch. 329 is as follows :

dvandvārāmeṣu bhūteṣu ya eko ramate muniḥ /
viddhi prajñānatṛptaṁ taṁ jñāna-tṛpto na śocati //

60b-61a. It is the auspicious acts that enable the individual to attain Devahood, while the mixture of auspicious and inauspicious activities enables one to attain human birth. Through inauspicious *karmas* one attains the birth as lower animals. Due to his *karmas,* he is helpless and cannot avoid it.

61b-62a. The worldly existence is always tormented by death, old age and other miseries. Every creature realises it.* Why don't you get enlightened?

62b-63a. You have given the term *Hita* (beneficent) to what is *Ahita* (non-beneficent). You regard a thing as *Dhruva* (permanent) to what is *Adhruva* (transitory). You have given the term *Artha* (Meaningful) to what is *Anartha* (harmful). Why don't you get enlightened?

63b-64a. Just as the silkworm in the cocoon entwines itself by means of the threads originating from itself, you are also entwined. Why don't you awake to the correct apprehension of these ?

54b-65a. Enough of attachment to objects of this world, for attachment to worldly objects engenders evils. The silk-worm which weaves a cocoon round itself is at last bound down by his own acceptance of ties.

65b-66. All beings passionately attached to one's sons, wives and families become the victims of destruction at last, even as wild elephants sunk in the mire of a lake become gradually weakened (and meet death). Have a look at extremely miserable creatures who are dragged by the vicious net of delusion.

67. The family, sons and wives, the physical body, the mass of accumulated wealth—all belong to others. They are unstable. What is that which one can call one's own ? The merits and the sins (committed by oneself).

That person who leads a self-contented happy life in the midst of people who take pleasures in sexual intercourse, should be known as a person whose thirst has been satiated by knowledge. And (it is known to all that) a person whose thirst or covetiousness is satisfied by perfect (spiritual) knowledge, never feels any misery.

*v. l. *Saṁsāre pacyate* (Mbh. *ibid*). 26.

A living being is cooked (in the cauldron of) Saṁsāra.

68. When one has to leave everything under duress and go, helplessly to the next world, why are you getting involved in a wrong and harmful activity ? You don't pursue your own interest (your real, durable wealth).

69. How will you by yourself traverse the pathway enveloped in darkness, without rest, without a support, without food and drink to be partaken of, and without a guide?

70. No one will follow you behind, as you set off from here. But the merit and the sin shall follow you (wherever) you go.

71. One seeks* one's objectives by means of learning, acts of bravery ('purity' in the Mbh. original) and great knowledge. When that objective is achieved one becomes liberated from *Saṁsāra*.

72. The (social) desire that one feels for living in the midst of human neighbourhoods (or habitations) is a rope-like bondage. People possessing merits succeed to cut it asunder and liberate themselves. Sinful persons are incapable of breaking it.

73. You find men of your own age and caste and having the same comely features taken away by the (god of) Death. You don't feel dejected and depressed even nominally. Indeed your heart is (made) of steel.

74-75. The river (called the world or life) has personal beauty or form as its banks, the mind, the speed of its current, (the sense of) touch, an island (in it), taste, its stream or current, smell, the mud, sound its waters. The special part leading towards heaven is full of grave difficulties. In this boat called intelligence, forgiveness is the oar for propulsion. Truth is the material forming the boat (*Satya-mayīm*) and practice of *dharma* is the stabilising ballast. Renunciation is the wind that propels (the mast of) the boat. Driven with speed it is with this boat (of intelligence) that one should cross the river.

76-77a. After eschewing both *Dharma* and *Adharma*, eschew both truthfulness and falsehood. Eschew Dharma by

* NP reads *anuśiryante* for *anusāryante* in the Mbh. As the reading in the Mbh. is appropriate in the context (and is also the original text from which the NP borrowed), it is accepted here.

means of non-conception (*A-Saṁkalpa*) and *Adharma* by means of non-violence. With the aid of intelligence eschew both truth and falsehood and at last cast off understanding itself by the Supreme knowledge.

77b-79a. Do you throw away this physical body having bones for its pillars, sinews for its binding cords, flesh and blood as its plaster, the skin (NP reading is 'Dharma') for its outer binding (packing ?) ; full of urine and faeces and hence emitting putrid smell; exposed to the attacks of sorrow and senility; the very seat of diseases and unsteady; dominated by the attribute of *Rajas* and impermanent—a temporary habitation for the being.

79b-80a. This whole universe which is both mobile and immobile, consists of the great elements and hence is material (full of atoms).

80b-82. Five sense-organs, the three attributes—*Tamas*, *Sattva* and *Rajas*. These (together with others mentioned above) constitute a group of seventeen and are called *Avyakta* (unmanifest). These with all those which are *Vyakta* (manifest) viz. the five objects of senses, consciousness, Intelligence, form and the group of twentyfive manifest and unmanifest ones.

When endowed with all these, it is (still) called the impermanent.*

83-85. He who knows the *Trivarga* (i.e. virtue, wealth, and love) happiness and misery, life and death perfectly well undertands the origins and dissolution. Whatever is perceived by means of the sense organ is called *Vyakta*. That should be known as *Avyakta* which is beyond the scope of the sense organs, that which can be grasped only through signs and symptoms. By means of the perfectly controlled sense organs, the embodied being is propitiated as if by means of continuous downpours. He sees the *Ātman* pervading the world and also the world fixed in the *Ātman*.

86. Being rooted in spiritual knowledge, the spiritual

---

* The NP reads *Samāyuktam anityam abhidhīyate*. But the reading is not satisfactory, though I have accepted it for translation. Mbh. (*ibid*) v. 47a reads *Samāyuktaḥ pumān* etc. and means "When endowed with (the above mentioned twentyfour possessions) he is called *Pumān* (Man). The Mbh. reading is better.

power is never lost* to a man who perceives the Supreme Soul in his own soul—the man who always sees all creatures in all conditions in his soul.

87-88. He who has become one with *Brahman* (transcends) by his spiritual knowledge all errors or miseries) never contacts any evil by contact with all creatures. Such a man never finds fault with practices or course of conduct prevailing in the world. A person who knows Liberation well, says that the Lord (or the Supreme Soul) is without beginning and end. It abides as a witness in all beings and is imperishable.

89. He (the soul) is inactive, non-stupefied (Mbh.—formless); only the being meets with grief as a result of his misdeeds.

90. For the purpose of counteracting his grief, he kills numerous creatures. As a result of these sacrifices, the performer has to undergo rebirth and perform (innumerable) new *Karmas*.

91. Such a person regards that what is really a source of misery as happiness. And he continuously becomes unhappy like an ailing person who eats unwholesome food not permissible in that sickness.

92. By his terrible acts, such a person is bound, pressed and tormented. Freed from them, he being bound by his *karmas*, obtains rebirth and thus rotates like a wheel in *Saṁsāra* without an axle.

93-94. Receding therefrom and being released from his own bondage, he wanders in the wide world as a result of the uprising of the activities. He revolves like a wheel without its axle (?) Many have attained *Siddhis* that gave rise to happiness and that had not been hindered. (That was possible for them) thanks to self-control, refraining from contacts and to the power of penance.

---

* The NP reads : *Parāvara-dṛṣaḥ śaktir Jñānavelāṁ na paśyati* |
The statement does not stand to reason. Hence the original reading from the Mbh. (*ibid*) v. 51 which is logical is accepted. The translation above is of the following :

Parāvara-dṛśaḥ Śaktir Jñāna-mūlā na naśyati |

CHAPTER SIXTY

1. Vv 1-36 in this chapter are mainly taken from *Mbh. Śānti* ch. 328 vv. 10-57.

2. In the *Mbh.* it is Nārada who advises Vyāsa to recite the Vedas.

3. NP. reads: *dvāvetau pratyayaṁ yātau* But the second line 12b becomes unconnected with 12a. Mbh. (ibid) v. 30 *dvāvetau pretya panthānau* etc. is better. It means: 'these are the two paths in the worlds hereafter.'

4. The term denotes the common tendencies of sense-organs or the common factors of Sādhyas and other beings.

5. v. 1 *Prāṇanāt*—(all are) enabled to live (Mbh. *ibid* v. 35)

6. The NP. reads : yo...*dadate cāpo jīmūtebhyovanenilaḥ* I took *avane* for *vane*, for this process is not limited to the forests : Mbh. (ibid) 39 reads: *ambarenilaḥ* 'in the sky'. The reading in Mbh. is worth considering.

7. v. 1. *Jayatāṁ varaḥ* : the foremost of all in energy.

8. This is the probable interpretation of the text of the NP. *yena vṛṣṭyā parābhūtās toyānyena nivartate* / The Mbh (*ibid*) v. 52a reads : *yena spṛṣṭaḥ parābhūto yātyeva na nivartate.* Being touched by which he is so overwhelmed that he goes away permanently (i.e. liberated from Saṁsāra) and never returns (gets Mokṣa).

9. Thus reads NP : *anāramantā sarvāntā sarvagāḥ sarva-cāriṇaḥ.* But the sentence has no predicate. The Mbh. (ibid) reads : *anāratam te saṁvānti sarvagāḥ sarvadhāriṇaḥ* They blow incessantly, have access everywhere and uphold everything.

10. Here ends chapter 328 in the Mbh. *Śānti.* It is significant that NK gives a secondary—Yogic—explanation to all these verses. But he, however, concludes with the mundane common sense remark : Hence one should not recite the Veda while a stormy wind blows."

11. In *Mbh* (*Śānti*) ch. 329, it is Nārada who approached Śuka.

CHAPTER SIXTYONE

The greatness of Nivṛtti[1] *Dharma*

Sanatkumāra[1] *said* :

1. Having heard such scriptural texts as are auspicious, dispelling sorrow, conducive to mental peace and happiness, one attains pure intelligence, whereby one attains really happy state.

2. Every day, thousands of incidents causing delight (sorrow-Mbh.) and hundreds of happenings causing sorrow affect a person devoid of wisdom, but not a person endowed with understanding and learning.

3. Persons of little intelligence and understanding become overwhelmed with mental sorrow of every kind due to advent of, and association with what is undesirable and severance from what is agreeable.

4. One should not nostalgically brood over the merits of the articles which one possessed in the past. One who does not think of them with reverent affection, becomes free from the bondage of love.

5. One should try to detect faults in things to which one feels attached. He should attribute undesirability to them. Then alone he becomes resplendent[2] immediately.

6. A person bewails for what is past (and lost permanently), does not acquire either wealth or religious merits or fame. He should reconcile himself with their loss. But that returns to him (?)[3]

7. Living beings sometimes gain and sometimes lose worldly objects. It should not be the cause of sorrow, to a person.

8. He who bewails the past, that which is dead or lost, attains miseries through miseries. He incurs greater loss and injury.

9. When a calamity causing physical or mental grief visits and cannot be warded off, one should not brood over it.

10. This is the antidote against misery that it should not

be brooded over. On being mused over, it does not decrease. Nay, it increases again.

11. One shall dispel mental misery by means of intellect and remove the physical pain by means of medicines. This is the power of knowledge; one should not behave like commoners in such matters.

12. No learned and sensible man shall yearn for these evanescent things viz.—the life, (comely) features, youth, hoarded wealth, health and association with beloved persons.

13. Misery is born of ignorance alone. It does not behove any one to bewail over it. Without bewailing, one shall try to remedy it, if one finds out its source.

14. In this life, undoubtedly misery is more pleasing* than happiness; (for) one will (try to) uplift the beloved *Ātman* from the miseries of old age and death.

15. Like the sharp-pointed arrows discharged by a good archer, physical and mental ailments affect the bodies deeply.

16-19. In order to destroy the ailment of a patient, who is afraid and who yearns for life, the body is being dragged about by means of treatments. The ducts of the body continue to flow. Like the current of the rivers they do not turn back. (The sun) takes away the life of men by day and by night again and again, during the two fortnights dark and bright; he makes the born man become old; he never tarries even for a moment. Himself free from old age, he takes away the lives of men overwhelmed by happiness and misery. Again and again, the sun sets, again and again he rises.

20. Taking with them the good and evil incidents that befall men according to their destiny and hence are not expected by them, the nights too pass away** ceaselessly.

21. Whatever one may desire, one shall attain, provided the fruit of actions of men does not depend on other factors.

---

* Mbh. reads *bahutaram* "the amount of sorrow and pain is greater than that of pleasure in this world."

** *matam* in the NP is not relevant. Hence *Astam* from *Mbh. Śānti* 331.1 (the corresponding verse of the NP) is accepted. In the NP v. 20 above
iṣṭāniṣṭā manuṣyāṇām mataṁ gacchanti rātrayaḥ |
matam seems to be a misprint for *mastam*.

22-23. Clever, intelligent men of unrestrained senses if destitute of efforts (or *karmas*), never succeed in earning any fruits. Other persons though destitute of intelligence and without any accomplishments and who are useles[4] and really the basest of men, are seen prompted by desires, and are seen indulging in all desires.

24. Another man attempts always to inflict violence on all living beings. He becomes old in deceiving but blessed with happiness throughout his life.

25. Fortune blesses someone who never stirs out but who sits (idle). Some one does everything but never obtains desired objects.

26. In order to recount the faults of men, the semen created in oneself at the sight of another, goes to still another person.[5]

27. When the semen is absorbed in the womb, it becomes a human foetus.[6] The recession (of semen or failure of conception) resembles a mango tree which blossoms fully without producing a single fruit.

28. To some persons who desire sons, who wish to perpetuate their lines and who (by worshipping deities etc.), strive for its achievement, not even an egg (an embryo in the womb) is born.

29. Some persons who dread the birth of an embryo as one fears a furious serpent, a long-lived son is born. How verily he is like his departed father ! (who has as if returned after departing from this life—Mbh. *ibid.* v. 17)

30. Some persons dejected due to sonlessness and with a burning desire for sons, at last get a son after performing penance and offering sacrifices to gods. The sons, duly borne for ten months (in the wombs by their wives) are born to be the banes and disgrace to their families.

31. Thanks to these blessed rites and observations, others inherit the hoarded wealth and grains and other diverse sources of enjoyment earned and stored by their forefathers.

32. When a man and a woman come in contact with each other, in the act of sexual intercourse, the embryo is formed in the womb like a calamity visiting the woman.

33-34. Due to excessive attachment to objects of senses

and due to delusion, death becomes unpleasant. A person who gives up both (the concepts of) pleasure and pain transcends (these) and goes to Brahman and enjoys the highest bliss.

It is with great difficulty that wealth (or objects of senses) are renounced. Nor it is pleasant or easy to retain them.

35-36a. One should not be worried on hearing about the destruction of riches or when they are not obtained. Some Men of peculiar nature become dissatisfied and are doomed on attaining adverse monetary conditions. But learned men are contented.

36b-38a. All things are hoarded only to be destroyed in the end. All ascents end in downfall; all contacts and unions end in separation; life ends in death; there is no end to the thirst (desire to get more and more); satisfaction alone is the greatest happiness. Hence, learned men praise satisfaction alone as the real wealth or an asset.

38b-39a. (Defective) When he does not stand even for a moment after acquiring (the body), what should he ever (constantly) brood over when the bodies (themselves) are impermanent and momentary.

39b-40a. Comprehending the real state of (created) beings, those who through the dint of their intelligence have traversed the path beyond darkness, do not come to grief but see the highest goal.

40b-41a. Like a tiger pouncing on an animal, the god of death picks out and snatches away a person whose desires are not satiated.

41b-42a. For securing escape from this misery, one should find a remedy. One should eschew grief, should not undertake (sacrifices and secular) activities. He should engage himself (in yoga) and be free from this misery (or fruitless efforts).

42b-43a. Whether in the case of a rich man or a destitute there is nothing more higher than merely the enjoyment of objects of senses such as sound, touch, taste, colour and smell.

43b-44a. Not that there is no misery without ailment to creatures by employment of speech. It is neither through speech nor learning (or knowledge) that all are separated (from life ?)

44b-45a. Restraining one's affection or attachment to things praised and others (not so praised), he who wanders freely (without the bonds of attachment) is really happy and learned.

45b-46a. Completely absorbed in spiritual pursuits with no expectations and free from desires or lustful enjoyments (*nirāmiṣa*), he who moves about with his self as his help-mate, becomes (really) happy.

46b-47. When an interchange or reversal of pleasure and pain takes place, neither his intellectual faculty nor manliness protect him from him. He must naturally exert himself. And a person who goes on doing efforts, is not lost or ruined.

48-49a. The embryo takes birth in the womb like an undesirable calamity. Those previous bodies (envelop) the soul who is eternal. After the suspension of the vital breaths of creatures (i.e. after the death of the body in the previous birth) he is invested with another (physical body) constituted of flesh and phlegm (according to his *karmas*).

49b-50a. When the previous body is destroyed, by another body which is as weak or strong[7] as the previous one is kept reserved for the transmigration of the creature whose previous body is burnt, like one boat is taking to another boat kept stationary and ready for the transfer of passengers.

50b-51a. (I enquire of you :) By whose efforts you see that the foetus continues to be alive (in the womb) when in the act of sexual intercourse a drop of inanimate semen is deposited in the womb.

51b-52a. The food stuffs taken in and beverages imbibed become digested in the stomach. Why then does not the foetus too become digested like the food?

52b-53a. It is Nature which has ordained the stay (of the *jīva*) in the urine and ordure in the womb. The *jīva* which is to take birth is helpless and he is not the agent (nor has any choice) in the matter of residence or escape from the womb.

53b-54a. Some come out from the womb alive; others die there (before birth) as their death is inevitable due to the arrival of others (their future bodies ordained by their previous *Karma*).

54b-55a* The person who in the course of sexual inter-

* The verse in NP is obscure.

course sprays out (sows) the seed, obtains from it some issue. The child thus brought forth indulges in the act of copulation in due course.

55b-56a. (It is not the soul but) the gross elements (constituting the physical body) at the close of one hundred years attain this type of seventh stage* (i.e. old age) and then cease to exist.

56b-57a. There is no doubt that when persons are afflicted by diseases, they lose the power of getting up or moving about like petty animals attacked by tigers.

57b-58. Despite their best possible efforts, physicians are not able to alleviate the pains of patients.

59. Even those various physicians though experts and equipped with medicines are themselves dragged (attacked) by diseases like beasts assailed by tigers.

60. Even though they imbibe many astringent and different kinds of medicated ghees, they are seen broken down by old age like big trees (*naga*)** by elephants.

61. Who administers medicines to ailing animals, birds, beasts of prey and poverty-striken people? These are not generally seen to be suffering from diseases.

62. A disease attacks and captures even terrible unassailable kings of ferocious energy, just as Caṇḍālas or roasters of beasts do to beasts.

63. In this way, people gagged and unable even to groan, submerged in delusion and sorrow are (seen to be) carried away in the big powerful current in which they are thrown.

---

etasmād yoni-sambandhād yo jīvan parimucyate |
Pūjāṁ na labhate kāñcit punar dvandveṣu majjati ||

"He who, while alive, is liberated through this sexual intercourse does not get any worship or honour but sinks in *dvandvas*. This is obviously strange. The original Mbh. verse has :

yo bījam parimucyate | prajāṁ ca labhate kāṁcit sajjati ||

The Mbh. verse is translated above.

*The comm. NK states the following 10 stages of human life : (1) stay in the womb (2) birth (3) infancy upto 5 years (4) childhood upto 12 years (5) Paugaṇḍa (6) youth (7) old age (8) decrepitude (9) suspension of breath and death. The Mbh (ibid) v. 28 reads *gatāyuṣaḥ* for *śatāyuṣaḥ* in the NP and the body is said to attain the 7th or the 9th stage out of the above 10 stages.

***nāga* in the NP is a misprint.

64. Neither by wealth nor by power of austere penance can embodied beings seeking to conquer nature, overcome it.

65. All persons desire to attain gradually to the top of the world. They strive to the best of their ability. But the result does not tally with their cherished desire.

66. If people were to obtain the fruit of their attempt (or cherished objective), they would never die, would never grow decrepit and would never have to experience anything unpleasant.

67. Persons who are careful as well as crooked, cruel and brave pay homage to men inebriated with the flush of affluence and puffed up with arrogance (Mbh. reads: those intoxicated with spirituous liquors).

68. In the case of some, griefs or sorrows recede even before they are glimpsed (by the prospective sufferer) while others who possess nothing of their own overstep[8] them.

69. A great disparity is seen in the fruition of the conjunctions of acts. Some bear a palanquine on their shoulders while others ride in them.

70. All persons aspire after affluence or prosperity. Out of them a few have chariots ahead of them in processions. Some men have no wealth (v.l. in the MBh. 'are wifeless') while others have hundreds of wives.

71. The opposite pairs—pleasure and pain—exist side by side. People have either one or the other. Have a look at this or that. You should not succumb to delusion.

72. Eschew both *Dharma* as well as *Adharma*, cast off (the dualistic concept of) truth and falsehood. After eschewing all the notions, be established in your own Self, be happy and free from all ailments.

73. O excellent sage I have recounted to you in details that secret and mysterious teaching. It is due to such knowledge that the gods (who were formerly human beings) could transcend the earth and go to settle in the heaven."

Sanandana said:

74. Having addressed thus Śuka, the son of Vyāsa, and bidding good-bye to him, the great sage Sanatkumāra

who was worshipped by Śuka with deep reverence, went his way.

75. After understanding the whole philosophic position, Śuka, the greatest of the Yogins, became eager to explore the region of the Brahman and went to his father.

76. Thereafter, after meeting his father and bowing him down, the great sage Śuka circumambulated him (clockwise) and proceeded to mount Kailāsa.

77. Vyāsa, being overcome with filial affection (for his son and pained at separation from him and grieved at heart, cried out, "O son, wait at least for a moment."

78. Śuka who was above all expectations, became freed from affection and bondage. He thought only of Liberation (from *Sāṁsāra*) and attained the highest region.

CHAPTER SIXTYONE

1. This chapter is compiled from the Mbh. *Śānti* chapters 330 ff., the only difference is that here the interlocutor is Sanatkumāra while in the Mbh., it is Nārada.

2. Mbh. (*ibid*) v. 6. reads : *virajyate* 'gets disgusted with them'.

3. NP reads : *taccāsya tu nivartate*, '*tu*' in the NP makes this a confused statement. The Mbh. reads *na nivartate* never returns to him and this is a better reading.

4. *niṣphalāḥ* but Mbh. (ibid) v. 11 reads *bāliśāḥ*.

5. These two lines in the NP seem independent or unrelated. In the Mbh. (ibid) v. 14a reads : "you should ascribe the above to the faults of man."

6. The Mbh. (ibid) v.15 reads *vā na vā* for NP *mānavāḥ*. The Mbh. means : "When at the sight of some other person semen is created but is actually imparted to another women, there may or may not be any conception."

7. This verse is the same as Mbh. (ibid) v. 22 with the following change : *calācalam* for *balābalam* in the NP and *nāvam ivā'hitām* for *nāvam ivā' calām* in the NP.

8. The reading *adhigacchati* in its original in the *Mbh.* (*Śānti* 331.40) has *na kiñcid adhigamyate* 'through possessing no wealth are free from miseries of every type.'

CHAPTER SIXTYTWO

The exposition of Mokṣa-dharma

Sūta said:

1. On hearing these words, the holy sage Nārada asked the Brahmanical sage once again about Śuka's departure.

Nārada said:

2. O holy lord, everything has been recounted by you with a very sympathetic heart. On hearing it, my mind has attained the most perfect quiescence.

3. O great sage, impart again unto me the philosophy of liberation. The thirst is never quenched by the ocean of the attributes of Kṛṣṇa.

4. In what region do those persons who are liberated from Saṁsāra and who are expert in the philosophy of *Mokṣa*, abide? This is my great doubt.

5a. O highly fortunate one! Do dispel that doubt as there is no other person (superior to you) amongst the knowers (of *Mokṣa-Śāstra*).

Sanandana said:

5b-6a. In accordance with the injunctions laid down in the Śāstras, Śuka who was conversant with *Krama-Yoga* (the order of the successive process of Yoga) fixed his soul (performed Dhāraṇā) in due course from his feet (upwards).

6b-7a. When it dawned (lit. the world became lighted with the light of the sun before its rise) that learned sage Śuka sat with his face eastward with his hands properly folded in an attitude of humility.

7b-8a. The place wherein the son of Vyāsa started to proceed by the path of Yoga was free from any flock of birds or sounds or any disturbing sight.

8b-9a. He then beheld his own soul liberated from all bonds of attachment. When he saw the (disc of the) sun, he gave out a loud laughter (in ecstasy).

9b-10. With a view to attain the path of liberation, he

again set himself up for Yoga. Becoming the master of the great yoga, he transcended the sky (or the element called the sky or space). The glorious son of Vyāsa became definitely the traverser of the path in the sky.

11. All beings gazed (agape) at the incessantly speeding prominent-most Brāhmaṇa with the effulgence of Garuḍa traversing through the sky with the velocity of the wind or the speed of the mind.

12. According to their ability and with due formalities they worshipped him. The residents of heavens rained showers of heavenly flowers on him.

13. All the bevies of celestial damsels and tribes of Gandharvas became filled with amazement at his sight. The sages as well as the Siddhas (or sages who have mastered Siddhis) were wonderstruck as to who was the person who had attained such a Siddhi.

14. Then that highly resplendent Śuka, being full of (spiritual) joy told those sages his name, O Nārada.

15. "If my father follows after me crying out "O Śuka", you should respond to him (promptly and) with attention.

16. When he was assured by them positively in the matter, he gave up the four worlds.* He then shed off the eight varieties of the attribute *Tamas* and five kinds of the attribute *Rajas* (which tempts men to five kinds of objects of senses.)

17. Thereafter, the intelligent Śuka cast off the attribute *Sattva* and it was a wonderful miracle. Śuka settled in himself that eternal position, devoid of attributes where the *Liṅga* was being worshipped.

18-19 He then (espied) two unparalleled peaks similar to the mountains Himalayas and Meru,** in close contacts. They were made of gold and silver and hence were yellow and white in colour. Those auspicious peaks were a hundred Yojanas in height. With a fearless heart Śuka alighted there.

20. Though the peaks were very closely united, they were seen suddenly torn asunder into two (at Śuka's impact). It was such a wonderful miracle, O excellent Brāhmaṇa.

---

*Mbh. Santi ch. 333.1 records the v. 1. *Yogān* which NK. explains as (1) *Vitarka* (2) *Vicāra* (3) *Ānanda* (4) *Asmitā*.

**vide v. 27 p. 909.

21. Thereafter, he suddenly broke through* and soared away from the two peaks of the mountain and that excellent mountain could not obstruct his passage.

22. Coursing from above, the pious-souled Śuka beheld the river ** Mandākinī (the 5th stage in the spiritual progress in the (*Vāyu-Vidyā*-NK) and a forest full of blossoming trees.

23. In the waters of the Mandākinī, a bevy of celestial damsels were indulging in sports while bathing. Those naked ladies of good form saw the formless sage.

24. Knowing that Śuka was traversing (towards *Brahma*) the father, overwhelmed with affection followed him closely from behind taking to that excellent course.

25. But Śuka directed his course far above the aerial region of the wind (i.e. above the *sūtrātman*—NK) and having thus shown his Yogic prowess, became all-pervading (identical with the Brahman).

26. Vyāsa, the performer of a great, austere penance, adopted the path of Yoga and within the twinkling of the eye reached the spot where Śuka alighted (with a dash).

27. He saw there the mountain peak split in two and the passage through which Śuka passed. The Siddhas and sages praised the (yogic) passage and achievement of his son.

28. Thereafter, crying out loudly upon the name of Śuka it was lamented so loudly by the father (Vyāsa) that the three worlds resounded with the cry.

29. The pious-souled Śuka who had access everywhere (as he became one with the Brahman), was the soul of all and hence with faces all round responded by uttering vibrantly the word *Bhoḥ* (as if in an echo).

30. Thereupon, echoing the mono-syllabic sound *Bhoḥ* (O Sire!), the whole world consisting of the mobiles and immobiles responded loudly to the reply of Śuka.

31. Since then, even to this day, when sounds are uttered in mountain caves or plateaus they still echo them as if in answer to Śuka.

---

*See v. 27 below.

**In the Mbh. (ibid) ch. 333.17 this is the adj. of Mandākinī. In view of the next verse, the Mbh. is correct though I have followed the NP.

32. Having thus displayed his latent prowess, Śuka cast off all attributes beginning with *Sattva* and attained the highest position (*Mokṣa*).

33. Having witnessed the great (Yogic) prowess of his son of unlimited brilliance, Vyāsa was consoled by Lord, Rudra O Nārada.

34. "Why are you so much distressed (in mind) and are so much agitated for your son, O sage? Don't you see O Brāhmaṇa, your son who has become identical with the Brahman coming near you?"

35. Thus consoled, the sage Vyāsa again returned to his hermitage while Śuka being one with the Brahmaṇ moved about in various worlds.

36. Thereafter, on another occasion, O Brāhmaṇa, Vyāsa, the son of Satyavatī, went to the hermitage of Badarikāśrama in order to see Nara and Nārāyaṇa.

37. On seeing those two lords performing great penance there, he himself began the practice of penance with the memory of Śuka still fresh in his mind.

38. O dear one, while Vyāsa stayed there, Śuka the knower of the great Yoga, went to Śvetadīpa where you have already gone formerly.

39. The glorious Lord Nārāyaṇa, the God of gods, Janārdana is sought after by the Vedas and his prowess was witnessed (by Śuka).

40-41. O Nārada, the lord was eulogised by Śuka of divine nature. He became pleased and said :

Śrī Bhagavān said

O leading Yogin, I, who am stationed in the mysterious secret of all Devas (Vedas), have been seen by you. O Vāḍava (Brāhmaṇa) become a Siddha by means of the Yoga imparted by Sanatkumāra. Stationed in the path of Sadāgati (i. e. the wind god), see the worlds as you wish.

42. Thus advised by Vāsudeva, the sage born of the Araṇī, O Brāhmaṇa, went to Vaikuṇṭha the region bowed to by all the worlds.

43. It was resorted to by Devas moving about in aerial chariots. It was surrounded by the (river?) Virajā, O

Nārada, as this world shines so too the other worlds (by its reflection).

44. The tanks there, are bedecked in diverse ways by means of gold and jewels; the steps are studded with corals: They (tanks) are fully covered with blue lotuses; they are agitated by the sports of celestial women.

45. The tanks reverberate loudly, thanks to the divine flocks of swans; the clear water is always full. The gatekeepers have four hands (each) and are bedecked in different kinds of ornaments.

46-50a. He was not prevented by the gate-keepers, followers of Viṣṇu, the Siddhas like Kumuda and others, from entering within. After entering, Śuka perceived the four-armed lord of Devas, the slayer of Madhu. He was quiescent. His face beamed with pleasure. He was clad in yellow silken garments. He was served by Śaṅkha, Cakra, Gadā and Padma (lotus) in their bodily form. He shone with the Kaustubha jewel on his chest. His (consort) Lakṣmī too shone on his chest. He was adorned with a girdle, a sacred thread, bangles and bracelets. His armlets and coronet as well as the gemset anklets shone (brilliantly). He was being served day and night by the groups of Siddhas. On seeing him, Śuka, overwhelmed with devotion eulogised Him thus:

Śuka said:

50b. (Śuka's prayer)—
Obeisance unto you, the son of Vasudeva, to the cosmic witness of all the worlds.

51. Bow to one who is in the form of the seed of the universe; to the perfect one; to the silent *Ātman*; (obeisance) to Hari the resident of Śvetadvīpa; to one who is resting on Vāsuki.

52. Hail to *Haṁsa* (the supreme being); to one of the form of the fish; to one who had assumed the body of the Boar; (obeisance) to the man-lion; to the one adored by Dhruva; to the master of Sāṅkhya and Yoga (systems of philosophy).

53. (Obeisance) to Catussena (one with four armies); to Kūrma (the divine tortoise); to Pṛthu (the big being); to one of the nature of happiness; to *Nābheya* (the Paramount lord);

to the creator of the universe; to the dispenser of destiny; to the annihilator.

54. Obeisance to the leading scion of the family of Bhṛgu (i.e. Paraśurāma); to Rāma, the descendant of Raghu; to the great one; (obeisance) to Kṛṣṇa, the originator of the Vedas; (obeisance) to one, of the form of Buddha and Kalki.

55. Hail to *Caturvyūha* (having four manifestations): to *Vedya* (one who should be known); to *Dhyeya* one who should be meditated upon); to the Supreme *Ātman*; to one called Nara and Nārāyaṇa; to *Śipiviṣṭa* (one pervaded by rays of light), to Viṣṇu.

56. Bow to Ṛtadhāman (with the majestic splendour of Ṛta); to *Vidhāman* (one devoid of abode); to Suparṇa (of good wings); to *Svarociṣ* (self-luminous); to *Ṛbhu* (Divinity) to one of good rites and lustre; to *Sudhāman* (one of good abode); to Ajita (the unconquered).

57. Obeisance to one of universal form; to one identical with the universe; to the cause of creation, sustenance and annihilation (obeisance) to the *Yajña* and the enjoyer of the *Yajñas*; (obeisance) to the biggest one, to the minute one and to the *Arthin* (the suppliant).

58. Obeisance to one whose eyes are the sun and the moon; to one who possesses power, virility and lustre; to one worthy of being worshipped; to the witness; to the unborn; to one who has many heads, legs and arms.

59. (Obeisance) to the lord of Śrī, to Śrīnivāsa, to one who is subservient to the devotees, to *Śārṅgin* (the wielder of the bow Śārṅga); to the overlord of the eight *Prakṛtis*; to Brahman of infinite power.

60. Bow to one who is comprehensible (only) through *Bṛhadāraṇyaka Upaniṣad*; to Hṛṣīkeśa; to Vedhas; to one whose eyes resemble the lotus; the Kṣetrajña (individual soul); to the luminous one.

61. (Obeisance) to Govinda, the creator of the universe; to the lord of the universe; to the truth; true to promise; to Vaikuṇṭha, to Acyuta.

62. Hail to Adhokṣaja, to Dharma, to Vāmana; to one having three *Dhātus*; to one who holds lustre; to Viṣṇu; to you the infinite one, to Kapila.

63. Obeisance to Viriñci (creator); to *Trikakud* (one who has three ensigns of Royalty); to one who has the forms of Ṛk, Yaju and Sāman; obeisance to *Ekaśṛṅga* (one with a single supremacy); to one of pure fame; to *Śāstrayoni* (the source of origin of the scripture).

64. (Obeisance) to Vṛṣākapi, to the prosperous one, to the lord, to one of universal activities; to one of the form of *Bhūḥ*, *Bhuvaḥ* and *Svaḥ*, to the slayer of Daityas; to one devoid of attributes.

65. Bow to the unsullied one; to the permanent one; to the unchanging one; to the imperishable one; obeisance to you, O Lord favourably disposed to those who seek refuge, Save me.

66. On being eulogised thus, the lord, the wielder of *Śaṅkha*, *Cakra* and *Gadā*, very favourably disposed to those who bow down, spoke thus to the sage born of the *Araṇi* (viz. Śuka).

Śrī Bhagavān said :

67. O son of Vyāsa, O highly blessed one of good rites, I am delighted with you. Attain learning and devotion; you are a perfectly wise one adopting many forms.

68. O Brāhmaṇa, this is the same form of mine formerly seen by you in the Śvetadvīpa. I am stationed here in the same form for my incarnation, in the form of the pervader of the Universe.

69. O blessed one, by (constant) thought over *Mokṣa-dharma* (virtue leading to liberation) you have become a Siddha. (Attain) excellent worlds such as those of Vāyu, firmament and the sun (?)

70. You are permanently liberated (from Saṁsāra). You are worshipped by gods and men. Devotion unto me who am gracious unto all is very difficult to obtain.

71. Once you have attained that devotion, nothing remains to be attained. The sages Nara and Nārāyaṇa are engrossed in penance, till the end of the Kalpa.

72. At their behest, Vyāsa, your father of holy rites, will be composing the scripture called the *Bhāgavata*. Learn it. Go down to the Earth.

73. He is now performing a penance on the mountain

Gandhamādana. He is much dispirited in his mind due to separation from you. Make him pacified. He is dear unto me."

74. O Brāhmaṇa, thus advised, Śuka bowed to the four-armed deity. Returning by the way he had gone, he came back to his father.

75. Thereafter, on seeing his son near him, the valorous son of Parāśara became delighted much in his mind. He desisted from his penance.

76. After bowing to Nārāyaṇa as well as to Nara, the most excellent among men, he returned to his own hermitage accompanied by his son born of the Araṇī.

77. O leading sage, at the behest of Nārāyaṇa through you he composed the divine compendium that consists of many anecdotes. (viz. the *Bhāgavata*).

78. He taught his son Śuka engaged in renunciation, the compendium of the *Bhāgavata* which is on a par with the Vedas and which increases devotion to Hari.

79. Śuka, the holy son of Vyāsa, took utmost delight in the Ātman. Yet he learned every day that compendium which is a favourite scripture of Viṣṇu's devotees.

80. Thus O sinless one, these *Mokṣadharmas* (virtues leading to liberation) have been related to you. They cause devotion to Hari of those who read and listen to it attentively.

———ooo———